D1589184

DEMOCRACY, EDUCATION, AND MULTICULTURALISM

DEMOCRACY, EDUCATION, AND MULTICULTURALISM

Dilemmas of Citizenship in a Global World

Carlos Alberto Torres

ROWMAN & LITTLEFIELD PUBLISHERS, INC.
Lanham • Boulder • New York • Oxford

ROWMAN & LITTLEFIELD PUBLISHERS, INC.

Published in the United States of America
by Rowman & Littlefield Publishers, Inc.
4720 Boston Way, Lanham, Maryland 20706

12 Hid's Copse Road
Cumnor Hill, Oxford OX2 9JJ, England

British Library Cataloguing in Publication Information Available

Library of Congress Cataloging-in-Publication Data

Torres, Carlos Alberto.
    Democracy, education, and multiculturalism : dilemmas of
citizenship in a global world / Carlos Alberto Torres.
        p.   cm.   23369310
    Includes bibliographical references and index.
    ISBN 0–8476–8534–9 (cloth : alk. paper). — ISBN 0–8476–8535–7
(paper : alk. paper)
    1. Critical pedagogy.   2. Education and state.   3. Multicultural
education.   4. Citizenship.   I. Title.
LC196.T65   1998
370.11'5—dc21   98–4047
                                                                CIP

Printed in the United States of America

Contents

Acknowledgments

Writing is an intellectual journey of discovery and dialogue. In writing this book, I have become indebted to a number of friends and colleagues who tolerated my obsessive interest over the last three years in discussing the relationships among the state, education, citizenship, democracy, and multiculturalism, even at the price of spoiling a good meal or a pleasant conversation.

I am grateful to Michael W. Apple, Robert Arnove, Atilio Alberto Boron, Sol Cohen, the late Paulo Reglus Neves Freire, Moacir Gadotti, Walter Garcia, Zelda Groener, John Hawkins, Pat McDonough, Ted Mitchell, Marcela Mollis, Pilar O'Cadiz, Raj Pannu, Raymund Paredes, David Plank, Thomas S. Popkewitz, Adriana Puiggrós, José Eustaquio Romão, Daniel Schugurensky, and Welford (Buzz) Wilms.

A few colleagues and friends read large parts or the entire manuscript and provided me with immensely insightful suggestions and criticisms. I am particularly indebted to Nick Burbules, Ray Rocco, Doug Kellner, Todd Gitlin, and Gloria Ladson-Billings. Raymond Allen Morrow, with whom I have spent the last decade discussing and writing about sociological theory and education, has provided, as always, insightful and critical suggestions.

A number of graduate students discussed the manuscript and provided most useful suggestions, showing me, once again, that the student is the teacher and the teacher the student. While I might not have done justice to their talents in responding to their questions, queries, and criticisms, I would like to recognize their insightful suggestions. I am thankful to María Beatriz Santana, Octavio Pescador, Saúl Duarte, Aly Juma, Carmen Laura Torres, Peter Kipp, Jeniffer Jafnosky, Xochitl Perez, Gabino Aguirre, David Victorin, Karen McClafferty, Julie Thompson, and Analee Haro. I am also grateful to Dean Birkenkamp, my friend and executive editor at Rowman & Littlefield, for his professionalism, warmth, and solidarity and his care for the enterprise of publishing as a contribution to the creation of a democratic public sphere.

I put finishing touches on this manuscript while continuously traveling in Mexico, Brazil, and Argentina. The candor and gentleness of Mexican, Brazilian, and Argentinean friends, with their many demonstrations of love and care for people, helped me to go back constantly to the Latin adage *"ad fontes."* That is to say, we should always come back to our senses of humanity, compassion, and love—true sources of intellectual inspiration.

I dedicate this book to my mother, who in her humanity has always showed me that compassion has no limits, that love transcends personalities and behaviors, and that living a democratic life should never be a mysterious feat.

I would also like to dedicate this book to my daughter Laura Silvina, who constantly teaches me that a curious intellectual mind and a loving personality with an immense thirst for dialogue can change the world, at least the world of the people who have the privilege to meet her. Her wide range of readings in contemporary sociological theory, particularly in issues of ethnicity and gender, helped me to engage and understand the subject better. My son, Pablo Sebastián, who read with his particularly inquisitive mind and wit—the mind of the philosopher—parts of the manuscript, offering very valuable, candid, at times overwhelmingly critical comments, deserves a similar dedication. I learned a lot interacting with him and with his passion for the truth. I also dedicate this book to my oldest son, Carlos Alberto, who, being the one who has studied in three countries, in three different languages, embodies better than many I know the notion of enfleshed interculturalism. His charming demeanor and his positive outlook on life taught me that migratory experiences may constitute, in the end, an endowment, a kind of invisible asset for people who know, as Carlos does, how to capture the serenity of life. This dedication goes as well to the newest members of my family, Nicole Toma and Rosanna DiSalvo. As always, María Cristina Pons, my *compañera* for twenty-five years, has a special place in this acknowledgment. With her sensibility, intelligence, and disarming smile and her talent as a literary critic and writer, she has made my life more meaningful and has helped me to understand and appreciate the immensely beautiful world of Latin American literature.

In closing, I would also like to dedicate this book in memoriam to my friend and *"maestro,"* the late Paulo Reglus Neves Freire, conscience of Latin America, who passed away as I was finishing this book. I am grateful to him for so many things that to list them here would be an impossible undertaking. We will remember him for his legacy represented in his teachings and writings, for his constant testimony of democratic coherence, for his uncompromising ethics and utopian thinking, for his boundless love for the people, and, above all, for teaching us his epistemology of curiosity.

1

The Secret Adventures of Order: An Introduction

The State, Power, and Education

> "The perfectioning of order begins in chaos."
> —Carlos Monsivais, *The Rituals of Chaos*

Politics, the state, education, all can be seen in a chaotic state. The rituals of chaos may be understood, in the figurative narrative of the Mexican chronicler Carlos Monsivais, as an invention of the social order. Jorgé Luis Borges (1996) talked about the secret adventures of order. Borges and Monsivais, to cite two renowned Latin American authors, show that sometimes literature attempts to understand reality, without always succeeding. Other times, literary work, with the imaginary that becomes real without canonical or analytical pretensions, suggests ways of understanding the dynamics of transformation of reality that social scientists, despite their efforts, methods, and scholarship, cannot capture in its multifarious dimensions. Thus, I have chosen the suggestive phrase of Borges as the title of this introduction. "The secret adventures of order" is more than a metaphor—it is an ingenious symbol of the intricate relations between the state, power, and education and indeed will be a central part of the dilemmas of citizenship in a multicultural society.

But are the rituals of chaos a part of the secret adventures of the social order? If so, the social construction of the educational reality, with its rituals, its chaos, and its symbolic order, would constitute a central aspect of the reproduction of the social order (Morrow and Torres, 1995). This is inevitable to such an extent that including those processes that appear to be challengers of the social reality, those practices that rupture the social, material, and symbolic order, and those transgressing movements of the social order could be reincorporated, in chaos, into defending the reproduction of the social order itself.

The reproduction of social structures at the symbolic level calls for rationalities

1

codes, routines, and practices that are deeply embedded in social struggles, in the technical and bureaucratic management of public education, as well as in the figure of the state, and they all play a pivotal role in social reproduction. Perhaps Borges's phrase, with the rich lyricism of its prose, captures a process that is eminently social. The secret adventures of order, in its constitution and transgression, link the state and education. And this is exactly what happens in the realm of educational discourses, policies, and practices and in daily class-room experiences. It is this way because the state plays a decisive role in requiring public and private education to set the norms, legislate, program, finance, and evaluate educational management. Yet, despite the importance of the state for education, there is, with few exceptions, no analytical discussion about the links between the state and education, much less a text that explores the links between theories of the state and education.[1] This work attempts to fill that gap, offering an analysis that unites a political sociology of education with the formation of citizenship and democracy.

This is a book about political philosophy and education—that is to say, about the symbolic realm of people's lives, their cognitive and affective under-standing of rationalities and utopias, and their agonic perception of how to find the appropriate ways for the "pursuit of liberty and happiness" in more egali-tarian and democratic societies.

By definition this is a theoretical book, but it claims not to be a book that is incomprehensible or inaccessible to the nonspecialist. This book tries not to be just another stone nested in that wall representing the mass of theoretical con-structs that only philosophers can decipher. It seeks to clarify analytically some of the key dilemmas of our time for educational practitioners, teachers, and researchers; but it also seeks to help parents, adults, youth, and children embedded in all sorts of educational milieus to understand the connections between citizenship, democracy, and multiculturalism.

I know that I don't have the answers to the multitude of questions (theoret-ical and practical) that this book addresses. I just hope that I have succeeded in identifying the most relevant questions involved in the theoretical problem.

Citizenship, Democracy, and Multiculturalism: The Theoretical Problem

> The test of a first-rate intelligence is the ability to hold two opposed ideas in mind at the same time and still retain the ability to function. One should, for example, be able to see that things are hopeless and yet be determined to make them otherwise.
>
> —F. Scott Fitzgerald, "The Crack-Up"

Theories of citizenship and theories of democracy mark the advent of modern political science and reflect, in their complexities, the theoretical and practical challenges of democracy in contemporary societies. Both theories of citizenship and theories of democracy also underlie the dilemmas of negotiating power in democratic societies.[2]

Theories of citizenship relate to every problem of the relations between citizens and the state and among citizens themselves, while theories of democracy relate clearly to the connection between established—hidden and explicit—forms of social and political power, the intersection between systems of democratic representation and participation and systems of political administrative organization of public governance. Ultimately, theories of democracy need to address the overall interaction between democracy and capitalism.

Finally, theories of multiculturalism, so prevalent in the educational field in the last twenty years, have emerged as a particular response not only to the constitution of the pedagogical subject in schools or to the interaction between the pedagogical subject and the political subject in democratic societies but also as a way to identify the importance of multiple identities (and hence narratives, voices, and agency) in education and culture. In short, theories of multiculturalism are intimately connected to the politics of culture and education.[3]

Thus, theories of multiculturalism relate to the main analytical purpose of theories of citizenship. Both attempt to identify the sense and sources of identity and the competing forms of national, regional, ethnic, and religious identity. Yet theories of multiculturalism have addressed the implication of class, race, and gender for the constitution of identities and the role of the state in a way that, by and large, mainstream theories of citizenship have not.[4] While these interconnections between identity and citizenship are not at all evident in the specialized bibliography, they have a practical grounding that brings them also closer to theories of democracy. This is so because theories of democracy are concerned not only with participation, representation, and checks and balances of power but also with ways to promote solidarity beyond particular interests or specific forms of identity.

Not only do theories of citizenship, theories of democracy, and theories of multiculturalism, in their specific spheres of influence and empirical loci, strive to define a sense of identity (for the notion of a democratic citizen and a multicultural political subject) including all its contradictory sources, but also they seek to define vigorously the limits and possibilities of forms of sociability that will promote the ability in individuals to tolerate and work together with people who are different from themselves. Likewise, these theories may enhance people's (or in a more restricted formulation, citizens') ability and desire to participate in the political process of promoting the public good and accountability. Finally, these theories will help individuals' willingness to exercise self-restraint and personal responsibility in their economic demands and in personal choices that affect the health and wealth of society and the environment as well as the process of community(ies) formation (Kymlicka and Norman, 1994: 152–153). This is so because, as Habermas (1992) so aptly has argued: "the institutions of constitutional freedom are only worth as much as a population makes of them" (7).

The Thesis Advanced in this Book

> "Equality of opportunity can mean . . . an equal right to a fully human life for all who will exert themselves . . . or an equal right to get into the competitive race for more for oneself."
> —C. B. Macpherson, *The Real World of Democracy*

The dilemmas of citizenship in a democratic, diverse, multicultural society can be outlined, at the beginning of our analysis, as follows: Theories of citizenship have been advanced, in the tradition of Western political theory, by white, heterosexual males who have identified a homogeneous citizenship through a process of systematic exclusion from, rather than inclusion in, the polity. That is, women, identifiable social groups (e.g., Jews, Gypsies), working-class people, and people representing specific ethnic and racial groups—in short, people of color—and individuals lacking certain attributes or skills (e.g., literacy and numeracy) were in principle excluded from the definition of citizenship in several societies and hence "from [the] ideas of individual entitlement on the one hand and of attachment to a particular community on the other" (Kymlicka and Norman, 1994: 352).

Theories of democracy, while effective in identifying the sources of democratic power, participation, and representation in legitimate political democratic systems, had been unable to prevent the systematic exclusion of large segments of the citizenry.[5] Thus, formal democracy differs drastically from substantive democracy. More worrisome indeed is the fact that theories of democracy have been unable to differentiate the roots of representative democracy (based on the notions of equal representation, equity, and equality) from the foundational principles that articulate capitalist societies. By definition, capitalism requires differential representation in power and politics and fosters inequity through hierarchies and competing interests and inequality through the workings of a profit-seeking system.

Theories of multiculturalism—while effective in discussing the politics of culture and identity and the differential sources of solidarity across and within specific forms of identity, and even insightful in showing the remarkable complexity of multiple identities, multiple voices, multiple narratives, and the contradiction of multiple solidarities as well as the need to promote border crossings in education—had been unable or unwilling to embrace a theory of citizenship and of democracy that could be workable in practical procedural terms, ethically viable in moral terms, and politically feasible in the context of capitalist civil societies.

This book cannot accomplish a systematic analysis and criticism of the theoretical gaps, silences, or omissions and the practical limitations of these three sets of theories as they relate to education. It attempts, however, to discuss in detail the intersections between theories of citizenship and multiculturalism, using as a backdrop theories of democracy and the state. I attempt to show that to address the key dilemmas of citizenship in multicultural societies, a theory of multicultural citizenship will be necessary.

Yet we need a theory of multicultural citizenship that will take seriously the need to develop a theory of democracy that will help to ameliorate (if not eliminate altogether) the social differences, inequality, and inequity pervasive in capitalist societies, and a theory of democracy that will be able to address the severe tensions between democracy and capitalism, on the one hand, and social, political, and economic democratic forms on the other. Finally, we really need a theory of multicultural citizenship that can provide a reasonable theoretical answer to the neoconservative cry about the ungovernability of modern democracies in capitalist societies.[6]

The Structure of This Book

To address these concerns, chapter 2 offers a discussion of the capitalist state in democratic societies. This chapter argues that theories of the state, the nature of the state, and the nature of public policy have substantive importance for understanding the political nature of education and public policy formation, and particularly for understanding the connections between education, citizenship, democracy, and multiculturalism. Yet theories of the state based on the political philosophy that came of age in the nineteenth century center on the notion of the state as part of the nation, and therefore the nation appears as a central unit of analysis. The question, then, is what happens to the state (and by implication to democracy and citizenship, and indeed to multiculturalism) when the globalization of economy, culture, and politics is taken into account. In other words, does the state wither away? These are exactly the concerns of chapter 3, which discusses the process of globalization in the context of the worldwide division of labor, its implications for capitalist economic restructuring, and the potential implications for citizenship, democracy, and multiculturalism.

With theories of the state and of globalization in the background, chapters 4, 5, and 6, on theories of citizenship, democracy, and multiculturalism, respectively, offer a systematic appraisal, from a political philosophical perspective, of the complexities associated with these theories and some of their dilemmas for public policy. Also, these chapters offer a systematic definition of the concepts and key theories involved in each area.

Finally, chapter 7, "Towards a Theory of a Democratic Multicultural Citizenship," revisits most of the theoretical issues presented in this book, shows systematically the dilemmas and contradictions associated with these theories and their potential intersections, pinpoints some gaps and theoretical "silences," and offers a set of themes that deserve further scrutiny.

Cornel West (1993a) has said that people do not live on arguments although they might be influenced by arguments. West is right when he claims that people live on love, care, respect, touch. While writing this book, I was very much influenced by people's love, care, touch, and respect. I have always been influenced by what West has defended so eloquently, that we should always preserve in our intellectual work a "nuanced historical sense" (19).

Reading West's (1993a) *Prophetic Thought in Postmodern Times* helped me to revisit, once again, why we all conduct educational research, or at least why we should, and why we should take seriously the contradictions between education, citizenship, and democracy. West says that there is an undeniable cultural decay in America that frightens him more than anything else: "By unprecedented cultural decay I mean the social breakdown of the nurturing system for children. The inability to transmit meaning, value, purpose, dignity, decency to children" (16).

While historically situated, his remarks, I believe, apply to many societies. Facilitating the nurturing and learning of children, youth, and adults is what public education—jointly with the family and a few other societal institutions—is supposed to do. That is what educational research should be about: understanding the indissoluble linkages of theory and practice. This is another practical reason why, periodically, we should revisit the theoretical relationship between state, education, citizenship, democracy, and multiculturalism and why we should strive, as Paulo Freire has told us on innumerable occasions, to build a world that is "less ugly, less cruel and less inhumane." This is exactly the sentiment that inspired my reading of political philosophy, trying to understand the connections between citizenship, democracy, multiculturalism, and the field of education.

Notes

1. In the English-language and French literature, there are examples. See, e.g., Michael W. Apple, ed., *Cultural and Economic Reproduction in Education: Essays on Class, Ideology, and the State* (London: Routledge & Kegan Paul, 1982); Pierre Bourdieu, *La noblesse d'état: Grandes écoles et esprit de corps* (Paris: Minuit, 1989); Martin Carnoy and Henry M. Levin, *Schooling and Work in the Democratic State* (Stanford, Calif.: Stanford University Press, 1985); Roger Dale, "The Political Sociology of Education," *British Journal of Sociology of Education* 4, no. 2 (1983): 185–202; Ron Everman, Lennart G. Svensson, and Thomas Söderqvist, eds., *Intellectuals, Universities, and the State in Western Modern Societies* (Berkeley and Los Angeles: University of California Press, 1987); Henry A. Giroux and Peter McLaren, eds., *Critical Pedagogy, the State, and Cultural Struggle* (Albany: State University of New York Press, 1989); Liz Gordon, "Beyond Relative Autonomy Theories in Education," *British Journal of Sociology of Education* 10, no. 4 (1989): 435–448; Daniel Morales-Gómez and Carlos Alberto Torres, *The State, Corporatist Politics, and Educational Policy-Making in Mexico* (New York: Praeger, 1990); Raymond Morrow and Carlos Alberto Torres, *Social Theory and Education: A Critique of Theories of Social and Cultural Reproduction* (Albany: State University of New York Press, 1995), esp. the section about education, the state, and the logic of reproduction, 341–447; Claus Offe, "Notes on the Laws of Motion of Reformist State Policies," n.d., mimeograph; Michael Pusey, "The Legitimation of State Education Systems," *Australian and New Zealand Journal of Sociology* 16 (July 1980): 45–52; George M. Thomas and John M. Meyer, "The Expansion of the State," *Annual Review of Sociology* 10 (1984): 461–482; Carlos Alberto Torres, "State and Education: Marxist Theories," in *International Encyclopedia of Education: Research and Studies,* vol. 8, ed. T. Husén and T. N. Postlethwaite (Oxford: Pergamon Press, 1985), 4793–4798; Gordon W. West, "Education, Moral Reproduction, and the State: Some Implications of Activistic Interpretations of Recent European State Theories for Canadian Educational Policy," *Interchange* 12, nos. 2–3 (1981): 86–101.

2. A preliminary version of this chapter was presented to the Symposium on Postmodernism's Challenge to the Social Sciences and the Humanities, Universidad Complutense de Madrid–University of California, Madrid, 22–25 April 1997.

3. Critical pedagogy is at the crossroads of intellectual fertilization between critical modernist and postmodernist positions. It is fundamentally concerned with the centrality of power in the understanding of "how schools work" and the fact that critical theorists have "produced work centering on the political economy of schooling, the state and education, the representation of texts, and the construction of student subjectivity." Peter McLaren, *Life in Schools* (White Plains, N.Y.: Longman, 1989), 159. Yet little if any work has been produced by the variant of multiculturalism that endorses critical pedagogy to address the question, intersection, and contradictions of theories of citizenship, democracy, and multiculturalism.

4. A distinguished counterexample is Carole Pateman's classic work advancing a feminist perspective for theories of democracy. See, e.g., Carole Pateman, *The Problem*

8 *Democracy, Education, and Multiculturalism*

of Political Obligation: A Critique of Liberal Theory (Cambridge, England: Polity Press, 1985).

5. David Held has argued that democracy took its distinctly contemporary form in the nineteenth and twentieth centuries as "a cluster of rules, procedures and institutions permitting the broadest involvement of the majority of citizens, not in political affairs as such, but in the selection of representatives who alone can make political decisions. This cluster includes elected government, free and fair elections; universal suffrage; freedom of conscience, information and expression; the right of all adults to oppose their government and stand for office; and the right to form independent associations." David Held, "Democracy and the New International Order," in *Cosmopolitan Democracy: An Agenda for a New World Order* (Cambridge, England: Polity Press, 1995), 97–98.

6. This intersection between capitalism and democracy is analyzed in chapter 5. For substantive work in this direction, see Samuel Bowles and Herbert Gintis , *Democracy and Capitalism: The Contradiction of Modern Political Life* (New York: Basic Books, 1986).

2

The State and Education

This chapter argues that theories of the state, the nature of the state, and the nature of public policy have substantive importance for understanding the political nature of education as public policy and the connections between citizenship, democracy, and multiculturalism. The definition of what are the "real" problems of education and what are the most appropriate (i.e., cost-effective, ethically acceptable, and legitimate) solutions depends greatly on the theories of the state that underpin, justify, and guide the educational diagnoses and proposed solutions. This chapter reviews classical theories of the relationship between the polity and education and liberal, neoconservative, and neoliberal reformulations of these theories, as well as neo-Marxist, poststructuralist, and postmodernist critiques of these formulations. The analysis of theories of the state and education is further enriched by examining the contributions of feminist theories and by beginning to explore how all the above theories relate to issues such as democracy, citizenship, and multiculturalism—an analysis that will be expanded in chapters 4, 5, and 6. Any analysis of the relationship between education and the state should take into account the multilayered, complex, and dynamic nature of this relationship, which reveals the multitude of tensions and contradictions that emerge out of the historical and social forces buffeting political and educational institutions.

The State: Problems of Definition

Nations may have passed a long life before arriving at this their destination, and during this period, they may have attained considerable culture in some directions. . . . But it is the State which first presents subject-matter that is not only adapted to the prose of history, but involves the production of such history in the very progress of its own being.
—G. W. F. Hegel, *Lectures on the Philosophy of History*

The legal state was conceived by Plato, a philosopher prone to speculate about the deep-seated presence of mythical thought in human endeavors, as the administrator of justice (Plato, 1941:70). The state is the general regulatory principle of order, unity, and lawfulness of what, many centuries later, Rousseau defined as the *volonté générale,* or "general will." For Hegel, the state was the supreme and most evolving reality of history, the "spirit of the world," the real incarnation of the Idea, and, like a demiurge, the producer of history. Thus, in the rich tradition of political philosophy that extends from Plato to Hegel, the state has been conceived of as the personification and guarantor of collective wishes. Hence, discussions about theories of the state are part of an *orgueilleux* heritage preoccupying generations of thinkers and philosophers, political activists and common citizens concerned with definitions of the nation and the state and how these concepts relate to notions of democratic culture, power, and citizenship.

Max Weber (1964) provides a clear discussion of some of the central features of states in modern societies:

> The primary formal characteristics of the modern state are as follows: It possesses an administrative and legal order subject to change by legislation, to which the organized corporate activity of the administrative staff, which is also regulated by legislation, is oriented. This system of order claims binding authority, not only over the members of the state, the citizens, most of whom have obtained membership by birth, but also, to a very large extent, over all action taking place in the area of its jurisdiction. It is thus a compulsory association with a territorial basis. Furthermore, today, the use of force is regarded as legitimate only so far as it is either permitted by the state or prescribed by it. . . . The claim of the modern state to monopolize the use of force is essential to it as its character of compulsory jurisdiction and of continuous organization. (156)

I will discuss the Weberian formula below, particularly Weber's notion of the state as a monopoly of force, compulsory jurisdiction, and continuous administrative organization.[1] What is important is to identify the relevance of the notions of democracy and citizenship in the context of the relationships between the state and education.

The notion of democracy entails the concept of a democratic citizenship, where agents are responsible, able to participate, and choose their representatives and monitor their performance. From liberal or neo-Marxist perspectives, these are not only political but also pedagogical practices, since the construction of the democratic citizen implies the construction of a pedagogic subject. Individuals are not, by nature, ready to participate in politics. They have to be educated in democratic politics in a number of ways, including normative grounding, ethical behavior, knowledge of the democratic process, and technical performance. The construction of the pedagogic subject is a central conceptual problem, a dilemma for democracy. To put it simply: democracy implies a process of participation where all are considered equal. However, education involves a process whereby the "immature" are brought to identify with the principles and forms of life of the "mature" members of society. Thus, the process of construction of the democratic pedagogic subject is a process of cultural nurturing, but it also involves manipulating principles of pedagogic and democratic socialization in subjects who are neither tabula rasa in cognitive or ethical terms nor fully equipped for the exercise of their democratic rights and obligations.[2] Yet in the construction of modern polities, the constitution of a pedagogical democratic subject is predicated on grounds that are, paradoxically, both a precondition and a result of previous experiences and policies of national solidarity (including citizenship, competence building, and collaboration). With this brief clarification of the importance of democracy for a political culture and the role of the state, let us continue with the discussion about the definition of the state.

The state is usually defined as the totality of the political authority in a given society. In Roman law *potestas* denoted official legal power, which is distinct from *auctoritas,* "which means influence or prestige, and ensured that one's view would be accepted" (Vincent, 1987:32). Several key elements institutionally and functionally define the notion of the state. First, the state is a set of institutions manned by the state's own personnel or bureaucracy. These institutions vary from institutions responsible for law and order (and hence violence and coercion), including the courts, police force, and army, to institutions responsible for symbolic and ideological functions, including institutions linked to social policy and education. State institutions are geographically located in a bounded territory, hence the notion of the nation-state. The relationship between the state and civil society is located within the same boundaries: "The state monopolizes rule making within its territory. This tends towards the creation of a common political culture shared by all citizens" (Hall and Ikenberry, 1989:1–2).

From a critical modernist position,[3] two of the most outstanding problems in defining state power from functional, legal, and institutional standpoints are historical and cultural. Historically, not every state controlled civil society, national boundaries, and markets nor enjoyed the monopoly of legitimate force as portrayed in the Weberian formula.[4] The Weberian definition begs the question: What is, or should be, understood by "legitimate force"? If, as Boudon and Bourricaud argue, we substitute monopoly of power for monopoly of force, then it is evident that in every society legitimate if not effective powers other than the state exist (Boudon and Bourricaud, 1989:381). For instance, the Indian uprising in Chiapas on 1 January 1994 exposed the collusion of interests between ranchers and their so-called white armies (salaried vigilantes working for private ranchers in southern Mexico), bureaucratic groups of the ruling party, and elements of the Mexican state. The massacre of indigenous people in the tiny village of Actual, in Chiapas, on 22 December 1997 in which nine men, twenty-one women, and fifteen children who were attending a religious ceremony in a church were killed is a sobering reminder of this collusion of interest and the presence of armed groups connected to hardliners of the ruling party. Indeed, ranchers shared this monopoly of force with the Mexican government. Another example is imperialist intervention in domestic policies. Influenced either by multinational corporations, such as ITT during Salvador Allende's presidency in Chile, or by direct action of colonial powers, such as France or Belgium in several African and Asian nations, or by endless interventions of the United States government and the former Soviet Union and its specialized agencies in many areas of the globe, imperialist interventions have all deeply undermined the power of postcolonial states. Not only imperialism but also domestic and international institutions constrain the power of the state. While nation-states historically attempt to control (through law, ideology, and coercion) what happens in their own territories, other institutions have disputed that control (e.g., the Catholic Church in European and Latin American Christendom trying to exercise cultural control, and on occasion, political hegemony) (Torres, 1992). In economic and financial terms, current "national" economic policies are deeply affected, challenged, and on occasion overtly determined by the overall trends of the globalization of economics, culture, and society and outside economic forces. This question of globalization is the subject of chapter 3.

Culturally, the term "common culture" (with its implications of a common cultural heritage, a basic literacy, and a political culture nurturing all citizens) may apply, to a certain extent, to specific state experiences (e.g., Sweden, Denmark, to some extent Japan), but it fails to capture the reality of other state experiences as expressed in the debates on multiculturalism in the United States or in the experience with hybrid cultures in Latin America (García Canclini, 1992). Thus, the common-culture argument is usually articulated by conservatives locating culture as a forum of consensus and harmony rather than a process of disputed citizenship. I will challenge this connection between culture and canon in my discussion of multiculturalism and, more specifically, in the conclusions about developing a democratic multicultural citizenship.

Historical and regional variability; the elusiveness of racial identity; power differentials based on class, gender, race, ethnicity, religion, and sexual orientation; and the complexity of intergroup relations within formal institutions all conspire against the notion of a common culture, the blueprint for an official knowledge, and the social construction of a political culture.[5] I will revisit this discussion in chapters 5, 6, and 7.

Modern political philosophers have seen the state as half-beast and half-human. In the words of Machiavelli, the state simultaneously reflects the pattern of the fox and the lion:

> Therefore it is necessary for a prince to understand how to avail himself of the beast and the man. This has been figuratively taught to princes by ancient writers, who describe how Achilles and many other princes of old were given to the Centaur Chiron to nurse, who brought them up in his discipline; which means solely that, as they had for a teacher one who was half beast and half man, so it is necessary for a prince to know how to make use of both natures, and that one without the other is not durable. A prince, therefore, being compelled knowingly to adopt the beast, ought to choose the fox and the lion; because the lion cannot defend himself against snares and the fox cannot defend himself against wolves. Therefore it is necessary to be a vox to discover the snares and a lion to terrify the wolves. (Machiavelli, 1993:137–138))

The dual nature of the modern prince has worried educators, preventing to some extent a systematic analysis of the implications of theories of the state in education. Educators have tried—I am afraid, unsuccessfully—to place the world of politics and the state strictly outside the realm of education and schools. This is a futile attempt to prevent the clever (and yet elusive) nature of the fox and the sanguinary (although at times passive) nature of the lion from undermining the noble purposes of education. Does it matter that the mythological Chiron the Centaur was himself an educator of rulers? Is it this dual nature of the state, half beast and half human, that makes it possible to think theoretically of school socialization as an integral part of processes of indoctrination, ideological manipulation, and/or the formation of a "common sense," as Antonio Gramsci has suggested?

Gramsci proposed a suggestive hypothesis: Education, as part of the state, is fundamentally a process of formation of "social conformism." Educational systems, and schools in particular, appear as privileged instruments for the socialization of a hegemonic culture. The state as an "ethical state" or as educator in Gramsci's perspective assumes the function of constructing a new civilization. The state thus constitutes an instrument of rationalization. In the Gramscian analysis schools and churches are seen as the largest cultural organizations in each country, and as ultimately producing hegemony. This notion of hegemony in Gramsci refers to a process of intellectual and moral leadership established as a consensus that is shared on the basis of common sense. This consensus, however, is dynamic and not static. It invariably emerges from a struggle or confrontation among social forces, ideologies, philosophies, and general conceptions of life. Despite Gramsci's antinomies,[6] he understands hegemony as a process of social and political domination in which the ruling classes establish their control over the classes allied to them through moral and intellectual leadership. Hegemony acquires a pedagogical character; but Gramsci also refers to hegemony as the dual use of force and ideology to reproduce social relations between the ruling and the subordinate classes.[7] If Gramsci's hypothesis is plausible, then the examination of the relationships between the state and education becomes central for understanding politics and culture in capitalist societies.

Education and the State

> Almost all analyses of educational problems have implicit in them a theory of
> the state, but few tell us what this theory is.
>
> Martin Carnoy, "Education and the State"

Why is the notion of the state so important for understanding educational policies and practices or the connections between citizenship, democracy, and multiculturalism? There is no simple answer to this question. For an approximation to the contours of the problem, we need to explore a triple context: the relationships between education and government, the relationships between education and the economy, and the relationships between education and citizenship building.

Theories and research on the state show that an analysis of the educational system cannot be separated from some explicit or implicit analysis of the role, purpose, and functioning of the government. Particularly during the twentieth century, education has increasingly become a function of the state. Educational systems and practices are sponsored, mandated, organized, and certified by the state. Indeed, "public education is not only a state function in terms of legal order or financial support; the specific requirements for degrees, teachers requirements and qualifications, mandated textbooks, and required courses for basis curriculum are controlled by state agencies and designed under specific public policies of the state" (Torres, 1985:4793).

Similarly, it has been argued that the state plays an important role in linking education and the economy. Human capital theory has argued that school expansion fosters economic growth (Psacharopoulos, 1988; Hanuschek, 1986). However, theories of credentialism and political economy theories challenged the basic premises of human capital theories.[8] Facing the criticism of credentialism, human capital scholars hypothesize that some conditions must be met before educational expansion can have an appreciable and positive effect on economic growth. First, a standard curriculum should be in place, and a sizable number of children in the age cohort beyond grade 6 should be enrolled in school. Second, there should be fluid linkages between education and the economy. Third, and a precondition for the first two relationships to succeed, the state must ensure the quality of education over time. Using the case of France in the late nineteenth century, it is argued that an active state played an important role in linking education and the economy, in securing a standard curriculum, and in ensuring the quality of educational offerings. The French case is then compared and contrasted with findings in the United States that are considered consistent to test empirically the hypothesis (Hage, Hage, and Fuller, 1988:824–837).

Notwithstanding the difficulties in identifying the exact contributions of education to economic growth, it is clear that the state, through public policy and public expenditures, contributes a great deal to facilitating the linkages between the educational system and the economy. Hence, the nature of the state and of the political regime and explicit state intervention (or lack thereof) will have decisive consequences for educational development and economic growth.

An educated citizenry is seen as a prized asset from all political perspectives (Meyer, 1977). Educational institutions are said to socialize individuals in peculiar ways, creating specific political orientations towards democratic or nondemocratic structures. The political culture is a set of "attitudes towards the political system and its various parts, and attitudes toward the role of the self in the system. It is a set of orientations towards a special set of social objects and processes" (Almond and Verba, 1963:13). Whether pursuing explicit corporatist goals[9] or seeking to develop a political culture based on the modern creed of democracy,[10] the state is said to play a major role in providing for the socialization of the citizenry and in creating the appropriate symbolic conditions for nurturing the political culture of the people.

The relationships among education, politics, and the state cannot be discussed only from the perspective of mainstream political culture. Despite what proponents of "technocratic" or "technicist" views of educational research, curriculum, and educational policy would like to believe, education is neither politically neutral nor technically "objective." As Paulo Freire has consistently claimed in his work, there is an inherent "politicity" of education. This has epistemological, analytical, and ethical implications. McLaren notes: "Not only is it impossible to disinvest pedagogy of its relationship to politics, it is theoretically dishonest" (McLaren, 1994:321). This politicity relates foremost to the explicit as well as the subtle linkages between education and power. At the same time, it is related to the political nature of the state and public education as contested arenas and sites for the exchange of goods and services and competition of political-economic projects (Freire, 1996). It is appropriate then, to define in detail the concept of the state and its implications for theories of the multiple relationships among state, society, and education.

The Concept of the State

> Wherever, therefore, any numbers of men so unite into one society, as to quit every one of his executive power of the law of nature, and to resign it to the public, there, and there only, is a political, or civil society.
> —John Locke, *On Civil Government*

The concept of the state is different from the concepts of government, political system, or political regime. The importance of the concept of the state has been eloquently argued by Atilio Boron (1994a):

> The concept of the state has become one of the very few in contemporary social sciences endowed with the capacity to foster a rich theoretical and methodological debate, not to mention the inflamed political controversy raised by its practical existence. This is all the more surprising because, for some time before this impressive comeback, the concept of the state had been excommunicated from the academy, its theoretical value condemned due to its allegedly inherent vagueness and formalistic bias as well as its equally reproved heuristic worth. It was in 1953, the time of the end of ideology, of the miraculous capitalist recovery after the war, and of the institutionalization of the class struggle, when David Easton eloquently voiced the prevailing consensus among the social scientists by saying that "neither the state nor power is a concept that serves to bring together political research." However, in less than three decades the real movement of history has made of this author an astonished witness of the "resurrection" of the concept, "now risen from the grave to haunt us once again." (1)

Thus the notion of the state has gained new recognition as a key concept in the history of political research (Boron, 1994b). Discussions about theories of the state acquired new vigor at the beginning of the 1970s when they were associated with debates in Marxist political theory of the state and the work of Antonio Gramsci. The discussions have also acquired new luster in the 1980s in mainstream political science discussions of the autonomy of the democratic state[11] and the process of redemocratization in authoritarian societies (Stepan, 1988; O'Donnell, Schmitter, and Whitehead, 1986). Additionally, recent discussions on state-education relationships have incorporated debates around issues of racial, ethnic, class, and sexual identity; political choices, nationhood; and democratic theory as well as notions of social regulation derivative of Foucault's approach (Morrow and Torres, 1995; Popkewitz, 1994b).

There is the need to clarify terminology, including the concepts of the state, political regime, political system, civil society, and public sphere because these concepts are subject to intense debates. They are familiar to specialists trained in political science or sociology, but they may not be commonly used by educational specialists and practitioners. Given the scope, intensity, and complexity of debates around these concepts, it will only be possible to outline the broadest contours of their definitions with the purpose of clarifying terminology rather than producing an exhaustive taxonomy or glossary of terms.

The notions of state and government are not synonymous, and the complexity of the modern state cannot be reduced to the notion of "government." Likewise, the notion of government cannot be defined in purely descriptive terms as merely a collection of agencies, organisms, and offices that without coherence or unity carry out administrative chores and tasks in administering the government's business in society or the so-called public good. Neither can the government or the state be conceived of as merely a collection of institutions and/or individuals performing roles and functions that are deemed necessary for the functioning of contemporary societies, including the administration of justice, the economy, defense, the legislature, and the executive (Boron, 1990–91). In this regard, Weber's definition suggested that the state must be considered as something more than the notion of the government.

The notion of the state—despite different competing interpretations, as we will see below—is generally seen as more comprehensive than the notion of the government. The state involves the workings of the government but cannot be restricted to it. Theda Skocpol (1979) argues that:

> The state properly conceived . . . is a set of administrative, policing, and military organizations headed, and more or less coordinated by, an executive authority. Any state first and fundamentally extracts resources from society and deploys those to create and support coercive and administrative organizations . . . [P]olitical systems . . . also contain institutions through which social interests are represented in state policy making as well as institutions through which non-state actors are mobilized to participate in policy implementation. Nevertheless, the administrative and coercive organizations are the basis of state power. (29)

Not only is the concept of the state different from (and more comprehensive than) the notion of government, but also it interacts with (and sometimes includes) the notion of political system. The state is then an institutional structure that includes:

> the incumbents within this structure, and body of law that make up the public sector. It thus includes the government (in the sense of the head of state and the immediate political leadership that surrounds the head of state), the public bureaucracy, the legislature, the judiciary, public and semi-public corporations, and the legal system. (Collier, 1979:403)

In theoretical terms, the notion of political system refers to the overall configuration of the model of governance in the context of a specific political regime, including the dominant coalition and public policy that characterize political life in a given society. Hence, different traditions in political science distinguish between different types of political systems, including democratic, authoritarian, and totalitarian political regimes. These political systems certainly differ in dominant ideology, patterns of political representation and participation, and leadership style.

The notion of the government or the state has usually been subsumed in political theory under the concept of political society, which is counterpoised against the notion of civil society. Whereas the concept of civil society cannot be separated from the concept of the state,

> the latter, by providing the overall legal framework of society, to a significant degree constitutes the former. Nonetheless, it is not unreasonable to claim that civil society retains a distinctive character to the extent that it is made up of areas of social life—the domestic world, the economic sphere, cultural activities, and political interaction—which are organized by private or voluntary arrangements between individuals and groups outside the direct control of the state. (Held, 1989:180–181)

Sometimes the notions of political society and civil society are translated into an opposition of concepts: the "public" sector and the "private" sector. "Public" refers to the Roman notion of *res publica,* an artificially constructed community that preserves the overall rights and interests of practically or historically constituted communities or any aggregate of individuals per se. For political philosophers such as Hobbes and Rousseau (even preserving the differences between them), the raison d'être of the state as the political society and the embodiment of the public is to preserve the liberty of individuals, even at the risk of having to regulate, in the view of many, the exchanges of individuals who interact in the private sphere of voluntary arrangements and domestic interactions. While private and public are seen as distinct and opposite poles and private interests are seen (and even glorified in the figure of the market) by many as more important than public ones, W. L. Weinstein's (1971) analogy draws a useful distinction: the notions of publicness and privateness are analogous to the layers of an onion. Just as every layer that is outside another layer will be inside another, then something that is public with regard to one sphere of life may be private in relation to another. Yet, the notion of public sphere is relevant for our purposes to clarify the relations between theories of the state and education.

"Public sphere" is a concept elaborated by Jürgen Habermas (1989) in *The Structural Transformation of the Public Sphere*. Different intellectual traditions use different terms to refer to similar concepts that, in turn, are supposed to account for specific phenomena of reality. A social phenomenon, however, is actually constructed and given life through our conceptualization (in itself an interpretation or understanding) of it. With this short and obviously incomplete word of epistemological caution, I must say from the beginning that the notion of public sphere could be seen as overlapping, but distinct from, the notion of civil society in classical eighteenth-century philosophy.

To avoid a very extensive discussion of the notion of public sphere, I shall quote Nancy Fraser (1997), who, with her customarily sharp analysis, critically captures the dimensions of Habermas's proposal:

> [The public sphere] designates a theater in modern societies in which political participation is enacted through the medium of talk. It is the space in which citizens deliberate about their common affairs, hence, an institutionalized arena of discursive interaction. This arena is conceptually distinct from the state; it is a site for the production and circulation of discourses that can in principle be critical of the state. The public sphere in Habermas' sense is also conceptually distinct from the official economy; it is not an arena of market relations but rather one of discursive relations, a theater for debating and deliberating rather than for buying and selling. This concept of the public sphere permits us to keep in view the distinction between state apparatuses, economic markets, and democratic associations, distinctions that are essential to democratic theory. (70)

Hence, the public sphere is distinct from the state; it is, in Habermas's definition—which Fraser criticizes as not wholly satisfactory—a body of private individuals constituting a public through deliberation and discursive interaction. The concept of the public sphere, as Fraser (1997) aptly notes, cannot be equated with the concept of community because this

> suggests a bounded and fairly homogeneous group, and it often connotes consensus. "Public," in contrast, emphasizes discursive interaction that is in principle unbounded and open-ended, and this in turn implies a plurality of perspectives.

Thus the idea of a public, better than that of a community, can accommodate internal differences, antagonisms, and debates. (97)

Given the scope, cultural diversity, and complexity of late capitalist societies, a fundamental question is the following: exactly where is the locus of the public sphere? The public cannot be subsumed under the operation of the state, nor can the realm of the public and public opinion be premised in the operation of the mass media, which is in general privately owned and operated for profit. The media report and form opinion, but they also circulate and construct views that are particular rather than universal. The notions of commodification of cultures, knowledge, and the role of media and advertisement preclude the media per se from embodying the locus of the public. Indeed, the media reflect, construct and signify a consumer culture and lifestyle (Featherstone, 1991). Moreover, the views of minorities and groups traditionally excluded culturally are not represented in the political economy portrayed by the media as often as in community and public settings or with the full range of deliberations that occur there. With a lament for the loss of the "joining and neighboring" approach to citizenship building, fifty years ago two of the most prominent scholars from the structural-functionalist tradition, and indeed quite clever cultural critics, Paul Lazarfeld and Robert K. Merton ([1948], cited in Morley, 1992) wrote on what they saw as the narcotizing dysfunction of the media deeply undermining citizenship:

> The individual reads accounts of issues and problems and may even discuss alternative lines of action. But this rather intellectualized, remote connection with organized social action is not activated. The interested and informed citizen can congratulate himself on his lofty state of interest and information and forget to see that he has abstained from decision and action. In short he takes his secondary contact with the world of political reality, his reading and listening and thinking, as a vicarious performance. He comes to mistake knowing about problems of the day for doing something about them. He is concerned. He is informed. And he has all sorts of ideas about what should be done. But, after he has gotten through his dinner and after he has listened to his favorite radio programs and after he has read his second newspaper of the day, it is really time for bed. In this peculiar respect, mass communications may be included among the most respectable and efficient social narcotics. (252)

Yet, a word of caution is important here. Even in societies with mass media fully controlled by multinational corporations, though with a set of rules and regulations that represent the best of the liberal tradition, there is always the possibility that autonomous journalism will expose illegal, immoral, or unethical behavior of government, corporations, cliques, or elite enclaves. Exposés of this kind help to reshape the nature and texture of the political debate. Without making of this an analytical remark, there is no doubt in my mind that the Watergate investigation in the United States constituted a watershed in the public perception of the integrity of the office of the executive (and not only in the figure of a politician like Richard Nixon with a penchant for corruption) and that it deeply affected the legality of the office in the eyes of the common citizen. Or shall I say with Nietzsche that this symbolizes for the citizen that "the instinct of the nation no longer comes out to meet him" (Nietzsche, 1991:82)?

Thus, if Lazarfeld and Merton (1948; as cited by Morley, 1992) are right, the choice seems to be between promoting a narcotizing of the citizenship and rampant cynicism that damages the fabric of democracy. However, in societies with unstable legal configurations, and even in which liberal democracy has not been fully attained, an honest, autonomous, and brave press and mass media can indeed represent the voice of reason criticizing established powers, including the government and private interests. This is the case, for example, of the Argentinean press and to some extent the mass media, which during the last years have become the key critics of government initiatives that otherwise would have remained unchecked, given the overwhelming control (until 1997) of the legislature and the judicial system by the Peronist government of Carlos Menem. Moreover, in the case of the assassination in 1996 of newspaper photographer José Luis Cabezas by what appears to be a serious conspiracy of business mafias connected with political operators in the state, the press has kept the investigation alive despite serious personal risks for many journalists, developing a central focus in the constitution of a democratic public sphere in the country.

Although a discussion on the public sphere is not the focus of this chapter, several comments are in order. First, not everybody agrees with Habermas that identities are formed before individuals participate in the public sphere. As our discussion on identity in chapter 5 suggests, identities are not formed once and for all in a particular period of life; their formation is a lifelong process. They are an integral part of the process of symbolic meaning-making resulting from our changing existential situation; they are deeply affected by political economy factors, and they are ever changing, elusive, and contradictory. I wholeheartedly agree with Nancy Fraser about the formative importance of the post-Oedipal discursive interaction out of the nuclear family, which can explain identity shifts over time (Fraser, 1997:97). Indeed, "public spheres are not arenas only for the formation of discursive opinion; in addition they are arenas for the formation and enactment of social identities" (Fraser, 1997:83).

Second, as is clear in Fraser's criticism and a host of other theoretical analyses from feminist perspectives, Habermas's normative ideal seems not to incorporate, analytically or historically, the notion of gender exclusion in the constitution of public sphere, which is obviously unacceptable to feminist scholars (Meehan, 1995). Third, the notion of the public sphere as a rational bourgeois discourse, while perhaps interesting as a heuristic notion for understanding the historical formation of public spheres, cannot in itself encapsulate all rational discourses that interact and construct public spheres in capitalist societies. In fact, it is quite difficult to accept that a rational discourse promoting models of radical democracy can be totally encapsulated under the guise of bourgeois discourse. Fourth, it is dangerous to assume, as Habermas does, that the public sphere is merely a space for deliberation. There are institutions, rules, practices, and behaviors that transcend discourses and that cannot be subsumed to narratives or exchanges. Fifth, it is equally dangerous to assume that the public sphere can be restricted to a homogeneous definition of citizenship without recognizing the large number of exclusions—based not only on gender but also on race, ethnicity, class, religion, sexual preference, etc.—that prevail in the practice of realpolitik in the structural-historical dynamics of capitalist societies. Despite Marx's suggestion that the experience of modernity is marked by the fact that "all that is solid melts into air,"[12] there is no reason to assume that if the Habermasian formulae of constitution of public spheres and ideal speeches can be practically implemented, these practices and narratives of exclusions, prevailing structural hierarchies and powers, and homogenizing definitions of citizenship will simply go away without a fight. Last, it is clear that a public sphere cannot be created without contributions from the democratic state (i.e., a state working to enhance the role of democracy in capitalism, while intervening to ameliorate structural trends of social inequality).

The preceding should not distract one from the central focus of this chapter. Whatever the locus of the public sphere, schools have been considered, in traditional terms, part of the state because they are supposedly engaged in helping students gain the knowledge and skills necessary for citizenship. The notion of citizenship, however, cannot be considered self-explanatory and nonproblematic, as I argue in chapter 4, and this is a point where the notion of public sphere becomes useful. From a critical perspective, the notion of citizenship is taken as a concept that should account for the pluralistic and hybridized nature of capitalist societies, including the diversity of social subjects. Critical pedagogy is seen as a form of cultural politics, arguing for the need to struggle for schools as democratic public spheres.[13] Moreover, "critical pedagogy is more than a desacralization of the grand narratives of modernity, but seeks to establish new moral and political frontiers of emancipatory and collective struggle, where both subjugated narratives and new narratives can be written and voiced in the arena of democracy" (McLaren, 1991:172). As part of the democratic public sphere (and not only as an integral part of the state's legal action), schools could constitute arenas of discourses incorporating diverse knowledge-guiding interests, including empirical-analytical, historical-hermeneutic, and critical-emancipatory knowledge.[14]

After discussing the relationships between state and education, providing as well a systematic discussion of the definition of the state and related basic concepts in political science, it is imperative to return to the discussion of political philosophy. Any analysis of the relationships among democracy, the state, citizenship, and education should consider the classics, particularly classical theories of the state, including liberalism and Marxism.

The Capitalist State in Democratic Societies, or the Democratic State in Capitalist Societies?

> The notion of the state refers to the basic alliance, the basic pact of domination, that exists among social classes or factions of the dominant classes and the norms which guarantee their dominance over the subordinate strata.
>
> —Fernando Henrique Cardoso, "On the Characterization of Authoritarian Regimes in Latin America"

> It is spirit which is *for itself*, since it maintains itself by being reflected in the minds of the component individuals; and which is *in itself* or substance, since it preserves them within itself. *Qua* actual substance, that spirit of a Nation (Volk); *qua* concrete consciousness, it is the Citizen of the nation. This consciousness has its essential being in simple spirit, and is certain of itself in the actual realization of this spirit, in the entire nation; it has its truth there directly, not therefore in something unreal, but in a spirit which exists and makes itself felt.
>
> G. W. F. Hegel, *The Phenomenology of Mind*

The liberal conception of the state is centered on the notion of separate public powers (for the government and the governed), and the state is conceived of as the supreme political authority within precise limits (Held, 1989:12). This liberal notion of political authority should be reconsidered from the perspective of contemporary political science. There is, without doubt, a tradition of liberal political analysis that primarily addresses the question of sovereignty of the state and citizenship, that is to say, the formation of the citizen and the political culture of the nation. A second tradition, that of liberal democracy, questions problems of political representation and accountability; that is, how the actions of individuals, institutions, and the state itself are subject to controls and checks and balances. This is particularly relevant in regard to the actions of individuals, institutions, corporations, and state agencies in the constitution of the democratic pact and the extent to which their actions damage or betray the democratic pact. A third tradition, Marxism, emphasizes the question of the power of the state, especially those aspects that concern the relationship between social class structure and the forces and instruments of political coercion. This analysis supposes that obtaining consensus and implementing measures that guarantee the fair representation of interests is not outside the realm of pressured persuasion or coercion, nor is it outside the realm of social relations of domination and exploitation. Finally, the perspective of political sociology, with the extraordinary contributions of Max Weber, focuses on the study of institutional mechanisms of the operation of the state, and especially on the exercise of the authority of the state and the relationships among nation-states.[15]

From the critical perspectives of liberalism, and especially those that are rooted in the theories of democracy, neo-Marxism, and political sociology, the discussion of the state takes on new dimensions. In a preliminary approach, the notion of the state appears as a heuristic instrument, as a concept that differs radically from the classical notions of political regime, government, and public power. In regard to this heuristic instrument, the notion of the state includes the idea of the condensation of power and force in the society. The exercise of the power of the state occurs by the exercise of actions of power and coercion over civil society by means of specialized state apparatuses. This notion of the condensation of power also refers to another central aspect of the state—the notion that the state exercises power. This power is independent of the major social actors, and on occasion it is exercised according to specific interests represented in society—for example, state action on behalf of specific elites. Thus, the power of the state can reflect a specific political project, a class alliance, or a coalition of specific economic, social, cultural, or moral interests. In short, the state appears as an alliance or a pact of domination.

There is a central idea in these perspectives of domination in which the state is also an arena of confrontation for conflicting political projects. As an arena of confrontation, it reflects not only the vicissitudes of social struggles and the tensions inherent in agreements and disagreements between social forces but also the contradictions and difficulties of carrying out unified and coherent actions within the parameters of a specific political project. Every public policy, even though it is part of a project of domination, serves as an arena of struggle and a sounding board for civil society and its inherent tensions, contradictions, and political agreements and disagreements.

Approaching the state strictly as an actor in the struggle between social classes de-emphasizes other important variables related to social action. In addition to class distinctions, other aspects of race, ethnicity, gender, geographical location, or ethical-moral or religious differences among individuals produce social relations and social actions that require the state to legislate, sanction, manage, and punish. According to Claus Offe, one of the central issues related to the state is the contradiction between the state's need for capitalist accumulation and the legitimacy of the capitalist system itself. Offe proposes an analytical approach, based on systems theory, that complements and extends Gramscian analysis and Poulantzas's interpretation. For Offe, the state is a mediator in the crisis of capitalism, and it acquires specific functions in the mediation of the basic contradictions of capitalism—the growing socialization of production and the private appropriation of surplus value. In order to measure this fundamental contradiction, the state is obliged to increase its institutional functions (Torres, 1989).

For Offe, the state is a self-regulating administrative system that reflects a group of institutional rules, regulations, and conventions that have historically developed in capitalist societies. Furthermore, the capitalist state does not necessarily respond directly to those who temporarily exercise power (the government of a particular political regime or party), nor does it directly respond to the dictates of particular social sectors (economic interests) or dominant classes. Given that the state appears as a pact of domination that mediates recurrent crises of the capitalist system and attempts to prevent them from affecting the conditions of production and reproduction of that system, the class perspective of the state is not based on representing specific sectoral interests, nor does it reflect the policies of the dominant classes or of a specific political group that may control governmental institutions (Carnoy, 1984:131–140).

The state, as a pact of domination and a self-regulating administrative system, plays a central role as mediator in the context of the crises of capitalism, especially regarding the contradictions between accumulation and legitimation. The discussion of theories of the state is particularly important for education for several reasons. First of all, as I have already argued, the definition, interpretation, and analysis of educational problems and their solutions depend to a large extent on theories of the state that justify and underlie the diagnostic and solution. In addition, new kinds of state intervention, often defined as the neoliberal state, reflect a substantial change in the logic of public action and involvement of the state, particularly in the developing world. At the same time, this change in the character of the state can also reflect new visions of the nature and limits of the democratic pact and of the character and role of education and educational policy in the global spread of capitalism. An extensive discussion on globalization and democracy can be found in chapters 3 and 5, respectively.[16]

Classical Theories of the State and Education:
From Liberalism to Marxism

It is not necessary to wait until Kings do philosophy or until philosophers become Kings. It is not even desirable because possessing power inevitably corrupts the free exercise of reason.

—Immanuel Kant, *Scriti Politici*

The state in liberal political philosophy constitutes the supreme political authority within precise limits (Held, 1989:12). The liberal idea of the state rests on the notion of public power as different from the ruling and the ruled. Indeed, according to this approach, the state has great independence from civil society, which enables "it to serve as an arbiter or conciliator among the social classes" (Easton, 1981:308). Liberalism argues that the state is above the fray of interests and societal conflicts; represents a neutral terrain ready to be occupied by different political parties (or alliances) according to shifting voting patterns; acts independently of particular groups or interests; legislates, preserves, and enforces the law without prejudice or particularistic goals; and above all represents the public interest.

This classical liberal perspective of political authority can be discussed from the perspectives of contemporary traditions in political science. A major tradition of liberal political analysis focuses primarily on questions of state sovereignty and citizenship. A second tradition of liberal democracy focuses on problems of political representation and accountability; that is, how the actions of individuals, institutions, and state agencies can be subject to checks and balances, while the rules that regulate, but also reflect the actions of, individuals, institutions, corporations, and state agencies find their legitimacy in the democratic pact or "social contract." Questions of state legitimacy, representation, and participation relate to how social and political practices of individuals and institutions are regulated within the framework of the democratic pact, thus enhancing rather than diminishing the democratic tradition of political negotiation. Tensions and contradictions between individual rights and collective rights (or the general will) are central theoretical constructs in the discussion about political participation, representation, and legitimacy. A third tradition emphasizes the question of state power, particularly state actions that relate to class structures, including means, models, and institutions of political coercion. Indeed, the state is seen as institutionalized political power. A basic assumption is that political life is not divorced from the basic determinants of social and economic life. Therefore, domination, exploitation, oppression, inequality, and discrimination are an intrinsic part of state activities, reverberating in the constitution and exercise of state power. While the characteristics of the political regime play a major role in the exercise of state power, its nature is intrinsically related to the role and function of the state in capitalist societies. The processes of securing and reproducing consensus and implementing measures that guarantee interest representation cannot be exempted from coercion and force. In the same vein, consensus building does not remain unrelated to relationships of domination and exploitation between individuals and among individuals, social regulations, structures, and institutions. The influence of Max Weber has shaped the study of the institutional mechanisms of operation of the state, especially the exercise of state authority, and the role of bureaucracy (including instrumental, legal, and bureaucratic rationality) in state actions. State action refers both to the actions of the state regarding the individuals and communities that define and play out their different interests, passions, and ideologies within the context of the nation and to the interactions between states in the world system (Held, 1983, 1989, 1991; Sonntag and Valecillos, 1977; Vincent, 1987). While Weber considered the notion of domination as central to his analysis, notions of exploitation or oppression were outside his analytical framework.

For critical perspectives of classical liberalism, those that are an extension of liberalism (including theories of democracy and political sociology), and those that are a critical reelaboration (including neo-Marxism), the discussion of the state acquires a new profile. At first glance, the state appears as a heuristic instrument, a concept that radically differs from the classic notions of government, political regime, public power, and public sector. As a heuristic concept, the notion of state reflects the condensation of both power and force in society. The power of the state is exercised through a specialized state apparatus and implies actions of force and coercion of civil society. For instance, individuals may voluntarily pay taxes, but the regulatory and coercive powers of state agencies enforce the probability that they will do it. The notion of condensation of force refers to another central component of the notion of the state: the state not only represents the exercise of the legitimate political authority but also exercises its authority in a vast array of domains and activities. The notion of the state as the condensation of force refers to the ambivalent nature of state power, which appears as relatively independent of the main social actors in civil society. At times, state power is exercised, if not on behalf of, at least in consonance with key demands of, special interest groups and classes. Thus without resorting to conspiracy theories (which refer to purposeful, singular, and coordinated actions of actors, groups, or institutions), some branches of political theory argue that state power may reflect a specific political project or a class alliance and, as such, may represent specific social, economic, cultural, ethical, and moral interests. The state appears as an alliance or a pact of domination in which, through elective affinities and not necessarily through preordained or concerted actions, certain interest groups or elites in civil society may exercise undue influence in the production of public policy.

An understanding that domination is always disputed, resisted, and challenged is central to viewing the state from the perspective of domination. That is, political domination is a historical process; it is rarely completely achieved, and therefore social control is never completely consummated. Challenges to political domination and hegemony may come from outside the ruling alliance (e.g., by contestatory social movements or classes, as I explain in chapter 5), but they also may result from disputes within the dominant clique or ruling alliance.

Domination and hegemony as theoretical notions suggest that the constitution of the state as a pact of domination is one that is continually and invariably a work in progress. The state, then, appears as a contested terrain, as an arena of confrontation of political projects. As such, the state not only reflects the vicissitudes of social struggles, the tensions in the agreements and disagreements between social groups and elites, but also the difficulties and contradictions resulting from the attempts to establish a coherent and unified action within the framework of a given cultural, social, and political project. Public policy, as part of a project of domination, is both an arena for struggle and a sounding board for civil society. When public policy is defined and implemented, tensions and contradictions, agreements and disagreements between social movements, elites, bureaucratic groups, individuals, and communities are played out daily. This explains the definition that Nicos Poulantzas formulated of the state and state power as social relationships. The state is the condensation of social power, but, at the same time, it has power and relative autonomy from social classes and interests or power groups.

The state appears as an arena for confrontation of social classes. The capitalist state for Poulantzas is an arena of class struggle; it is simultaneously a product of class struggle and an actor that intervenes in the constitution of class relations. For Poulantzas, departing from Althusser's (1971) interpretation of Gramsci, the distinction between state practices of consensus and state practices of coercion is too subtle and does not reflect the practical operation of the state. It becomes difficult to identify the two dimensions separately at the level of social practices. It is not possible to govern merely by force; there is always a need for a minimum of consensus. Likewise, it is impossible to establish repressive practices (and institutions) without an ideological basis. Repressive activities count on the ideological support of those in charge of the repression and various sectors within civil society. Finally, in the presence of divergent and contradictory interests, there is no consensus that can be established without force—either at the level of actual implementation of physical force to achieve a given end or in terms of the probability of exercising physical force. Similarly, no ideological or scientific rhetoric can, by itself, justify and sustain indefinitely state action.

Poulantzas views Althusser's interpretation of Gramsci as too limited because of his emphasis on the negative and restrictive aspects of state action. In his latest work, Poulantzas argues that Gramsci's view of the state as part of the ideological hegemony of the dominant classes along with the coercive state apparatus (police, the army, the judicial system, and the prison system) should be reconstructed. Poulantzas quite eloquently argues that the capitalist state was part of the class struggle and that it played a decisive role in the reproduction of the conditions of production. The state has a very important role as a capitalist relation, increasing the capacities for accumulation and legitimation of the capitalist system (Torres, 1985; Carnoy, 1984).

However, to understand the state strictly as an actor in class struggle is to downplay other important variants of its social action. The reason is that the state not only is a central actor in preserving (or challenging) class distinctions but also is crossed by, and is the location of, a host of other key social struggles based on race and ethnicity, gender, geographical location, and ethical, moral, religious, and sexual preference. These differences generate social relations, and the state is forced to intervene either as a legislator, regulator of social exchanges, executor of laws, or coercive disciplinarian.

From a critical theory perspective, Claus Offe takes as the central question for state action the contradictions between capital accumulation and legitimation. The state has to promote capital accumulation, which in a capitalist structure always generates inequalities. At the same time, the state has to promote and sustain the legitimacy of the overall political and economic system. Offe incorporates into a new theoretical synthesis theories of systems and Gramsci's and Poulantzas's analysis of the state as a social relation. The state acquires specific functions trying to mediate in the basic contradiction of capitalism: the growing socialization of production and the private appropriation of surplus value. To be able to mediate this fundamental contradiction, the state in late capitalism has to expand its traditional institutional functions and role (Torres, 1989).

For Offe, the state is a self-regulating administrative system. It is the condensation of legal foundations, rules, and regulations as well as the formal and informal institutions and codes that have become crystallized historically in capitalist societies. A capitalist state does not necessarily respond to the ruling elite that may control the government in a given political regime, nor does such a state necessarily completely respond—in democratic regimes—to the will of the elites or dominant classes. Although the state appears as a pact of domination trying to mediate and avoid recurrent crises of capitalist production and trying to prevent threats to the conditions of production and reproduction of the system, a class perspective of the state does not rest on the ability of the state to represent the specific sectoral interests of a group or class nor to represent the will of specific groups in control of the institutions of government (Carnoy, 1984). On the contrary, the specific class component of the capitalist state results from the structural and historical imperatives of the capitalist system and its reproduction and depends on its own secular dynamics as a regulatory institution in capitalism.

These regulatory functions are as follows. First, the state, considering that it cannot control or regulate capitalist production itself (given that capital accumulation takes place in units of private production), creates the conditions for the continuation of private relations of production. Second, the social actors that control the apparatus of the state depend for their survival and the achievement of their political objectives on resources that, via taxes, can be extracted from private capitalist production. When there is a crisis of capital accumulation, state resources diminish. Third, the state has not only the authority but also the "mandate" to sustain and create the conditions for capital accumulation and social reproduction and for the capitalist social relations of production. Finally, given that the political personnel who control the state do not themselves hold power but instead require a mandate for action, the notion of a state that represents the generalization of social interests can be justified.

According to Offe (1973), the state can only function as a capitalist state by appealing to symbols and resources that conceal its nature as a capitalist state. In other words, its very existence above the fray of social conflict is dependent upon its systematic denial of its capitalist nature. The legitimation of the capitalist state and of the capitalist system implies that state institutions and state bureaucracies strive to reconcile the just-mentioned regulatory functions in promoting capital accumulation while struggling to implement the democratic demands of its citizens; demands already established in the democratic framework. Thus the state must undertake not only political, ideological, social, and cultural but also economic actions to counter the legitimacy deficit of late capitalism (Torres, 1989, 1991; Levin et al., 1986).

This legitimacy deficit is sometimes expressed as the ungovernability of democratic systems. The notion of governability of democratic systems is discussed by Offe (1984) in the following terms:

> Its connotations are "rising expectations" on the part of competing interest groups and parties, disseminated by the media; a resulting "overload" of the state bureaucracies which find themselves, under the impact of fiscal constraints, unable to satisfy such expectations; a breakdown of government authority which

would be required for a firm resistance to proliferating demands; an increasing level of distrust, suspicion and frustration among the citizens in their attitudes vis-à-vis the state, and a creeping paralysis of the foundations of economic stability and growth potential. (164)

The state performs its basic functions, including the execution of a preventive strategy of crisis management, the establishment of a system of priorities with respect to social needs and potential threats, and the creation of a long-term avoidance strategy to defuse future threats to political stability while building consensus. The notion of compensatory legitimation refers to the state's need to cope with a deficit of legitimacy in the overall system. This crisis of legitimation has several sources. One of the most important is the disparity between growing social demands on welfare policies and diminishing fiscal revenues to meet those demands. To confront the crisis of legitimation, the state calls upon scientific and technical knowledge and expertise, increasing policies of participation, and legalization of educational policies with a growing role for the judicial system in education as a last resort to settle disputes in the educational arena (Torres and Puiggrós, 1996; Weiler, 1983). Therefore, education as compensatory legitimation implies that the state may use educational policies as a substitute for political rights and for increased material consumption while simultaneously creating a system of legitimizing beliefs that will assure the loyalty of its citizens. In synthesis, the state is a pact of domination and a set of self-regulating institutional apparatuses, bureaucratic organizations, and formal and informal codes seeking to represent the public and private spheres of society. A central role of the state is to act as mediator in the context of the crisis of capitalism, especially in the contradictions between accumulation and legitimation.

Martin Carnoy (1992) has argued that the majority of analyses of educational problems have implicit in them a theory of the state but that seldom are the fundamentals of that theory recognized or spelled out in educational research and practice. Becoming self-reflective about our own assumptions seems to be a precondition for solid scholarship. However, since the role of the state has become even more complex and problematic in contemporary societies, this new role poses new conceptual problems for theoretical analysis, and the development of state theories creates more practical problems as well. David Harvey (1989) has correctly argued that

the state is now in a much more problematic position. It is called upon to regulate the activities of corporate capital in the national interest at the same time as it is forced, also in the national interest, to create a "good business climate" to act as an inducement to transnational and global finance capital, and to deter (by means other than exchange controls) capital flight to greener and more profitable pastures. (170)

Changes in the nature of the alliance controlling the state, and in the nature of the state itself, are reflected in the logic of public policy and state action. At the same time, changes in the character of the state and public policy may reflect new visions of what democracy should look like. They may also reflect new visions of what education can do for a certain definition of democracy, multiculturalism, and citizenship, and whether and how schooling and nonformal education should intervene in the constitution of the democratic political culture. Finally, an important question is whether changes in educational systems and educational policies are compatible with the globalization of capitalism in the world system, a question addressed in chapter 3 and in the conclusion of this book. The next section will provide a systematic overview of different perspectives on the state and education.

Contemporary Educational Theories and the Capitalist State

The Liberal State and Education

> The Enlightenment philosophers wanted to utilize this accumulation of specialized culture for the enrichment of everyday life, that is to say, for the rational organization of everyday social life.
> —Jürgen Habermas, "Modernity versus Postmodernity"

Liberal-pluralist theories of the state conceive of the state as a political system, as an autonomous political institution independent from the system of production and class structure. The state appears, then, as a neutral referee overseeing and regulating the clashes between interest groups. State intervention takes place either when different interest groups and possibly elites competing for resources conflict with the general interest of all citizens or when the state, pursuing independent activities, attempts to modernize society.

The liberal view suggests that the state is the collective creation of its individual members, providing a set of common social goods, including defense, education, the legal system, and the means of enforcing that system to all or the majority of citizens and legal residents (Held, 1983, 1991; Cerroni, 1992; Carnoy, 1984; Hall and Ikenberry, 1989; Zaretsky, 1983; Evans, 1991; Moran and Wright, 1991). This normative, rather than analytical, position was epitomized by Thomas Jefferson when in 1776 he began the American Declaration of Independence with these famous words:

We hold these truths to be self-evident, that all men are created equal; that they are endowed by their Creator with certain inalienable rights; that among these are life, liberty, and the pursuit of happiness. That, to secure these rights, governments are instituted among men, deriving their just powers from the consent of the governed.

There is a principle of autonomy in liberalism (shared to some extent by Marxism as an offspring of earlier classical liberal thought) that is well expressed in Held's (1989) synthesis: "Individuals should be free and equal in the determination of the rules by which they live; that is, they should enjoy equal rights (and accordingly, equal obligations) in the specification of the framework which generates and limits the opportunities available to them throughout their lives" (165).

Two key meanings of the principle of autonomy should be highlighted: on one hand, the notion of the autonomy of individuals, as aptly discussed by Held, and on the other hand, the notion of state autonomy and the independence of state bureaucracy (Carnoy, 1984:1992). There are several implications of this principle of autonomy, particularly if we remember that Kant equated the principle of autonomy with free will. First, "Citizenship theory was grounded in the primacy of the practical politics of universal social obligations and rights" (Culpitt, 1992:6). This assumption has implications for the role and functions of the state, as discussed below. Second, the state should remove any impediment to the full exercise of freedom and facilitate the pursuit of happiness by all individuals. Hence liberalism emerges as the champion of tolerance and the archenemy of despotism (e.g., totalitarianism and authoritarianism). Finally, the state should work to remedy or prevent confrontations that could alter the nature of the social pact.

State autonomy "allows the state to translate its preferences into authoritative actions to the degree to which public policy conforms to the parallelogram of the public officials' resource-weighted preferences" (Nordlinger, 1981:19). Indeed, the state in classical liberalism was conceived of as an arena in which "societal conflicts are fought out, interests mediated, and the ensuing results authoritatively confirmed" (5). Yet, Nordlinger goes on to argue that a state-centered view of the liberal democratic state shows, whether from pluralist or neo-pluralist perspectives,[17] that public officials have societally unconstrained volitions; therefore, public officials not only witness the struggle for resources, the definitions of societal needs, and the adaptation of preferences but also intervene authoritatively in pursuing specific goals. For a state-centered tradition, the liberal democratic state plays a critical role in balancing, aggregating, and reconciling conflicting demands, acting continuously as a broker and mediator, and facilitating the acceptance of policy compromises. The development of the welfare state highlights the highest level of autonomy of the liberal democratic state in the achievement of the democratic pact.

The welfare state is a particular form of the democratic liberal state in industrialized societies. Its origins have been associated with Scandinavian state experiences at the turn of the century, particularly Sweden's social democracy, and the industrial and financial reconstitution of the post-depression era in the United States, based on a "social pact" (New Deal) and coordination of policies between employers and labor (Moran and Wright, 1991; Offe, 1984, 1985; Therborn, 1979a; Torres and Puiggrós, 1995). A striking feature of the welfare state is its interventionist role in the economy, including enlarged public spending in both productive and nonproductive sectors. Welfare policies are defined as government protection of minimum standards of income, nutrition, health, housing, and education. As Wilensky (1975, 1976) argues, these welfare benefits were assured to every citizen as a political right rather than as charity (see also Popkewitz, 1991).

In this century, schooling has reflected the key features of the liberal state in public policy. While education was perceived by nineteenth-century liberals as a tool for enlightenment and as the great equalizer, in the twentieth century, schooling played a key role in the action of the welfare state. School expansion has been associated with the extension of citizenship rights and welfare policies to the majority of citizens.[18] Central concerns for liberal and social-democratic planners were how to analyze the social and economic changes, how to conceptualize the functional relationship between schools and society, and, when societies become more specialized and diversified, what implications might follow from the transformations in schooling that have accompanied changes in the division of labor.

The analysis of the role of schooling in the liberal perspective of the welfare state was accompanied by an almost complete neglect of the contradictory aspects of the division of labor, including class conflict, and a very truncated conception of individualization implied by theories of socialization popularized by key functionalist theories, particularly the work of Parsons (see Morrow and Torres, 1995). The manifest and limited number of latent functions of education was stressed, and positive functions were analyzed to the exclusion of negative or dysfunctional ones. In addition, there was an uncritical acceptance of assumptions such as the high level of systemic integration of society and the methodological principle that the "whole" served by the "part" (i.e., education) was indeed society as a whole rather than some powerful class, dominant ethnic groups, or castes within society taking advantage of positions of wealth, influence, and power.[19]

Post–World War II euphoria facilitated the liberal and social democratic options' portrayal of a vision of equality of opportunity and educational reform in democratic societies. This vision was certainly considered an option between the equally unacceptable choices of bolshevism and fascism. Parallel and complementary economic doctrines in the form of Keynesian economic theory paved the way for a mixed economy balanced by central fiscal and monetary policies (indicative planning), as well as, in the 1960s, the theory of human capital that justified educational expenditures as part of a long-term strategy of economic growth. Thus, educational planning in industrial advanced societies played a central role in the conception of the interventionist welfare state, a state that was necessary for controlling the self-destructive tendencies of capitalist growth. The emergence of the postcolonial state, a sizable worldwide economic surplus, and modernization theories, coupled with the diffusion of human capital theory for educational planning, helped to fuel educational expansion in the developing world to unprecedented levels (Carnoy, 1977; Carnoy and Samoff, 1990; Fagerlind and Saha, 1983; Fuller, 1991; Russell, 1989; Selowsky, 1980; Torres, 1990).

Liberal educators see educational systems performing three major functions: cognitive and moral socialization, skills training, and certification. These functions contribute to a rational allocation of resources and social mobility (Banks, 1989; La Belle and Ward, 1994). Educating people with universal cognitive skills is held as essential, while economic and political socialization functions are decisive in the welfare of individuals, communities, and the overall society. Educational systems perform an allocative function, preparing individuals for their roles in the division of labor, thus facilitating an efficient distribution of talent through competitive selection. The economic function, conceived of primarily as producing human capital, links education to higher levels of productivity by individuals in the labor force. Finally, the role of schooling in political socialization is acknowledged as indispensable to social integration and social control. With the notion of social differentiation, ascriptive statuses are legitimated through academic achievement by converting them into acquired statuses.

Perhaps the best examples of liberal policies in the U.S. educational system are represented by the programs of the War on Poverty. These programs were based on a set of assumptions: first, that the elimination of poverty in the United States requires helping children born in poor families to escape from their situation (under the presupposition that there is no falling back into poverty); second, that the principal reason that children do not escape poverty is that they do not acquire the basic cognitive competencies for succeeding in the world; and finally, that the best and most efficient mechanisms for breaking the vicious circle of poverty are educational reforms based on compensatory programs for families and neighborhoods to keep them above a minimal acceptable threshold (Jencks et al., 1972).

Because of the dominant theory of the state held by liberal policy planners in the welfare state, the transmission and legitimation of inequality may have resulted as a (latent) function of the school, perpetuated by curricular and teaching practices. For instance, the debate on tracking highlights how school experience varies by students' social class, resulting in ability grouping and curriculum grouping that perpetuate segregationist practices in U.S. schools, to the detriment of students of color, women, immigrants, and working-class students (Oakes, 1985; Wells and Oakes, in press).

Thus, through educational planning and social engineering, liberal functionalist theories of educational reform advanced personal and civil rights, including a movement toward equality of opportunity and economic redistribution. In the United States, particularly, liberal education confronted the issues of unequal status attainment and the effects of race in education. At the same time, through a functionalist theory of stratification, liberalism provided a rationale for a hierarchy of rewards, rejecting notions of absolute equality, while paradoxically placing equality of educational opportunity at the center of social efficiency and civil rights movements. The failure of functionalist educational theory stemmed therefore from its inability to explain fully the causes of inequality and problems of unequal opportunity, let alone suggest a plausible strategy for dealing with the role of the educational process in perpetuating social inequalities.

The general disillusionment with North American "liberalism" led social theorists either back toward a more pessimistic neoconservative position or to an emergent, if marginal and divided, democratic socialist left. In other advanced liberal democratic societies (all characterized by the existence of a significant social democratic party with roots in labor, and in some cases a significant communist party), the reception and appropriation of functionalist theories of education was rather different. In Europe, generally speaking, the existence of a conservative tradition in education and politics allowed the American combination of progressive education, comprehensive secondary schools open to all, and a tertiary system with relatively open admission standards, or contest mobility (which evolved from functionalist education theory), to be associated with progressive reform. Hence we find the irony of European labor parties supporting policies that were rationalized—partly because of their effectiveness against the claims of defenders of traditional elitist education—in accordance with American functionalist theory and empirical mobility and status attainment research (Morrow and Torres, 1995; in press b).

Most significant here is the case of Britain, where the sociology of education had its roots in the work of Karl Mannheim, who was exiled in England,

and of T. H. Marshall, whose work will be discussed extensively in chapter 4. Marshall's influential analysis of the welfare state and the principle of citizenship gave hope for the reconciliation of liberty and equality in a democratic society, a theme that was complemented in Mannheim's work on social planning (Marshall, 1950, 1983; Mannheim, 1953, 1960; Whitty, in Torres, 1998; Zeitlin, 1968). Though the existence of a powerful labor movement made equality of opportunity a central theme, the problem of efficiency and the waste of human resources was also central (Karabel and Halsey, 1977:10).

The fusion of social democratic politics, technocratic functionalism, and empirical research in education took into account neither the relationship between school outcomes and societal structures nor the cultural processes involving education. Also, it did not seriously consider the implications of implementing a radical democratic educational policy within a welfare state subject, to some extent, to the contradictions of capitalist development. Research continued to show "that policies, informed by sociological understandings, did not in fact remove inequalities. On the contrary, they seemed to produce, with monotonous regularity, the same or similar educational outcomes" (Baron et al., 1981:130, cited by Morrow and Torres, 1995:72).

Liberalism was caught in the crossfire between the Left and the Right. Various social forces undermined the educational agenda of liberalism. From the left, reproduction theories linked education with the social and cultural reproduction of capitalist societies, challenging key assumptions of educational liberalism. Reproduction theories emphasize that power and knowledge are always intertwined in education. Thus, educational policies, classroom practices, and curriculum are an integral part of a contradictory process of socialization of children and youth into a given social order, while at the same time educational sites, policies, and practices may develop forms of resistance to a hegemonic culture.[20] From the right came the growing dissatisfaction with the welfare state, particularly its fiscal performance. In addition, the liberal rhetoric on equality of educational opportunity was counterbalanced by a rhetoric about educational achievement and excellence in the United States and by a new neoconservative rhetoric emphasizing individual rights over public obligations and social rights.[21]

Central flaws of liberal reformers and researchers of the liberal persuasion are their lack of a historical-structural analysis of educational processes in capitalist societies (e.g., their lack of a political economy of education); their refusal to tackle head-on the implications of domination and exploitation in capitalist societies and, by implication, in education; and particularly their acritical acceptance of the role of the state in promoting citizenship on the basis of the primacy of the practical politics of universal social obligations and rights while at the same time a set of exclusions (based on economics, race, ethnicity, or gender) remains stubbornly in place. Nancy Fraser (1997) says it very nicely:

> Liberal political theory assumes that it is possible to organize a democratic form of political life on the basis of socioeconomic and sociosexual structures that generate systemic inequalities. For liberals, then, the problem of democracy becomes the problem of how to insulate political processes from what are considered to be nonpolitical or prepolitical processes, those characteristic, for example, of the economy, the family, the informal everyday life. The problem for liberals, thus, is how to strengthen the barriers separating political institutions that are supposed to instantiate relations of equality from economic, cultural, and sociosexual institutions that are premised on systemic relations of inequality. (79)

A theory of the state that does not address the nature and distribution of power in society is seriously flawed. Indeed, if we assume that power in Western societies—as criticized by British Marxist Ralph Miliband—is competitive, fragmented, and diffused, and if everybody, directly or in organized groups, may have some power, how can the liberal state effectively regulate the appropriation and usufruct of power, influence, and wealth on behalf of all citizens? Can public education charged with the mandate to facilitate egalitarian social change be an effective tool in the presence of established social hierarchies, economic structures, and interest groups?

If institutional democracy, including universal suffrage, free and regular elections, representative institutions, and effective citizenship rights, is preserved, then both individuals and groups will take advantage of these rights under the protection of the law and an independent judiciary. For liberal multicultural researchers and policymakers, however, political culture is not homogeneous but diverse, hence intergroup relations become a problem to be addressed. The goal of multiculturalism "is to reform the school and other educational institutions so that students from diverse racial, ethnic, and social-class groups will experience educational quality" (Banks, 1993:3). The liberal state and its attempt to change individual preferences as the preferred means for solving the dilemmas posed by multiculturalism have been contested by neoconservatives, neoliberals, reproduction and parallelist theories, and critics of official knowledge.

The Neoconservative State and Education: Choice and Cultural Pluralism

> It is not a very satisfactory and plausible hypothesis to think of human culture as the product of a mere illusion—as a juggling with words and a childish play with names.
>
> —Ernst Cassirer, *The Myth of the State*

Traditional conservatism emerged as a response to the French Revolution and the politics and ideology of the Enlightenment. As such, conservatism opposes progressivism. The concepts of nation, family, duty, authority, standards, traditionalism, self-interest, competitive individualism, and antistatism have usually been linked to traditional conservatism, and they represent a clear reaction to the basic values of liberalism (Apple, 1993b; Bobbio, Matteucci, and Pasquino, 1987–88). The neoconservative ideology and the neoconservative state are usually associated with drastic political economy shifts away from the welfare state in the 1980s, including Thatcher's program of government (Thatcherism), Reagan's "conservative revolution" (Reaganomics), and Brian Mulroney's Progressive Conservative Party agenda in Canada. The basis of the model was forceful privatization of state enterprises and large sections of public property; loosening of regulations of the market and private enterprise; control of inflation rather than support for full employment; and the growing importance of the executive with the corresponding decline in the role of Congress or Parliament (Therborn, 1989).

There are, however, differences among the British, American, and Canadian neoconservative experiments, resulting in contradictory policy outcomes. For instance, opportunity structures, including institutions, political alignments, and ideology, show differences across nations. The personality, personal style of government, and general ideological profile of the leaders show remarkable differences. For instance, Margaret Thatcher developed a bitterly intransigent conservative approach to governing that involved taking to task trade unions, local governments, the political opposition, and virtually anyone who challenged or questioned her program (even from within the ranks of her own party). Ronald Reagan's supply-side economics was embellished with moral conservatism on social issues, with the rising importance of neoconservative forces such as the Moral Majority. Despite Brian Mulroney's admiration for, and friendship with, Thatcher and Reagan, his neoconservatism was tempered by his pragmatic nature as a broker politician, by the opportunity structure of Canada with its decentralized policy orientation, by the entrenchment of equality rights in the Canadian Charter of Rights, and by the heterogeneous configuration of ideological positions within Mulroney's coalition (with Western Canada and Quebec representing distinct positions on a host of issues). Likewise, the contradictions between program rhetoric and program implementation became evident in Reagan's supply-side economic solution that included a massive budget deficit and increasing national debt (Stockman, 1986). Despite these differences and contradictions, privatization and market-driven policies became centerpieces of the neoconservative agenda.

Privatization and market-oriented reforms are appealing to the neoconservative state for a number of reasons. On the one hand, they help to release some of the pressures on fiscal expenditures. On the other hand, they provide a convenient avenue to depoliticizing the regulatory policies of the state in important areas of public policy formation. Transferring public services outside the direct administration and/or control of the state helps to avoid conflictive exchanges with stakeholders and consumers (clientele). Privatization plays a pivotal role in the neoconservative model, because "purchase of service contracting is both an administrative mechanism for addressing the particular issues of the social legitimacy of the state involved in direct social services and an attempt to borrow from the managerial ethos of private enterprise (and entrepreneurial development) systems of cost-benefit analysis and management by objectives" (Culpitt, 1992:94).

Neoconservatives have argued that "the state" and "the market" are two diametrically opposed social systems. They are considered clear choices in the organization of production as well as in the delivery of services (Moran and Wright, 1991). Why favor the market over the state? Neoconservatives consider markets more versatile and efficacious than the state's bureaucratic structures for a number of reasons. Markets respond more quickly to changes in technology and social demands than the state. Markets are more efficient and cost-effective in providing services than the public sector, and market competition will produce greater accountability in "social investments" than bureaucratic politics. The argument is not merely economic but moral, as Milton Friedman (cited in Dahrendorf, 1975) let us know: "Every act of government intervention, [he says] limits the area of individual freedom directly and threatens the preservation of freedom indirectly" (5). Similar arguments have been defended by von Hayek (1960).

Is this drive towards the market an indication of changes in the constitution and operation of capitalism per se? Capitalism moved in the 1970s and 1980s into a stage that David Harvey (1989) characterizes as "flexible accumulation." This late capitalist model

> rests on flexibility with respect to labor processes, labor markets, products, and patterns of consumption. It is characterized by the emergence of entirely new sectors of production, new ways of providing financial services, new markets, and above all, greatly intensified rates of commercial, technological, and organizational innovation. (147)

A central outcome of the economic process is the growing polarization in income distribution between the haves and the have-nots in capitalist democracies (Przeworski, 1991; Reich, 1991; Thurow, 1992). Harvey (1989) sees these changes in flexible accumulation giving rise to a peculiar culture, characterized as postmodernist, with its emphasis on "ephemerality, collage, fragmentation, and dispersal in philosophical and social thought [which] mimics the condition of flexible accumulation. . . . all of this fits in with the emergence since 1970 of a fragmented politics of divergent special and regional interest groups" (302). Notwithstanding Harvey's insights, flexible accumulation as a mode of production highlights a parallel process of concentration and centralization of economic power, with an increasing role for multinational corporations in the process of capital accumulation and production in the world system. The cultural features of ephemerality, collage, and fragmentation seem to fit better the description of what is happening to social classes, social movements, and subordinate cultures than what is happening to transnational corporations in the world system.[22]

These cultural changes are not independent of the experience of social struggles in advanced industrial democracies and the developing world, including the anti–Vietnam War movement, feminist and women's movements, peace movements, antinuclear movements, or liberation movements *tout court*. Nor are these cultural changes totally independent of specific ideologies. Hence, there is a neoconservative backlash to the "excesses" of liberalism, and state intervention (or conversely in some areas lack of, or timid, intervention) in culture and education.

Neoconservatives in the United States see the origin of the contemporary crisis not in the economy or politics but in the moral and cultural spheres. For them, the social pact that brought together labor and capital at the turn of the century, and particularly the Democratic New Deal, has run its course. Paradoxically, neoconservatives believe that the rise of the welfare state has weakened class conflict by providing a safety net and benefits, resulting in the declining political significance of social class in postindustrial societies (Clark, Lipset, and Rempel, 1993).

For U.S. neoconservatives, the philosophical premises of liberalism are bankrupt. From this principle it follows that the liberal tradition has exhausted its ability to respond to the cultural and moral demands of the day. Liberals strategically placed in the mass media, schools, arts and humanities, and "tenured radicals" in higher education are blamed for the moral and cultural decay of capitalist America. Their moral permissiveness and refusal to sustain the traditional heterosexual family has resulted in increased teen pregnancy, academic truancy, sexual promiscuity, gang behavior, and gay and lesbian movements requesting recognition of alternative lifestyles and sexual preference. Neoconservatives see the liberals' contempt for authority, their disdain for cultural and historical traditions, and their reliance on "big" government and welfare policies ads the root of the crisis evolving in America.

The fiscal crisis of the state is seen as a proof of what neoconservatives have been claiming all along in the United States: Society cannot sustain a social welfare safety net with increasing costs of entitlement programs because the system will be financially bankrupt and will create dependency. Individuals will rely on state support rather than on their own efforts and work ethic and will avoid the performance of their individual duties and obligations while pressing for their rights. Hence the seeds of the country's moral and cultural bankruptcy are planted.

Solving the cultural crisis will entail the creation of a legitimate system based on individual responsibility rather than state handouts. Dismantling the heavy welfare state programs, deregulating the private sector, and privatizing the public sector are considered appropriate recipes for America to remain competitive internationally and to thrive economically and politically, although in an enriched cultural atmosphere emanating not from decaying liberals but from "born-again" Christians (Boron, 1981; Coser and Howe, 1977; Habermas, 1990; Torres, 1986). Thus many different roles are assigned to education in the neoconservative state. A central component of the neoconservative restoration is a critique of the liberal notion of autonomy and its implications for classroom practices. Autonomy is interpreted as lack of accountability. Thus,

> National curricula and assessment, greater opportunity for "parental choice," tighter accountability and control, the marketization and privatization of education—all of these proposals may be internally contradictory as a set of "reforms," but all are part of the conservative package that has been formed by the Neoliberal and Neoconservative wings of this movement. (Apple, 1993b:5; see also Apple, 1993a)

The neoconservative state in education rests on two central claims, one of accountability and parental rights, and another dealing with race and a particular appraisal of multiculturalism and diversity in the United States. School choice and vouchers are predicated as an attempt to link schools and markets. In this chapter we discuss the former, and the latter will be discussed in chapter 6. The proposals of John E. Chubb and Terry M. Moe's (1990) *Politics, Markets, and America's Schools* are part of school reform agendas that have been launched in the United States and elsewhere. These reforms focus on "'restructuring' rather than merely transforming the efficiency of existing systems, which suggests the transformation of purposes, assumptions, and methods of schools systems" (Darling-Hammond, 1993:xi).

Not surprisingly, this reform agenda is taking place in times of serious financial retrenchment in public education everywhere. Because much of the schools-are-failing literature blames the teachers, the relationships between teachers and educational authorities are also being reconsidered. Even where there is less focus on blame, there is a good deal of attention to competency testing, certification, national exams—in short, diverse attempts to improve excellence in instruction and learning. Reducing expenditures in financially overburdened school districts and attempting to make the systems more cost effective involve layoffs and substitution of lower-paid instructional personnel for more expensive, fully trained teachers.[23] This situation and recent initiatives concerning school finance, such as vouchers, have placed teachers' organizations at the center of disputes on educational policy and practice.

Chubb and Moe's analysis is a pristine example of the neoconservative argument that is based, ostensibly, on a libertarian political philosophy. Theoretically, they rely on public choice theories and a secularized theology of free markets:

> Political control, rooted in public authority and the group and constituency pressures that surround it, inherently operates to bury the schools in bureaucracy, deny them autonomy, and inhibit the emergence of effective organization. Market institutions, rooted in the decentralized choices of those who use and produce educational services, inherently tend to discourage bureaucracy, nurture school autonomy, and promote effective organization. (Chubb and Moe, 1993:222)

What is original about their approach is that they focus not so much on the operation of markets (for Chubb and Moe, theories of markets are already well developed) but on theories of government, particularly those linking governments to schools. A theory of school governance is needed because the "way to improve schools, then, is to decentralize, make them smaller, and promote community" (Chubb and Moe, 1993:222). They argue that gains in individual achievement are influenced by the quality of school organization and that schools should be considered government agencies. Hence, the question is whether market-driven schools are better than democratically controlled ones (Sujstorf, Wells, and Crain, 1993). Wells (1993) contends that the complexities of the school choice process are usually ignored by free-market school choice advocates. Behaving more like private, profit-driven corporations and responding in this way to consumers' demands ignores critical issues "that make the school consumption process extremely complex" (47–48).

At a theoretical level, by focusing on theories of the state, we may find ways to criticize, and even improve upon, public choice theory, particularly when "in this view individuals are rational utility maximizers and it is accepted that the pursuit of self-interest in the market place will yield socially and economically desirable outcomes" (Peters, in press). Yet, as Wells rightly points out, the neoconservative promise of school choice falls prey to a simple fallacy: competition between schools will not necessarily lead to school improvement because other variables are beyond the control of school quality. Racial attitudes, alienation, powerlessness, parental involvement, and lack of accurate information are part of the social context of family life. Wells (1993) argues that school competition does little, if anything, to surmount structural and subjective determinants. Moreover, as Carole Pateman (1996) remarks, "privatization means that potential channels of democratic accountability are being closed" (24).

While the debate on neoconservatism has been vigorous in the United States, the influence of neoconservative educational policies reaches beyond the United States's borders. Neoconservative developments in curriculum, textbooks, and teaching, like changes in the international division of labor and the dynamics of the marketplace, were observed by Carnoy and Torres (1994) in Costa Rica in the 1980s. Costa Rican policymakers tried to solve the dilemma of lower enrollment, increased student dropout rates, and dissatisfied teachers by blaming teachers publicly for "mediocre" education (Carnoy and Torres, 1994). Blaming teachers would give teachers' organizations less support in their demands for higher salaries and would legitimize alternative (non-teacher-centered) means of improving education. This was precisely the same policy advocated by the Reagan and Bush administrations in the United States.

Thus, while criticizing teachers and school personnel in general, a new Costa Rican administration launched a back-to-basics educational "modernization" program shortly after it took office in 1986. The reform's proposal, intended to improve the "efficiency" of educational production, consisted of three specific projects: First, the introduction of microcomputers and computer literacy in the classroom; second, the creation of a national testing system for the first, second, and third cycles, including tests in mathematics, Spanish, science, social studies, and English and a test for high school seniors that required a passing grade in all subjects, including a foreign language, writing and orthography, grammar and literature, sciences, mathematics and social studies, for graduation; third, the creation of the Costa Rican Scientific Colleges for gifted children as a way of improving Costa Rica's international competitiveness through advances in science and technology.

In addition, a number of controls were imposed on teachers and students. These included, among others, a canon of the minimum content to be taught, mandatory reintroduction of cursive writing for all pupils, the same uniform for students in all public schools, compulsory daily written lesson plans for teachers, more quizzes and semester examinations, and a longer school year. Emphasis on rationalization of educational administration; a more efficient accounting, administrative system, data base, and school registry; and functional decentralization by regions—despite the small size of the country—were also part of the package.

In Brazil, in moves similar to the neoconservative reaction to the threat posed by multiculturalists, neoliberal governments at the state and local level have promoted educational policies of "quality control" based on North American and Japanese models of managerial efficiency and accountability. These moves encountered opposition from the left, which advances the notion of "public popular schooling," seeking to address the specific cultural experience of the poor. In Brazil, too, neoconservatives argued that teachers' lack of technical expertise and the inefficiency of administrators were the main causes of school failure (O'Cadiz, Wong, and Torres, 1998).

Despite the power of their proposals, neoconservatives have accepted in advanced industrial countries, paradoxically, the notion of citizenship rights and obligations that are intrinsic to a welfare state model. Thus, neoconservatives

> cannot easily retreat from welfare. . . . the overall pattern is that structural obligations remain. . . . What seems inevitable, despite the enormous power of the Neoconservative argument, is that social and economic survival depends in part on further resolving the classic political problem of the proper relationship between individual autonomy and public obligations. (Culpitt, 1992:192–194)

While the neoconservative state is strong in its cultural critique, many of its key economic and social proposals reemerge in neoliberal pragmatic models.

The Neoliberal State and Education: The Question of Autonomy

> The mere existence of state autonomy poses grave problems for liberal-democratic theory.
> —Atilio Boron, "Estadolatria y teorías 'estadocéntricas'"

While neoconservatives struggle with the dilemma of promoting individual autonomy and public obligations, neoliberal political economy implies a related contradiction between individualistically conceived preferences and rational social choice (MacIntyre, 1988). This contradiction is aptly presented by Williams and Reuten (1993):

> Though markets aggregate individual preferences in a way agnostic to any particular notion of the public good, like democratic political aggregation, they only work when there is considerable convergence in the preference orderings of the individuals—they do not reconcile fundamental conflict; rather they are

premised on a stable structure of behavioral norms, supported by a mature state. (82)

Williams and Reuten (1993:82) use Arrow's paradox to convey the full meaning of this problem. If the place of the individual in the capitalist economy is crucially and solely as a preference-ordering subject, there must be a serious questioning of the liberal idea of the state as a site for bargaining between individuals with autonomous preferences. In other words, why should individuals subject themselves to any order, much less to the rule of the state? Moreover, why accept that there are social needs to be met?

The answer of the welfare state to these questions has been quite straightforward. After a lengthy period of social upheaval, welfare policies were concessions to the working class in exchange for more predictable economic outcomes during Fordism (e.g., prevention of work stoppages or strikes). A perceived "social peace" and public investment in job-creation strategies would bring prosperity for all. More satisfied, better educated workers would be more productive, and they, their communities, and society at large would prosper. In effect, social expenditures were insurance against class conflict. Yet, with the growing need to locate the place of the individual vis-à-vis the notion of the greatest societal good, the liberal state defended its welfare policies as attempts to create solidarity and community by providing basic social goods and services.

Are there any connections between the neoconservative and the neoliberal state? Michael Apple has argued that both types are wings of the same rightist movement. Extending Apple's argument, and taking a world system approach based on Wallerstein's work, I argue that the distinction between metropolitan, semiperipheral, and peripheral countries plays an important role in determining the nature of the state.[24] Neoconservative political economy has emerged partly as a reaction to welfare states in metropolitan state formations. Many of these state formations have been characterized as advanced industrial societies or late capitalism. Indeed, the majority of neoconservative experiences have taken place in states that have not historically been subject to colonization.[25] Moreover, with few exceptions, they have been colonizers. They have either profited from, or become, colonial powers themselves, colonizing regions of the world that were later identified as the Third World.[26] Culturally speaking, the tradition of conservatism, or more generally the social forces associated with the Right in Europe, Canada, the United States, Australia and New Zealand (i.e., countries of the North) are quite different from the political experience of the Right in the Third World (i.e., countries of the South). Countries in the South have experienced authoritarian governments, military dictatorships, or authoritarian populism with rightist affiliations. With the exception of fascism or authoritarian corporatist experiences, the Right in metropolitan countries, despite the growing power of the executive in neoconservative states, has negotiated its differences with liberalism within the framework of parliamentarism. This is not the experience of the Third World, where parliamentarism itself, given the power of the executive and strong leaders *(caudillos)*, has often been a nominal rather than a substantive political practice.

In sum, differences in historical traditions, social and economic endowments, and political culture affect the theory and practice of democracy. The lack of a lasting (rather than an ephemeral) liberal democratic tradition in many of the countries of the South, the lack of an extensive welfare state experience, and the strong presence of corporatism and populism account for important differences in the configuration of the right vis-à-vis countries in the North. These differences can also be noted between a rightist movement with no oligarchical past in the United States and the right connected with the experience of feudalism and nobility in Europe.

Neoliberals, while drawing upon the tradition of liberalism and simultaneously having serious reservations about the theory of democracy, have joined neoconservatives in their criticisms of the welfare state. A key component of their critique is the notion that the fiscal crisis of the state is the result of state overload, of an "overburdened" state trying to satisfy increased demands from citizens, thus creating a gap between increasing fiscal expenditures and decreasing fiscal revenues. These disparities, and the dissatisfaction of taxpayers because of the higher taxes needed to pay for entitlements, result in the ungovernability of democracies. Ungovernability stems from the institutionalized arrangements of mass democratic reforms in a welfare state, including the creation of state subsidies and handouts that are disincentives for workers and that squeeze profits via taxes from corporations and individuals.

The notions of neoliberalism and the neoliberal state appear to be "exported" from the center to the periphery and semiperiphery.[27] No doubt, there is a neoliberal ideology and narrative consolidated in the central countries. Given the implications of the liberal past of metropolitan societies, the specific debates within the political parties (e.g., the discussion in the United States about the role of the New Right in the Republican Party), and the influence of neoconservative economics in regard to globalization, the notion of neoliberalism in central countries appears as almost interchangeable with the notion of neoconservatism in political economy. This is not the case in terms of cultural, social, or ethical preferences.

What are the differences in the political sociology of education of neoconservatism and neoliberalism? The neoconservative state is partly a backlash against the so-called excesses of the welfare state and its fiscal crisis. The model of the neoconservative state under the Reagan and Bush administrations attempted to place the United States in a hegemonic position in the context of a rapidly changing international system. These administrations were faced with growing economic competition from Germany and Japan and an overblown fear of the military might of the Soviet Union. Education was associated with national security and economic competitiveness in the world system. The neoconservative vision of educational reform reflects an attempt to socialize American children and youth for the exercise of power and domination on a global scale. It is a project that distances itself from the singular idea of an education for democracy, as originally defended by liberalism and its pedagogical counterpart, progressivism. Hence the emphasis on the quality of education, excellence, and particularly the support for science and technology in the schools. Central players in the context of neoconservatism are the Business Roundtable, some private foundations, state governors, and professional associations seeking to develop standards for teaching of disciplines.

Neoliberalism offers similar prescriptions, but there are a few differences. The politics of neoliberalism, when transported to the countries of the periphery, constitute a set of proposals that refer to the condition of the countries of the South in the international context, and particularly in the division of labor. Neoliberalism strives to pass the cost of educational services to the clientele through imposing user fees, increasing the participation of the private sector in education (i.e., privatization), and promoting decentralization of educational services as a means of redefining the power and educational relations among federal, provincial, and municipal governments. These are standard policy prescriptions that overlap heavily with neoconservatism.

Is there an alternative to neoconservative and neoliberal analyses of the role of the state in educational development? Neo-Marxist analyses differ from the theoretical accounts of neoliberalism and neoconservatism. Neo-Marxist theories analyze the interactions between state and education in historical context, trying to show the contradictory dynamics between economic and political structures and human agency. Regarding schooling, neo-Marxism focuses on the role of official knowledge as a state practice and develops a parallelist analysis of race, class, and gender as independent but interactive dynamics.[28]

Parallelist Theories and Official State Knowledge: Neo-Marxist Theories of the State and the Critique of Neoconservatism and Neoliberalism

> The concrete is concrete because it is the synthesis of multiple determinations, hence unity in diversity.
>
> —Karl Marx, *Grundrisse*

Neo-Marxist theories discuss the state as intimately related to notions of power and its distribution in society. Ralph Miliband (1969), one of the most prominent Marxist political scientists of this century, said it nicely:

> A Theory of the State is also a theory of society and of the distribution of power in that society. But most Western "students of politics" tend to start, judging from their work, with the assumption that power, in Western societies, is competitive, fragmented and diffused: everybody, directly or through organized groups, has some power and nobody has or can have too much of it. In these societies, citizens enjoy universal suffrage, free and regular elections, representative institutions, effective citizenship rights, including the right of free speech, association and opposition; and both individuals and groups take ample advantage of these rights, under the protection of the law, an independent judiciary and a free political culture. (2)

Michael Apple (1993a) has highlighted the difficulties of classical Marxism in the treatment of class, race, and gender (163–182; see also Torres, 1998). This position is defined by McCarthy and Apple (1988) as a "nonsynchronous parallelism." Apple (1986a) argues that:

> A paradigm case in point here is the criticism leveled against traditional Marxist interpretations by feminist authors. Many of their arguments have been devastating to orthodox assertions, . . . so much so that many people on the left believe that any attempt at understanding our social formation that does not combine in an unreductive way analyses of class and gender together is only half a theory at best. . . . The same, of course, needs to be said of race as well. The rejection of major aspects of the received orthodox Marxist tradition and the emerging sensitivity to the truly constitutive nature of gender and race demonstrate not a weakness but the continued growth and vitality of a tradition of critical analysis that is attempting to deal honestly and openly with the complexity of life under present conditions of domination and exploitation. (320–321)

A central issue of nonsynchronous parallelist theories is not to sideline the importance of class in the political sociology of education while, at the same time, avoiding essentializing class in theories of social and cultural reproduction. Apple (1992), discussing the work of Basil Bernstein, has argued that class itself is increasingly becoming gendered and raced. Thus,

> we cannot marginalize race and gender as constitutive categories in any cultural analysis. If there are indeed basic cultural forms and orientations that are specifically gendered and raced, and have their own partly autonomous histories, then we need to integrate theories of patriarchal and racial forms into the very core of our attempt to comprehend what is being reproduced and changed. At the very

least, a theory that allows for the contradictions within and among these dynamics would be essential. Of course, this is one of the multiple areas where Neo-Gramscian analysis and some post-structuralist positions that have not become cynically depoliticized intersect. (143)

What, then, in this theoretical reconstruction is the role of the state in cultural reproduction and schooling? To begin with, the state is a site of multiple conflicts based on class conflict and gender, race, and ethnicity struggles. Apple (1992:141; see also Apple, 1989) suggests that because the state is a locus of ideological struggle, "to win in the state you must win in civil society" and that the politics of common sense of neoconservatives reflects a new consensus. He has aptly characterized this new consensus an "authoritarian populism" that attempts to build a new social accord (Apple 1993b:21).

Apple (1992) notes that Bernstein contributes to our understanding of

> market-oriented visible pedagogies where educational policy is centered around programs of school choice. This, he correctly believes, is but a "thin cover" for a restratification of schools, students, and curricula. . . . The issue of restratification also points to the crucial role the state plays as a sponsor of such market-oriented programs and as a site of class conflict. (142)

Better textbooks and teacher-proof curricula are seen as an imperative for restoring order in classrooms and achieving excellence in education. Apple (1992:36–37) argues that "the history of the state, in concert with capital and a largely male academic body of consultants and developers, [is one of] intervening at the level of practice into the work of a largely female workforce." Apple (1988b:37) suggests that to understand the dynamics of the history of curriculum, "one must integrate an analysis of the state, changes in the labor process of state employees, and the politics of patriarchy." In order to do so, a dialectical approach is necessary. Privatization and market-oriented policies, "especially if they have been articulated through the State, are the results of conflicts, compromises, and accords within various levels of the State, and between the State and a wide array of social movements and forces in the wider society." (Apple, 1992:142; see also Apple and Weis, 1986).

The call is for a more subtle analysis of the state, "one that parallels the advances currently being made on the study of gender and race in economy and politics. This would certainly complement the current discussions of the central place of democratic conflicts in the State itself" (Apple, 1988a:122; see also Carnoy, 1984). Such a study would offer a comprehensive analysis of the four trends that Apple (1993b) identified in the conservative restoration in the

United States and Britain: privatization, centralization, vocationalization, and differentiation.

Changes in state formation entail a change in the production of hegemony and commonsense interpretations of everyday life, and particularly a change in the political alliances controlling the state—from liberalism to neoconservatism and neoliberalism. Replacing the role of the state with the logic of the market in determining educational policy is criticized as a class strategy in the neoliberal state (Ball, 1993; Dale, 1989). A similar argument is made in regard to the withdrawal of state investment in public education in Latin America and how that would affect the constitution of citizens as pedagogical subjects (Puiggrós, 1990; Torres and Puiggrós, 1997). Changes in the labor process relate to the changes from a mode of production defined as the transformation of Fordism into a post-Fordist model with implications for the process of skilling and deskilling of the labor force and the logic of technical control in curriculum (Apple, 1982b).

The post–World War I model of industrial development was mass production, superseding the nineteenth-century craft paradigm. Fordism as a mass production model was concerned with the production of standardized commodities for stable mass markets. Fordism and Taylorism were systems of production based on capital-intensive industrial manufacturing, scientific management, increases in plant utilization and productivity through stringent control over labor, the use of time-motion and controlled studies of labor work inside the factory, intense fragmentation of work tasks based on the separation of conception and execution, the acceleration of productive operations, and the famous Ford assembly line, which restructured the technical division of labor inside the factory (Braverman, 1974; Clarke, 1990; Gramsci, 1980; Manacorda, 1977).

Post-Fordism is characterized by flexible specialization and labor flexibilization:

> Whereas work under the mass production paradigm was characterized by an intense division of labor, the separation of conception and execution, the substitution of unskilled labor for skilled labor and special purpose for universal machines, the quest for specializations prompts a more flexible organization of production based on collaboration between designers and reskilled craft workers to make a wide variety of goods with general purpose machines. (Tomaney, 1990:30)

While Fordism and Taylorism were characteristic of industrial development in the United States, flexible specialization is characteristic of changes in labor management models in Japan and Germany. The distinction between conception and execution of tasks has been deliberately blurred by a change to reliance on teamwork, where foremen regarded as part of the work teams are representatives of the workers to management. In addition, there is extensive job rotation to familiarize workers with the context of their work and to increase their flexibility (Piore and Sabel, 1984). Quality circles were implemented around the mid-1960s to promote the idea of labor and management teams working cooperatively to improve the different phases of production. In Germany, with more trained workers on the shop floor, there is an explicit effort to eliminate the distinctions between blue-collar and white-collar workers. The overall model of institutionalization of long-term employment is not based so much on contract agreements in negotiations between labor unions and management under the supervision of the state as, particularly in Japan, on workers' dependence on the company for lifetime employment, family welfare, and welfare provision. This model, however, calls for job rotation and teamworking, which intensify the levels of commitment and productivity of workers and very often demand working overtime on short notice to meet production shortfalls. There are of course, other areas of job enhancement and flexibilization, including the institutionalization of unregulated labor activities through nonformal or informal labor markets and the like. Quality control and just-in-time production are other salient traits of the Japanese model.[29]

Political economists have seen these changes in the workplace as attempts not only to increase productivity relative to wages but also, and more important, to discipline labor. The neoconservative approach that seeks to bring school expansion and practices in line with a disciplined labor force is seen as an integral part of a general process of struggle over control of workplaces and schools (Carnoy and Levin, 1985). There are a number of implications for teacher training and curriculum reform. The obvious one is the erosion of teacher autonomy through the push for "prepackaged" curricula, textbooks, and computer/video technology that could be more "predictable" than individual craft implemented in the classroom when the door is closed. More control is sought through implementation of managerial techniques associated with labor flexibilization, including total quality control—hence the emphasis on standardized testing. A second direction is to promote the direct presence of the marketplace in the classroom through direct advertisement and linkages between corporations and schools (e.g., the presence of groups such as the Business Roundtable, which presses for educational reforms; or the implementation in public schools of Channel One, which mixes commercial messages with educational instruction).

Michael Apple (1989) lists several educational policies gaining momentum in the United States that have been instrumental in shifting the debate towards the pastures of the right, reconstituting the prevailing common sense in education:

(1) Proposals for voucher plans and tax credits to make schools more like the idealized free market economy; (2) the movement in state legislatures and state departments of education to "raise standards" and mandate both teacher and student "competencies" and basic curricular goals and knowledge, thereby centralizing even more at a state level the control of teaching and curricula; (3) the increasingly effective assaults on the school curriculum for its supposedly anti-family and anti–free enterprise bias, its "secular humanism," its neglect of the "western tradition," and its lack of patriotism; (4) and the growing pressure to make the needs of business and industry into the primary goals of the educational system. (27)

A primary goal is the flexibilization and centralization of teacher training through a unified curriculum that is compatible with total quality models. A desirable by-product—and indeed a precondition—is to curb the power of trade unions. This is important because, given the present process of teacher certification, teachers' unions and the teaching profession per se are among the few unions and professions in capitalism that are somewhat protected from international competition. However, as Picciotto (1991) argues, the state must not counter the trend of internationalization:

The capitalist state, although territorially defined, was born and developed a loose network of interrelated and overlapping jurisdictions. The regulatory framework for corporate capitalism which emerged from the last part of the 19th century was based on the nation state but involved emulation and transplantation of forms, as well as international coordination; and it facilitated international ownership of capital through the transnational corporation which became the dominant form in the 20th century. Transnational corporations have favored minimal international coordination while strongly supporting the national state, since they can take advantage of regulatory differences and loopholes. Processes of international coordination of state functions, relying on national legitimation, have taken the form of bureaucratic-administrative corporatist bargaining through a motley network of informal structures as well as the more visible and grand organizations. The growing globalization of social relations has put increasing pressure on both national and international state structures. (43; see also Ruccio, Resnick, and Wolff, 1991)

The growing internationalization of the state is still an open question in terms of its scope and dynamics. Likewise, the implications of this internationalization and globalization for educational policies, textbooks, and curricula are thus far lacking empirical and theoretical research. However, there are a few exceptions. In an eight-country study of reform practices in teacher education, Popkewitz and Pereira (1993) argue that international organizations such as the Organization for Economic Cooperation and Development and the European Union are playing crucial roles in promoting changes in regulations of teacher education.

Postmodern perspectives on the state, however, blur the distinction between private and public and between the state and civil society, posing a fundamental question to the notion of governability: Do we explain how power works by explaining the state, or do we explain the state by explaining how power works?

Social Regulation, Public Sphere, and State Intervention: Postmodern Perspectives on the State and Education

> If power were never anything but repressive, if it never did anything but to say no, do you really think one would be brought to obey it? What makes power hold good, what makes it accepted, is simply the fact that it doesn't only weigh on us as a force that says no, but that it traverses and produces things, it induces pleasure, forms knowledge, produces discourse. It needs to be considered as a productive network which runs through the whole social body.
> —Michel Foucault, *Power/Knowledge*

Classic principles of liberal political theory that conceive of the state as a great mediator of divergent interests are challenged not only by critical modernist political theories but also by postmodernist criticism.[30] Thomas Popkewitz (1991), for instance, argues that in a postmodern world, the state does not necessarily represent the public interest and that professional knowledge is not privileged over common sense. With the collapse of the modernist project, and by implication the collapse of the established modernist educational reform agendas, specific social movements, limited agendas, and particularistic claims represent the focus of politics.

Postmodernist analyses are based on explicit views of power as fragmented in capitalist society. Despite this fragmentation, as Miliband points out, the state remains firmly at the center of debates on the articulation of power in civil society, the constitution of democratic communities, and democratic political cultures. One may add that any definition of the relationships between power and state should consider the role of education and its potential contribution to political representation, participation, and citizenship in late capitalism. Let us, however, examine some of the premises of postmodernism and how theories of the state and power are accounted for in recent postmodernist analysis.

Postmodernism argues that there is a "new" epoch in society and thus a new cultural paradigm. For current purposes some of the key sociological implications of postmodern society and culture can be summarized as involving various processes of fragmentation, including: (1) a decentering and fragmentation of power that calls into question theories of domination and hegemony; (2) an uncoupling of material interests and subjective expressions in collective action, resulting in the shift of the demands of social movements from distributional to cultural-ethical issues; (3) the emergence of heterogeneity as opposed to the homogenization that has been characteristic of the world system; and (4) a growing distrust and disillusionment with democracy resulting from the fragmentation of political communities and identities.

Consider briefly each of these points. Postmodernism argues that power has become decentered and fragmented in contemporary societies. Thus, to suggest the notion of a ruling elite conducting its business and having decisive influence in the formulation of public policy or education will obscure—in a postmodern view—the multiplicity of powers that interact in society, as well as policy outcomes (Bowles and Gintis, 1986). How does one define power that is fragmented and lacking a unifying principle? Does this fragmentation undermine the nonsynchronous, parallelist conception of the relations of class, gender, and race in cultural reproduction? In short, does the fragmentation of power undermine conceptual frameworks and "grand narratives" such as those of hegemony and domination?

The so-called death of "grand narratives" poses political and epistemological questions. For Foucault, truth depends on strategies of power rather than epistemological criteria. This is a central concern for a theory of the state and power. Does this mean that if we rely on skeptical poststructuralist accounts we cannot define some "master signifier" that helps us to ground, ethically and politically, political action? Otherwise we cannot validate *ex ante* any policy recommendation in education from a theoretical standpoint, nor can we validate ex post facto the same principles for political action. The most obvious implication is the lack of direction and the absence of a political program. One possible consequence of this is "a false radicalism which engages in constant but ultimately meaningless transgression of all defended viewpoints" (Hulme, 1986:6). This political activism highlights Harvey's (1989) concern that we may end up with philosophical and social thought that is characterized by ephemerality, collage, fragmentation, and dispersion.

Political activism based on "false radicalism" does not challenge the fragmented politics of divergent special and regional interest groups. This situation, added to the secular internecine struggles of progressive groups, the structural and historical action of the capitalist state, and actions from the right, undermines the communities of learning and political action, hindering the ability of progressive groups to challenge preponderant differential resources (influence, power, and wealth) of elites and dominant classes in education. This transgressive activism may challenge the narratives of neoconservative and neoliberal projects in education, an important accomplishment considering the power of the "common sense" narrative of the right. However, it offers few, if any, guidelines for practical politics. The problem is compounded when social subjects are considered to be politically decentered.

The notion of the decentering of social subjects implies an uncoupling of the close link between objective social interests and subjective expressions (e.g., class consciousness) assumed by a great deal of modernist social theory. The resulting contradictory loyalties of individuals increasingly undermine a central organizing principle of struggle. One oft-noted consequence of this relative uncoupling of social position and political action is that the "new" social movements are more concerned with cultural (and ethical-political) than distributional demands. Decentered individuals are not supposed to have "class consciousness" in classical terms, yet, in Giddens's (1991) social psychological analysis, they strive to achieve "self-actualization."

Postmodernism argues that the power of nation-states is now being diminished in the context of an increasingly interdependent world and in the context of more local struggles. Yet, as Immanuel Wallerstein (1991) argues, the history of the (capitalist) world system has been a historical trend towards cultural heterogeneity rather than cultural homogenization. Thus, the fragmentation of the nation in the world system is happening at the same time that there is a tendency towards cultural differentiation or cultural complexity, that is, globalization. Globalization and regionalization seem to be dual processes occurring simultaneously. This fact has not been overlooked by certain strands of postmodernism, providing an avenue to understand the simultaneous rise of ethnicity and nationalisms with globalization; these are not necessarily contradictory or unrelated phenomena.

In this increasingly complexly organized, multicultural, and multilingual world system, the bases of traditional forms of political community have been eroded. There is an emerging theory and practice of distrust in democracy. Hence, the previous models of democratic checks and balances, separation of powers, and the notion of a democratic accountability no longer work, not even at the level of formal rather than substantive democracy. Distrust in democracy and democratic theory as part of a modernist discourse cannot be associated with all postmodernist strands per se. However, it poses problems for the changing patterns of power in education and raises concerns about the narrowing of the meaning of democracy. The redefinition of democracy needs to be extricated from the forming patterns of social regulation because "not only have the interests represented been narrowed; participation exists within a restricted range of problems and possibilities" (Popkewitz, 1991:215).

Any redefinition of the notion of democracy situates the school at the center of the modernist-enlightenment project. Postmodernism would argue, however, that the ethical, substantive, and procedural elements of democratic theory should be reexamined in light of postmodern culture. The challenge for educators, parents, students, and policymakers is to think critically about the failures of the past and about the myriad exclusionary practices that still pervade schooling—hence bringing to the forefront issues of power and domination, class, race, and gender. The validity of the notion of instrumental rationality guiding school reform should also be examined because it gives attention to administration, procedures, and efficiency as the prime criteria for change and progress and because it assumes that there is a common framework structuring the experience of all people (Popkewitz, 1987; Torres, 1996a).

On a different front, professionalization, as Foucault has argued, also defines the limits of governmentalization and the different realms of governance: "The Foucauldian perspective suggests that those cognitive and normative elements that operate to establish the boundaries between associations of professional experts and the state must be viewed, in terms of process, as means of negotiation used by discourses that define the possible realms of governance" (Johnson, 1993:150). Popkewitz (1994a) argues, in a similar vein, that the state "entails a variety of actors in the educational arena including government agencies and professional and social organizations which organize and administer policy." State reorganization reconstitutes the patterns of social regulation for Popkewitz (in press), and it is clearly expressed in decentralization processes that, on the surface, are changing the patterns of state regulation of schooling. A second set of patterns of social regulations relates to Foucault's governmentality as described by Popkewitz (1994a):

> A second form of regulation and one which ties together different layers of social/political life is the construction of scientific discourses by which the individuals manage the "self" in the social world. I argue that there is a governmentality as certain reform discourses internationally circulate to shape and fashion teachers' dispositions towards practices, such as those found in constructivist psychologies that reform didactics. The construction of school reform discourse is a practice that normalizes social relations through the strategies for constructing and organizing the "objects" of schooling. (21)

In short, from a postmodernist perspective such as Popkewitz's (drawing from Foucault and Bourdieu), the state must be seen as a multilayered historical and relational concept. He presses his claim by stating:

> While most state theories have focused solely on actors and structures, my argument has sought to consider the state as an historical problem of relations; considering the production of social regulation through the position of actors and the deployment of discourses in the educational arena. This view of the state is one of an epistemological concept that is continually historicized. (Popkewitz, 1994a:24; see also Popkewitz, 1994b)

This research agenda offers a path for microanalysis of power, the state, and education that could be politically useful. In such an approach Foucault's "pedagogical devices" and discursive relations may have their own independent power of macrostructural relations and discourses. There is always a risk of delinking microanalysis from macrodynamics of a structural and historical nature and hence losing the "nuanced historical sense" of the phenomena that we are analyzing. However, there should be no doubt that a multilayered approach, such as the one proposed by Popkewitz, opens up avenues for exploring simultaneously the discourses of educational reform as social regulation and the patterns of transformation of the state and schooling as school rituals change (with strong implications for the discourses and practices [e.g., the pedagogical devices] that regulate the construction of language, discourse, and the social construction of "self").

Innovative comparative and international work shows the importance of this dual pattern of state regulation and how it is changing the practices of teachers' education, at the level of the nation-state and globally (Popkewitz, 1991; 1993). Expert knowledge appears as a deployment of power. For Popkewitz, a historical view of the state—and a global perspective on international organizations regulating capitalism—should be seen as two strategies or patterns of regulation, one the product of the practices (ideologies, discourses, narratives, and social action) of the actors in the arena of education, and one a product of the discourses themselves (with a growing internationalization of the rules that regulate the discourses of educational reform). These discourses deploy power and, in education, usually affect lives of teachers, most of whom are women.

Against the Patriarchal State? Feminism and the Color of the State

> There is nothing about "being" a female that naturally binds women. There is not even such a state as "being" female, itself a highly complex category constituted in contested sexual scientific discourses and other social practices. Gender, race or class consciousness is an achievement forced on us by the terrible historical experience of the contradictory social realities of patriarchy, colonialism, and capitalism.
>
> Donna Haraway, "A Manifesto for Cyborgs"

Feminist theories can be classified in terms of theories of difference, theories of inequality, and theories of oppression (Lengermann and Niebrugge-Brantley, 1992). Theories of difference include biosocial, institutional, and social psychological explanations of the differences between men's and women's experiences and situations. Theories of inequality refer to the explanations of why women have fewer privileges and resources than men as analyzed by liberal and Marxist theories. Connell distinguishes three models of feminist analysis—"class first" theory, "social reproduction" theory, and "dual systems" theory—exemplifying the wide array of theoretical approaches that attempt to explain women's inequality in education and the role of the state (Connell, 1983, 1987; see also Fraser, 1997:151–188).

Class first theory argues that capitalism is the root cause of all inequalities and class struggle is primary. The social reproduction model, with the influence of structural Marxism, suggests that "the family, sexuality or gender relations at large were the site of *reproduction* of 'relations of production'" (Connell, 1987:43). Hence, this theory suggests a systemic connection between the subordination of women and economic exploitation in capitalism. Dual systems theory is a third approach suggested by Connell. Dual systems theory (see Eisenstein, 1979; Hartman and Sargent, 1990) argues that the basic idea is that capitalism and patriarchy are distinct and equally comprehensive systems of social relations that meet and interact.

Theories of oppression imply that women are oppressed by men, not merely unequal to or different from them. Psychoanalytic, socialist-feminist, radical feminist, and third-wave feminist theories have addressed these issues in different ways. With the growing presence of postmodernist discourse and its implications for feminism, third-wave feminist theories are offering one of the most compelling theoretical arguments (hooks and West, 1991). Third-wave feminism looks at the notion of "difference" and focuses on women of color in industrially advanced societies and on women in the Third World. This approach assumes that one cannot use the concept of "women" as a generic category in stratification. Third-wave feminism focuses instead on the factual and theoretical interpretations of differences among women: "The differences considered are those that result from an unequal distribution of socially produced goods and services on the basis of position in the global system, class, race, ethnicity, and affectional preference as these interact with gender stratification" (Lengermann and Niebrugge-Brantley, 1992:341).

What has happened with feminism and women's movements in neoconservative and neoliberal states? The feminist and the women's movement agendas have fared differentially during recent neoconservative governments, especially when compared to the gains achieved in the liberal welfare state. An assessment of women's movement outcomes in legislative and judicial commitments in Canada, the United States, and Britain studied decisions regarding equal rights legislation, including legislative and judicial commitments to women's equality; reforms to family laws, including policy on divorce laws affecting women and children; choice and reproduction policies, particularly women's access to safe and affordable abortion services; violence against women, including domestic violence and rape; and employment rights, including equal pay for equal work, affirmative action policies, and child care delivery (Bashevkin, 1994). This study shows that between 1971 and 1980, approximately 75 percent of legislative and judicial outcomes in Britain and the United States and 56 percent in Canada were favorable to women and feminists. A most striking reversal of this trend was found during the Reagan administration, with legislative and judicial decisions going against feminist positions: "From a success to failure ratio of 24:7 before Reagan's election, these figures dropped to 13:15 afterward" (Bashevkin, 1994:289). Some decisions seen as favorable to women's demands were the result of Reagan's efforts "to offload responsibilities from federal to state government and to reduce public spending on social welfare" (Bashevkin, 1994:289). In Britain and Canada the feminist agenda did much better, particularly in Canada, with a success rate of 80 percent, despite women's decreased access to federal elites during the Mulroney years. This analysis, however, considers only judicial and legislative decisions in the three governments, a small portion of the policy context. Major budget cuts in housing, child care, and education during the Reagan administration; Thatcher's policies undermining trade unions and local government; and the budget cuts by the federal government in Canada that affected women's groups were not evaluated. If these sectoral policies had been included, the analysis would have shown the negative impact of sectoral outcomes and budgetary policy on the feminist and women's movements.

It is clear, particularly in the United States, that despite the practical difficulties and pervasiveness of male chauvinism in politics, the women's movement thrived in the 1960s and 1970s in comparison with the neoconservative administrations of the 1980s. As a result of the struggles of women, the liberal state promoted women's equality through antidiscrimination policies in employment, salary, and wages, as well as promoting women's reproductive rights and child care delivery and prevention of violence against women. These policies were highly favorable to women and to the feminist movement. The neoconservative state undermined some of those gains, and women, the feminist movement, and other progressive movements learned not to take the state for granted, particularly when patriarchal relations were brought to the fore.

Patriarchal relations—and their representation in education—are a central concern for the feminist movement (Zaretsky, 1983). It is known that Marx devoted just a few pages of his magnum opus to the situation of women and children. Marx saw women as wageworkers and wage earners, or conversely as unproductive labor. Their significance for capitalism was the generation of surplus value. Working women were perceived as part of the general category of the proletariat. Hence they were "perceived as exploited rather than oppressed and there was no sense of patriarchal structuring of the economy" (Coole, 1993:181).

Nelly Stromquist (1991) argues that patriarchal states are at the root of the oppression of women. Looking at the relationship between gender and education and analyzing data for illiteracy and higher education, Stromquist (1991) concludes that every state, regardless of its model of governance or mode of production,

> engage[s] in activities that either continue to assign domestic responsibility to women or leave undisturbed social representations of women's "proper" role in society. These representations, though maintained through ideological forces, have a clear material foundation and are supported by an implicit coalition of men and women of upper and middle-classes that permits wealthier women to share some benefits with men while extracting resources from lower-class women. (111)

Feminist theory of color points to the role of the state and class in the discrimination, exploitation, and oppression of women of color and working-class women. This is an important point because, as Diana Coole (1993:179) argues, some postmodernist feminists "have shifted attention to [the] cultural aspect with little attempt to integrate the economic aspects of sexual politics." This charge cannot be applied in toto to the different varieties of postmodernist feminism, including expressions as different as those represented in the work of Dorothy Smith (1987), Nancy Fraser (1989, 1997), and Judith Butler (1993). The paradox is how to move away from a Hegelian concept of universality and, at the same time, define the universal features of feminist struggles against patriarchal states.

Drawing from Hegel, one of the peculiarities of the Marxist concept of class was its inherent universalism: the working class was destined to be the class to end all classes. There was little basis for the hardening of class *difference* into anything more than a recognition of different trajectories of socialization and experience. The decline of the notion of a universal class left open the question of the ultimate meaning of class differences. The partial decline of class concepts in post-Marxist theory reflects the loss of any sense of anchorage that would allow some external attribute, such as participation in wage labor or productive versus unproductive labor, to define an essential category of humanity. As neo-Marxist critics point out, however, this undermines the basis for collective strategies of change and creates a theoretical vacuum in considering the role of the state in social reproduction. Paradoxically, the emergence of gender, ethnicity, and race as central components of the reproduction of domination has suffered a similar but quite distinctive fate. As subjects of suppressed and colonized identities, women and people of color clearly have a need to recognize and celebrate their inevitable differences (at least those not contaminated by domination itself).

If, at the level of social theory (and metatheory), feminist theory calls for historical specificity, the same analytical logic calls for a structural and historically specific analysis of the form of state that is considered the embodiment of patriarchy. A definition of the nature and praxis of the state as patriarchal is just the beginning of an integrative and historically informed explanation. It is imperative to analyze the historical configuration of the state as a social formation; its dominant symbolic narrative (with its contradictions); and its modes, means, and methods of patriarchal (and classist and racist) action (Block, 1989; Gordon, 1989; Jessop, 1983; Morrow and Torres, 1994; Torres, 1990). For theoretical as well as practical reasons, we need a concrete examination of the patriarchal role of the state in capitalist societies, its limits and capacities, including institutional and economic endowment; the nature of the policy process; the social history of the state apparatus; the distinction between levels of state intervention; its intersections and contradictions (e.g., among federal, state, and municipal levels) and historical specificities, including the location in the world system; the challenge of scale (e.g., a city-state like Kuwait, a small island state like Santa Lucia in the Caribbean, or a small country like Nicaragua, versus the dimensions of megastates, such as Brazil, India, China, the United States, or Russia); colonial/postcolonial experiences; and the nature of race, ethnicity, gender, and religious relations in the society.

An integrative theory of the patriarchal state and its influence on gender discrimination may be difficult to accomplish, given the current conditions of social theorizing. However, specific, timely, historically informed, cross-cultural, and comparative studies of the interrelations between patriarchy and capitalism in modern states and how those relationships affect schooling and educational policies are not only feasible but crucial for political action. Gender, race, and class need to be linked in any historically informed study of gender discrimination and state practices. Historically, limitations of middle-class feminist theorizing were evident in the early emancipation movements in the

United States, and they failed to recognize the claims of lower-class women and those of color: "The convenient omission of household workers' problems from the programs of 'middle class' feminists past and present has often turned out to be a veiled justification—at least on the part of the affluent women—of their own exploitative treatment of their maids" (Lorde, 1984, cited in Grant and Sleeter, 1986:196; see also Grant and Sleeter, 1988; hooks, 1990; hooks and West, 1991; Jelin, 1990; Lengermann and Niebrugge-Brantley, 1984; Sternbach et al., 1992).

Feminist theory and particularly third-wave feminism have provided insights for a thorough understanding of the praxis of new social movements and the practice of the state in the Third World and in advanced industrial societies (Jelin, 1990; Scott, 1990).

Summary

Prevailing notions of the state held by policymakers and researchers influence the dominant research agenda, the analysis of educational problems, and policy prescriptions. Theories of the state also influence educational research per se. At a concrete level, theories of the state held by government coalitions and educational bureaucracies will influence not only research but also planning and operation of educational systems. Discussions about theories of the state and education encompass a broad range of views regarding the relationships among education, the state, and civil society. By implication, theories of the state define the nature, purpose, and role of educational research, policy, and practices. Therefore, any discussion of educational reform; the relationships between teachers, students, and administrators; curriculum policy and work; teachers' training; educational financing; multiculturalism; citizenship; democratic education; or educational policy in general involves competing and contradictory views and perceptions of the relationships between the individual and the community, a basic tension in the constitution of Western thought (Wolin, 1960). Different notions of community, in turn, relate to different notions of the state. They also involve different views of what democratic governance of societies and schools should be, including notions of power, participation, representation, and democratic decision making. Despite their increasing historical specificity, and because of their normative and analytical orientations, critical and mainstream perspectives have, by and large, focused on the nation-state as the locus of politics and education. The notion of globalization, however, has transformed the debate, increasing the stakes for emancipatory politics in education.

Notes

1. Max Weber, "The Fundamental Concepts of Sociology," in *The Theory of Social and Economic Organizations,* ed. Talcott Parsons (New York: Free Press, 1964), 156. For a good discussion of Weber's views, see Richard Bendix, *Max Weber: An Intellectual Portrait* (New York: Doubleday, 1962).

2. I am thankful to Walter Feinberg for this suggestion in a personal communication to the author.

3. A critical modernist position is outlined in Raymond A. Morrow and Carlos Alberto Torres, *Social Theory and Education: A Critique of Theories of Social and Cultural Reproduction* (Albany: State University of New York Press, 1995), esp. 339–445. For an extension of the analysis in sociology of education, see Carlos Alberto Torres and Ted Mitchell, eds., *Sociology of Education: Emerging Perspectives* (Albany: State University of New York Press, in press).

4. Max Weber, *Economy and Society* (New York: Bedminster, 1968); Bendix, *Max Weber*; Max Weber, *From Max Weber: Essays in Sociology,* ed. H. H. Gerth and C. W. Mills (New York: Oxford University Press, Galaxy Books, 1958).

5. Peter McLaren, "Critical Pedagogy, Political Agency, and the Pragmatics of Justice: The Case of Lyotard," *Educational Theory* 44, no. 3 (Summer 1994): 325; Linda M. McNeil, *Contradictions of Control: School Structure and School Knowledge* (New York: Routledge, 1988), 166–178; Cameron McCarthy and Warren Crichlow, eds., *Race, Identity, and Representation in Education* (New York: Routledge, 1993), xiii–xvii; Michael W. Apple, *Official Knowledge: Democratic Education in a Conservative Age* (New York: Routledge, 1993), 1–63; Madeleine Arnot, "Male Hegemony, Social Class, and Women's Education," in *The Education Feminism Reader,* ed. Lynda Stone (New York: Routledge, 1994), 84–104.

6. Perry Anderson, *Las antinomias de Antonio Gramsci* (Barcelona: Fontanara, 1978). See also Morrow and Torres, *Social Theory and Education,* 249–281.

7. Antonio Gramsci, *Selections from the Prison Notebooks of Antonio Gramsci,* ed. and trans. Quintin Hoare and Geoffrey Nowell Smith (New York: International Publishers, 1980). For a commentary on Gramsci, education, and the state, see Carlos Alberto Torres, *The Politics of Nonformal Education in Latin America* (New York: Praeger, 1990), 23–28; Carlos Alberto Torres, *The Church, Society, and Hegemony: A Critical Sociology of Religion in Latin America* (Westport, Conn.: Praeger, 1992), 39–57. For a good discussion of the relationships between education, common sense, and hegemony, see Apple, *Official Knowledge,* 15–43.

8. Two of the best examples of credentialist theories are Ronald Dore, *The Diploma Disease: Education, Qualification, and Development* (Berkeley and Los Angeles: University of California Press, 1976); and John Oxenham, ed., *Education versus Qualifications? A Study of Relationships between Education, Selection for Employment, and the Productivity of Labour* (London: George Allen & Unwin, 1984). Several political economists succeeded in casting doubt on the premises of human capital theory, arguing that the contribution of education to growth is much smaller than the early human capital theorists and development economists thought. In addition, the correla-

tion between earnings and education includes many other influences on earnings that are also correlated with schooling but should not be attributed to it. Martin Carnoy et al., *Can Educational Policy Equalize Income Distribution in Latin America?* (London: Saxon House, 1979); Martin Carnoy et al., "The Political Economy of Financing Education in Developing Countries," in *Financing Educational Development,* by International Development Research Centre (Ottawa: IDRC, 1982), 39–68. Carlos Alberto Torres, Rajinder S. Pannu, and M. Kazim Bacchus, "Capital Accumulation, Political Legitimation, and Education Expansion," in *International Perspectives on Education and Society* 3, ed. Abraham Yogev and Jaap Dronkers (Greenwood, Conn.: JAI Press, 1993), 3–32.

9. Corporatist Portugal offers an invaluable illustration of a process of conservative modernization propelled by the state, with specific roles assigned to the educational system. Stoer and Dale argue: "The state became increasingly concerned in the educational domain with the ideological contribution of education to a definition of national development. . . . the state embarked upon a course that led to a very high degree of centralization of power and control over teachers and to the extreme ideologisation and elitisization of schooling." Cited in Stephen R. Stoer and Roger Dale, "Education, State, and Society in Portugal, 1926–1981," *Comparative Education Review* 31, no. 3 (1987): 405.

10. Offe and Preuss have argued that the notion of democracy increasingly appears to be "a secularized version of the most elementary tenets of Christian theology." See Claus Offe and Ulrich K. Preuss, "Democratic Institutions and Moral Resources," in *Political Theory Today,* ed. David Held (Stanford, Calif.: Stanford University Press, 1991), 146.

11. Eric A. Nordlinger, *On the Autonomy of the Democratic State* (Cambridge: Harvard University Press, 1981); David Easton, "The Political System Besieged by the State," *Political Theory* 9, no. 3 (August 1981): 303–325. From a class analysis perspective, highlighting the principles of state autonomy following Poulantzas's analysis, see Martin Carnoy and Henry Levin, *Schooling and Work in the Democratic State* (Stanford, Calif.: Stanford University Press, 1985), 37–51.

12. I refer here, of course, to the analyses of Marx and modernity as discussed by Marshall Berman in his insightful *All That Is Solid Melts into Air: The Experience of Modernity* (New York: Simon & Schuster, 1982).

13. Henry A. Giroux, *Schooling and the Struggle for Public Life: Critical Pedagogy in the Modern Age* (Minneapolis: University of Minnesota Press, 1988), 136–137. Henry Giroux and Peter McLaren, eds., *Between Borders: Pedagogy and the Politics of Cultural Studies* (New York: Routledge, 1994).

14. I refer to Habermas's three guiding-knowledge interests. For a discussion, see Morrow and Torres, *Social Theory and Education,* 19–38.

15. Held, *Political Theory and the Modern State* (Stanford, Calif.: Stanford University Press, 1989), 11–55; David Held, *Political Theory Today* (Stanford, Calif.: Stanford University Press, 1991); Heinz Rudolf Sonntag and Héctor Valecillos, *El estado en el capitalismo contemporáneo* (Mexico City: Siglo XX Editores, 1977); David Held et

al., eds., *States and Societies* (Oxford: Martin Robinson, 1983); Andrew Vincent, *Theories of the State* (Oxford: Basil Blackwell, 1987).

16. Carlos Alberto Torres, "La universidad latinoamericana: De la reforma de 1918 al ajuste estructural de los 1990," in *Curriculum universitario siglo XXI,* by Carlos Alberto Torres et al. (Paraná, Argentina: Facultad de Ciencias de la Educatión, Universidad Nacional de Entre Rios, 1994), 13–54; Carlos Alberto Torres, "The State and Education Revisited, or Why Educational Researchers Should Think Politically about Education," *AERA, Review of Research in Education* 21 (1995): 255–331; Atilio Alberto Boron and Carlos Alberto Torres, "The Impact of Neoliberal Restructuring on Education and Poverty in Latin America," *Alberta Journal of Educational Research* 42, no. 2 (June 1996): 102–114.

17. The former differ from the latter on a number of issues, particularly in that a few interest groups are especially able to influence the state and that "the ineffectiveness of the others is further diluted because they are underutilized." Nordlinger, *Autonomy of the Democratic State,* 157.

18. The institutionalist approach argues that public education plays a major role in the legitimation of political systems and in the integration and modernization of countries. Compulsory schooling has been associated with different theories of Westernization, modernization, social control, and status-group competition. The institutionalist approach instead argues that educational development is not the result of domestic (internal) processes resulting from economic and social differentiation, especially industrialization and urbanization. Likewise, mass schooling did not develop as a deliberate attempt to establish social control (over the lower classes or immigrants) or to reorient traditional attitudes of populations. Institutionalists argue instead that mass schooling "is a prominent consequence of the development of the cultural framework of the West as a whole." This Western framework implies developing the nation of the nation-state, a modern conception of citizenship that is seen as a source of compulsory mass schooling. Hence, schooling serves as a "ceremonial induction" into modern society, as "an extended initiation rite that symbolically transforms unformed children into enhanced individuals authorized to participate in the modern economy, polity, and society, and it does so by definition." See J. Boli and F. Ramirez, "Compulsory Schooling in the Western Cultural Context," in *Emergent Issues in Education: Comparative Perspectives,* ed. Robert Arnove, Philip G. Altbach, and G. P. Kelly (Albany: State University of New York Press, 1992), 28, 30.

19. A paradigmatic analysis of this approach is presented in Talcott Parsons's classic text, "The School as a Social System: Some of Its Functions in American Society," in *Education, Economy, and Society: A Reader in the Sociology of Education,* ed. A. H. Halsey (New York: Free Press, 1961), 434–455. To be sure, there are critics within and outside the tradition who have developed positions connected with the previous work of Durkheim but in a direction very different from the Durkheimian interpretation introduced by Parsons. See Robert Merton, *Social Theory and Social Structure* (New York: Free Press, 1968). Outside the functionalist tradition, the work of Basil Bernstein and Pierre Bourdieu stands out. See Basil Bernstein, *Class Codes and Control,* vol. 1, *Theoretical Studies towards a Sociology of Language* (London: Paladin, 1973); Basil Bern-

The State and Education   67

stein, *Class Codes and Control,* vol. 3, *Towards a Theory of Educational Transmission,* 2nd ed. (Boston: Routledge & Kegan Paul, 1977); Pierre Bourdieu, "Structuralism and Theory of Sociological Knowledge," *Social Research* 35 (1968): 681–706; Pierre Bourdieu, *Outline of a Theory of Practice,* trans. Richard Nice (Cambridge: Cambridge University Press, 1977); Pierre Bourdieu and Jean-Claude Passeron, "Sociology and Philosophy in France since 1945: Death and Resurrection of a Philosophy without a Subject," *Social Research* 34 (1967): 162–212; Pierre Bourdieu and Jean-Claude Passeron, *Reproduction in Education, Society, and Culture,* trans. Richard Nice (London: Sage, 1977).

20.   Samuel Bowles and Herbert Gintis's work illustrates radical economists' preoccupations with educational functions in liberal societies in the 1970s. See their classic *Schooling in Capitalist America: Educational Reform and the Contradictions of Economic Life* (New York: Basic Books, 1976); Samuel Bowles and Herbert Gintis, "Education as a Site of Contradictions in the Reproduction of the Capital-Labor Relationship: Second Thoughts on the 'Correspondence Principle,'" *Economic and Industrial Democracy* 2 (1981): 223–242. For a critical yet sympathetic commentary, see Mike Cole, ed., *Bowles and Gintis Revisited: Correspondence and Contradiction in Educational Theory* (London: Falmer Press, 1988); Michael W. Apple, "Standing on the Shoulders of Giants: Class Formation and Capitalist Schools," *History of Education Quarterly* 28, no. 1 (1988): 231–241. It is instructive to mention, however, that a central critique of Bowles and Gintis's approach, in addition to its perceived mechanistic views of the relationships between schools and societies and their economicism, is their lack of a theory of the state in their argument criticizing schooling in capitalist societies. It is this theoretical flaw in their argument that prevented them from accounting for contradictory trends towards equality and democracy in education (i.e., correspondence and contradiction as organizing principles structuring social life and schooling). Carnoy and Levin, *Schooling and Work,* 22. For a systematic analysis of reproduction theories, see Morrow and Torres, *Social Theory and Education.*

21.   Neoconservative preoccupations, themes, and rhetoric are present in a number of works. See, e.g., National Commission on Excellence in Education, "A Nation at Risk: An Imperative for Educational Reform," *Education Week,* 27 April 1983, 12–16; and Mortimer Adler, *The Paideia Proposal* (New York: Macmillan, 1982).

22.   In Latin America, and perhaps applicable to other areas of the world, García Canclini defines the neoconservative models as a contradictory process of selective modernization and regressive cultural and social decadence. See Néstor García Canclini, "Una modernización que atrasa: La cultura bajo la regresión neoconservadora," *Revista de Casa de las Américas,* no. 193, October-December 1993, 3–12.

23.   I am grateful to Joel Samoff for bringing this to my attention.

24.   For a useful discussion of these categories, see D. Chirot, *Social Change in the Twentieth Century* (New York: Harcourt Brace Jovanovich, 1977); Immanuel Wallerstein, *The Capitalist World Economy* (Cambridge: Cambridge University Press, 1979).

25.   Let us be clear. This claim has verisimilitude in terms of the legal foundations and historical experience of the nation-state. The experience of "people" within the boundaries of the nation-state is altogether a different matter. Consider, for instance, the

exploitation of labor through the slavery of blacks, the treatment of Latinos and women, the systematic extermination of immigrants, guest workers, and indentured labor, etc.

26. The terms "Third World," "Third World states," "Southern countries," and "countries of the South" are used interchangeably.

27. "Neoliberalism" or "the neoliberal state" are terms used to designate a new type of state that has emerged in Latin America in the past two decades. Tied to the experiences of the neoconservative governments, the first experience of neoliberalism implemented in Latin America is the neoliberal economic program carried out in Chile after the fall of Salvador Allende, under the dictatorship of General Pinochet. More recently, the market models implemented by the governments of Carlos Saúl Menem in Argentina, Carlos Salinas de Gortari and Ernesto Zedillo in Mexico, and Fernando Henrique Cardoso in Brazil, to name a few, represent, with the particularities of the Argentinean, Mexican, and Brazilian circumstances, a neoliberal model.

Neoliberal governments promote notions of open markets, free trade, the reduction of the public sector, the decrease of state intervention in the economy, and the deregulation of markets. Larissa Lomnitz and Ana Melnick (*Chile's Middle Class: A Struggle for Survival in the Face of Neoliberalism* [Boulder, Colo.: Lynne Rienner, 1991]) point out that historically and philosophically neoliberalism is associated with structural adjustment programs. Structural adjustment is defined as a set of programs, policies, and conditionalities that are recommended by the World Bank, the International Monetary Fund, and other financial organizations. Although the World Bank distinguishes between stabilization, structural adjustment, and the policies of adjustment, it also recognizes that the use of these terms is "imprecise and inconsistent" (cited in Joel Samoff, "More, Less, None? Human Resource Development: Responses to Economic Constraint" [Palo Alto, Calif., June 1990], 21; mimeographed). These programs of stabilization and adjustment have given rise to a number of policy recommendations, including the reduction of state spending, the devaluation of currencies to promote exports, reduction of tariffs on imports, and an increase in public and private savings. As I have emphasized, a central aspect of this model is a drastic reduction in the state sector, especially via the privatization of state enterprises, the liberalization of salaries and prices, and the reorientation of industrial and agricultural production towards exports. Thus, structural adjustment and stabilization policies seek to free international exchange, reduce distortions in price structures, do away with protectionism, and facilitate the influence of the market.

The premises of the neoliberal state can be synthesized as follows. The political rationale of the neoliberal state is made up of a mixture of theories and interest groups that are tied to supply-side economics, monetarism, neoconservative cultural sectors; groups opposed to the redistributive policies of the welfare state; and sectors worried at all costs about the fiscal deficit. In other words, it is a contradictory alliance. These state models respond to fiscal crises and the crisis of legitimacy (real or perceived) of the state. In this way, the citizens' crises of confidence are important crises for the exercise of democratic representation and confidence in governments. In this culturally conservative and economically liberal model, the state, state interventionism, and state enterprises are part of the problem, not part of the solution. As has been pointed out on several occasions by neoliberal ideology, the best state is the small government.

The prevailing premises of the economic restructuring of advanced capitalism and the premises of structural adjustment are highly compatible with the neoliberal models. They imply the reduction of public spending, reduction of programs considered wasteful, privatization through the sale of state enterprises, and the development of mechanisms of deregulation to diminish state intervention in the operation of the business world. In addition, it is proposed that the state should participate less in the provision of social services (including education, health, pensions and retirement, public transportation, and affordable housing) and that these services should be privatized.

28.   Up to this point, and quite consciously, I have constructed my discussion of the liberal, neoconservative, and neoliberal states in empirically grounded and informed experience, linking that to political philosophical theories. The following discussions of parallelist theories, postmodernism, and feminism are largely theoretically derived. Because of space constraints, I will not discuss transitional states (e.g., transitions from capitalism to socialism, or from socialist experiences to capitalism) and socialist state experiences per se.

29.   The model includes special industrial arrangements (i.e., "special relationships") between buyers and supplier companies, with a specific role played by the Ministry of International Trade and Industry. Nick Oliver and Barry Wilkinson, *The Japanisation of British Industry* (London: Basil Blackwell, 1988); Paul Hirst and J. Zeitlin, "Flexible Specialization versus Post-Fordism," *Economy and Society* 20, no. 1 (1991): 1–56; Bob Jessop, "Regulation Theory, Post-Fordism, and the State," *Capital and Class* 34 (1988): 147–168.

30.   In this section, I borrow from my work with Raymond Morrow in *Social Theory and Education*.

3

Globalization

This chapter suggests that the phenomenon of globalization limits state autonomy and national sovereignty. These limits are expressed in the tension between global and local dynamics in virtually every decision and policy domain in the social, cultural, and economic spheres. Globalization therefore not only blurs national boundaries but also shifts solidarities within and outside the national state. Globalization cannot be defined exclusively by the post-Fordist organization of production but emerges as a major characteristic of a global world economy. Issues of human rights, regional states, and cosmopolitan democracy will play a major role affecting civic minimums at the state level, the performance of capital and labor in different domains, and particularly the dynamics of citizenship, democracy, and multiculturalism in the modern state.

The Phenomenon of Globalization

> The passage from the state of nature to the civil state produces in man a very remarkable change, by substituting in his conduct justice for instinct, and by giving his actions the moral quality that they previously lacked.
> —Jean-Jacques Rousseau, *The Social Contract*

Globalization has been defined as "the intensification of worldwide social relations which link distant localities in such a way that local happenings are shaped by events occurring many miles away and vice versa" (Held, 1991: 9). Held suggests, among other things, that globalization is the product of the emergence of a global economy, expansion of transnational linkages between economic units creating new forms of collective decision making, development of intergovernmental and quasi-supranational institutions, intensification of transnational communications, and the creation of new regional and military orders.

The process of globalization is seen as blurring national boundaries, shifting solidarities within and between nation-states, and deeply affecting the constitutions of national and interest group identities. Neil Smelser (1994) captures the spirit of this theme quite well when he writes:

> A convenient starting-point for depicting the world situation is to consider the status of the nation-state. Once commonly supposed to be the natural and sovereign focus of the loyalty and solidarity of its citizens, this idea of the state has recently been challenged with respect to all of these constituent elements. The international boundaries of the state have become permeable through the greater globalization of production, trade, finance, and culture with a resultant loss of control of all states over their own fortunes. The sovereignty of states has been further compromised through shifting patterns of regional political federations and alliances. At the sub-national level, the state has found itself challenged by the efflorescence and revitalization of solidarity groupings with multiple bases—regional, linguistic, religious, ethnic, gender, and life-style— as well as a bewildering array of novel social movements that generate their own solidarity. All of these compete with the state for the loyalties of peoples and sometimes for jurisdiction over territory. In a word, the contemporary state has been pressured from both above and below by contested boundaries and shifting solidarities.[1] (5)

Globalization is indeed a social construct that, as Douglas Kellner (1997) has suggested, needs to be considered critically from the perspective of critical theory. Kellner suggests that the concept of globalization is ubiquitous and entails everything from the Westernization of the world to the ascendancy of capitalism. Some people see globalization as increasing the homogeneity of societies, while others, on the contrary, see globalization as increasing the hybridization of cultures and diversity. For still others, globalization is an evolving operation of power by multinational corporations and states, while, in contrast, others see in globalization the linchpin of environmental action, democratization, and humanization. Some people see the concept of globalization as a contemporary ruse to hide the effects of imperialism or modernization, while some others would claim that modernization will open a new "global age" that differs from the "modern age." Moreover, while some theorists claim that globalization is the defining concept of a new epoch in the history of humankind, others disagree, claiming that the novelty and centrality of globalization have been exaggerated (Kellner, 1997:2). Kellner concludes, Solomonically, that globalization is all of the above and that in many ways the discourse of globalization can be articulated with modern and postmodern theories; in fact, for Kellner (1997) we are in an "interregnum period between an aging modern and an emerging postmodern era" (3).

What is important about Kellner's analysis is that he has captured very well the spirit of the epoch as far as social theory is concerned: globalization cannot be analyzed only in terms of discrete polar opposites but should be seen as a transitional situation between two historical epochs. As such, it is a complex, multidimensional phenomenon "that involves different levels, flows, tensions, and conflicts, such that a transdisciplinary social theory is necessary to capture its contours, dynamics, trajectories, problems, and possible futures" (Kellner, 1997:4).

Kellner is skeptical that historical epochs rise and fall with neatly defined chronological boundaries, and he sees the current epoch as a period that is parallel in many ways to the Renaissance, a transitional period between historical eras. In fact, Kellner (1997), despite his knowledge and defense of postmodernism as more than a historical fad, does not see globalization as responding to a clear "postmodern" condition because "capitalist relations of production still structure most social orders and the hegemony of capital is still the structuring force of most dimensions of social life" (31).

From the perspective of critical modernism—that is, a position that sees class, race, and gender as distinct and autonomous modes of domination that nevertheless have systematic interactions that deserve to be studied from interdisciplinary perspectives (Morrow and Torres, 1995)—I turn now to analyze the globalization of capitalism and economic restructuring worldwide.

The Globalization of Capitalism and Economic Restructuring

> When the accumulation of wealth is no longer of high social importance, there will be great changes in the code of morals. We shall be able to rid ourselves of many of the pseudo-moral principles which have hag-ridden us for two hundred years, by which we have exalted some of the most distasteful of human qualities into the position of highest virtues. . . . But beware! The time for all this is not yet. For at least another hundred years we must pretend to ourselves and to everyone that fair is foul and foul is fair; for foul is useful and fair is not. Avarice and usury and precaution must be our gods for a little longer still. For only they can lead us out of the tunnel of economic necessity into daylight.
> —John Maynard Keynes, "Economic Possibilities for Our Grandchildren"

Economic globalization is the result of a worldwide economic restructuring that involves the globalization of economies, science, technology, and culture, as well as a profound transformation in the international division of labor (Harvey, 1989). Along with this transformation of the international division of labor there has been a readjustment of economic integration among nations, states, and national and regional economies. In large part, this globalization is a result of changes in communications and computer technology that increase the productivity of labor, replace labor with capital, and lead to the development of new areas of high productivity (e.g., software technology and computers that helped multibillionaire Bill Gates and Microsoft reach world markets). These changes are redefining relations between nations, and they involve the mobility of capital via international exchanges, as well as short-term, high-risk financial instruments—what some critics have called "the casino economy" ruled by currency speculators (Barnet and Cavanagh, 1996b). There is an enormous concentration and centralization of capital and production at the international level (Carnoy et al., 1993).

The process of globalization has affected labor in contemporary capitalism. Yet labor markets are not homogeneous but segmented. The segmentation of labor markets implies that there are at least four kinds of markets: one, usually transnational, that responds to the demands of monopoly capitalism; a second that responds to the demands of competitive capitalism, representing the secondary labor market, and is more oriented toward exchanges in the domestic market of good and services; a third, the public sector, one of the few labor markets relatively protected from international competition—although with the predominance of neoliberalism and the neoconservative criticism of "big government," public sector employment has been affected by the process of privatization and is shrinking; and finally, a rapidly growing marginal labor market that includes everything from illegal transactions (such as narcotraffic) to self-employment, domestic work, family enterprises, small-scale subsistence production, and innumerable other economic activities that have been called marginal, underground, or informal work. Interestingly enough, this marginal labor market is segmented as well, with some sectors that are clearly tied to globalization (such as narcotraffic or child pornography as an industry) while others are extremely local in their roots, operation, and economic projections (such as street vendors).

A central characteristic of this highly globalized capitalism that has greatly affected labor markets is the global dispersion of the factors of production. Furthermore, the marginal profit rates are growing because of the continued increase in per capita productivity (whose rate of growth continues to increase in some advanced capitalist countries) and a reduction in costs (via layoffs, intensification of production, replacement of more expensive workers with less expensive ones, or the replacement of labor with capital). With the growing segmentation of labor markets in which the primary markets offer more income, stability, and perquisites, there has been a replacement of hourly wages by payment for piecework. This creates a clear distinction between the nominal and real salaries and wages of workers and the social wage via indirect loans and state actions. At the same time, this set of transformations implies the decline of the working class and a reduction of the power of organized labor in negotiating economic policies and in the constitution of the social pact.

Following the long-term tendency of the last three or four decades, service sectors continue to grow, outstripping the importance of the primary and manufacturing sectors in the gross national product. Even in the service industries, which tend to be labor intensive, there are clear indications of the substitution of technology for "middlemen," as is evident, for instance, in the declining importance of travel agents and real estate agents in their respective economic markets.

These changes in the global composition of labor and capital are taking place at a time when there is an abundance of labor and when the conflicts between labor and capital are decreasing. The increase of supernumerary workers is also associated with an increase in international competition and the conviction on the part of the working class and labor unions that it is not always possible to pressure companies in search of more and better social services or salaries. This is because of the abundance of labor, as well as the awareness that the falling profit margins of companies in the transnational and competitive environment have resulted in job losses and the accelerated migration of capital from regional markets in advanced capitalistic countries to areas where labor is highly skilled and poorly paid. The threat of free-trade agreements such as the North American Free Trade Agreement or the new arrangements proposed by the World Trade Organization mark the limits of protectionist policies. Well-known examples are trained engineers and computer experts from India who enter the payroll information of North American companies in data bases for a fraction of the cost of employing American white-collar workers; low-cost mass production by Chinese workers, sometimes subject to forced labor; and young Indonesian girls who manufacture tennis shoes for ten cents an hour.

In order to deal with falling rates of profits, transnational capitalism seeks to achieve more productivity per capita or the reduction of the actual costs of production, as well as transferring production activities to tax-free zones where there is cheap and highly skilled labor; limited organized labor; easy, efficient, and cheap access to natural resources; favorable political conditions; access to better infrastructure and national resources; larger markets; and tax incentives (*Fortune*, 1992).

This new global economy is very different from the former national economy. National economies were previously based on standardized mass production, with a few managers controlling the production process from above and a great number of workers following orders. This economy of mass production was stable as long as it could reduce its costs of production (including the price of labor) and retool quickly enough to remain competitive at the international level. Because of advances in communications and transportation technology and the growth of service industries, production has become fragmented around the world. The new global economy is more fluid and flexible, with multiple lines of power and decision-making mechanisms, analogous to a spider's web, as opposed to the static pyramidal organization of power that characterized the traditional capitalist system (Przeworski, 1991; Ohmae, 1990; Reich, 1991; Thurow, 1992; Mander and Goldsmith, 1996).

These changes in the globalization of capitalism have serious implications for culture and education. As Kellner (1997) so insightfully argues: "culture is an especially complex and contested terrain today as global cultures permeate local ones and new configurations emerge that synthesize both poles, providing contradictory forces of colonization and resistance, global homogenization and local hybrid forms and identities" (11).

While the public education system in the old capitalist order was mostly oriented toward the production of a disciplined and reliable workforce—and yet resistance to systemic reproduction and political radical alternatives takes place in school settings—the new global economy requires workers who can learn quickly and who can work in teams in reliable and creative ways (Wilms, 1996). The most productive workers in a global economy are those whom Robert Reich (1991) defines as symbolic analysts, and they will make up the most productive and dynamic segments of the labor force.

Along with the segmentation of labor markets, globalization implies the replacement of full-time workers by part-time workers (with a substantial reduction in the cost of labor owing to fewer employer contributions to health, education, and social security), an increase in female participation in labor markets, a systematic fall in real salaries, and a growing gap that separates salaried workers from the dominant sectors of society and from self-subsistence wage earners. A similar international phenomenon can be identified in the growing social and economic gap between developing countries and advanced capitalist nations.

Globalization thus has deep implications at the levels of economic exchanges and the symbolic constitution of the social order worldwide. The next section explores the intersection between structural and symbolic changes in the process of globalization.

Globalization and Citizenship: Sovereignty, Markets, and Human Rights

> Moralists and theologians have been saying for a long time that we have got our values all wrong, in putting acquisition ahead of spiritual values. This has

not cut much ice in the last three or four centuries because it was inconsistent with the search for individual and national power to which market societies have been committed. But if I am right in saying that national power from now on is going to depend on moral advantage, on moral stature, then the claims of morality and power will coincide. The way to national power will be the recognition and promotion of equal human rights.

—C. B. Macpherson, *The Real World of Democracy*

Changes in the conditions of production and in the domains of politics, information technology, consumer taste, and capital flows in the overall economy and, more importantly, in the politics of culture worldwide have implied theoretical and practical challenges to the notion of citizenship as predicated by most political philosophy traditions. Here I would like to consider the connections between globalization, rising concerns with worldwide markets and free trade, and the way in which market competition in the context of neoliberalism affects the notion of citizenship and democracy on a global scale.

In the same vein but from the very different political-ideological standpoint of universal human rights, I would like to offer a systematic appraisal of the limits of citizenship given the growing awareness and globalization of the discourse and institutions of universal human rights. These two paradoxically similar arguments from disparate—even antinomical—political philosophical perspectives underscore the complexities associated with globalization and its cultural implications for citizenship.

Citizens and Markets

Nation states are political organisms, and in their economic bloodstreams cholesterol steadily builds up. Over time, arteries harden and the organism's vitality decays.

Kenichi Ohmae, *The End of the Nation State*

Kenichi Ohmae (1995), a most respected Japanese business strategist, advances the thesis in his most recent work, *The End of the Nation State,* that the nation-state is economically sclerotic and that, although still a player in the world system, it has lost its capacity to control its national economy, especially to control exchange rates and to protect its currency. Moreover, the nation-state can no longer generate real economic activity and has lost its role as a critical participant in the global economy. Instead, the four I's (that is, investment, industry, information technology, and individual consumers) that Ohmae indicates drive the expansion and operation of the global economy have taken over the economic power once held by the nation-state.[2] The result of this economic process is the rise of the region state, defined simply as an area that often comprises communities situated across-border that developed around a regional economic center having a population of a few million to 20 million people (Ohmae, 1995:143).

Thus, the nation-state has lost its ability to cope with its own economic dynamics and political tensions, because, as Ohmae (1995) argues:

> Buffeted by sudden changes in industry dynamics, available information, consumer preferences, and flows of capital; burdened by demands for the civil minimum and for open-ended subsidies in the name of national interest; and hogtied by political systems that prove ever-less responsive to new challenges, [nation-states] no longer make compelling sense as discrete, meaningful units on an up-to-date map of economic activity. (79)

For Ohmae, the nation-state has become a dysfunctional unit in terms of economic organization. As the creation of an earlier stage of industrial history, it lacks incentive, credibility, tools, legitimacy, and even the political will to play a central role in today's borderless economy in terms of real flows of economic activity: "as the workings of genuinely global capital markets dwarf their ability to control exchange rates or protect their currency, nation states have become inescapably vulnerable to the discipline imposed by economic choices made elsewhere by people and institutions over which they have no practical control" (Ohmae, 1995:12).

These changes, which are the result of the "new discipline" imposed by the process of globalization over the nation-states, will write the obituary of what Ohmae considers a long-dead body of thought: liberalism and, by implication, liberal democracy. For Ohmae, the central tenet of the liberal ideal in civic life is a philosophical position to sustain extensive public investments in education and to facilitate the action of responsible individuals, at the same time fostering cultural diversity. Liberalism will promote these twin aims except where either goal may conflict with the perceived *volonté générale,* or common good (Ohmae, 1995:75)

Yet, argues Ohmae, for liberalism to work, mutual respect is necessary so that differences in choices, lifestyles, or consumer preferences are not interpreted as challenging the social order or specific individual interests. In addition, to sustain the liberal edifice there must be mutual trust among citizens so that state actions are legitimated as necessary for the social pact and not as merely an imposition or caprice. The third condition is transparency in the actions of the state and in the ability to produce and disseminate information, so that all members of the society can be confident that the decisions reached after a broad debate are fair, even if they don't particularly like the decisions or obtain any benefits from them.

For Ohmae, neither the behavior of individuals nor the behavior of the governments in liberal democracy meet these three criteria. Today in capitalist democracies there is no civic participation but low voter turnout; there is increased competition among individuals following pure self-interest rather than increased solidarity; and governmental information has become opaque rather than transparent, leading to what Ohmae (1995, 75–76) defines as the Iron Triangle of decision making, in which lawmakers, bureaucrats, and special interest groups dominate the process. Thus, for Ohmae, the state is a nostalgic fiction because managers in the public enterprise or in private enterprises cannot any longer be treated as part of discrete national units. Moreover, the production of goods and services cannot be easily attached to a particular national label.

Therefore, growing desires for low-cost products override traditional choices of domestic products. This new culture is embedded in a new form of international cultural taste that Ohmae defines as the "Californianization" of taste. This seems to be particularly relevant in the world of teenagers, who show a fundamental convergence in taste worldwide (e.g., the dominance of rap music, Levi's jeans, or Nike shoes). This shows a growing convergence of worldviews, mind-sets, even thought processes, a commodity consciousness that is multimedia driven and that is, at the same time, creating a serious generational rift between the "Nintendo kids" generation and its predecessors (Ohmae, 1995:15–16; Barnet and Cavanagh, 1996a:72–73).

Technology plays a central role in the globalization of information and culture, particularly because at a macroeconomic level, technological change has made it possible to shift capital anywhere in the world with virtually no restrictions. Thus, capital flows, which have increased dramatically worldwide, need not be tied to any physical movement of goods or services.[3] By extension, traditional forms of trade represent only a fraction of trade across borders and of the borderless economy. Not only capital but also, at the level of companies, information technologies have made it possible for managers to achieve quick, effective, and interactive information about their customers, markets, products, and organizational processes. This, in turn, permits managers to be more responsive to customers and more flexible in organizing the way to provide their services worldwide. Finally, at the market level, technological changes (and particularly exposure to mass media) have changed the way customers know and appreciate how other people live, what kinds of goods and services are available to them, and the relative value of those goods worldwide. This way, then, traditional notions of economic nationalism will have only a small influence on purchase decisions (Ohmae, 1995:27–28).

Not only do the nation-states lose their prestigious position in the world of trade facing the emergence of the regional states, but also, to add to their burden, according to Ohmae (1995), while their economic position weakens, their political position, facing growing demands for the civil minimum, follows suit: "Adding to these burdens, of course, is the steadily growing share of the civil minimum demanded of government in the form of broad-based social programs—welfare, unemployment compensation, public education, old-age pensions, health insurance, and the like" (55).

This demand for the civil minimum shows an important schizophrenia in liberal democracies: citizens do not want these benefits reduced, but they do not want to pay for them either. When facing civil discontent, Ohmae (1995:46) argues, the nation-state can respond in three possible ways. First, if the information monopoly of the state is quite solid and challenges are diffused, the nation-state may face these threats with force, or simply the threat of force. This is, indeed, a short-lived solution that may eventually lead to the demise of "outlaw" regimes. Second, if the monopoly of information is incomplete but the state is still powerful in facing unrest, it could "tough out" disobedience and unrest. However, if the monopoly of information is leaky and public pressure substantial, the nation-state may try to "buy off" the opposition.

For Ohmae (1995), in developed economies the last option is the response of choice. Yet, the solution is worse than the problem because

> Once it becomes known that they [states] are willing to respond to the many claimants to their resources by buying them off as cheaply as possible, the number of claimants lining up for their turn inevitably skyrockets. As does the level of support that satisfies. Worse, as public expectations about the legitimacy of such support harden, it becomes progressively more difficult for governments to revoke the principle or to exclude, as a matter of either policy or discretionary judgment, any but the most marginal categories of people with outstretched hands. Worse still, once the entitlement mentality gets so fully entrenched that demands on the nation's resources exceed the available supply, the reaction of interested constituencies is not to adopt a more moderate stance or to offer to accept less in the name of the common good. It is, rather, to turn with a vengeance on competing constituencies in hopes of discrediting them or otherwise capturing part of their share. And it is precisely this kind of intramural skirmishing that produces the acid most likely to eat away the fabric of the nation state. (47)

This entitlement mentality compounds the political economic troubles of the nation-state and the excesses of the demand for the civil minimum. What are the possible solutions to the problems of the nation-state? The answer is self-evident for Ohmae (1995): the emergence of successful regional states and the possibility of utilizing different organizational forms to tackle and resolve the problems, which are, overall, organizational problems—the product of the human condition—and which can be solved, or at least ameliorated, by organizational solutions that take human nature into account. At this point, Ohmae resorts to a populist call, arguing that economic and political problems are mostly organizational problems, not fundamental questions of ideology. Therefore, these problems cannot be answered by imposing any ideological answer on the nation-states, be it liberal democracy, market economy, socialism, or communism: "the goal, after all, is not to legitimize this or that political establishment or power arrangement. It is to improve the quality of life of people, regular people—us—no matter where they live. People come first; borders come afterwards. It is time for economic policy to remember this simple fact" (148).

In short, in today's borderless economy, with the growing mobility of investment, industry, information technology, and individual consumers, central governments have only one option to avoid economic sclerosis and restore sustainable and self-reinforcing vitality to their economy without mortgaging the long-term prospects of their citizens. That solution is to put global logic first in entering the global economy. To do this, nation-states should allow full operational autonomy to the region states that emerge within or across their borders: "The only hope is to reverse the postfeudal, centralizing tendencies of the modern era and allow—or better encourage—the economic pendulum to swing away from nations and back toward regions" (Ohmae, 1995:142).

Ohmae in both his 1995 book, *The End of the Nation State,* and in his earlier and popular book *The Borderless World: Power and Strategy in the Interlinked World Economy* (1990) seems to advance the idea of global citizenship as consumer and producer in region states. Succinctly put, his argument rests on the assumption that the market discriminates (that is to say, determines) who belongs to, and who has fallen out of, the realm of citizenship. In fact, for Ohmae, corporations, some state institutions, and some citizens have found perfect niches of science, technology, capital, and labor from which they can compete favorably in the world system of commodity production and exchange. These regional niches—whose only legitimacy rests on their ability to compete successfully in a world dominated by free trade and the fact that they are examples of comparative advantage in the allocation of resources and endowments—are in fact the only productive units that can build the polity around them, with all its philosophical, economic, and political implications.

A natural corollary of this analysis is that the nineteenth-century notions of the nation-state are totally obsolete today. Nation-states have allowed regional trading blocs to flourish without controlling them, and sometimes even without levying taxes on them. Therefore, on a global scale, worldwide competitive activities of state institutions, capital, labor, and corporations constitute the only viable sense of organized community, of economic citizenship—

which overrides any sense of political citizenship—and even any viable sense of cultural-national homogeneity. This is particularly so when popular mass culture has become the norm worldwide, and the mass media are stimulating and even regulating consumption as well as values worldwide.

For Ohmae (1995; 1990), there is certainly no reason to strive for any notion of citizenship's rights or obligations nor to substantiate any needs of citizen virtues, given the fact that the state has little, if any, power to regulate exchanges between "trading states" and the fact that pressures for the civil minimum in liberalism have had disastrous results. Therefore the notion of citizenship without market sponsorship is meaningless.

Citizens, National Sovereignty, and Universal Human Rights

> The first state of being is the Power of the State, the second its Resources of Wealth. The state-power is the simply spiritual substance, as well as the achievement of all, the absolutely accomplished fact, wherein individuals find their essential nature expressed, and where their particular existence is simply and solely a consciousness of their own universality.
> —G. W. F. Hegel, *The Phenomenology of Mind*

The exact opposite political-philosophical view argues, however, that while the limits of citizenship as described by Ohmae can be substantiated in the experience of industrialized advanced nations, the real basis for these limits is not merely or exclusively economic circumstances but the predominance of human rights, which creates a new and more universal concept of citizenship. The human rights movement has unfolded in the postwar era, and is, for instance, clearly represented in the human rights policies developed for guest workers in Europe. It is the predominance of universal human rights rather than simply the predominance of market rules that underlies not only the new demands for citizenship but also citizenship's limits within the nation-states.[4]

Personal rights, through the universal extension of the notion of human rights, are becoming available to individuals who fall outside the status of national citizenship. Human rights appear as a new normative framework and a new transnational discourse and structure that not only celebrates but also actively promotes human rights as a world-level organizing principle. Thus, the predominance of universal personhood over national status undermines the national order of citizenship. Nuhoglu Soysal (1994) challenges the popular notion, well entrenched in the tradition of political philosophy, that national citizenship is an imperative for acquiring membership in the polity. She claims that incorporation into a system of membership rights does not inevitably require incorporation into the national collectivity. . . . [In Europe] the guest worker experience attests to a shift in global discourse and models of citizenship across two phases of immigration in the twentieth century. The model of national citizenship, anchored in territorialized notions of cultural belonging, was dominant during the period of massive migration at the turn of the century when immigrants were expected to be molded into national citizens. The recent guest worker experience reflects a time when national citizenship is losing ground to a more universal model of membership, anchored in deterritorialized notions of persons' rights. (3)

Nuhoglu Soysal (1994) describes this new model where rights are institutionalized on the basis of personhood as postnational citizenship: "Postnational citizenship confers upon every person the right and duty of participation in the authority structures and public life of the polity, regardless of their historical or cultural ties to that community" (3). Her analysis is based not only on a faithful acceptance of human rights as a preordained normative framework superseding national, regional, or local cultures (and the politics of identity per se) but also on the preponderance of a new institutionalism and organizational rules that are the result of the consolidation of a new world order—with education playing a central role in the world system.

Institutions are built around routines, rules, norms, and structures, and, within certain limits and frames of behavior, they can guide the transformation of social action. For this new institutionalism, changes in the relationships between the economy (deindustrialization, export-oriented models, globalization), politics (diminishing roles of the state in the private sector, withdrawal of public investment, shrinking state employment), and education (higher user fees, privatization, decentralization, and problems in quality of education) challenge the role of education in development.

Compulsory schooling has been associated with the processes of Westernization, modernization, social control, and status group competition. The early institutionalist approach represented by the work of J. Meyer (1977) and J. Boli and F. Ramirez (1992), among others, argues that educational development is the result not of domestic (internal) processes but of economic and social differentiation, especially industrialization and urbanization. Thus, mass schooling did not develop as a deliberate attempt to establish social control (over the lower classes or immigrants) or to reorient traditional attitudes of populations. Boli and Ramirez (1992) argue, instead, that mass schooling "is a prominent consequence of the development of the cultural framework of the West as a whole" (28). Undoubtedly, the politics and discourse of universal human rights appears as a cornerstone of this new cultural framework of the West.

This Western framework implies developing the notion of the nation-state and a modern conception of citizenship that is seen as a source of compulsory mass schooling. It also implies, as Boli and Ramirez (1992) put it, that schooling serves as a ceremonial induction in modern society, as "an extended initiation rite that symbolically transforms unformed children into enhanced individuals authorized to participate in the modern economy, polity, and society, and it does so by definition" (30).

For these purposes, the role of the state as a modernizer is paramount. Yet, more recently, the state appears as inefficient, even when playing with symbols. In Bruce Fuller's (1991:12–24) view, the state is a bounded institution responsive to a mix of interests or interdependencies, and, showing its own weakness, it simply creates a "signaling theory of schooling." The state must acquire material capital and technical know-how as it fights for legitimation and organizational efficacy required for its own survival. Thus, the state's fragility in developing societies and the contradictions it faces have more to do with fragile states competing with other modernizing institutions than with external and internal forces that erode state autonomy, particularly in the context of the globalization of world economies. Similarly, the state's inability to govern (including the ungovernability of democratic systems) occurs when the state provides conflicting signals to communities.

There are obvious problems with this approach that cannot be explored in detail here. However, posing the question of the global paradoxes of membership, Nuhoglu Soysal (1994) hints at some of the most intractable questions in the analysis of the new institutionalists:

> In the postwar era, if one facet of the discourse and praxis of immigration is the closure of national polity, the other is the expansion of the same polity beyond national closure. While the first involves boundary construction through restrictive policy measures and national(ist) narratives, the other is about "'border crossing" . . . a constant flux of people, the extension of rights of membership to foreigners, and narratives of multiplicity. This apparent paradox is only intelligible if world-level institutional frameworks and processes are taken into consideration. (6)

Two principles then become antagonistic, namely, national sovereignty and universal human rights. For Nuhoglu Soysal, "These two global precepts simultaneously constrain and enhance the nation-state's scope of action" (7–8). This creates an incongruity between the normative and the organizational bases of rights as well as between constitutional prescriptions and laws. There is incoherence, also, in the factual application of those laws in disputed social contexts. In short, in the context of disputes for identity and the politics of culture as performed in social formations, racism and ethnic tensions, sexism and patriarchy, and class exploitation and patrimonialism cannot be ignored as constitutive of the daily experience of people, both at the level of the elites and the socially subordinated sectors.

Challenging traditional assumptions about access to citizenship and exercise of membership rights in a polity, Nuhoglu Soysal (1994), departing from key assumptions of the early institutionalist theory, argues:

> The state is no longer an autonomous and independent organization closed over a nationally defined population. Instead, we have a system of constitutionally interconnected states with a multiplicity of membership. [Hence] . . . the logic of personhood supersedes the logic of national citizenship, [and] [i]ndividual rights and obligations, which were historically located in the nation-state, have increasingly moved to a universalistic plane, transcending the boundaries of particular nation-states. (164–165)

Yet, in the name of preserving universal human rights in the face of deteriorating societal and state conditions, atrocities have been committed—evidenced, for instance, by revelations of human rights abuses by the peacekeeping mission in Somalia in 1991 in which Canadian and Italian soldiers were charged with torturing and killing Somali teenagers (Fox, 1997).

Nuhoglu Soysal's (1994) analysis of the limits of citizenship has implications at three levels: first, at the level of citizenship, where notions of identity and rights are decoupled; second, at the level of the politics of identity and multiculturalism, where the emergence of membership in the polity "is multiple in the sense of spanning local, regional, and global identities, and which accommodates intersecting complexes of rights, duties and loyalties" (166); and finally, given the importance of the international system for the attainment of democracy worldwide, Nuhoglu Soysal highlights the emergence of what could be termed cosmopolitan democracies, that is, international political systems relatively divorced in their origins and constitutive dynamics from the nation-states' codes.

Globalization and Multicultural Citizenship: Postmodernism's Children?

"What helped you today was not the leaves, but power."
"Your power, Don Juan?"
"I suppose you could say that it was my power, although that is not really accurate. Power does not belong to anyone. Some of us may gather it and then

it could be given directly to someone else. You see, the key to stored power is
that it could be used only to help someone else store power."
　　　　　　　—Carlos Castañeda, "Sorcery: A Description of the World"

Citizenship has always been associated with the constitution and operation of
the modern nation-state. The question, in the face of increased globalization, is
whether the nation-state and citizenship are withering away. Paradoxically,
these assumptions are related to the postmodernist view.

Postmodernism argues that nation-states are losing importance in the context of an increasingly interdependent world and of more local struggles. Yet,
as Immanuel Wallerstein argues, the history of the (capitalist) world system
has been a historical trend towards cultural heterogeneity rather than cultural
homogenization. Thus, the fragmentation of the nation in the world system is
happening at the same time that there is a tendency towards cultural differentiation or cultural complexity, that is, globalization. Globalization and regionalization seem to be dual processes occurring simultaneously. This fact has not
been overlooked by certain strands of postmodernism, providing an avenue to
understanding the simultaneous rise of ethnicity, nationalisms, and globalization, not necessarily as contradictory but as related phenomena.

Held (1995) has persuasively argued that there is a new world order associated with the globalization of capitalism,

> an international order involving the conjuncture of a global system of production
> and exchange which is beyond the control of any single nation-state (even of the
> most powerful); extensive networks of transnational interaction and communi-
> cation which transcend national societies and evade most forms of national reg-
> ulation; the power and activities of a vast array of international regimes and
> organizations, many of which reduce the scope for action of even leading states;
> and the internationalization of security structures which limit the scope for the
> independent use of military force by states. (101)

Held's overall argument overlaps with Ohmae's arguments about regional
states and rests on the assumption that, in the past, trade routes and empires
linked distant populations with networks of interaction of limited sophistica-
tion. In the present, however, the contemporary new social order is defined by
multiple systems of transaction and coordination linking people, communities,
and societies in such a complex way that territorial boundaries are rendered
virtually useless in controlling economic, cultural, and political activities.
Needless to say, this situation generates new political uncertainties.

One may agree with Kenichi Ohmae's or David Held's notion of a new
social order with the globalization of capitalism and the predominance of tech-

nology, but there are other very powerful facts that cannot be ignored. Among them is the fact that capital continues to be loosely regulated within national borders, while labor continues to be strongly regulated within state borders. Therefore, the question of what kind of government is more suited to advance the logic of the business world is not redundant for some factions of capital. That is, not every government or government alliance is always welcomed by capital, nor does every capitalist society have the same type and extent of regulations. For instance, there is no doubt that regulations pertaining to capitalist transactions differ quite dramatically between, for instance, Japan and the United States. Thus, what is a legal and usual practice in the former could even be considered illegal and be regulated by antitrust laws in the latter.[5]

Technology has national "hotbeds," such as California's Silicon Valley, with some countries having a larger critical mass of information technologies, brains, capital, and resource endowments than others. Finally, while there are tax paradises where multinational corporations can locate and avoid taxes on profits, (e.g., Andorra, the Canary Islands, the Cayman Islands), other large and small local or multinational business corporations continue to be tied to their headquarters and areas of operations and continue to be taxed at the local/national level.

In this historical context, what are the implications for citizenship, democracy, and education of this notion of globalization? Any redefinition of the notion of democracy situates public schooling at the center of the modernist-Enlightenment project. Postmodernism would argue, however, that the ethical, substantive, and procedural elements of democratic theory should be reexamined in light of postmodern culture. The challenge for educators, parents, students, and policymakers is to think critically about the failures of the past and about the myriad exclusionary practices that still pervade the process of schooling—hence bringing to the forefront issues of power and domination, class, race, and gender. For instance, as I said before, the validity of the notion of instrumental rationality guiding school reform should also be examined because it gives attention to administration, procedures, and efficiency as the prime criteria for change and progress, and because it assumes that there is a common framework structuring the experience of all people.[6] This certainly challenges some key postmodernist approaches.

Human rights, in fact, constitute the basis for identity politics, and the notion of tolerance appears as a central foundation for diversity and citizenship premised as human rights. Todd Gitlin (1995) explains:

> A humane respect for difference, an understanding that one aspect of the human condition is to live in a distinct milieu, an acknowledgment of the limits of what anyone can know—these remain the basis for common human rights. The

Enlightenment's enduring ideal of universal rights, once extended logically, guarantees the right to be different—although it is also a reminder that human beings have good reason not to differ about one elementary right: the right to be who one wishes to be. (215)

Gitlin's (1995) passionate defense of the Enlightenment poses a central problem for postmodernist perspectives: by ignoring the critical contributions of critical modernism, many postmodernist approaches fall into the trap of depoliticizing the process of human empowerment and liberation. Henry Giroux (1988) poses the problem bluntly: "The flight from foundationalism is at the same time often a flight from politics" (61). He continues:

Various brands of postmodernism, poststructuralism, and neo-pragmatism have declared war on all the categories of transcendence, certainty, and foundationalism. First principles are now seen as mere relics of history. The unified subject, long the bulwark of both liberal and radical hopes for the future, is now scattered amid the valorizing of decentering processes. Moreover, the attack on foundationalism has resulted in a one-sided methodological infatuation with deconstructing not simply particular truths, but the very notion of truth itself as an epistemological category. (61)

In the same critical vein, Habermas's ethical rationalism provides the basis for a powerful counterattack against the flight of postmodern philosophy from ethics and politics and constitutes, to be sure, a central referent for emerging perspectives in the sociology of education, including a systematic appraisal of the conditions for citizenship formation given the dynamics of education (Morrow and Torres, in press a). What we need, then, is to study in some detail the relationship between the process of globalization and citizenship as solidarity building.

Globalization, Citizenship, and Solidarity

A community or *polis* is not something that can be made or engineered. . . . There is something of a circle here. . . . The coming into being of a type of public life that can strengthen solidarity, public freedom, a willingness to talk and listen, mutual debate, and a commitment to rational persuasion presupposes the incipient forms of such communal life. But what then is to be done in a situation in which there is a breakdown of such communities, and where the very conditions of social life have the consequences of furthering such a breakdown?

More poignantly, what is to be done when we realize how much of humanity has been systematically excluded and prevented from participating in such dialogical communities?

—R. J. Bernstein, *Beyond Objectivism and Relativism: Science, Hermeneutics, and Praxis*

If globalization is deeply undermining the position of nation-states in the world system, globalization is also reshaping the movement of labor across national boundaries and the social milieu. As a corollary, it has also increased the diversity within nation-states. If multiculturalism is one of the results of the process of globalization of culture and society at the level of the nation-state, the connections between globalization and multiculturalism have immediate implications for theoretical debates and practical politics relating to the constitution of bicultural and multicultural identities, multilingualism in schools, and the new cultural demands on curriculum, teaching and learning, evaluation, and intergroup relations in schools. This is so because mass schooling policies were historically developed by the welfare state to foster, among other things, national solidarity, as I argued in chapter 2. Education, as public policy, was developed, mandated, supervised, and regulated by the modern state and has played a major role in the constitution and operation of the welfare state.

It was Emile Durkheim (cited in Bardis, 1985) who argued that the state was central in moving capitalist societies from mechanical into organic solidarity:

Even when society relies most completely upon the division of labor, it does not become a jumble of juxtaposed atoms, between which it can establish only external, transient contacts. Rather the members are united by ties which extend deeper and far beyond the short moments during which the exchange is made. There is above all, an organ upon which we are tending to depend more and more; this is the state. The points at which we are in contact with it multiply as do the occasions when it is entrusted with the duty of reminding us of the sentiment of common solidarity. (271–272)

Echoing Durkheim, several political scientists, such as Peter Flora and Jens Alber (1991), have argued that the nation-state is the main source of solidarity in capitalist societies. The nation-state as provider of solidarity in the European context goes back to the nineteenth century, but it has a predecessor in the Roman Catholic Church, which provided welfare for the needy.[7] The transformation of solidarity by the nation-state has brought about reflections on the subject of citizenship. As early as 1950, Gunnar Myrdal (1960, 1973) argued that large-scale systems such as the nation-state are related to citizenship, ethnicity, and cultural identity. Thus the main (but not by any means the only) source of solidarity in the welfare state is related to the creation of citizenship rights and the rhetoric to build a homogeneous society.

From this perspective, the nation-state appears as the framework for institutionalized solidarity and citizenship rights. Otherwise, one would ask why the rich should be in solidarity with the poor. Why should there be any solidarity between generations? Or solidarity between different neighborhoods or regions within the nation-state? Or solidarity between individuals of different genders and occupations? Or, simply put, any solidarity among citizens themselves?

This issue has immense implications for political philosophy, a fact that was amply recognized by Karl Marx (Tucker, 1978) when he argued in *The German Ideology* that

> Just because individuals seek only their particular interest, which for them does not coincide with their communal interest (in fact the general is the illusory form of communal life), the latter will be imposed on them as an interest "alien" to them, and "independent" of them, as in its turn a particular, peculiar "general" interest: or they themselves must remain within this discord, as in democracy. On the other hand, too, the practical struggle of these particular interests, which constantly really run counter to the communal and illusory communal interest, makes practical intervention and control necessary through the illusory "general" interest in the form of the State. (161)

This analysis, however, immediately invites a discussion of the notion of radical democracy as proposed by the citizen of Geneva, Jean-Jacques Rousseau (1976). If the constitution of the state, as Rousseau suggested, implies forcing individuals to adapt to the social and democratic pact, then what motive do individuals have for creating relations of solidarity beyond certain limits of self-interest? What interest do they have in creating the conditions for minimum levels of tolerance and social articulation through organic rather than mechanical integration? Moreover, who will be able to enforce legitimately this limited solidarity? These are important questions if we consider Rousseau's views (Chapman, 1956).

For Rousseau, people should be forced to become democratic. When individual protest is suppressed, we are forcing the individual to be free. Rousseau (1976) argues in *The Social Contract* that

> it will be asked how a man can be free and yet forced to conform to wills which are not his own. How are opponents free and yet subject to laws they have not consented to? I reply that the question is wrongly put. . . . The unvarying will of all members of the State is the general will; it is through that that they are citizens and free. . . . Had my private opinion prevailed, I should have done something other than I wished; and in that case I should not have been free. (113)

Therefore, in capitalist societies it is the nation-state that articulates the principles that regulate social exchanges and solidarity. Yet, a number of changes are affecting the process of solidarity building, as I have already outlined. In the Western world, there is increased competition among Western powers. With the erosion of the hegemony of the United States in international relations in the post–Cold War era, the competition between Japan, Germany, and the United States shows not only different capitalist states competing for markets (and multinational corporations usually associated with their national origins) but also different types of capitalism and democratic states.

In Eastern Europe, the collapse of an organized system of solidarity after 1989 calls for the establishment of another system of solidarity, but this time a system that can be regulated through the market. The question arises of how to do away with a welfare system that, despite its inability to preserve freedom of choice, did in fact guarantee a minimum level of housing, employment, education, and health care subsidized or provided by the state. The transition from a system based on state provisions to one based on market exchanges is certainly plagued by difficulties. A very important problem, given the cultural and historical configuration of several artificially constructed Eastern European societies, is to establish the basis for solidarity beyond what is mostly ethnicity and national identity. The conflict in Bosnia is a tragic yet telling example of the sharp division along ethnic lines in several Eastern European societies. Finally, moving away from the previous sphere of influence of the Soviet Union, the creation of the European Union implies a different type of solidarity, perhaps at a metanational level that will alter the equilibrium of the world system.

Globalization and the worldwide division of labor imply that solidarity is still organized at the level of the nation-state, but they also imply that tensions and determinants generated within the process of globalization are affecting the constitution of solidarity at the level of the nation-state when no institution in the international system is replacing the role of social welfare once performed by state institutions. Despite these issues, the process of globalization, usually associated with movement of capital and labor, may not be such an entirely new phenomenon as it seems.

For Harold Wilensky (1994), the process of globalization underscores labor policies that have been fully in place at least since the 1960s. If market-oriented democracies exist in many forms and the process of globalization is also part of the process brought about by changes in technology, communications, and trade, what changes can in fact be attributed to globalization (Gourevitch, 1986)? There are different institutional varieties of nation-states, not only with regard to differences in performance, but also with regard to the way forces external to the nation-states command power in the context of the world system—that is, multinational corporations and bilateral and multilateral international agencies. The corporatist arrangement between management, labor, and the welfare state has also been dramatically altered. Economic performances explain shifts in trade and taxation, but we should not underestimate the importance of power, ideology, and political parties in contemporary democracies.

Another issue is the relationship between the process of globalization and the transnationalization of identity. While it is indeed debatable whether globalization is a planetary event, new notions of social marginality cut across the duality of North-South relationships. Thus, key issues of politics of solidarity, including governance, accountability, and citizenship, enter into conflict with the historical process of centralization that has been embedded in national territories. Globalization is perceived as denationalization of territories defined by the growing power of transnational corporations, interventionism of foreign states, and a pervasive transnational culture fostered by mass media, all of which seem to prevail over peripheral nation-states, domestic capital, and local, regional, or national cultures. Reaction to such a process of denationalization is exemplified well in the Chiapas conflict, entering its fourth year in 1998, and the struggle of the Zapatista Liberation Front to establish an Indian identity (and rights) beyond, and indeed opposed to, the legal commitments accepted by the Mexican state and reflected in the North American Free Trade Agreement between Mexico, the United States, and Canada (Marcos, 1994).

These conflicts take place in the context of multiple circuits of globalization, including an "inner" and "outer" circuit in terms of capital accumulation. The inner circuit refers to international migration, transnational identities, and the struggle of women and people of color. The outer circuit of globalization refers to new technologies that are changing the information process and institutions and the mobility of capital. Thus, there are different forms of social control and regulation in the inner and outer circuits of globalization. A good example is that currency markets are out of control because technology involves a speed of transactions that escapes existing forms of state regulation and control. This is fascinating, since technology itself is designed not only as a form of exchange but also as one of control. These are, however, forms of control that are not easy for governments to handle, and technology may result in reversals of fortune for governments, as the following vignette of former finance minister Ricupero of Brazil illustrates.

Conducting research for this book in Brazil in 1994, I witnessed a political scandal in the Brazilian state that rocked the souls and hearts of many citizens. A former university professor and seasoned Brazilian diplomat, Rubens Ricupero, then minister of finance and the Brazilian candidate (with the support of all Latin American countries) for the presidency of a new international organism that will implement the GATT (General Agreements on Tariffs and Trade) agreements, unintentionally disclosed to the public a number of his private thoughts on the Brazilian economy and politics. While he was waiting to fix a technical problem for a public television interview, his private conversation with a journalist was picked up by an open microphone. The conversation was (apparently) involuntarily aired and captured with unfiltered sound by parabolic antennas in several places in Brazil. What was labeled as "the crisis of the parabolic antennas" by the Brazilian media showed that technology is not only social regulation but also can be used for empowerment. Among other things, Ricupero said that he had no qualms (scruples) about hiding or downplaying economic information that might damage the campaign of the candidate supported by the government, sociologist Fernando Henrique Cardoso. His actual words, as reported in the 7 September 1994 *Journal ISTOE,* were, "Eu não tenho escrúpulos. O que é bom a gente fatura; o que é ruim, esconde." He also was inclined to deceive the public about economic indices, boasting that he was extremely useful to the TV network Rede Globo—a network that is representative of the most conservative sectors of the Brazilian bourgeoisie. This is so, according to Ricupero, because instead of giving its open public support to Cardoso, the network simply reports Ricupero's arguments, as current minister of finance, supporting the project of economic stabilization launched by Cardoso as the previous minister of finance. Nobody will object to the word of Ricupero, a distinguished public official.

Needless to say, this private conversation shocked the public, and Ricupero had to resign two days later. The implications of this affair loomed over Brazilian politics for a while. Ricupero had the demeanor and reputation of an extremely honest politician, a public servant who was above the fray of competing interests and mediocrity. He was always projected as a mystical, monklike figure among the Brazilian elite. Until that infamous conversation, his ethics and reputation as a state functionary were impeccable.

Many Brazilians of different social conditions and political affiliations felt deceived, betrayed. The whole political discourse was vitiated, casting doubts on the legitimacy of the upcoming government. This episode underscored for me, as an educational researcher, the importance of discussing the relationships between the state and education when facing complex moral choices in public policy. After all, a public interview by a public official is usually considered a pedagogical act of educating (or forming) public opinion. The art of persuasion is a pedagogical art. Not by chance Lacan insisted that a good teacher is a great seducer. The interview also reinforced my concern for continuing a critical scrutiny of state affairs based on a healthy skepticism of state rhetoric. The same applies, from a critical theory perspective, to every level of social exchange and narrative in the public sphere and civil society. Finally, it reinforced my conviction that authentic moral indignation is a most relevant political weapon for cultural criticism and practical politics. Moral indignation, however, cannot be construed as "another" narrative. It is authentic only when it is nourished by anger and hope, two of the most important sentiments for a true renewal of states and civil societies in this critical time.

Coming back to the connections between technology and citizenship, it is possible for one to question whether new technologies are contributing to the overriding of traditional loyalties to the nation-state and historical forms of citizenship. Globalization has implications for issues of power and legitimacy at several levels, and most certainly, in light of the debates about liberal education and human emancipation, it has implications for what Cornel West (1993a) so properly calls "the irreducibility of individuality within participatory communities" (32), a basic premise of democratic pragmatism, U.S. style.

Economic globalization relocates certain components of power and authority. In so doing, new forms of nonstate power, legitimation, and authority appear. Examples are the International Monetary Fund, the World Bank, the World Trade Organization, and other international organizations that have acquired new roles and legitimacy in the last decades. Although the autonomy of the national elites and scientific communities to deal with regulatory institutions of capitalism like the World Bank and their educational proposals is quite limited, the legitimacy of these institutions does not go uncontested. Nevertheless, these international institutions have become especially prominent in these times of economic retrenchment and fiscal crisis in the Third World (Coraggio and R. M. Torres, 1997; De Tommasi, Warde, and Haddad, 1996; Tussie, 1997).

One example of how international economic players can work to create nonstate forms of power is the reaction of bond markets to the industrial-incentive package that the Clinton administration tried to pass upon taking office. The perception that accelerated economic activity would lead to higher inflation, which in turn would lead to higher interest rates, created worrisome expectations for conservative, long-term investors holding bonds. An overheated economy and inflationary pressures led to higher interest rates and a selloff of the bonds, which increased fiscal pressure on the government. Bond markets and their economic logic had set clear limits for new economic policies of a new administration in the United States that had inherited a large fiscal deficit and internal debt from the Reagan and Bush administrations. After realizing the strength of the opposition, Clinton, who had lobbied the Democratic Congress hard to pass the industrial policy package, quickly withdrew the package, creating ill will with legislators of his own party who had risked their own positions in their districts by pushing for the presidential initiative.

A final point needs to be emphasized. As I argued in chapter 2, globalization also relates to the new role that professional associations play in setting national standards in the United States (e.g., the association of teachers of mathematics for new mathematics standards) and other industrially advanced countries (Popkewitz, 1993). Is this process of social regulation operating independently of the ideologies (e.g., neoconservatism or neoliberalism)? Is this process of social regulation through professional associations a specific way of building hegemony by defining occupational and educational futures, as postmodernism seems to imply? Is the allegiance (and overall strategic formulation) of these new forms of nonstate authority related to specific national policies or to transnational, abstract formulae of world system integration? These questions are, again, of the utmost importance in considering the question of citizenship in the context of globalization and declining economic resources.

Are Cosmopolitan Democracies the Answer?

> "Democracy" is today an intensely contested word that means different things to different people, even as everyone claims to be for it.
> —Nancy Fraser, *Justice Interruptus*

Political theorists are not oblivious to the paradoxes and contradictions that the new institutionalism and globalization suggest. In this increasingly complexly organized multicultural and multilingual world system, the bases of traditional forms of political community have been eroded; and coupled with this erosion is an emerging theory and practice of distrust in democracy. Hence, the previous models of democratic checks and balances, separation of powers, and the notion of democratic accountability no longer work smoothly, not even at the level of formal rather than substantive democracy. Yet distrust in democracy and democratic theory as part of a modernist discourse cannot be associated with all postmodernist strands per se. The growing distrust in democracy poses problems for the process of educational reform and its eventual connections with citizenship building and raises concerns about the narrowing of the meaning of democracy in capitalist societies.

The redefinition of democracy needs to be extricated from the forming patterns of social regulation that prevail in contemporary societies. Italian philosopher Norberto Bobbio (1995) contends that this issue may be at the heart of the possible survival of the democratic system: Can a state be fully democratic in a world that is not (as yet) democratic? Posing a Kantian dilemma in considering the relationships between domestic and international systems, Bobbio (1995) points to a vicious circle: "States can become democratic only in a fully democratized international society, but a fully democratized international society presupposes that all the states that compose it are democratic. The completion of one process is hindered by the non-completion of the other" (39).

For David Held (1995), the answer to this dilemma is the notion of cosmopolitan democracy. Held is very clear about the need to develop a cosmopolitan democratic model, one in which democracy "can be secured in a series of interconnected power and authority centers [because] . . . the possibility of democracy today must, in short, be linked to an expanding framework of democratic states and agencies" (106). Held is very positive about a series of developments that give impetus to the extension of democracy worldwide, including:

> (1) the development of transnational grass-roots movements with clear regional or global objectives such as the protection of natural resources and the environment, and the alleviation of disease, ill-health and poverty; (2) the elaboration of new legal rights and duties affecting states and individuals in connection with the "common heritage of humankind," the protection of the "global commons," the defense of human rights and the deployment of force; and (3) the emergence and proliferation in the twentieth century of international institutions to coordinate transnational forces and problems, from the United Nations and its agencies to regional political networks and organizations. (114)

In the last instance, this model of a cosmopolitan democracy requires a new international political culture and a serious examination of distinctive national, ethnic, cultural, and social identities that offer the limits as well as the possibilities of developing a cosmopolitan democracy and citizenship. Held (1995) is sanguine about this issue when he argues that in order for the plurality of identities that constitute societies to persist in sustainable ways, "each has to recognize the other as a legitimate presence with which some accommodation must be made; and each must be willing to give up exclusive claims upon the right, the good, the universal and the spatial" (116). This is certainly easier said than done, particularly since Held himself recognizes that the globalization of communications and information has not created a sense of common human purpose but has served to reinforce the politics of identity and difference, hence "further stimulating the 'nationalization' of politics" (115).

It is at this level that the discussion of multicultural citizenship acquires new dimensions. Likewise, new appeals to the notions of enlightenment and reason as a way to sort out conflicts about citizenship, both at local and global levels, are being heard through the voices of contemporary cultural critics. For instance, as Gitlin (1995) points out:

The paradox is that as investment, communication, organization, migration, and trade become more intensely global, the reality that people experience, the one that comforts them and fills them with feelings of membership, becomes even more stubbornly local—all the more so because competing claims of commonality feel hopelessly abstract and remote. (226)

Therefore, the idea, anticipated by Marx and a host of Enlightenment theorists, of the contradictions between the interest of the community and that of the individual is magnified by the new contradictions, on the one hand, between the interests of the nation-state postulating the idea of sovereignty as supreme and," on the other hand, by rules, regulations, and structures of the new global institutionalism, arguing that the precepts of universal human rights and the rights given by personhood (and not merely by national birth or naturalization) are in dialectical tension (Nuhoglu Soysal, 1994:158–159).

Karl Marx (Tucker, 1978) was very clear in his early writings. He said in *The German Ideology:*

Out of this very contradiction between the interest of the individual and that of the community the latter takes an independent form as the State, divorced from the real interests of individuals and community, and at the same time as an illusory communal life, always based, however, on the real ties existing in every family and tribal conglomeration—such as flesh and blood, language, division of labor on a larger scale, and other interests—and especially . . . on the classes, already determined by the division of labor. (160)

The stakes are high because, as Marx argued, "Just because individuals seek only their particular interest, which for them does not coincide with their communal interest (in fact the general is the illusory form of communal life)," the latter will be imposed on them as an interest "alien" to them, and

independent of them, as in its turn a particular, peculiar "general" interest: or they themselves must remain within this discord, as in democracy. On the other hand, too, the practical struggle of these particular interests, which constantly really run counter to the communal and illusory communal interest, makes practical intervention and control necessary through the illusory "general" interest in the form of the State. (161)

Interestingly enough, Held's (1995) notion of the sovereignty of a cosmopolitan democracy, along with the notion of human rights as the universal rights of personhood, not only reaffirms Marx's (Tucker, 1978) suggestion of the contradiction between community and individualism—the classic contradiction that underlies most of the arguments in contemporary political philosophy appearing as a most serious theoretical and practical conundrum, as Wolin (1960) so aptly formulated years ago—but now this contradiction reaches a world level, in the tension between national sovereignty and human rights and between the nation-states and the region states. This new contradiction increases the complexity of the democratic design of the notion of citizenship, which seems to lose its clear articulation in the twin principles of territorial anchorage and shared cultural traditions and history. And, finally, naive conceptions of a homogeneous citizenship are challenged by the very same notion of multiculturalism and the politics of identity so predominant in the politics of culture and education in the world system. Human rights are crucial because they give standing to individuals based on their humanity and not because they are tied to a particular state. Moreover, human rights open the door to a process of democratization and citizenship that is not state-centered (Pateman, 1996: 24).

After discussing the theoretical constructs of the state and globalization and the perpetual tensions between the two in this and the previous chapter, I now turn to a detailed analysis of the the three components of the theoretical dynamics and relationships that I am trying to clarify: theories of citizenship, democracy, and multiculturalism.

Notes

1. This is well documented in the sociological literature. The Thirteenth World Congress of Sociology, which took place in Bielefeld, Germany, 18–23 July 1994, had as its central theme "Contested Boundaries and Shifting Solidarities." See Neil Smelser, "Contested Boundaries and Shifting Solidarities," *International Sociological Association (ISA) Bulletin* 60 (Spring 1993): 5.

2. The theoretical notion of the state covers federal and state governance. Yet the presence of "provincial" or single states with premier economies makes matters more complicated. For instance, in Canada there is a clear division of labor between federal and provincial states. The federal state is charged with key symbolic processes to increase the legitimacy of the political system, including, e.g., immigration and constitutionalism. The provincial state is primarily in charge of specific roles in promoting capital accumulation, and hence education is fundamentally a provincial responsibility. Another example is the differential might of single states in a union, as is the case of the state of California in the United States. Journalistic reports remind us periodically that in terms of output California ranks seventh (above Canada and following very closely Great Britain) in the world, with an annual output of $1,037 billion, because of its position at the crossroads of one of the busiest trade routes in the world, linking Asia and Latin America, and California's powerhouse in terms of agricultural products, entertainment, computers, electronics, etc. The top G-7 countries are the United States

($6,773 billion), Japan ($4,321 billion), Germany ($2,075 billion), France ($1,355 billion), Italy ($1,101 billion), Great Britain ($1,069 billion), and Canada ($900 billion). Dave Lesher, "California Is Golden and Global," *Los Angeles Times,* 8 January 1998, A1, A20.

3. Goldsmith (1996:502) asserts that since World War II global GNP has increased fivefold and world trade twelvefold. Money itself, Barnet and Cavanagh (1996b:368) tell us, has become a global product. For instance, the worldwide total of eurocurrency accounts in 1973 was $315 billion; by 1987, the total was nearly $4 trillion.

4. For a compelling analysis of the the limits of citizenship given the predominance of human rights, see Yasemin Nuhoglu Soysal, *Limits of Citizenship: Migrants and Postnational Membership in Europe* (Chicago: University of Chicago Press, 1994).

5. See Lester Thurow's analysis of the interlocking ownership of business and strategy plotting in his much-acclaimed *Head to Head: The Coming Economic Battle among Japan, Europe, and America* (New York: William Morrow, 1992), 64 ff.

6. The notion of instrumental rationality is central to critical theory. It is defined here combining the Weberian notion of rationality as purposive-instrumental action and Habermas's notion of instrumental action. For Max Weber, purposive-instrumental action is "determined by expectations as to the behavior of external objects and of other men, and making use of these expectations as 'conditions' or 'means' for the rational success-oriented pursuit of the agent's own rationally considered ends" (McCarthy, 1979:28). The notion of instrumental action in Habermas "is governed by technical rules based on empirical knowledge. In every case they imply empirical predictions about observable events, physical or social" (McCarthy, 1979:391). I should add, following Marcuse's criticism of technical reason, that every form of instrumental rationality, insofar as it represents an adequate means to a given end and is governed by technical rules based on empirical knowledge seeking to forecast and control social and physical events, involves a substantive purpose of domination that is exercised through methodical, scientific, calculating, and calculated control.

7. See, e.g., the teachings of the "social bishop" of the time, Wilhelm Emmanuel von Ketteler, *The Social Teachings of Wilhelm Emmanuel von Ketteler: Bishop of Mains (1811-1877),* trans. Rupert J. Ederer. (Washington, D.C.: University Press of America).

4

Citizenship

_____

This chapter offers a systematic appraisal of theories of citizenship, including an analysis of the connections between citizenship, state theories, and democracy. In this regard, this chapter succinctly summarizes the contribution of British social scientist T. H. Marshall and its refutation by the insights of the neoconservative movement. Once the foundations for the theory of citizenship are established and its critique is advanced, the most serious challenges to the notion of citizenship in the liberal tradition are considered. These include contributions from feminist theories—and particularly their critique of T. H. Marshall's work—postcolonialism and subordinate spaces theories, critical race theories, and theories of social movements. An argument is made showing that without the proposals of the Enlightenment, a theory of citizenship cannot be accomplished. Yet, and following the insights of T. H. Marshall, without an acceptable distribution of resources, it can be argued that growing poverty levels drastically affect the constitution of a democratic citizenship, thus resulting in the dualization of society and consequently the dualization of citizenship.

The Citizen

> Viewing dialogue as a process of openly negotiated meaning and value has a close kinship with a metatheory about how generalizable moral values can be identified and justified.
>
> —N. Burbules, _Dialogue in Teaching_

Traditionally, the notion of citizenship was associated with the inhabitant of the city: a bourgeois, _civis Romanus,_ or _citoyen,_ as Max Weber (1966:233) tells us. Yet, it would be simplistic to define citizenship as a group of citizens enjoying limited rights within the context of a given city. There are a number

101

of fascinating accounts of how citizenship developed historically, including an analysis of the constellations of variants in the constitution of citizenship considering whether citizenship formation resulted from ruling-class strategies or from a host of social struggles (i.e., citizenship "from above" versus citizenship "from below"); how citizenship differs given distinct legal traditions (e.g., Roman continental systems versus British common law); or differences in the types of political systems in which the notion of citizenship is articulated (e.g., liberal, reformist, authoritarian, monarchist, fascist, and authoritarian-socialist) (T. H. Marshall, 1950, 1963, 1981; Mann, 1989; Weber, 1966; Somers, 1993; Turner, 1986).

To undertake a discussion of theories of citizenship and their importance to education, it is important to move beyond historical or legal considerations. Likewise, it is important to move beyond the notion of citizenship as a kind of personal status, a combination of rights and duties that all legal members of a nation-state hold. The discussion of theories of citizenship requires stating a premise from the outset: a theory of what a good citizen is should be relatively independent of the formal premises of the legal question of what it is to be a citizen. This is so because of the dual theoretical concerns of citizenship: citizenship as identity and as a set of civic virtues. Yet, as it will be argued later on, while citizenship as legal identity has predominated in the formulations of theories of citizenship, I emphasize in this text the importance of moving beyond this threshold to the notion of citizenship as civic virtues. However, without considering the political economy dimension and the need for a historical structural analysis of citizenship, any suggestion that citizenship is primarily a function of the civic virtues could be seen as an idealistic belief. Civic virtues need a civil minimum that can be found only in a historical-structural context where these civil minimums overlap with basic material conditions—as explained in the postscript of this chapter—that serve as basic premises in the constitution of full citizenship.

Moreover, theories of citizenship are context dependent. In ancient Greece, the title of citizen was closely related to the patrician class. Indeed, citizenship helped to differentiate individuals who could manage the affairs of the state (the *raison d'état*) from the plebeians, the individuals who had no choice but to follow the dicta of the state, and, of course, to differentiate citizens from slaves, who had no civil rights. Democratic citizenship, however, has come a long way from the primitive forms of citizenship in the city-state of Athens. Citizenship now faces the complexity of contemporary capitalist nations besieged by the globalization of technology, capital, and labor—that is to say, the globalization of economics, culture, and politics—as well as significant challenges for contemporary social theory. Yet it would be grossly misleading to consider that citizenship has a unitary character or a set of features that remain historically static (Turner, 1990). With these words of caution, I will begin the analysis of citizenship theories.

The Enlightenment as the Foundation of Citizenship

> Those postmodernists who propose to discard the Enlightenment as an excrescence of male, imperialist, racist, Western ideology are blind to their own situation. For all their insistence that ideas belong to particular historical moments, they take for granted the historical ground they walk on. They fail, or refuse, to recognize that their preoccupation with multiculturalism, identities, perspectives, incommensurable world views, and so forth would be unimaginable were it not for the widespread acceptance of Enlightenment principles: the worth of individuals, their right to dignity, and to social order that satisfies it.
> —Todd Gitlin, *The Twilight of Common Dreams*

The movement of the Enlightenment suggests that there is a historical and social construction of human identities, and therefore socialization in rational principles is considered important, with educational institutions—as key institutions of the Enlightenment—playing a central role. As Gitlin (1995) has enunciated: "That ideas carry the marks of experience, that individuals have the right to be individual—these are offshoots of the value placed by Enlightenment thinkers on the critical life" (215).

There are three elemental aspects of a theory of citizenship for the Enlightenment: first, the Kantian proposal that sustains the hypothesis that socialization processes, especially as related to cognitive thinking, have a place within structures that precede individuals' coming of age, or their becoming knowledgeable; second, the Hegelian proposition that suggests that the capacity to be socialized should be recognized as a civilizing technique, that is, as part of a process that depends to a large extent on the circumstances that inhibit or facilitate progressive social change (Morrow and Torres, in press); third, the Marxist contention that suggests that without access to the production and distribution of resources, that is, without access to the material benefits of the economy, it is impossible to sustain citizenship in political terms.

Karl Marx (Tucker, 1978), one of the most influential thinkers of the Enlightenment, who in his early work draws his analysis from Hegel while criticizing the idealism of the German philosopher, argued in his *Contribution to the Critique of Hegel's Philosophy of Rights* that: "All other state forms are definite, distinct, particular forms of state. In democracy the formal principle is at the same time the material principle. Only democracy, therefore, is the true unity of the general and the particular" (20–21).

With the Hegelian reconstruction of Kant, a philosophy of consciousness—

which later has in Marx and in the entire historical materialistic tradition a non-positivistic conception—begins. This philosophy includes a notion of consciousness that surpasses the Kantian image of a universal abstract subject whose capacity to understand reality was measured a priori by cognitive categories that permitted learning and the construction of empirical facts emanating from science. For Hegel and all the Enlightenment tradition—which granted importance to the nonpositivistic educational humanism that predominated in the development of educational systems of the twentieth century—the origins of consciousness emanate from a process of mutual recognition of self-consciousness and of the "other" as exteriority (Marcuse, 1967, 1970; Smith, 1989; Torres, 1976a, 1976b). Self-consciousness, according to Hegel (1976:111), exists in and for itself and, for this reason, exists for another. In other words, it exists only to be recognized as such.

It is necessary to acknowledge that a theory of citizenship based on a philosophy of consciousness runs the risk of considering all citizens as subject to the same rights and obligations. In other words, this theory of citizenship sees reality constituted by a totality of homogeneous individuals (insofar as they all confront work, nature, and fear) but with a diversity of interests. However, it is clear that the complex configuration of social reality is different from any homogenizing perspective. The issue is not only diverse (and at the same time antagonistic) interests but diverse identities per se. The diverse identities of class, gender, race, ethnicity, sexual preference, religion, regional factionalism, and many other differences in the perceptions, preferences, and experiences of social actor cannot be easily subsumed under a diversity-of-interest perspective, thus challenging essentializing notions of citizenship and inviting us to analyze social formations and experiences, as Cornel West (1993a) points out, with a "nuanced historical sense."

An anthropology and a philosophy of consciousness point to the possibility of intersubjective recognition and the necessity to establish a philosophy of the rights of individuals. It was only within this framework of a political-philosophical interpretation, advanced by diverse thinkers from Plato, Aristotle, and Machiavelli to seventeenth- and eighteenth-century contributors such as Locke, Hobbes, and Rousseau, up to the twentieth-century work of Dewey, Freire, and Habermas, that it was possible to develop a theory of citizenship in the Enlightenment—a theory that obviously did not remain uncontested.[1]

As a creature of the Enlightenment, the liberal state, in designing a public education system to incorporate all sectors of the population under the same institutional network, conferred on the educational system the responsibility of "educating the sovereign," in the fortunate, although undoubtedly contradictory, phrase of leading Latin American school reformer Domingo Faustino Sarmiento.

As was pointed out in chapter 2, a systematic study of the relationships between education and citizenship leads us to explore the theories of the state as well as theories of citizenship. This is why, as C. B. Macpherson pointed out two decades ago in a well-known article considered to be a landmark in the revitalization of discussions on theories of the state, it is necessary to rely on a theory of the state in order to understand politics. The same could be said about the need for a theory for the state to develop a theory of citizenship.[2] Like Canadian political scientist C. B. Macpherson, British sociologist Thomas Humphrey Marshall has produced exceptionally lucid work that is a landmark in the discussion of citizenship and democracy.

Citizenship, State and Democracy: The Contribution of T. H. Marshall

> One who becomes a prince through the favor of the people ought to keep them friendly, and this he can easily do seeing they only ask not to be oppressed by him.
> —Nicolo Machiavelli, *The Prince*

> To have to bargain for a living wage in a society which accepts the living wage as a social right is as absurd as to have to haggle for a vote in a society which accepts the vote as a political right.
> —T. H. Marshall, *Sociology at the Crossroads*

The most significant development in citizenship theory in this century has undoubtedly been linking the welfare state and its network of services with the full expression of democratic citizenship. T. H. Marshall's celebrated and much-cited "Citizenship and Social Class" article, written in 1949, articulates, as do few other works, the new postwar consensus about the notion of the liberal welfare state as a precondition for the exercise of citizenship in capitalist societies (1950, 1963, 1983).

For Marshall, citizenship developed over 250 years in England, classifying citizenship into three elements: civil, political, and social rights. Western civil society obtained civil rights in the eighteenth century, political rights in the nineteenth century, and social rights in the twentieth century. Civil rights encompass all rights required for individual freedom (i.e., the right to own property, the right to freedom of speech, and the right to justice). Political rights comprise all rights surrounding the electoral process (the right to vote, to elect and be elected, etc.). Finally, social rights, the most controversial of all rights, include not only a modicum of economic welfare and security but also what is necessary for individuals to live a full life: "to share to the full in the social heritage and to live the life of a civilized being according to the standards prevailing in society. The institutions most closely connected with welfare are the educational system and the social services" (Marshall, 1963:74).

Marshall's arguments on citizenship are embedded in the arguments of the ongoing democratization of society, which illustrates a central principle of the Enlightenment. Yet, as Pateman (1996:6) points out, citizenship is not synonymous with democracy.

As David Held (1989) notes, Marshall sought to show that:

> civil rights were the first to develop, and were established in something like the modern guise before the first great Reform Act in 1832. Political rights developed next, and their extension was one of the main features of the nineteenth century, although it was not until 1928 that the principle of universal political citizenship was fully recognized. Social rights, by contrast, almost vanished in the eighteenth and early nineteenth centuries, but were revived in the latter part of the nineteenth century. Their revival and expansion began with development of public elementary education, but it was not until the twentieth century that social rights in their modern form were fully established. Marshall's principal evidence for this is the history of the modern welfare state. The great distributive measures of the post-war welfare state, including measures introducing health care, social security, new forms of progressive taxation and so on, created better conditions and greater equality for the vast majority of those who did not succeed in the free market. They also provided a measure of security for all those who are vulnerable in modern society, especially those who fall into the trap of the "poverty circle." Marshall's proposal is that social rights form a vital element in a society which is still hierarchical, but which has mitigated the inequalities—and mellowed the tensions—deriving from the class system. (191)

Marshall's influential work has been criticized for a number of reasons, particularly on the grounds that his approach is based on context-specific processes and therefore cannot be applied beyond the English experience.[3] Marshall, however, was very careful to show that this process has an appeal beyond the British boundaries, and, more important, he did not see this process of acquisition of civil, political, and social rights as irreversible. Moreover, his concern was to understand to what extent modern citizenship modifies social class just enough to create a truce in the overall dynamics of social conflict. If that were the case, for Marshall (1950) citizenship would be the architect of co-optation and its end result would be the prolonging of inequality: "Is it still true that basic equality . . . embodied in the formal rights of citizenship, is consistent with the inequality of social class? I suggest that our society today assumes that the two are still compatible, so much so that citizenship has itself become, in certain respects, the architect of legitimate social inequality" (70).

Yet, he thought that the notion of a social pact (i.e., of a compromise between different social and political forces) underscored the establishment of democratic citizenship in its full expression in the welfare state. However, this notion of consensual politics did not preclude Marshall (1973) from highlighting that the achievement of citizenship has always been a contested process, a process of struggle, and he cautions us that "it may be that some of the conflicts within our system are becoming too sharp for the compromise to achieve its purpose much longer" (122).

The Neoconservatives and Citizenship

> I know who is a liberal. Blindfold me, spin me like a top, and I will walk up
> the single liberal in the room without zig or zag and find him even if he is hid-
> ing behind the flower pot.
> —William F. Buckley, "Did You Ever See a Dream Walking?"

Marshall's words of caution may have been premonitory. The emergence of the neoconservatives in the last two decades has signified a serious challenge to the notion of citizenship sponsored by welfare state liberals. First is the criticism that a welfare state promotes passivity among the poor by creating a culture of dependency. Second is the criticism that by drawing resources from exhausted fiscal coffers, welfare liberals have created the conditions for a fiscal crisis of considerable magnitude without improving the real life chances of the people on welfare. Finally, neoconservatives see the permissiveness of the welfare state, particularly in culture and institutions of higher education, as responsible for the moral crisis (including the family crisis) in American and European cultures.

What is the neoconservative answer to the perceived value crisis in capitalist societies and to the crisis of citizenship? The neoconservative answer is quite different from the logic of rights prevalent in liberal circles. Neoconservatives do not necessarily accept the notion of citizenship as a political or legal status. Rather, neoconservatives counterpoise two logics, the logic of the state and the logic of the market, giving to the latter the ability to create able consumers who can, by the dynamism of the market, construct a more viable and workable social agreement. Even though the question of citizenship is not neglected, neoconservatives refuse to grant an a priori citizenship status to individuals without a sensible counterpart of economic standing (see Kenichi Ohmae's position outlined in chapter 3).

Thus for neoconservatives, the task of citizenship means to fit rights to obligations, making sure that the language of rights incorporates the language of responsibilities and vice versa. Yet, feminist scholars have argued that males tend to emphasize the language of rights and justice, while females tend to feel more comfortable with the language of responsibilities and care. This distinction is drawn to the point that one may ask the Kantian question of whether we face two distinct moralities and, by implication, epistemologies and ethics (Noddings, 1995). There is also an important tension, as Derek Bell argues, between human rights and property rights in the U.S. Constitution (Bell, 1987:239).

Following Bell, Ladson-Billings and Tate (1995) argue that the history of the United States "is replete with tensions and struggles over property—in its various forms. From the removal of Indians (and later Japanese-Americans) from the land, to military conquest of the Mexicans, to the construction of Africans as property, the ability to define, possess, and own property has been a central feature of power in America. . . . Thus, we talk about the importance of the individual, individual rights, and civil rights while social benefits accrue largely to property owners" (53).

Thus, the neoconservative argument on citizenship faces two key objections. The first is that rights and justice do not comprise the whole spectrum of moral choices but that care and responsibility need to be incorporated in any moral design of public policy. This, of course, puts very serious limits on the individualistically conceived neoconservative logic. But there is more. The contrasting logic of property rights as viewed by neoconservatives and human rights is seen as a central tension in the U.S. Constitution with its egalitarianism. Indeed, the question of human rights posits limits to citizenship and further constrains the neoconservative philosophical claim.

At a sociological level, the New Right's critique of the notion of social citizenship and the welfare state has been counteracted by a set of critical observations of the neoconservative premises. First, the notion of dependency as a result of the welfare state is challenged on the grounds that it is the rise of unemployment, in the context of the global economic restructuring, and not the availability of welfare that is responsible for the situation of the poor in advanced industrial societies. Conversely, the experience of the most extensive welfare states, particularly the Scandinavian states, was made possible because these states have enjoyed surprisingly low unemployment rates in this century. This critique of neoconservatives argues that as a result of the political economy of the right, class inequalities have been exacerbated and the working poor and the unemployed have fallen below levels of minimum economic participation in the system and have, in fact, become politically disenfranchised. This is what Claus Offe (1985) a decade ago called the commodification of labor, which produces social instability and ungovernability of capitalist societies facing a crisis of legitimation.

As explained in chapter 2, the neoconservative and neoliberal agendas do not differ much in their social policies. Instead of accepting citizenship as a political and social status, they have sought to reassert the role of the market, rejecting the idea that citizenship confers a status independent of economic standing. Yet, despite the neoconservative and neoliberal visions, what is becoming clear is that poverty is creating a serious challenge to the attainment of citizenship, a challenge that, drawing from the experience of Latin America, is discussed in the postscript of this chapter.

What, however, are the implications for education and citizenship of this reliance on the market? The next section, which draws from the contributions of Geoff Whitty, will offer the answer that the citizen has been replaced by the consumer.

Education, Citizenship, Consumers, and the Market: Geoff Whitty's Critique

> The state receives, and often takes, the child from the arms of the mother to hand it over to official agents; the state undertakes to train the heart and to instruct the mind of each generation. Uniformity prevails in the courses of public instruction as in everything else; diversity as well as freedom is disappearing day by day.
>
> —Alexis de Tocqueville, *Democracy in America*

As explained in chapter 2, in the liberal state, education has always been seen as playing a pivotal role in the constitution of citizenship. Although education has been publicly provided, with the growing emphasis on market forces in education, the citizen has become a consumer, affecting social modes of solidarity and forms of political consciousness and representation. Geoff Whitty (in press) says it very nicely: "I will suggest that the currently fashionable preference for institutional autonomy and parental choice within many education systems is unlikely to assist in the empowerment of the majority of citizens in inegalitarian societies. Rather, the celebration of diversity and choice amongst individuals with unequal access to cultural as well as material resources is likely to inhibit rather than enhance their chances of emancipation" (1).

Whitty (in press) has argued that recent neoconservative reforms in education move toward the market, diminish state involvement, and pursue multiple goals. First and foremost, these reforms can be understood in terms of projecting changing modes of regulation from the sphere of production into other areas, such as schooling and welfare.[4] There is indeed a comparable shift between the establishment of markets in the provision of social services and a shift in the economy away from Fordism towards a neo-Fordist mode of accumulation, as analyzed in chapter 3. Second, the emergence of new schools with greater specialization is also seen as the equivalent of the rise of flexible specialization in the economy driven by the imperatives of differentiated consumption, replacing the old assembly-line world of mass production. (Whitty, in press:7–8). Third, taking into account the changes in the mode of production and in the symbolism of educational systems in more fragmented cultural domains, these reforms are also seen as an account of postmodernist forms of representation, choice, and diversity in the "new times"—that is to say, a move away from modern bureaucratized state education systems.

Yet, empirical evidence suggests that rather than benefiting the disadvantaged, the emphasis on choice and school autonomy (including vouchers and charter schools in the United States and grant-maintained schools in England) further disadvantages those unable to compete in the market (Smith and Noble, 1995; Plant, 1990; Apple, 1997). After a detailed analysis of these policies, Whitty (in press) concludes that:

> The growing tendency to base more and more aspects of social affairs on the notion of consumer rights rather than upon citizen rights involves more than a move away from public-provided systems of state education towards individual schools competing for clients in the marketplace. While seeming to respond to critiques of impersonal over-bureaucratic welfare state provision, this also shifts major aspects of education decision making out of the public into the private realm with potentially significant consequences for social justice. . . . As the new education policies foster the idea that responsibility for welfare, beyond the minimum required for public safety, is to be defined entirely as a matter for individuals and families, then not only is the scope of the market narrowed, but civil society will be progressively defined solely in market terms. (15)

Whitty (in press:26) suggests the creation of new forms of association in the public sphere in which citizen rights in the process of public policy formation can be reasserted against the trends of a restricted version of the state and a marketized civil society. Education policymaking should be an integral part of democratic life and a legitimate public sphere (26).

Whitty's concern with the marketization of social relations in schools and the drive toward a consumer society, while advanced from a social democratic position on the left, is nonetheless compatible with the traditional liberal notion of public schools that help to teach responsible citizenship insofar as public schools require children of different races and religions to work together and learn to respect each other.

From the liberal trenches, Amy Gutmann (1987) has persuasively argued that education for citizenship should focus on the justification of rights rather than responsibilities and, at the same time, that schools should foster general virtues (courage, law-abidingness, loyalty), social virtues (autonomy, open-mindedness), economic virtues (work ethic, capacity to delay self-gratification), and political virtues (capacity to analyze, capacity to criticize). From this perspective, schools should teach children how to engage in the kind of critical reasoning and moral perspective that define public reasonableness (Kymlicka and Norman, 1994:368). These civic virtues not only form the citizen but also enhance the chances of democracy working in contemporary capitalist societies because, as Turner (1986) suggests, "citizenship must play an independent normative role in any plausible political theory and . . . the promotion of responsible citizenship is an urgent aim of public policy" (194). Yet, when people live below certain levels of welfare, the cultivation of civic virtues may be insufficient to nourish citizenship—or to put it in T. H. Marshall's terminology, social rights—that allow them to take advantage of rights and fulfill their obligations as citizens.

A central impediment to the fulfillment of citizenship is the growing poverty of many citizens, and particularly their decommodification, with their inability to sell their labor in formal markets—hence the growing importance of informal labor markets for subsistence. The postscript to this chapter, focusing on the experience of poverty and citizenship in Latin America—which is by no means unique in the context of globalization—shows the complexities of the problem of attaining citizenship when minimum basic economic needs are not met.

Beyond poverty, there are other serious challenges to the notion of citizenship as outlined by the liberal tradition. Among the most important are the challenges presented by the theory and practice of feminism, postcolonialism, critical race theory, and social movements. The next section presents these arguments, and the last section focuses on the interactions between markets, citizenship, and education.

The Challenges of Feminism, Postcolonialism, Critical Race Theory, and Social Movements

Feminism

> I am located in the margin. I make a definite distinction between the marginality which is imposed by oppressive structures (sites of domination and deprivation) and marginality one chooses as a site of resistance—as location of radical openness and possibility.
>
> —bell hooks, *Yearnings*

T. H. Marshall—and with him many scholars—took for granted that in the eighteenth century, all people in England were legally free and therefore enjoyed civil citizenship. Yet, a most serious challenge to this assumption is the idea that adult English males enjoyed their legal freedom and citizenship because of the commodification of women's labor and women's lack of legal power in households controlled through patriarchal practices (see Gordon, 1990). As Pateman (1996) puts it:

> despite the increasing volume and range of criticism, his commentators typically fail to appreciate the peculiar narrowness of Marshall's interest in citizenship, which runs in one direction only. . . . He fails to ask whether rights are of equal worth to all citizens, or to make the point in another way, whether citizenship means the same for all individuals. He asked about the social integration, and the material and cultural conditions of the—male—working class. He did not consider whether there were other citizens who might be described as second class. (7–8)

This commentary by Pateman points to three most interesting criticisms of T. H. Marshall: (a) that his analysis, with the drastic emphasis on the ideology of the (male) working class, may not any longer account for changes in citizenship due to a restructured globalized capitalism; (b) that he failed to take into account the issue of ethnicity (which accounts for a sizable fraction of what Pateman chooses to call "second-class citizens"); and (c) that he obviously failed to account for the subordination of women in his analysis of citizenship. Hence, the importance of the feminist challenge to citizenship, which I now turn to discuss.

Feminism, like any contemporary social theory, is a mixture of currents with a cast of characters playing different roles according to different principles that, although interrelated, do not necessarily lead to the same theoretical conclusions or policy orientations. However, any critical reading of classic feminist texts will show how important feminism has been in deconstructing the prevailing inherent "maleness" of the traditional conceptions of citizenship and, therefore, how feminism can offer extremely insightful suggestions about how to construct a radical democratic project based on true equality and freedom.[5]

The question of identity is central for a discussion of the challenges to traditional liberal citizenship. Chantal Mouffe (1993), refusing to take an essentialist position but also taking advantage of poststructuralist contributions, has outlined epistemologically what is at stake in discussing citizenship from a feminist perspective: "It is only when we discard the view of the subject as an agent both rational and transparent to itself, and discard as well the supposed unity and homogeneity of the ensemble of its positions, that we are in a position to theorize the multiplicity of relations of subordination" (77).

Mouffe argues that relations of subordination are multilayered and that in fact one may play a dominant role in one relation and a subordinate role in another. In part, this has to do with the material and symbolic positionality of subjects and with the fact that identity is not a fixed essence but an ensemble of positions (i.e., status/role), narratives, and discourses constructed by the subject from his/her relations (and therefore experiences) and from her/his own positionality.

This is a mise-en-scène marred by contradictions and uncertainties in the lifeworld of social agents. Indeed, Mouffe's (1993) view calls into question the same notion of identity as an essence responding to certain codes, rules, or nature: "The 'identity' of such a multiple and contradictory subject is always contingent and precarious, temporarily fixed at the intersection of those subject positions and dependent on specific forms of identification. It is therefore impossible to speak of the social agent as if we were dealing with a unified, homogeneous entity" (77). The basic implication of Mouffe's analysis is that the notion of the identity of a subject should not be approached simply as the coexistence of a plurality of positions.

Mouffe's assertion is a most important challenge for the notion of citizenship. Since the social agent cannot be singled out as made up by a basic single identity, and since the notion of plurality defies easy definitions of what a citizen is, this analysis seriously challenges any simplistic definition of citizenship based on legal or territorial notions.

But there is more. While the plurality of identities exists, it cannot be simply understood as an aggregate of factors or as an amalgam of properties. For Mouffe (1993), identity should be seen as the product of the interaction between different discourses that construct the experience of a subject and the different positions that define this experience. Yet, since these positions are the product of "the constant subversion and overdetermination of one by the others" (77), the politicization of identities is evolving in new forms of struggle that are central, in Laclau and Mouffe's (1985) perspective, to the project of a radical and plural democracy.

From a radical and plural democracy perspective, Laclau and Mouffe (1985) advance the notion of democratic equivalencies. The idea is that it is necessary for the construction of radical democratic politics to link diverse democratic struggles and identities and to establish democratic equivalencies:

> the task of radical democracy is indeed to deepen the democratic revolution and to link diverse democratic struggles . . . for example, of antiracism, antisexism, and anticapitalism. These struggles do not spontaneously converge, and in order

to establish democratic equivalencies a new "common sense" is necessary, which would transform the identity of different groups so that the demands of each group could be articulated with those of others according to the principle of democratic equivalence. . . . In order that the defense of workers' interests is not pursued at the cost of the rights of women, immigrants or consumers, it is necessary to establish an equivalence between these different struggles. It is only under these circumstances that struggles against power become truly democratic. (19)

Mouffe (1993) professes a radical antiessentialism. While she accepts the existence of key signifiers to refer to collective subjects, the notion of "woman" will not have a unified essence, and therefore: "we no longer have a homogeneous entity 'woman' facing another homogeneous entity 'man' but a multiplicity of social relations in which sexual difference is always constructed in very diverse ways and where the struggle against subordination has to be visualized in specific and differential forms" (78). Once the notion of essential identities is called into question through what Fraser (1997) calls deconstructive essentialism, the dilemma of equality versus difference becomes meaningless for Mouffe, or simply a false antithesis for Fraser (1997:3).

How can this antiessentialist or deconstructed essentialism position take advantage of the contributions of feminism to a theory of citizenship? Mouffe (1993) criticizes radical feminism, represented by Carole Pateman's (1986a, 1986b, 1988, 1992, 1995, 1996) analysis of man/woman antagonisms. Mouffe argues that a central aim of feminism has been to seek specific demands that could reflect women's interest in the articulation of democratic politics.[6] Pateman's (1992) position is criticized by Mouffe as an essentialist position. Yet, before criticizing Pateman, Mouffe takes on maternal feminism for its inability to promote an adequate model of citizenship. Mouffe argues that because a mother-child relationship is an unequal, intimate, exclusive, and particular activity, it contrasts highly with democratic citizenship, which requires collective, inclusive, and generalized activities.

According to Mouffe, Pateman's analysis defines citizenship as a patriarchal category constructed in the masculine image, and the alternative is to create a sexually differentiated conception of citizenship recognizing the ability that women have and men lack: motherhood. For instance, criticizing domesticated feminism, Pateman (1986a, cited by Mouffe, 1993:80) argues that this view "gives due weight to sexual difference in a context of civil equality, requires the rejection of a unitary (that is, masculine) conception of the individual, abstracted from our embodied existence and from the patriarchal division between the private and the public" (24).

This argument, constructed by Mouffe from a 1986 unpublished paper by Pateman (1986a), is also presented in a major collection of works of feminist political science edited by Pateman (1986b), which appeared in the same year. First, there is a criticism of the private/public distinction: "One of the most important and complex legacies of the past for feminism is the construction of the ostensibly universal 'individual' within the division between private and public. The sexually particular character of the individual is at the heart of the problem of equality and sexual difference" (7). Second is the criticism of what, for the perspective of liberal social science, feminism is supposed to do to fill the theoretical gaps, omissions, and misconceptions in social and political theory:

> The difficulty . . . is that feminism is seen as a matter of fitting women into a unitary, undifferentiated framework that assumes that there is only one—universal—sex. Or, to put this another way, it is easy to suppose, in the face of the long history of assertion that women's capacities necessitate our exclusion from public life, that the only appropriate response is to insist that sexual difference is irrelevant. However, this line of argument leaves intact the sexually particular characterization of the public world, the individual and his capacities. (7)

Third, Pateman (1986b) then goes on to show the shortcoming of the liberal argument that since women have the same capacities as men, when properly educated, they should be fully integrated into civil life and the public sphere. She claims that "the argument is admirable, as far as it goes. What it glosses over is that there is a womanly capacity that men do not possess, and thus it implicitly denies that birth, women's bodies and the feminine passions inseparable from their bodies and bodily processes have any political relevance" (7).

More explicitly still, arguing about the politics of motherhood, Pateman (1992) states that: "The fact that only women have the capacity to become pregnant, give birth and suckle their infants is the mark of 'difference' par excellence. Childbirth and motherhood have synthesized the natural capacity that set women apart from politics and citizenship; motherhood and citizenship, in this perspective, like difference and equality, are mutually exclusive" (18).

Finally, Pateman (1986b) offers a synoptic argument of what the contribution of feminism to political theory can be: "It is, however, very apparent that distinctively feminist theory begins from the recognition that individuals are feminine and masculine, that individuality is not a unitary abstraction but an embodied and sexually differentiated expression of the unity of humankind. To develop a theory in which women and femininity have an autonomous place means that the private and the public, the social, and the political, also have to be completely reconceptualized; in short, it means an end to the long history of sexually particular theory that masquerades as universalism" (10).

Mouffe (1993) offers a most interesting counterargument to Pateman's analysis. She agrees with Pateman that the liberal category of 'the individual' is built as a universal, homogeneous public, therefore relegating the notions of particularity and difference to the realm of the private. Moreover, Mouffe also agrees with Pateman that this political philosophical conceptualization has been deleterious for women. Yet, Mouffe (1993) states that "I do not believe, however, that the remedy is to replace it by a sexually differentiated, 'bi-gendered' conception of the individual and to bring women's so-called specific tasks into the very same definition of citizenship" (81).

Mouffe concludes that Pateman's instincts are correct in trying to bring to bear the political value of motherhood to deconstruct the patriarchal foundations of citizenship. In a similar vein, Catherine MacKinnon et al. argue that "to make issues of gender turn on the so-called difference is, ultimately, to take a male perspective" (1985:21–22). But Mouffe claims that Pateman remains trapped in her own dilemma and is therefore unable to deconstruct the opposition men/women. Mouffe (1993) wants instead "to argue that the limitations of the modern conception of citizenship should be remedied, not by making sexual difference politically relevant to its definition, but by constructing a new conception of citizenship where sexual difference becomes effectively irrelevant" (82).

Mouffe is quick to point out that she is not arguing in favor of the disappearance of the notion of sexual difference as a valid distinction, nor is she postulating a gender-blind perception of social relations. Her view is, instead, that "what a project of radical and plural democracy needs is not a sexually differentiated model of citizenship in which the specific tasks of both men and women would be valued equally, but rather a truly different conception of what it is to be a citizen and to act as a member of a democratic political community" (82).

Pateman, in her *Sexual Contract* (1988), criticizes women's dominance and subordination as key to the lack of complete citizenship in contractual societies, and she links both processes to a master/subject model. Fraser (1997) argues that "in Pateman's view, the dyadic master/subject model constructs our understanding of masculinity, femininity, sexuality, and sexual difference. It is the symbol template of patriarchal culture" (226). Although she appreciates the boldness in Pateman's approach in the *Sexual Contract,* Fraser criticizes it on several grounds. First, Fraser argues that meanings of morality and femininity "do have some association with mastery and subjugation, but that those associations are neither exclusive nor fully authoritative" (233). Second, Fraser contends that Pateman's model fails to consider larger structural and political economic factors, in addition to subjugation and domination, that account for exploitation in capitalist societies. Third, she argues that those dyadic forms of mastery and subjugation are being transformed by important structural mechanisms that live through fluid cultural forms. Finally, Fraser argues that the model of master/subject is immensely contested and does not provide a template for the whole range of experiences, either in terms of exploitation and subjugation or in terms of political resistance and cultural confrontation.

Pateman (1992), however, replies that her goal is to move beyond equality and difference and that the heart of the matter is not sexual difference but women's subordination: "the vital question is overlooked of how to subvert and change the manner in which women have already been incorporated, and so to transform the relationships between equality and difference" (27).

This discussion highlights three rather intractable themes for the tradition-al liberal conception of citizenship. First, the notion of identity as an elusive, disputed, ever-changing assemblage of narratives and positions makes it very difficult to speak of citizenship as a single identity correlated either with a ter-ritory, culture, or experience. Hence, Mouffe's criticisms of essentialized posi-tions is based on the premises of "conceptualizing identities and differences as discursively constructed instead of as objectively given" (Fraser, 1997: 183). Second is the notion of the patriarchal foundations of liberal democracies and the indispensable criticism of, and changes in, those foundations needed if all men and women are to be considered full citizens. As Pateman (1992) instructs us, "By a genuinely democratic citizen, I mean that both sexes are full citi-zens" (28). This, in turn, invites criticism of the political usage of the notions of the public and the private. The feminist criticism of the "public" as a male, patriarchal concept and the need to understand democracy as method as well as content encompassing the private and public domains—a distinction that should incorporate the value of caring as related to, though not necessarily exclusive to, motherhood—are important challenges to the traditional notion of citizenship measured by voting patterns and participation rates. Finally, Mouffe suggests that the need to find a democratic equivalence in incorporat-ing the diverse struggles is built into the very notion of postulating alternative identities in the construction of a democratic citizenship and community. Mouffe's (1993) posture assumes the need to discuss citizenship not as one single identity enmeshed with others, or as a sum of identities, but as an artic-ulating principle "that affects the different subject positions of the social agent, while allowing for a plurality of specific allegiances and for the respect of indi-vidual liberty" (84).

Mouffe's overall approach avoids the construction of a specific and strictly feminist political project without losing the contributions of feminism to the deconstruction of the traditional notions of citizenship. Pateman, on the other hand, tries to criticize what she perceives as a polity built on male rights. Mouffe's point, however, is that understanding the constitution of the subject as constructed through different discourses and positions is more appropriate than reducing identity to a single attribute, such as class, race, or gender, or a single model, such as the master/subject construct, and is a prerequisite for understanding how relations of power are constructed and what forms of exclusion, despite the claims of liberal citizenship, prevail.

Yet, Mouffe and Pateman, two distinguished feminist scholars, seem to have overlooked one of the key problems for feminist theory, which is to address the connections between race and gender, avoiding privileging gender over race. A black feminist scholar criticizes the work of white feminists as follows: "the word 'black,' applied to women, is an intensifier: if things are bad for everybody (meaning white women), they're even worse for black women. Silent and suffering, we are trotted onto the pages (mostly in footnotes) as the ultimate example of how bad things are" (Harris, 1997:260). As a noted Chicana writer puts it, when we discuss the intersection of gender, class, culture, and ethnicity, we find ourselves in a "wild zone," "because Chicanos and other men of color are themselves members of politically and economically subordinated classes. Yet, to recognize the compound oppression . . . demands recognition of the additional burden of gender for women as it is interpreted within political hierarchies in all patriarchal societies." (Chávez Candelaria, 1997:248).

The idea of a multicultural wild zone, as proposed by Chávez Candelaria (1997), is an interesting social construct because it speaks of multiple cultural experiences but facilitates the examination of gender as a discrete attribute. Indeed, the notion of the multicultural wild zone is based on recognizing that experience develops differentially according to "such fundamental categories such as gender, race, and ethnicity, as well as according to political-economic categories of class and wealth distribution" (250). Fraser (1997:179) seems to agree.

This is a central insight, particularly for notions of radical democracy and democratic interactions at the level of the household and the family, as much as at the level of society at large. Race, class, and gender interact quite decisively in one of the most patriarchal forms of male dominance, machismo, which has long been considered a serious handicap in the construction of radical democratic and socialist behavior. The notion of machismo, usually attributed to the demeanor and attitude of Latino or Chicano men towards women in general, has been widely popularized in the mass media and the print press as almost a distinctive cultural characteristic, and hence it nowadays forms part of the folkloric prejudice about Latinos in general, given the implicit assumption that Latina and Chicana women, willingly or unwillingly, become accomplices of men's machista behavior.

However, there is enough meaning distortion and commodification in capitalism to make us forget the origins and intentions of the Spanish term "machismo'" and how it can be theoretically framed in looking at the experience of men and women of color in the United States. Feminist Chicana writer Gloria Anzaldúa (1997) reminds us of the origins of the term and the consequences of the resignification that took place in capitalist, patriarchal societies. Her analysis deserves to be quoted at length:

> The modern meaning of the word *"machismo,"* as well as the concept, is actually an Anglo invention. For men like my father, being "macho" meant being strong enough to protect and support my mother and us, yet being able to show love. Today's macho has doubts about his ability to feed and protect his family. His "machismo" is an adaptation to oppression and poverty and low self-esteem. It is the result of hierarchical male dominance. The Anglo, feeling inadequate and inferior and powerless, displaces or transfers these feelings to the Chicano by shaming him. In the Gringo world, the Chicano suffers from excessive humility and self-effacement, shame of self and self-deprecation. Around Latinos he suffers from a sense of language inadequacy and its accompanying discomfort; with Native Americans he suffers from a racial amnesia that ignores our common blood, and from guilt because the Spanish part of him took their land and oppressed them. He has an excessive compensatory hubris when around Mexicans from the other side. It overlays a deep sense of racial blame.
>
> The loss of sense of dignity and respect in the macho breeds a false machismo that leads him to put down women and even to brutalize them. Coexisting with his sexist behavior is a love for the mother which takes precedence over that of all others. Devoted son, macho pig. To wash down the shame of his acts, of his very being, and to handle the brute in the mirror, he takes to the bottle, the snort, the needle, and the fist. (769).

Machismo is the product of ignorance, perhaps even of deep psychological structures of family socialization, but also, as Anzaldúa claims, of capitalism, patriarchy, and Gringo dominance in the life of people of color. Machismo is indeed a serious deterrent to citizenship as the enjoyment and performance of civic values not only for the women subject to the machista behavior but also for the brutal macho himself, whose humanity is being affected with each brutal act, and who, by resorting to machismo as a way of self-identification, undermines the notion of democratic citizenship as civic virtues. It is clear, however, that the solutions to the machismo problem cannot simply emerge from psychological techniques or educational practices; they relate to a broader, systemic problem of race, class, and gender relations in increasingly globalized capitalist societies.

Hence the importance of the new contributions of border feminists, most predominantly Chicana feminists, criticizing as cultural imperialism white Eurocentric feminists' inability to imagine the needs, desires, and rights of their counterparts among women of color: "Feminism affects and influences Chicana writers and critics, but feminism as practiced by women of the hegemonic culture oppresses and exploits the Chicano in both subtle and open ways" (Saldivar-Hull, 1994:204).

The complexity of race, gender, and class dynamics, particularly as expressed through the contributions of border feminism, needs to be situated in the lifeworld of globalized postcolonial societies. Thus, it is important to discuss the contribution of postcolonial analysis to citizenship, especially if we take into account the title of Gloria Anzaldúa's well-known poem "To Live in the Borderlands Means You."

Postcolonialism

> It is only too tempting to fall into the trap of assuming that, because essentialism has been deconstructed theoretically, therefore, it has been displaced politically.
> —Stuart Hall, "When Was the 'Post-Colonial'? Thinking at the Limit"

Looking back at T. H. Marshall's contribution, we need to recognize that for him the "adult English male" subject was the citizen par excellence, and the one he had in mind. But, as Pateman (1996:9) points out, Marshall does not draw in detail the notion of the "British subject," nor does he look at the implications of a three-staged citizenship forged in England and fully supported by the expansion of British imperialism in the world. For instance, Pateman (1996:10–11) notes that a 1948 act separated those acquiring British nationality by virtue of birth or naturalization in the United Kingdom from those acquiring it as part of the status of Commonwealth countries. Hence it is important to discuss postcolonialism as a challenge to citizenship.

Colonialism is linked to the imperialist expansion of mostly European metropolitan societies over Third World societies, a historical process that Lenin defined as imperialism, a superior phase of capitalism.[7] Colonialism was also an attempt to force modernization through territorial, political, and technological invasion from industrial advanced societies onto less technologically developed societies. This process of forced modernization was not the product of authoritarian philanthropy, of bringing modernity to "traditional" people, but an attempt to solve some of the looming social problems of the colonial powers themselves and to exploit the untapped natural and human resources of the country to be colonized.[8]

For instance, the expansion towards "new territories" (Africa and Asia most prominently) served well to address the need to expel population from Europe, given the overpopulation and European crisis from the last quarter of the nineteenth century until World War I. Expansion also addressed the problems of the superabundance of labor and declining rates of return on capital in need of new markets for investments and raw materials. Finally, colonialism was based on geopolitical considerations of European nation-states and elites that were trying to enhance their planetary reach while attempting to settle (militarily and diplomatically) their differences in European nation building.

Postcolonialism, a theoretical perspective connected with liberation movements fighting against colonialism and racism, emerged as an attempt to criticize the rational foundations of colonialism and to decolonize "the mind," as Franz Fanon would say. Postcolonial thought is above all a criticism of the Enlightenment and its legacy of modernity. As does feminism, postcolonialism criticizes the notion of an unqualified reason, universality, the progressive unfolding of history, national sovereignty, and the integrity of a self-identity subject that holds specific, self-reflective interests. Like feminism, postcolonial discourse has had a significant impact on cultural studies, the discourse of minority representation, and most of the discussions in humanities on dramatic, literary, cinematic, artistic, and musical texts (Ashcroft, Griffiths, and Tiffin, 1995).

Political scientist Ray Rocco, in his poignant and insightful analysis of "new" and "old" migrants in Los Angeles, takes advantage of many of the key cultural categories brought forward by postcolonial analysis—namely, hybridity, borders, margins, the "third space," and the "in-between"—and refers to all of them with a fascinating social construct: "subaltern spaces."

In the best tradition of critical modernism, Rocco (1997) in his study of Los Angeles links theories of postcolonialism, theories of spatialization such as those advanced by postmodern geographies, and cultural studies. His starting point is that the critique of the European conceptualization of difference should take into account the colonizing-decolonizing axis, and he offers a critique and reexamination of the articulation between the previous colonial subjects and the previous colonial metropolis. He says, "Focusing on analyzing the way that differences between Europe and the U.S., on the one hand, and Third World cultural formations and configurations on the other, the postcolonialists problematize the notions of difference and elaborate theoretical constructs to capture the complexity of the conditions of articulation" (4).

Since culture is a battleground and postcolonialism's main goal has been to address the need to decolonize the mind and to advance the interest of oppressed people, the aim is to call into question the supremacy of the Western framework and the supremacy of white power in explaining how resistance to colonialism was articulated, how identities were constructed in the struggle, and how the relations of domination create radical cultural disjunctions. As

Rocco (1997) explains: "Hybridity, borders, third space and margins are all attempts to theorize the complexity of these relations in terms that reject the privileging of the West and which delineate the nature of institutional location of Third World people" (5).

The notion of the hybrid, the diaspora, or the border seems to capture theoretically this attempt to understand the location and political symbolic practice of people of the Third World, both in terms of their geopolitical inception in the cultural map of the globe and in their physical diasporic inception at the heart of metropolitan colonial societies.

While he is careful not to impose a theoretical construct like postcolonialism that may not capture the complexity of the current political situation of a racial formation like the United States, Rocco (1997) still feels that postcolonialism has something of value to offer in helping understand "the connection between the colonizing-decolonizing contexts and histories that are the root of much of the theorizing about these concepts, and the connections between the long-standing populations from previously colonized countries and the most recent immigrants from both the same countries and others from distinct regions and with substantially different cultural contexts" (7).

Theorizing subaltern spaces allows Rocco to understand, in his study of Latino migrants in Los Angeles, the dynamics of new immigrants and those Latinos who were already in the city and who have had a longer history of engagement with the U.S. culture and system of subordination and power. These dynamics need to be accounted for by considering not only institutional spaces and practices (economic, political, cultural) that create conditions that enable but also constraints, conditions, strategies, and choices for social and political action.

Rocco (1997) states that "the characteristics of fragmentation and cultural disjunction, and the emergence of subaltern spaces that contest U.S.-Eurocentric representations and dominance, are indeed found in urban centers such as Los Angeles. . . . [I]t has been the rapid and massive migrations of people from Asia, Latin America and Africa to European and U.S. megacities, their impact on cultural, economic and political institutional relationships, and the construction and interpretation of these as perceived threats to the maintenance of the cultural ground of national identity, that has occasioned the preoccupation with theorizing 'difference'" (10).

Of course, the incorporation of these concerns and concepts requires an analysis of the various dimensions of transnationalization, of what constitutes a nation, and what role the territorial spaces play in the articulation of the notion of national sovereignty. This also implies a serious challenge to homogeneous notions of political community and political identity, more so in the context of the process of globalization of labor as discussed in chapter 3. Rocco claims that it is precisely on the types of changes that he analyzed between nation, identity, community, territory, and state that the discourse on citizenship needs to be articulated.

In his study of Los Angeles Latino communities, Rocco (1997) finds that new and old Latinos engage in practices that fall within the notion of citizenship building: "they engage in practices within relational settings of civil society that under specific conditions, can be construed as in effect making claims that are about membership in the community, about having access to institutional settings, resources, and opportunities . . . about the freedom to develop and maintain culturally based associational networks, that challenge the criteria of inclusion/exclusion, and affirmations of spaces of cultural identities. [Rocco's studies] . . . revealed a number of such practices, which although not necessarily understood nor intended by the actors to be 'political,' nevertheless are in effect contestations of established boundaries, rules, and constructions of citizenship" (10).

Under specific conditions: this is the crux of the matter of theorizing citizenship from the postcolonialist perspective of hybridity, borders, and subaltern spaces. What specific conditions would make it possible for the contestations of established boundaries, rules, and the construction of citizenship to be incorporated into a discussion of how subaltern identities in multicultural societies may constitute a comprehensive, dynamic, and complex notion of citizenship? This is the challenge that postcolonialism poses to citizenship, as so well presented in Rocco's theoretical and empirical study.

The question, however, was not addressed in T. H. Marshall's classic studies because of the limited interest that he shows in discussing democratization and his failure to understand the construction of British citizenship in light of the construction of the British state as an imperial power. Yet, this failure to understand the role of ethnicity is not confined to Britain but has played a major role in the question of citizenship in the United States.

Critical Race Theory

That property will ever be unequal is certain.
—Thomas Paine, *Common Sense and Other Political Writings*

Even the most liberal of the Founding Fathers were unable to imagine a society in which whites and Negroes would live together as fellow citizens. Honor and intellectual consistency drove them to favor abolition, personal distaste, to fear it.
—Staughton Lynd, "Slavery and the Founding Fathers"

Despite T. H. Marshall's contribution to a theory of citizenship, his failure to consider ethnicity and race in the analysis was a glaring omission. Today this is more important than ever. Race and racism continue to be central concepts in understanding the racial formation in the United States. Despite much lip service paid to discussions on race and the liberal discourse of tolerance, race and racism are perceived by critical race theorists as muted and utterly marginalized in the analysis of public policy and citizenship (Ladson-Billings and Tate, 1995).

Critical race theory was born in the United States in the context of legal studies trying to address the differential treatment of people of color by the prison and legal systems. For many, critical race theory is the result of work by progressive legal scholars of color who see American law as permeated by racism and who make the elimination of racism in American jurisprudence a central goal in the elimination of all forms of subordination.

Critical race theory, as outlined by one of its key proponents, Derrick Bell (1995), views civil rights achievements in the United States in this century with growing skepticism: "In our era, the premier precedent of *Brown vs. Board of Education* promised to be the twentieth century's Emancipation Proclamation. Both policies, however, served to advance the nation's foreign policy intent more than they provided actual aid to Blacks" (2). Bell argues that in the United States the legal rights framework has been sacrificed on behalf of whiteness: "Even those whites who lack wealth and power are sustained in their sense of racial superiority by policy decisions that sacrifice black rights. The subordination of blacks seems to reassure whites of an unspoken, but no less certain, property right in their 'whiteness'" (7).

"Whiteness" appears as an organized principle of privilege: the privilege of being white and therefore of appearing to have no race. The legal construction of whiteness was linked to the legal construction of citizenship until 1952: "Congress in 1790 limited naturalization to 'white' persons. Though the requirements for naturalization changed frequently thereafter, this racial requisite to citizenship endured for over a century-and-a-half, remaining in force until 1952. From the early years of this country until just a short time ago, being a 'white person' was a condition for acquiring citizenship" (Haney Lopez, 1997:542).

Critical race theory, as Solorzano and Villapando (in press) explain, is related to five key insights: (1) the primary focus on race and racism; (2) the challenge to dominant ideology; (3) the commitment to social justice; (4) the importance of experiential knowledge; and (5) the use of an interdisciplinary perspective.

Richard Delgado (1997), one of the leading critical race theorists in the United States, introduces the key insights of critical race theory in the collection of essays that he edited reflecting the cutting edge of the movement as follows. First, critical race theory represents a new generation of writing about civil rights in the United States. Second, it is a "dynamic, eclectic and growing movement in law and about the young writers, many but by no means all of color, who have been challenging racial orthodoxies, shaking up the legal academia, questioning comfortable legal premises, and leading the search for new ways of thinking about our nation's most intractable and insoluble problem—race" (xiii). Third, a basic premise is that racism is a normal, not an aberrant, feature of American society, a secular feature marked by the social construction of "whiteness." Fourth, the social construction of race—like its legal construction—is made through discursive analysis. Starting with the premise that "a culture constructs social reality in ways that promote its own self-interest (or that of elite groups)" (Delgado, 1997:xiv), critical race theorists set out to construct a different reality, and therefore the use of narrative, and particularly autobiography, is central. Autobiographies are important because, as Jerome McCristal Culp Jr. (1997) argues: "Being black, I cannot stop, at least in the short run, being an anomaly to many people. I can only hope to shape the way in which that anomaly is understood. . . . Autobiography also influences my white colleagues. I believe I disquiet my colleagues when I raise issues about the composition of our student body or our faculty or what we teach, because it raises the issues about their own autobiography. My white colleagues think I am saying to them, 'How did you get here?' They would like me to join them in a conspiracy of silence that claims a common and simple autobiography. I will not" (415). Fifth, as Delgado (1995) claims, another central insight of critical race theory is interest-convergence: "White elites will tolerate or encourage racial advances for blacks only when they also promote white self-interest" (xiv). Hence, traditional civil rights law is seen as more valuable to whites than to blacks. Sixth, similar to standpoint theory within feminism, critical race theory adopts a form of perspectivism, as charged by one of its critics, Randall Kennedy (1997): "without the suffering that comes from being a person of color in a society dominated by whites, white scholars cannot see the world from the victims' perspective, and will, to that extent be prevented from creating scholarship fully attuned to the imperatives of effective struggle against racial victimization" (437). Similar to the feminist movement, which advanced the premise that "the personal is political," the movement of critical race theory has advanced the premise that "the personal is also legal" (Culp, 1997:411).

Locating the discussion in the realm of social inequality and school inequity, Ladson-Billings and Tate (1995) start with the premise that race continues to be a significant factor in determining inequality in the United States; and given the fact that U.S. society is based on the prevalence of property rights, not personal rights, the intersection of property and race creates an analytical tool to understand social and school inequity.

Critical race theory, then, will be useful to prove that racism is endemic and deeply ingrained in American life. These culturally sanctioned beliefs, no matter how symbolically concealed, involve the defense of preestablished social, cultural, and economic advantages. Therefore the challenge to racism entails a serious challenge to the superordinate position of whites over racial minorities. Ladson-Billings and Tate claim that the civil rights acts have been ineffective in addressing this racial inequality because, ultimately, not having challenged the basis for property subordination, whites have, paradoxically, benefited from school desegregation. Even more, when desegregation was launched, new models of resegregation through ability grouping came into operation, reproducing the conditions for a learning imbalance between whites and people of color (Oakes, 1995; Wells and Oakes, in press).

Another important premise of critical race theory, and one that is very prominent in the discussion of citizenship, is that claims of neutrality, objectivity, meritocracy, and the goal of a color-blind society should be challenged (Ladson-Billings and Tate, 1995:55–59; Farber and Sherry, 1995; Olivas, 1995). Thus, "For the critical race theorist, social reality is constructed by the formulation and exchange of stories about individual situations. These stories serve as interpretative structures by which we impose order on experience and it on us" (Ladson-Billings and Tate, 1995:57).

Racism is so deeply ingrained in America, critical race theorists contend, that any rethinking of citizenship needs to incorporate systematic challenges to the practice of racism in the legal system and, by extension, in the school system. Perhaps it is true that "members of different groups have different methods of understanding their experiences and communicating their understanding to others" (Farber and Sherry, 1995:284).

This rethinking of citizenship should challenge not only racism but also the prevalence of the logic of property rights over the logic of personal rights and the foundation of human rights as the basis for equality and justice. Given the magnitude of the task, there are no naive assumptions that antiracist positions can be easily organized in a coalition to challenge prevailing racist structures, sentiments, and values.

By putting the question of race first, critical race theory argues that the question of citizenship can no longer be treated as a homogeneous identity in search of the exercise of rights and obligations. Along the same lines of argument used by critical race theorists, another important claim on the state and the constitution of citizenship is provided by old and new social movements, which I discuss next.

The New Social Movements and Citizenship

> Because they could never be in power, they could maintain untouched their
> unifying if contradictory ideology and hence they would survive, and survive
> quite well, as movements. It was the weakening of the political carapace of
> capitalism which, by allowing the antisystematic movements to arrive at state
> power in large numbers, exposed the deep internal cleavage of these move-
> ments, the rift between those who sought upward mobility and those who
> sought equality.
>
> —Immanuel Wallerstein, *Unthinking Social Science*

Taking seriously the topic of social movements requires giving more
explicit attention to collective behavior and collective action, terms referring
to the range of more or less spontaneous activities (ranging from crowd out-
bursts to revolutionary movements) that challenge the structures of existing
institutions and cultural norms (Tilly, 1978).[9]

The social theory of the French sociologist Alain Touraine (1981) has made
social movements central to a theory of society, social change, and citizenship.
Social movements are different from nongovernmental organizations (NGOs).
These are usually defined by their autonomy from governmental control; the
term normally refers to "a nongovernment, nonprofit organization having a
principal fund of its own, managed by its own trustees or directors, and established to maintain or aid . . . activities serving the common welfare" (Emer-
son, 1956, cited by Arnove, 1980). NGOs may or may not be grassroots organizations, which, in turn, are often defined—for instance in Latin America—as
private, community-based organizations working to provide democratic leadership and improved economic opportunity for the poor through job creation,
education, health care, and productive microenterprises (Inter-American Foundation, 1990). Following Touraine, social movements refer to collective efforts
to promote some type of change in power. For Touraine (1981), there is a type
of conflictual action best characterized as defensive collective behavior. For
instance, attempts by grassroots organizations and NGOs to ameliorate the
impact of unemployment, housing shortages, and limited health-care or educational infrastructures can easily be classified as collective defensive behavior. Touraine also discusses a second type of conflict in which conflicts modify decision making and become social struggles. If groups seek to change the
social relations of power in cultural actions, ethical values, science, or production, they can be classified as social movements. Thus, the feminist, ecol-
ogy, peace, and antinuclear movements are examples of social movements. In
Latin America, for instance, social movements include the Christian Base
Communities, neighborhood associations, the feminist movement, the landless

peasants' movement, and ecological associations (Mainwaring and Viola, 1984; Slater, 1985; Jelin, 1987; Rodriguez Brandão, 1982).

If we understand politics as a struggle for power, these social movements should not be interpreted exclusively in political terms, as they also represent cultural and moral practices centered on the construction of collective identities and spaces. They originate around certain demands and specific social relations, becoming increasingly autonomous from traditional institutions of political representation of interests. This is so, argues Ernesto Laclau (1985)—joining other proponents of social movement theory—because individuals no longer exclusively define their identity in relationship to the means and relations of production, but also as consumers, residents of a particular neighborhood, members of a church or gender group, and participants in the political system (Calderón, Gutierrez, and Dos Santos, 1987; Lechner, 1987).

In fact, social movements may arise as alliances of grassroots and community organizations, NGOs, political parties, trade unions, church organizations, and even individuals such as intellectuals, artists, and others. Since new social movements challenge the increasing bureaucratization, commodification, and cultural massification of social life, they are the "expression of a more open and pluralistic form of democracy" striving to enhance "the diffusion of collective and participatory values and practices through an ever-widening range of sites of social struggle" (Slater, 1985:6).

The stricter meaning of social movements as a challenge to existing institutions should be clearly differentiated not only from the more diffuse notion of resistance but also from the quite different notion of "reform movements" in education, which for the most part have little to do with politically threatening mass mobilization outside normal political channels.

The numerous social and student movements in the 1960s revitalized social movement theory, and collective action ceased to be treated as irrational. Moreover, numerous approaches radically revised the analysis of self-interest in social movement mobilization—that is, the implications of a utilitarian conception of mobilization based on a drastic revision of the economic argument that informed Marx's conception of social interests. According to *rational choice theory*, the logic of collective action is paradoxical, because if human motivation is essentially based on individual self-interest, members of a collectivity have no rational interest in making sacrifices for collective gains when they can achieve the benefits without participation. The resulting "free rider" effect has the consequence of making mobilization extremely difficult given the weakness of ideals to motivate activism for the vast majority of movement members.

With neoliberalism, a call for developing and strengthening civil society—understood as the private sector—has been heard. Interestingly enough, while international organizations like the World Bank, the International Monetary Fund, and UNESCO have emphasized the importance of NGOs for assisting the poor and filling in for lack of state action, no reference is usually made to the contestatory character of social movements. Yet, social movements represent the dynamic actors in civil society in challenging the state and are often facilitated by various kinds of NGOs that have become significant actors in educational and other contexts.

A *new social movements* theory departs from classical Marxist theory in its attempt to understand the relative shift from the politics of distribution to social movements concerned with identity politics and the quality of life. Discussion has centered around the contested thesis of the distinctiveness of "new social movements," a conception of largely European origin that puts greater emphasis on cognitive and ideological factors, as well as the importance of civil society (as opposed to the state) as an arena for change (Keane, 1988; Cohen and Arato, 1992; Foweraker, 1995; Eder, 1993). This approach arose from the attempt from the late 1960s onwards to make sense of protest movements that appeared to focus on distinctive issues and drew upon new types of participants: student movements, peace and environmental movements, the women's movement, etc. According to this perspective, the new social movements differ in key ways with respect to ideology (quality of life, as opposed to growth and redistribution); basis of support (diverse interests and emergent networks, as opposed to social classes related to industrial labor, agriculture, or race); motivations for participation (more idealist, as opposed to objective social interests); organizational structure (decentralized, as opposed to bureaucratic); and political style (extraparliamentary, as opposed to integrated into neocorporatist processes of negotiation) (Dalton, Kuechler, and Burklin, 1990).

Social movements are also central to understanding the construction of a public sphere, with educational policy, particularly with respect to schools, playing a central role in the constitution of a democratic theater for social deliberation. Cultural reformist movements have often been aligned with broader social movements, as exemplified in the original experience of Paulo Freire as a policymaker in São Paulo, Brazil, at the beginning of the 1990s under the leadership of a democratic socialist political party (O'Cadiz, Wong, and Torres, 1998).

Along with peculiar combinations of socialist parties gaining control of segments of the state through democratic liberal elections and their attempts to link social movements to state policy, student movements also became important actors. This is not new in discussing a theory of citizenship if one remembers the free-speech movement in Berkeley and its implication for citizenship in the United States.

The problematic of student movements is largely associated with contexts where the university itself (and occasionally secondary educational institutions) becomes the site of social movement activity. Such student movements have had periodic influence in advanced industrial societies (e.g., the revolutionary uprisings in Europe after World War I, the 1930s European confrontations between fascists, socialists, and communists; and the worldwide student revolts of the late 1960s) (Willener, 1970; Wallerstein, 1991). In many underdeveloped contexts, student movements have remained a virtually continuous source of agitation against more or less authoritarian states that reproduce vast inequality of income and opportunity. In these settings, struggles over university "autonomy" have been triggered in part by the political threats posed by student movements (Mollis, 1996).

The politics of identity also plays a role in the constitution of educational policy and social movements. Educational policy may be an explicit part of a general social movement, as in the case of "old" social movement theory concerned with working-class mobilization. The classic example here is the role of education as part of the demands of European labor movements in the nineteenth and twentieth centuries (Simon, 1987, 1965; Wrigley, 1982). The rise of public schooling in the West can be broadly described as the outcome of the struggles of class-based social movements to gain state support for inclusion as part of a universal citizenship (Boli and Ramirez, 1992). Some of these have been associated with major social transformations. Following the Mexican revolution, for example, educational reform was officially linked with extensive efforts to expand rural schooling and assimilate the campesino and indigenous populations. The creation of the secretariat of public education in Mexico in 1921 under the leadership of a former president of the national university, José Vasconcelos, who over the years emerged as a major national *pensador,* was an attempt not only to unify the nation culturally but also to link the newly created revolutionary state with classic Western thought as a foundation of the new citizenship. Curiously enough, in a country devastated by a civil war that took more than 1 million lives in a population of scarcely fourteen million at the time, one of the first initiatives of Secretary Vasconcelos was the publication of the Greek classics and pre-Socratic philosophers, to be disseminated massively within the Mexican population.

Finally, new social movement theory has provided the basis for a dramatic shift in understanding the relationship between social movements and education. A distinctive characteristic of new social movements is their cognitive and ideological focus on rethinking preexisting social and cultural paradigms as part of a politics of identity. As a consequence, one of their key strategies is broadly educational, as opposed to a focus on gaining power, and the implications for citizenship are numerous. To cite just a few, consider the gains that the environmental movement has made in schools in promoting a democratic citizenship that is concerned about, at a collective and even a planetary level, the protection of endangered species, the levels of pollution in the air and water, and the presence of dangerous substances in food. Consider the role of the Zapatista movement in Chiapas in redressing the inequality built into the interaction of Mexican aboriginal people and the postrevolutionary Mexican state and the movement's consistent and bold political program linking those ethnic and political demands to the constitution of a true radical democracy in Mexico and the constitution of a democratic citizenship without exclusions. Consider the impact of the antitobacco movement in schools, challenging the idea that smoking is glamorous and linking advertisements to the powerful tobacco lobby and multinational tobacco corporations. By challenging the consumption of tobacco, all sorts of connections between the political system, the mode of production, and the risk to the quality of life of the citizens are critically exposed. Consider the case of the racially based civil rights movement in the United States: the dismantling of segregated schools constituted, despite its obvious limitations and the criticisms of critical race theory, perhaps the most fundamental and far-reaching demand linking race and education and eventually remaining a central tenet of American citizenship (Eyerman and Jamison, 1991; Carlson, 1997). The gains of the civil rights movement in redressing past inequalities have helped to create a notion of brotherhood and sisterhood among citizens that ameliorates the deleterious (and still strongly felt) symbolic and material impacts of slavery. Consider the growing importance of the feminist movement in affirming unequivocally the political, social, cultural, and economic equality between men and women and drastically changing the spectrum of social relations in the schools by promoting the principles and methods of feminist pedagogy and by creating a new level of social exchange between students, teachers, and parents in defending feminist goals.

The impact of this challenge to sexism in the multicultural curriculum is lamented by neoconservatives. For instance, in describing research about citizenship education in U.S. schools, it is argued that "textbooks have dramatically changed their treatment of women. While the earlier books treated women's issues as an interesting, but essentially peripheral, part of American history, more recent treatments have expanded and glorified the role of women at the expense of men" (Lerner, Nagai, and Rothman, 1995:5).

These are only a few salient examples of the vast array of serious contributions made by social movements, through education and educational policy, to citizenship and social change. Despite numerous failures to achieve dramatic changes in policy in response to new social movement demands, these new social movements have been more successful in these educational efforts, a process reflected in significant shifts in public opinion on various issues such as gender, race, the environment, peace, and sexual orientation. Virtually every new social movement has also been characterized by the advocacy of curricular change and has generally found a few sympathetic listeners within teacher education and among educational policymakers.

Moreover, the pluralist mandate of public educational systems in most liberal democracies requires ongoing updates of the agenda of "legitimate" issues to be presented as part of mass education and democratic citizenship. Such effects increase dramatically at the higher levels, thus precipitating recent debates about "political correctness" on university campuses, especially in the United States (Bérubé, 1994). To a great extent, this whole debate can be viewed in terms of the significant success of new social movements in reforming—if not fundamentally transforming—the content of higher education in the humanities and to a lesser extent in the social sciences (which have long been more attuned to inputs from social movements). For the most part, these changes have proceeded along the lines of the single-issue demands often typical of identity politics. One consequence has been the need to rethink the relationships between race, class, and gender in education (Morrow and Torres, 1994, 1995; Torres and Mitchell, in press).

Efforts to link and integrate new social movements with educational reform from the 1980s onward are most closely associated with the cultural movement most commonly identified with the term "critical pedagogy." Yet, the failure of critical pedagogies to effect significant change in policymaking and curriculum has elicited various forms of criticism. Most fundamentally, it has been argued that such efforts to develop a general critical pedagogy and apply it to eliciting counterhegemonic resistance in schools is inconsistent with Gramsci's theory of hegemony concerned with "social and political movements, as in 1968 in France and Mexico or in 1970 in the United States" (Carnoy and Levin, 1985:160). More negatively, it has been argued that the failures of critical pedagogy—as a "transformative pedagogy in general"— stem precisely from the lack of a historically specific relation to social movements: "The effect of critical pedagogy is to further distance new sociologists from past, contemporary and emergent social movements; to replace with generality, the specific requirements of an educational politics; and, finally, to diminish social understanding that prohibits flight from history and politics" (Wexler, 1987:87–88). Nevertheless, under the impetus of postmodernist and multicultural debates, critical pedagogy has consistently attempted to incorporate a multiplicity of voices from new social movements as part of the struggle against "the disconcerting proliferation of separatist forms of identity politics" (McLaren, 1995:187; see also Walsh, 1996).

Moreover, the criticism of critical pedagogy has even enlisted one of its most conspicuous representatives. Peter McLaren (1997a), in a paper entirely devoted to explicating the pedagogical implications of Ernesto "Che" Guevara thirty years after his assassination, laments that

> critical pedagogy has become so completely psychologized, so liberally humanized, so technologized, and so conceptually postmodernized, that its current relationship to broader liberation struggles seems severely attenuated if not fatally terminated. The conceptual net known as critical pedagogy has been cast so wide and at times so cavalierly that it has come to be associated with anything dragged out of the troubled and infested waters of educational practice, from classroom furniture organized in a "dialogue friendly" circle to "feel-good" curricula designed to increase students' self-image. Its multicultural education equivalent can be linked to a politics of diversity that includes "respecting difference" through the celebration of "ethnic" holidays" and themes such as "black history month" and "Cinco de Mayo." If the term "critical pedagogy" is refracted onto the stage of current educational debates, we have to judge it as having been largely domesticated. (3)

Despite these criticisms of the American rendition of critical pedagogy, the praxis of social movements offers potentially fertile ground for a "conscientization" approach à la Freire. Social movements typically build on the knowledge base and previous struggles of people, taking into account their organizational capabilities and grievances. This allows for the building of programs with and from the communities rather than for them, as Freire has illustrated in countless writings. His views can be assessed in the context of his experience as a policymaker in São Paulo, where a partnership between social movements and the municipal state was established, linking human resources from the movements with financial and technical resources from the state, not only resulting in a renewed effort for curriculum reform but also building the basis for a new understanding of citizenship in Brazil (O'Cadiz, Wong, and Torres, 1998).

Summary

"You are talking scandal, Harry, and there is never any basis for scandal."
"The basis of every scandal is an immoral certainty," said Lord Henry, lighting a cigarette.
"You would sacrifice anybody, Harry, for the sake of an epigram."
"The world goes to the altar of its own accord," was the answer.
—Oscar Wilde, *The Picture of Dorian Gray*

Bryan Turner (1990), extending T. H. Marshall's insights, argues that "Citizenship is, as it were, pushed along by the development of social conflicts and social struggles within such a political and cultural arena, as social groups compete with each other over access to resources. Such a theory of citizenship also requires the notion of the state as that institution which is caught in the contradictions between property rights and political freedoms. Finally, the possibilities of citizenship in contemporary societies are, or have been, enhanced by the problems of war-time conditions in which subordinate groups can make more effective claims against the state" (194). Perhaps we should add to Turner's analysis that new theories of critical modernism, including feminism, critical race theory, and subordinate social spaces theory nested within the theoretical net of postcolonialism, and the practice of new social movements have also enhanced the possibilities of citizenship, particularly in multicultural democratic societies.

Postscript: Poverty and the Dualization of Citizenship

Let me come back to T. H. Marshall's puzzling comments about living wages and suffrage: "to have to bargain for a living wage in a society which accepts the living wage as a social right is as absurd as to have to haggle for a vote in a society which accepts the vote as a political right" (Marshall, 1963:16). As Pateman (1996) rightly states, at the end of the millennium, while suffrage is now almost universally accepted as an entitlement, living wages as a guarantor of democratic standing are not. This is a parallel discussion that the relationship between citizenship and poverty is important for a number of reasons. For one, the neoliberal agenda that has so far prevailed in the context of globalization and the neoconservative reinterpretation of Marshall's model lead to the claim that social rights are merely instrumental in achieving other rights and are contingent upon the fiscal wealth of the state. From this perspective, social rights are therefore particular, not universal (as voting rights are); social rights are merely secondary rights, or not rights at all.

We cannot equate the process of globalization and the neoliberal programs; they have different rationales and dynamics, and the presence of one—that is, globalization as a historical process—does not justify the surge of the other— neoliberalism as a hegemonic process. Nevertheless, given changes in the process of globalization as discussed in chapter 3, and given the ideological underpinnings of neoliberalism, the state is assigned a less prominent role in the construction of citizenship and the provision of social services to large segments of the population. By implication, this results in a loss of the solidarity implicitly embedded in welfare policies, because private philanthropy cannot pick up the extent, diversity, and financial magnitude of the services involved. If there is a loss of solidarity in the community attributed to the changing role of the state, this poses important problems for democratic theory. Similarly, the impoverishment of growing segments of the population creates a quagmire for public policy and citizenship or, to put it in the vernacular, creates a dual citizenship or second-class citizens, given the gap between rich and poor in capitalist societies.

Dual Citizenship

From a political perspective, power is fragmented and diffused, as several versions of postmodernism argue (Morrow and Torres, 1995). Looking at the moral crisis of contemporary societies, a central element in the analysis is that the distinctions of *différance*—to paraphrase Bourdieu—lead people to construct the categories of otherness.[10] By placing the blame and responsibility for the perceived economic, social, or moral crisis on "the other" as scapegoats, the ethical and political dilemmas emerging in the constitution of working and caring communities are diffused or ignored. Thus, shifting the blame to "others" (illegal immigrants, lazy workers, "minorities," etc.) facilitates a pedagogical discourse that relocates the responsibility for providing high-quality education to all citizens from the hands of the state to the market. After all, the market, as a deus ex machina, will discriminate against less able individuals and will reward the most able individuals, and does so by definition. Hence, the most rational means of resource allocation (i.e., the market's supply and demand dynamics) will identify means and ends, making it possible for the most motivated, best educated, and most "productive" individuals to succeed.

With the logic of the market prevailing, the argument goes, individuals will then be free from state intervention and from clientelist and patrimonialist state practices. They will be able to pursue their free will without outside intervention in the context of a freer exchange of goods and services regulated by market mechanisms. This position may be considered a philosophy of libertarianism with its exacerbation of individualism, and it does little to develop forms of solidarity beyond kinship and small groups. An unqualified total market orientation will pit individuals and the social representation of the notion of free individuals against socially constructed notions of community and collective attempts at social change. The construction of community in contemporary and fragmented capitalist societies, given the exclusionary nature of capitalist development, demands the creation of social inducements—beyond individual ethics—to foster generosity and solidarity. In addition, it requires notions of social contracts (or a social pact) that can be achieved even though operational notions of individual autonomy and freedom may be, following the Rousseauian dilemma, qualified and occasionally restricted, so the whole community can have access to higher and convivial levels of freedom.

In the same vein, following the postmodern notion that the state is mostly social regulation, any crisis of social regulation refers not only to deep fractures in society—for instance, what Habermas called the legitimacy deficit in late capitalism—but also to typical problems of the state in late capitalism (Connell, 1987; Apple, 1993a, 1982c, 1988b). The paradox is that crises of social regulation, and by implication drastic changes in the role of the state, may explain the decline in solidarity.

However, a reconstructed theory of the pedagogical subject suggests that the notion of otherness has multiple expressions calling for a notion of cultural diversity in schools. Let us consider for a moment the situation in Latin America, where there are several indications of serious dislocations in the school systems. For instance, teachers may find students aloof, with no interest in learning cognitive skills or pursuing public deliberation. Students may find teachers (and adult society in general) distant from their own interests and social construction of knowledge—a knowledge base that is the result of the appropriation of a global mass culture.

Another example, closer to the experience of the United States, relates to debates on the politics of identity as discussed in this book. Taken in one of its most extreme versions, the politics of identity and representation of minority groups in schools and universities may agree with the theory of a zero-sum society. With a zero-sum approach, the affirmation of rights of one group of underrepresented individuals and the appropriation of resources to satisfy a historical grievance or modify an identifiable process of discrimination will imply, by definition, that resources are taken from one group at the expense of another group of underrepresented individuals. Thus, the result is the continuous conflict among diverse constituencies representing minority, women, class-based, ability, and other underrepresented groups, given the implicit (and widely accepted notion) that resources are fixed or inelastic.

What are the implications of dislocations of this magnitude for the relocation of the politics of identity and difference in Latin America and elsewhere? Is it possible to find a model or framework of solidarity that does not depend entirely on the performance of the welfare state or any reconstructed notion of state intervention that could be made sharply distinct from the neoliberal state? This question requires different levels of analysis. To begin with, the notion of social regulation set forth by Foucault is very useful to link the workings of structures and the process of reception, adaptation, resistance, and reelaboration of knowledge by individual actors. Can social regulation operate independently from competing ideologies? If so, then the gap between generations or declining state intervention in sponsoring solidarity should not be an issue. The rules and the instruments of regulation will simply have changed hands, giving a more prominent place to market exchanges.

Knowledge will be not only fragmented but also segmented by social hierarchies. Those who can afford to pay growing user fees will continue to send their children to school, and their offspring will be able to access the pool of knowledge that society has to offer. Those who are unable to pay the growing out-of-pocket expenses will simply become marginal to mainstream knowledge (and societal structures).

The same can be said regarding the socialization of children and youth who are introduced to new technologies, computers, or advanced communications devices. Technological literacy will become a central component in the context of social differentiation in the region. The best-endowed private and public schools will be able to take advantage of these new technologies in terms of both teaching and learning. This, in turn, will increase the exposure of middle- and upper-class students to the most creative and productive—not to mention the most profitable—technologies. Public schools that do not have access to additional funding to modernize their technological structure, to hire specialized teachers and technicians, and to attract the best students in their areas of influence will remain quite distant from the avant-garde training and socialization.

With these increasing processes of differentiation, the educational system will then be another form of exclusion rather than inclusion, reflecting the dualization of society. Dual societies reflect in dramatic ways how individuals differ in their access to wealth, power, influence, and political representation. There is no reason why, with the withdrawal of the state from its public mandate, society will provide free and compulsory education to its citizens. Schooling will become increasingly dualized.

Latin American societies, like many other societies around the globe, have become increasingly dual, with rich and poor sectors growing very much apart. This dualization of class structures is not exclusive to Latin America but is a phenomenon of worldwide proportions. Therefore, there are serious contradictions, tensions, and imbalances between social citizenship and political citizenship. Social citizenship is expressed by effective access to a certain quantity of goods and services, both material and symbolic, that decisively conditions the quality of life of individuals. Political citizenship is expressed by means of equal and universal suffrage and the exercise of rights and obligations.

This schism between the two types of citizenship, so insightfully argued by T. H. Marshall, will encourage the proliferation of attitudes, beliefs, and values antagonistic to the democratic stability and the legitimation formulae upon which democratic regimes are founded. Needless to say, with teachers' perceptions that they need to transmit the collective values of the nation to children and youth, it is no surprise that teachers' leaders and rank-and-file are visibly upset with diminishing investment in public education, which is seen as one more trend in this process of dualization. In this context, it is legitimate to ask whether the disequilibrium between these two citizenships explains the withdrawal of state investment in education and compulsory schooling. This withdrawal, perhaps forced by structural adjustment conditionalities, is reflected in educational budgets and eventually in declining enrollments, particularly in public secondary education.

The dualization of schooling will result in, and be an example of, the constitution of at least two broad types of citizens: one that I will call "triple-A citizens," to use a term in vogue in Latin America, emulating the nomenclature used to classify the quality of bonds and credit ratings of institutions, and another that I will call "dispensable" citizens, class B or second-class citizens. Triple-A citizens are those who can exercise any model of political representation and participation they wish, not only through their vote but also through political action, because they are connected to the networks of power. They can gather information quickly through new cybernetic technologies—and the navigation of the growing "information superhighway"—and can manipulate the symbols of the highbrow cultural capital.

Dispensable citizens are those whose marginality is constructed through the process of representation of mass media coupled with their political isolation and fragmentation. They also suffer serious economic pressures; many of them are already part of a poverty belt surrounding the metropolitan areas of Latin America or are located in deteriorating sectors of cities, particularly inner cities. Their strategies for survival in their everyday life take precedence over any other activity, including politics. Both types of citizens are exposed simultaneously to the multiple messages of increasingly internationalized mass media committed to the construction of possessive individualism, to use the term popularized by Macpherson in his insightful critique of liberal theories of democracy (Macpherson, 1962). In Latin America this is what a cultural critic called the unilateral North Americanization of the symbolic markets (García Canclini, 1992).

Dual Citizenship and Poverty

This issue of dual citizenship poses the perennial question of who is being included in, and who is being excluded from, compulsory schooling. The inclusion and exclusion of social groups from schooling should be discussed in light of increasing user fees, decentralization, privatization, and municipalization policies. These policies are not restricted to Latin America, and therefore this discussion has an intellectual and political appeal that goes well beyond idiosyncratic or regional considerations. What remains to be studied in detail is the extent to which the conditionalities of structural adjustment have increased the dualization of class structures and citizenship, or whether this process of dualization has independent dynamics that structural adjustment may have been unable to slow down or, on the contrary, has simply accelerated. Yet, the question of poverty still looms in thinking about citizenship in democratic societies.

It is evident that a theory of citizenship, a fundamental complement of a theory of the state and education, cannot be developed if one of the three principles regarding the acquisition of rights advanced by Marshall is not fulfilled. As has been pointed out elsewhere (Boron and Torres, 1996), a disturbing factor in the establishment of citizenship in Latin America and in educational practice and policy is the accelerated impoverishment of large sectors of Latin American societies (Boron and Torres, 1996). This situation has serious consequences for democracy and the implementation of economic modernization or social reform projects.

Recent data shows that there are 210 million people below the poverty line in Latin America. Moreover, the situation is also linked to the question of employment and salary level in the region. The Economic Commission for Latin America (ECLA) has pointed out that 1995 salaries are below 1980 salaries and that the minimum salary in 1995 for thirteen of the seventeen Latin American countries studied is below that of 1980. For instance, in Chile, in 1996 the top 20 percent in income received 57.1 percent of the national income, while in 1992 they had only 52.4 percent. The poorest 20 percent of the population in 1996 received only 3.9 percent of the national income, while back in 1992 they received 5 percent. Of the 14 million Chilean citizens, 3.3 million live below the poverty line. Argentina is not very different: the richest 20 percent in May 1997 received 52.9 percent of the national income, while the poorest 20 percent received only 4.3 percent. Twelve years earlier, the richest 20 percent received 49.4 percent of the income and the poorest 20 percent received 5.9 percent. Hence, not only has the disparity in income distribution between rich and poor widened, but also salaries for the poor have fallen and employment has become more precarious (Newspaper *Clarin,* 1997: 27).

The problem of poverty in Latin America appears to be intractable, given the onerous hegemony evident in the neoliberal economic reasoning of the dominant classes. Several studies have pointed out the dangerous contradictions that arise when an exclusionary and marginalizing economic model that permits previously unknown forms of social apartheid is juxtaposed with a democratic regime whose legitimacy rests on the masses' expectations of political integration or "real" citizenship (Boron, 1994a; 1994b). This is a situation where the cultural attributes of citizenship (i.e., citizenship as a public virtue) need to overlap with the structural dynamics of citizenship, guaranteeing for the majority of the individuals social rights, including a living wage, and a political economy that allows them to have the option to exercise citizenship as a public virtue.

This contradiction between neoliberalism and democracy is far from being a mere theoretical or rhetorical problem. Rather, it reflects the tremendous difficulties that await Latin American democracies in their efforts to reconcile three fundamental imperatives of this type of political regime: equity, access, and representation. Simultaneously, democratic regimes in Latin America face other harsh realities arising from the unexpected, yet desired, effects of structural adjustment[11] in a context in which, almost without exception, the public sector is incapable of functioning even at a minimal level of administrative efficiency.

Boron and Torres (1996) argue that there are three main problems in the relationship between poverty and democracy and that these problems have a direct impact on the role that education plays in the fight against poverty. The first is of an ethical nature: the serious attack on justice that is produced by the neoliberal policies that have burdened the lower socioeconomic classes with the costs of stabilization and structural adjustment. Despite different styles, the basic principles of these policies have been similar in the different Latin American countries: a general reduction in social expenditures; an increase in tax revenues through the increase of indirect taxes, which further aggravate the regressive nature of tax structures; the freezing of wages and salaries, especially in the public sector; and the "flexibilization" of labor markets, a euphemism for justifying massive layoffs, unemployment, and underemployment. Flexibilization is used to such an extent that there are countries, such as Nicaragua, in which it is possible to say that there are more unemployed than employed persons in formal labor markets. The poor are increasing in number, and poverty is growing to previously inconceivable levels.

The second problem is of an economic nature: up to what point is poverty compatible with the need to improve the macroeconomic "rationality" of Latin American capitalism and the economic reforms, directed towards the attainment of certain objectives, that harm the popular sectors by diminishing their income and consumption patterns and reducing their expectations of individual and collective progress? It is not necessary to adhere to a catastrophic vision of the world to understand that an impoverished society will have a difficult time expanding its consumption or being able to achieve the increased competitiveness that would permit it to compete in the turbulent waters of international markets—markets in which the "competitive advantages of nations" are based on higher levels of education, health, and quality of life of their labor forces.

The third issue is related to the effects of orthodox (structural) adjustment on the ideological foundations of new democracies. In Latin American societies, the principles of democratic legitimacy have lacked the strength found in other regions. This weakness in the ideological principles of democracy is a serious obstacle for the consolidation of democracy, especially given that for democracy to function effectively, it is necessary to count on a relatively high level of credibility in its administrative efficiency and a positive opinion of its capacity to represent the "general interests" of society.

Nevertheless, these menacing tendencies are not necessarily destined to lead to the collapse of democracy. The "economic reductionism" dominant in certain domains of social sciences during the 1970s, both on the right and on the left, was disputed by the perpetuation of Latin American democratic regimes during the tumultuous decade of the 1980s. A recent empirical investigation has convincingly shown that, at least in the short run, economic crises do not necessarily precipitate the disarticulation of democratic regimes. Furthermore, Latin American democracies have been shown to possess a surprising strength. Yet, even though these conclusions may serve to allay premature anxieties, it is still the case that democratic governments, insensitive to the urgent needs of the poor and indifferent to the growth of poverty, could very well be digging their own graves.

The tradition of Western political thought speaks with one voice: generalized indigence is incompatible with the spirit and the practices of democracy and liberty. Plato (1941) criticized oligarchic governments of the polis, because they resulted in the violent coexistence of two cities: that of the poor and that of the rich, joined "in a permanent conspiracy against each other, mother of the disorder which would put an end to liberty" (551.d, 552.d). Almost two thousand years later, Rousseau (1967) theorized about the conditions that would assure the existence/coexistence of democracy and liberty. To achieve this objective, he recommended reducing the differences between the "different classes, as much as possible," so that there would be neither beggars nor super-rich. These groups, two faces of the same coin, were considered dangerous for the future of democracy because "it is among them that the business of public liberty would be determined: some buy it and others sell it" (292–293).

Notes

1. Clearly, the notion of citizenship in the Enlightenment has not gone uncontested. For instance, just to show a particular criticism of the foundations of the Enlightenment, a central tenet of Enlightenment critics is the notion that it is a comprehensive master narrative that is too abstract and ahistorical and cannot understand the narrative of peoples situated in their temporality and location. Thus, it has been called "a self-

conscious—indeed belligerently self-conscious—antihistorical, antinarrative, anti-relational, naturalistic conceptual frame." Margaret Somers, "Narrativity, Narrative Identity, and Social Action: Rethinking English Working-Class Formation," *Social Science History* 16, no. 4 (Winter 1992): 593.

2. C. B. Macpherson, "Do We Need a Theory of the State?" *Archives Européennes de Sociologie* 18, no. 2 (1977). This reference to the importance of Macpherson to a fully developed theory of democratic citizenship is in agreement with a key criticism by Bryan Turner of T. H. Marshall's theory of citizenship, when Turner boldly states: "Any theory of citizenship must also produce a theory of the state, and this aspect of Marshall's work was the most underdeveloped." Bryan S. Turner, "Outline of a Theory of Citizenship," *Sociology* 24, no. 2:193.

3. A prominent critic is Anthony Giddens, who questions Marshall's three stages of development as a teleological and evolutionary logic. In addition, Giddens questions what he considers Marshall's oversimplification of politics and the state inasmuch as Marshall did not pay sufficient attention to the role of social struggles that, in their resolution, created the condition for state concession, and not vice versa. For a summary of Gidden's criticisms and a defense of Marshall's position, see David Held, *Political Theory and the Modern State* (Stanford, Calif.: Stanford University Press, 1989), 193–195; for a more cautious defense, see Turner, "Outline of a Theory."

4. We should keep in mind that, as historian David Tyack reminds us, "Regulation in American education has often aimed at correcting serious inequities such as segregation of blacks or neglect of disabled or immigrant children" (186). Deregulation, however, while enhancing decision making at the school, local, or district level, may produce opposite social results in terms of equity and equality. See David Tyack, "Restructuring in Historical Perspective: Tinkering toward Utopia," *Teachers College Record* 92, no. 2:170–191.

5. See chapter 2 for a short introduction to the varieties of feminism. See also Carole Pateman, *The Sexual Contract* (Stanford, Calif.: Stanford University Press, 1988); Donna Haraway, "A Manifesto for Cyborgs: Science, Technology, and Socialist Feminism in the 1980s," in *Coming to Terms: Feminism, Theory, Politics,* ed. Elizabeth Weed (New York: Routledge, 1984), 130–143; Donna Haraway, "Ecce Homo, Ain't (Ar'n't) I a Woman, and Inappropriate/d Others: The Human in a Post-Humanist Landscape," in *Feminists Theorize the Political,* ed. Judith Butler and Joan W. Scott (New York: Routledge, 1992), 86–100; Rosemary Hennessey, *Materialist Feminism and the Politics of Discourse* (New York: Routledge, 1993); Carmen Luke and Jennifer Gore, eds., *Feminisms and Critical Pedagogy* (New York: Routledge, 1992); and Raymond Morrow and Carlos Alberto Torres, *Social Theory and Education* (Albany: State University of New York Press, 1995).

6. This position, however, has taken many forms, from maternal feminism and the defense of an ethics of caring as opposed to the male ethics of justice that prevailed in liberalism, to an attempt to introduce feminine values in politics, to the idea of counterposing the realm of the public as the articulation of "the political" and in which male values predominate, to celebrating the realm of the private as the articulation of family values—a feminist politics of the private.

7. Of course, this description should include, in the case of the United States, its colonial experiences in the Philippines, Cuba, and Puerto Rico; and in the case of the former Soviet Union, its colonial dominion of East Europe and Afghanistan. To the dismay of many conservative analysts and given its socialist history, Cuba continues to be an exception to colonialist doctrine.

8. Interestingly enough, sociology as an empirical science and ethnography as modern anthropology were largely developed in the interstices of the process of colonization by scientists working in the colonial powers. For instance, without attempting a reductionist reading of a majestic research agenda, the work of Emile Durkheim, in France—for instance, his *Suicide*—was an attempt to address some of the key tensions in the transition from mechanical to organic solidarity in industrializing societies. Likewise, most of the original ethnographic work of the last part of the last century and the first quarter of this century, most notably French ethnography, was extremely instrumental and influential in increasing the understanding the culture, customs, and behaviors of the people being colonized.

9. This section is an elaboration of a text that was written with Raymond Morrow for another purpose and publication. See Raymond Morrow and Carlos Alberto Torres, "The State, Social Movements, and Educational Reform," in *Comparative Education: The Dialectics of the Global and the Local,* ed. Robert F. Arnove and Carlos Alberto Torres (Lanham, Md.: Rowman & Littlefield, in press).

10. I am using this category with a more structuralist bent than Derrida's notion of *"différance."* As Madan Sarup explains, "Derrida developed this concept to refer to two related but different concepts: first, the notion of 'to differ'—"to be unlike or dissimilar in nature, quality or form"—and to 'to defer'—"to delay, to postpone (the French verb *différer* has both these meanings). . . . Derrida's analysis of Husserl led him to portray language as an endless play of signifiers. Once an independent signifier was abandoned signifiers referred to other signifiers which yet again referred to signifiers. Language is thus the play of differences which are generated by signifiers which are themselves the product of those differences. Derrida incorporates into the meaning of différance the sense of deferring." Madan Sarup, *An Introductory Guide to Post-Structuralism and Postmodernism* (Athens: University of Georgia Press, 1989), 48–49. The notion of *différance* used here refers to a factor intimately related to Bourdieu's cultural capital insofar as different cultural practices are recognized and taught by the educational system. Four elements are distinctive in Bourdieu's analysis: (1) the notion that each social class transmits the cultural capital from one generation to the next; (2) the idea that the school system systematically legitimates and values the cultural capital of the upper classes, devaluing by implication that of the subordinate social classes; (3) the fact that cultural capital also explains how differential academic achievement is reproduced in differential wealth; and (4) the idea that the school system manages to reproduce the hierarchies (either social, cultural, or economic), converting social hierarchies into academic hierarchies. For an analysis of Bourdieu, see Morrow and Torres, *Social Theory and Education.*

11. "Neoliberalism" and "the neoliberal state" are terms used to designate a new type of state that emerged in Latin America in the past two decades. As explained in

chapter 2, related to the experiences of neoconservative governments such as those of Margaret Thatcher and John Major in England, Ronald Reagan in the United States, and Brian Mulroney in Canada, the first experience of neoliberalism implemented in Latin America is the neoliberal economic program carried out in Chile after the fall of Salvador Allende in 1973, under the dictatorship of General Pinochet. More recently, the market models implemented by the governments of Carlos Saúl Menem in Argentina, Carlos Salinas de Gortari and Ernesto Zedillo in Mexico, and Fernando Henrique Cardoso in Brazil, to name a few, represent, with the particularities of the Argentinean, Mexican, and Brazilian circumstances, a neoliberal model. Neoliberal governments promote the notions of open markets, free trade, the reduction of the public sector, the decrease of state intervention in the economy, and the deregulation of markets. Historically and philosophically, neoliberalism is associated with structural adjustment programs. Structural adjustment is defined as a set of programs, policies, and conditionalities that are recommended by the World Bank, the International Monetary Fund, and other financial organizations. Although the World Bank distinguishes between stabilization, structural adjustment, and the policies of adjustment, it also recognizes that the use of these terms is imprecise and inconsistent. These programs of stabilization and adjustment have given rise to a number of policy recommendations, including reduction of state spending, devaluation of currencies to promote exports, reduction of tariffs on imports, and an increase in public and private savings. As I have emphasized, a central aspect of this model is a drastic reduction in the state sector, especially via the privatization of state enterprises, the liberalization of salaries and prices, and the reorientation of industrial and agricultural production towards exports. Thus, structural adjustment and stabilization policies seek to free international exchange, reduce distortions in price structures, do away with protectionism, and facilitate the influence of the market in the Latin American economies. See Larissa Lomnitz and Ana Melnick, *Chile's Middle Class: A Struggle for Survival in the Face of Neoliberalism* (Boulder, Colo.: Lynne Rienner, 1991), 9–47; Joel Samoff, "More, Less, None? Human Resource Development: Responses to Economic Constraint" (Palo Alto, Calif., June 1990), mimeograph; Sergio Bitar, "Neo-Conservatism versus Neo-Structuralism in Latin America," *CEPAL Review* 34 (1988): 45.

5

Democracy

━━━━━━━━━━━━━━━━━━

This chapter discusses the connections between the traditions of the theories of democracy and the state, with a particular focus on the contribution of C. B. Macpherson. It shows that the prevailing form of democratic governance is liberal democracy and inquires about some of the reasons for the crisis of democracy in capitalist societies and its impact in education. A central focus of many critics is the social decapitalization that aggravates the crisis and hence the constitution of citizenship. Making the transition among theories of the state, theories of globalization, theories of citizenship, and theories of multiculturalism, this chapter, following the contribution of Paulo Freire, begins a systematic exploration of the conditions of democratic education and its political challenges. The chapter concludes with a postscript on democracy and post-socialism.

Theories of Democracy

> The paradox in the 1990s is that democracy is more popular than ever before, but the conditions under which all citizens can enjoy the standing of full members of the polity are under serious threat.
> —Carole Pateman, "Democratization and Citizenship in the 1990s"

In the theory of democracy, three historical traditions of political thought coincide. First is the classical Aristotelian theory of the three types of government, including democracy, the government of all citizens who enjoy the benefits of citizenship, which is different from the government of the monarchy, the government of only one ruler, which, in turn, is different from the government of the aristocracy, the government of few rulers. Second is the medieval theory, which incorporates Roman law and the notion of popular sovereignty, which creates a foundation for the exercise of power, leaving the supreme power in the hands of the people. By different means, this power is transferred, but only temporarily, to a given ruler—hence the right to rebellion when the ruler fails to uphold the rights of the people. The third historical tradition is the contemporary doctrine of democracy, based mostly on the work of Nicolo Machiavelli, which identifies at the beginning of the modern nation-state only two main forms of historically constituted government: the monarchic and the republican. In the same tradition, for Jean-Jacques Rousseau, the republic, which is the most genuinely popular form of government, coincides exactly with the characteristics of the democratic regimes (Bobbio, Matteucci, and Pasquino, 1987–1988).

Democratic regimes differ among themselves, depending on their organization. They can be distinguished by their juridical-institutional implementation (e.g., presidential versus parliamentarian); by the articulation of political parties in the implementation of a democratic regime (e.g., two-party versus multiparty systems); by the fragmentation of political culture (e.g., centrifugal versus centripetal political cultures); or, as in Robert Dahl's (1956) typology in his *Preface to Democratic Theory*, by the Madisonian, the populist, and the polyarchical models.

In this book I prefer to explore in detail the distinction between formal and substantive democracy. Before I do so, I would like to start with several models of democracy that have been identified by the tradition represented in the legacy of C. B. Macpherson (1962, 1973). Connolly (1993), following Macpherson's insights, identifies four key models. First is the notion of a *protective democracy*, which, "formulated by Jeremy Bentham and James Mill, presupposed the hegemony of a market economy. It sought regular elections to advance market interests and to protect against the tyranny of the state within this setting" (105).

Second is the notion of *developmental democracy*, which in Connolly's (1993) view "represents a notable advance in democratic idealism. Its best representatives were John Stuart Mill and T. H. Green. The key problem was to elevate working-class men into rational beings. . . . In the Millian conception, the 'model of man' as a possessive individualist—that is, of people as 'conflicting, self-interested consumers and appropriators'—is compromised by the conception of man as 'a being capable of developing his power or capacities.' Democratic participation also become the central route to self-development" (196).

The third notion is *equilibrium democracy*, also known as *pluralist democracy*, advanced by Joseph Schumpeter in 1942. This model "depreciates the value of participation and appreciates the functional importance of apathy. Apathy among a majority of citizens now becomes functional to democracy, because intensive participation is inefficient to rational individuals. Participation activates the authoritarianism already latent in the masses, and overloads the system with demands which it cannot meet" (196–197). Claus Offe's (1984, 1985) analysis, from a vantage point closer to the theory of the fiscal crisis of the state than to a theory of elitist democracy, shows a variant of this theory in his analysis of the crisis of legitimacy in late capitalism and the question of ungovernability. As outlined by Connolly (1993), "The equilibrium model protects against tyranny, but it performs poorly when measured by the standards of developmental democracy" (197).

We find, finally, C. B. Macpherson's theory of *participatory democracy,* built around Rousseau's paradox: "We cannot achieve more democratic participation without a prior change in social inequality and in consciousness but we cannot achieve the changes in social inequality and consciousness without a prior increase in democratic participation" (100). For Macpherson, very much along the same lines as T. H. Marshall and following, no doubt, the same reasoning as Rousseau, rough equality is a precondition for effective democratic models, while an effective democracy appears as a precondition for the attainment of rough equality. For Macpherson, participatory democracy brings a sense of community, of association, of neighboring and joining, of feeling part of a whole in the construction of a more tolerant but still politically efficient system. This is so because, as Macpherson (1973) argues, participatory democracy "brings with it a sense of community, . . . how the enjoyment and development of one's capacities is to be done for the most part in conjunction with others, in some relation of community" (33).

As Jane Mansbridge (1993) reminds us, this is the foundation for Carole Pateman's insightful analysis when Pateman (1970, cited in Mansbridge) claims, in *Participation and Democratic Theory,* that "the major function of participation in the theory of participatory democracy is . . . an educative one, educative in the very widest sense" (42). Moreover, Pateman (1970) also argues that the experience of participation "will develop and foster the democratic personality" (64). Pateman's own analysis is very close to Macpherson's theory of democracy, which, in turn, owes a great deal to developmental democracy because it presupposes, like Rousseau and very much against Hegel's dictum of the appropriation of consciousness by consciousness, that human capacities have the power to develop without preventing others from developing their capacities. Yet, a premise of Macpherson's (1962) analysis is the search for a society that is not regulated by domination or exploitative exchanges among human beings. However, Macpherson's theory of possessive individualism, which for him marks the unity of the different variants of liberalism as a tradition in political theory, hinges on the notion that ownership is constitutive of individuality, freedom, and equality and that, as Carens (1993) reminds us, "Democracy is conceptualized merely as a means of choosing one's governors, and this is justified as an extension of the principle that individual owners should be free to make choices about how best to pursue their individual interests, assuming that the basic system of property ownership is not itself in question" (2–3).

Equality and liberty are values that are contextualized in the historical experience of some societies and cannot be predicated as universal imperatives because their own definitions are contested. Yet, they are in fact considered ethical imperatives within the theories of universal human rights. Moreover, they are not easily reconcilable, and more often than not, the pursuit of public policy inspired by the pursuit of each principle shows very serious tensions and contradictions among them.

Therefore, in the vigorous tradition of liberalism, democracy appears as the most appropriate political milieu in republican societies, reflecting the premises of human behavior and choices: individuals are related to each other through market exchanges, and it is, as Tully (1993) points out, "their selfish pursuit of unlimited wants [that] would bring the greatest good to the greatest number" (37). This utilitarian perspective, which Macpherson so aptly describes and criticizes in his theory of possessive individualism, has permeated liberal thought, making freedom of choice and the pursuit of rational yet selfish choices the backdrop for the development of capitalist social relations of production in the context of the social-liberal-democratic contract. Yet a central question is the relationship between democracy and the state.

Democracy and the State

> Man is the only animal that robs his helpless fellow of his country—takes possession of it and drives him out of it or destroys him. Man has done this in all the ages. There is not an acre of ground on the globe that is in possession of its rightful owner, or that has not been taken away from owner after owner, cycle after cycle, by force and bloodshed.
>
> —Mark Twain, *Letters from the Earth*

In this book, the state has been defined as a terrain for struggle of national and sociopolitical projects, but also as a pact of domination, as a corporate actor assuming the representation of popular sovereignty, and as the political authority that enforces democratic rule. Democracy has also been defined as a system of political representation and political participation where subjectivities and rules are not (and should not be) reduced, in the end, to effects of power, gender, race/ethnicity, and wealth. Thus, the state plays a central role in the constitution of democracy and citizenship, particularly in multicultural societies.

To clarify the role of the democratic state, I have distinguished between democracy as method and democracy as content. As a method, democracy is primarily political representation that includes regular voting procedures, free elections, parliamentary and judicial systems free from executive control, notions of checks and balances in the system, the predominance of individual rights over collective rights, and freedom of speech. As content, democracy is associated with political participation by the people in public affairs. It is related to the power of the people (over any other regulatory institution, such as kingship or a government bureaucracy), the idea of equal rights for all citizens, and, particularly in the U.S. Constitution, a political philosophy of egalitarianism. In addition, democracy as content implies power changes in the interactions among individuals, both at the micro level (e.g., achieving nonexploitative gender relationships in families) and at the macro level (e.g., pursuing gender equality in social and economic exchanges).

When theories of democracy are considered, the notion of the state acquires new normative and political dimensions. In the liberal democratic tradition, the state upholds universalistic, rational, and consistent laws that should provide a level playing field. This is where the criticism of critical race theorists outlined in chapter 4 resonates with peculiar force in rethinking the democratic idea. At the same time, the democratic state uses public policy to create a modern citizenship, separating the particular interests of individuals from the general will. After more than two hundred years of democratic practice, it is clear now how difficult it is to accomplish this goal, and how visionary of Alexander Hamilton's words of warning sound now: "Happy will it be if our choice should be directed by a judicious estimate of our true interests, unperplexed and unbiased by considerations not connected with the public good. But this is a thing more ardently to be wished than seriously to be expected" (Hamilton, Madison, and Jay, 1961:33).

Critical views of theories of the democratic state argue that conflict is inherent in the constitution of the polity. Martin Carnoy and Henry Levin (1985) argue that public policy is a product of basic social conflict, a conflict that is played out in the state arena. In their research on the production of educational policy resulting from class conflict and social movements, advanced capitalist states appear as a terrain of social struggle. Carnoy and Levin argue that to grasp the transformation of education, one needs simultaneously to understand changes in labor processes and how these processes mutually condition each other. For this approach, educational change is perceived as part of a larger social conflict resulting from inequalities of income and the social power of capitalist production.

Thus, conceived as an administrative system of political domination, the state can be understood as the totality of political authority in a society, notwithstanding the level (national, provincial, or local) at which it operates. The democratic state, with its policies directed toward the constitution and reproduction of capitalism, protects the system of commodity production from various threats and guides its transformation. Concomitantly, it overcomes sectoral or factional short-term needs and disputes among individual capitalists or corporative groups.

But the state also reflects the dynamics of democracy. Basic human rights are protected by laws enacted and enforced by the democratic state, as discussed in chapter 3. In many democracies, the public sector, in an attempt to advance civil rights, has become the main source of employment for minorities and women. Health, welfare, and educational policies are particularly sensitive areas in efforts to satisfy the democratic aspirations of citizens. Thus, democratic states have also advanced the cause of democracy through welfare policies, the enforcement of progressive laws, and the employment of minorities and women. For instance, we have demonstrated that in the Brazilian context, the major figures in the pursuit of democratic goals are grassroots organizations, social movements, and political parties such as the Partido dos Trabalhadores, which has extensive grassroots support (O'Cadiz, Wong, and Torres, 1998).

Whether these new social and educational policies promoted by social movements are politically feasible and workable, technically competent, and ethically sound is an issue that deserves further discussion. Yet, it is evident that changes in the form of the state and in the political system, as well as changes in the legal foundations of democratic states, could have serious implications in advancing a democratic program, in the construction of democratic education, in the constitution of a citizenship built on legal foundations and civic virtues, and in addressing the sometimes intractable questions of race, class, gender, and culture, particularly in multicultural societies ruled by liberal democracies.

The Triumph of Liberal Democracy

> How difficult it is for error to escape its own condemnation.
>
> —Publius

The notion of democracy that has become hegemonic at the end of the twentieth century is liberal representative democracy with its principle of the active citizen. As it is defined by Held (1995), it constitutes "a cluster of rules, procedures and institutions permitting the broadest involvement of the majority of citizens, not in political affairs as such, but in the selection of representatives who alone can make political decisions" (97).

As I have argued above, it will be convenient to distinguish at the outset, as the Italian political scientist Umberto Cerroni (1976) does, between democracy as content and democracy as method. Democracy appears to be primarily a method of political representation. The notion of democracy as content is related to the notion of democracy as a system of political participation by the people in public affairs. However, a radical notion of democracy goes beyond the attempt to prevent forms of exclusion that preclude political and social participation. Radical democracy postulates radical equality in racial/ethnic, class, and gender interactions, both at the level of the public sphere and in the intimacy of the household. Thus, a first important tension occurs between democratic regimes that uphold formal rules but fail dramatically to uphold democracy in terms of class, race/ethnicity, and gender interactions.

A second important issue, then, is to explain how the notion of democracy became intimately intertwined with the notion that capitalism is the most conducive mode of production for the development of democratic systems. Samuel Bowles and Herbert Gintis (1986) offer a very persuasive argument. They argue that the dynamics of democracy rely on two logics of expansion of the capitalist system, personal rights and property rights, which are often opposed. The dynamics of the conflict between these two logics (represented perhaps in the clash between business ideology and social movements in advanced industrial capitalism and in dependent-development capitalism) are not only over the use and appropriation of societal resources but also about the question of setting ethical standards of social behavior.

However, capitalism as an economic and social system of accumulation, production, reproduction, and distribution of commodities is intrinsically conflictual and marked by internal contradictions. Claus Offe (1984: 244) signals the emergent functional discrepancy between the economic and political substructures of advanced capitalism. Offe describes the structural problem of the capitalist state in the following terms: "The capitalist state suffers from an 'overload' of demands and requirements which it cannot satisfy without destroying the capitalist nature of the economy nor ignore without undermining its own democratic institutional set-up and the regulation of class conflict provided by it" (246).

In late capitalist societies, social power is essentially heterogeneous and diffused, and the same dynamic of democracy has created over the last two centuries many social movements that strive to change the direction or the nature of the democratic system. These movements have revolved around issues of class and labor, race, gender, the environment, nuclear disarmament, and global peace. In fact, the most recent social movements in the United States, Western Europe. and Latin America (from both the right and the left), as I explained in chapter 4, are not distributional in nature, but they express moral and cultural aspirations and rage.

If capitalism is a conflictual system and democracy has two different logics of development, then the question is why democracy and capitalism become intermingled and why this working relationship of politics and economics does not fall apart. Bowles and Gintis (1986) claim that the connection between democracy and capitalism has been made through four historical accommodations of the system: (a) in Europe, the Lockean proposal that accommodates the system by limiting the political participation of the propertied; (b) in the United States, the Jeffersonian proposal that distributing property widely among the citizenry (of Anglo-Saxon origin) reaccommodates the system in the face of increasing political strains; (c) the political proposal of Madison to foster a sufficient heterogeneity of interest among citizens to prevent the emergence of a common political program of the nonpropertied; and (d) the Keynesian model, in which economic growth and distribution of income generate a communality of interests between the dispossessed and the wealthy.

Is there a new accommodation of the system in the face of the current crisis of democracy? What is the situation of democracy and capitalism at the end of the millennium? It can be characterized, following Offe (1984) once again, as the problem of ungovernability of democracy in capitalist societies—or to put it in Bowles and Gintis's terms, the lack of a new historical accommodation of the system entails a risky impasse.

Offe (1984) describes ungovernability in the following terms:

> Its connotations are "rising expectations" on the part of competing interest groups and parties, disseminated by the media; a resulting "overload" of the state bureaucracies which find themselves, under the impact of fiscal constraints, unable to satisfy such expectations; a breakdown of government authority which would be required for a firm resistance to proliferating demands; an increasing level of distrust, suspicion and frustration among the citizens in their attitudes vis-à-vis the state and creeping paralysis of the foundations of economic stability and growth potential. (164)

The notion of ungovernability is clearly related to the view of neoconservatives who criticize what they see as the corrosion of liberal politics and their promotion of voting backlash against the welfare state, particularly around the issue of increasing and progressive taxation. Thus, according to Offe (1984), ungovernability implies that the "conflict-generating potential of the institutions of the democratic policy far outweighs their conflict-resolving capacity" (164). Given this context, as the left argues, there is an authoritarian transformation of democratic politics characterized by the increasing veto power of large capital and corporations over the dynamics of democracy, leading some analysts from progressive standpoints to speak skeptically about corporations ruling the world and the buying out of democracy (Korten, 1996).

Offe (1984) recognizes that there is some truth to this claim of the left, but he also agrees with key elements of the diagnosis of the right that denounces democratic ungovernability, concluding that "both the institutional functions of conflict articulation and conflict resolution are reduced; and the polity becomes repressive and unmanageable at the same time. Neither of the two functions which, according to liberal-democratic theory, are to be performed by the institutional bridge linking the state and the individual can be performed" (166).

Ungovernability reflects a central tension in liberal democracy, that between the pursuit of freedom without restrictions and the aspiration to radical equality without qualification. Alexis de Tocqueville, in his famous study, stated boldly the conservative opinion that sooner or later democratic systems will seek greater equality at the expense of freedom. Liberals with a strong conservative bent like Tocqueville's will undoubtedly value freedom more than anything else. Therefore, Tocqueville was quite concerned with the democracy he saw in America: "For de Tocqueville, the democratic foundation of the nation was explained by the absence of aristocracy, the frontier, and the exclusion of the established church. Although there was a radical tradition of citizenship expressed in the idea of an independent militia, American democracy nevertheless continued to exist alongside a divisive racist and exploitative South" (Turner, 1990: 208).

Not only is this criticism of Tocqueville by Turner in order, but there is more. A century ago, Tocqueville argued about the wonders of the American democratic system, emphasizing that with the exception of the slaves, the domestics, and the poor sustained by the municipal systems, there was nobody in America who could not have been an elector and therefore participate, albeit indirectly, in the formulation of the law. Interestingly enough, for Tocqueville, to exclude women, slaves, domestics, and the poor on welfare—in other words, more than half of the U.S. population at the time—was not considered an infringement of the exercise of democratic rights by individuals. Quite the contrary. For Tocqueville, the justification of democracy is to understand that all those individuals who had been declared as electors by law can, and indeed may, cast their votes. This fact is in itself a sign of a typical democracy of procedures, or democracy as a method, and as such indicates and justifies the existence of a democratic system.[1]

Tocqueville's blank check for democracy should be challenged, drawing democratic distinctions that are imperative to avoid a sociological model of citizenship that is predicated as a monolithic and unified conception. Despite T. H. Marshall's immense contribution to the debates, his unified conception of citizenship needs to be criticized. We need to consider not only the elusiveness of identity but also the presence of borders and exclusions. It is also important to highlight again the distinction between democracy as method and democracy as content. This distinction helps to understand the notion of the formation of citizens through education, a prime goal of the Enlightenment, not as a monolithic or fixed identity, but as "public and private definitions of moral activity in terms of the creation of public space of political activity, and active and passive forms of citizenship in terms of whether the citizen is conceptualized as merely a subject of an absolute authority or as an active political agent" (Turner, 1990: 209). These distinctions are important for the notion of a democratic pedagogical subject constituted as citizen and the notion of the crisis of liberal democracy. But before I discuss the connections between the crisis of democracy and education, I shall address the notion of social decapitalization as one of the prime leitmotifs for this crisis, a position advanced by some neo-Tocquevillian theorists who see declining membership in civic associations as a serious problem for democracy.

Liberal Democracy and Social Capital

> Values are values, things immediately having certain intrinsic qualities. . . . The notion that things as direct values lend themselves to thought and discourse rests upon a confusion of causal categories with immediate qualities.
> —John Dewey, *Experience and Nature*

The crisis of governablity of democracies brought to the fore the role that education and civil society play in creating, reproducing, and consuming social capital. Alexis de Tocqueville (1969) in his *Democracy in America* was deeply impressed by the propensity of Americans for civic association. He stated, "Nothing, in my view, deserves more attention than the intellectual and moral associations in America" (513).

Following Tocqueville's lead, social scientists in the United States have argued that the performance of social institutions is powerfully influenced, as Putnam (1995) argues, by "norms and networks of civil engagement . . . [and] that successful outcomes are more likely in civically engaged communities" (66).

One social scientist who propelled the concept of social capital to fame is the late James Coleman (1988, 1990). Coleman identifies three aspects of social capital that are related to social networks: (1) obligations and expectations that depend on the trustworthiness of the social environment; (2) the information-flow capability of the social structure; and (3) the norms that regulate social networks, usually accompanied by sanctions for those who break the norms. The example that Coleman uses to illustrate his point is the higher performance of parochial Catholic schools compared to public schools. He argues that parochial schools have proved more effective in teaching basic skills because of a shared sense of trustworthiness translated into the relationships that predominate in the parish and the fact that, given those networks, the relationships between parents, teachers, and students allow for information to flow more freely and faster than in more anonymous and fragmented public schools. Finally, the existence of these social networks (that is, social capital), which contributes to a more successful educational outcome, produces a higher degree of human capital that, in an endless circular process, then produces a higher degree of social capital when networks are improved and perfected, and so on. A similar argument is made by Stanton-Salazar and Dornbusch (1995:116–135), who examined data on the information networks of a selected sample of Mexican-American high school students. Academic success is related to the formation of instrumental ties between students, teachers, and counselors.

These social networks are deemed central for a successful economic outcome, and these norms and networks of civil engagement are considered key elements affecting the performance of representative government. Drawing from his empirical analysis of subnational governments in Italy, Robert Putnam (1995) advances two key hypotheses: first, that "quality of governance was determined by long-standing traditions of civic engagement (or its absence)" (66); and second, that these networks of organized reciprocity and civic solidarity are not the result of modernization but rather are a precondition for it.

Hence, the notion of social capital that synthesizes the combination of norms and networks for civil engagement: "By analogy with notions of physical capital and human capital—tools and training that enhance individual productivity—'social capital' refers to features of social organization such as networks, norms, and social trust that facilitate coordination and cooperation for mutual benefit" (66). Thus, communities that have high stocks of social capital will perform better than those that lack it. Why? Because social capital affects the norms of generalized reciprocity (beyond the primary units of reciprocity and solidarity, such as the family) and at the same time encourages the emergence of social trust:

> Such networks facilitate coordination and communication, amplify reputations, and thus allow dilemmas of collective action to be resolved. When economic and

political negotiation is embedded in dense networks of social interaction, incentives for opportunism are reduced. At the same time, networks of civic engagement embody past success at collaboration, which can serve as a cultural template for future collaboration. Finally, dense networks of interaction probably broaden the participants' sense of self, developing the "I" into the "we," or (in the language of rational choice theorists) enhancing the participants' "taste" for collective benefits. (66)

Thus, social networks and civil engagement influence public life, increase the degree of participation, and also enrich private life. Yet, a central concern is that while the average number of years of education—which, according to Putnam, is considered the best individual-level predictor of political participation—has risen sharply over the last generation, actual political participation, measured by voting, has steadily declined in the United States. Putnam (1995) lists several causes explaining what may have prompted a decline in social trust despite the increases in education. First is the growing distrust of the American government. Second is the fact that religious sentiments are becoming less tied to institutions and more self-defined. Third is the fact that traditional associations that prompted political participation, such as unions and parent-teacher associations, are also declining in membership. Fourth, civic associations based on voluntarism, such as mainline civic associations (e.g., the Red Cross and the Boy Scouts of America), fraternal associations (e.g., Lions, Elks), or even the participation of Americans in organized forms of social entertainment, such as bowling leagues, are also declining. The decline of secondary associations is a worrisome trend that cannot be offset, in Putnam's analysis, by the relative increase in tertiary associations, such as national environmental associations like the Sierra Club, feminist associations like the National Organization for Women, or the American Association of Retired Persons, which are considered interest groups that do not represent the same level of social connectedness as primary or secondary associations for civic engagement.

Social decapitalization, then, is attributed to the loosening of social bonds in the family, both extended and nuclear. In turn, while associational membership increases social trust, increases in membership in nongovernmental organizations, especially nonprofit service agencies, which are on the rise (from Oxfam to organizations supporting a philharmonic orchestra) are not adding much to the social connectedness that is needed. And social support groups (e.g., Alcoholics Anonymous and Gamblers Anonymous), while they are an important form of social capital as far as emotional and intellectual support of individual endeavors is concerned, do not often play the same role as traditional civic organizations. They may play a more important role in the enrichment of private life than in the reinvigoration of public life.

Among the reasons for declining social capital, the massive entry of women into the labor force after War World II is counted as one trend that has drastically diminished "the time and energy available for building social capital" (Putnam, 1995:74). A second reason is the high mobility of the American population, which too frequently uproots individuals from their communities, creating the hypothesis of the "re-potting" problem. Technology also plays a major role, moving entertainment from the public to the private domain. Finally, changes in class structure affecting the middle classes, which were always considered more prone to political participation than the lower classes, are deemed responsible for social decapitalization. Thus, restoring social capital is a precondition for restoring civic engagement and social trust.

The theoretical usefulness of the concept of social capital is still debatable. What is clear is that it appears as a theoretical alternative to boost social connectedness and organized solidarity in advanced capitalist societies facing the shrinking of the welfare state and the dismantling of its network of services. One of the key questions about the notion of social capital, as discussed in Portes and Landolt's (1996) work, is its analytical utility. A similar problem is the corporative consciousness that could dramatically increase the social capital of an institution (e.g., the police) but that in turn may result in decreased social solidarity and welfare of the society at large. In fact, Putnam accepts the proposal of several critics "who stress that closely knit social, economic, and political organizations are prone to inefficient cartelization and to what political economists term 'rent seeking' and ordinary men and women call corruption" (76).

A second problem is, of course, the failure, by and large, to discuss race in developing the concept of social capital. While class and gender have a central role in Putnam's analysis, and to a lesser extent in Coleman's, race is virtually marginalized as a central identity. Importantly enough, the very theoretical notion of identity (not only racial or ethnic identity) is quickly bypassed in the analysis in favor of a notion of universality (for instance, the notion of societal trust) that at some point most if not all social agents are presumed to have enjoyed and that has recently deteriorated. In Putnam's analysis, the positive trends that he sees as related to the erosion of social capital, particularly a substantial decline in intolerance and in overt discrimination, are clearly related to the contribution of education (and multicultural education in particular) and social movements fighting for civil rights.

Therefore, while the notion of social capital is an ingenious concept to explain some of the problems (and possible solutions) to society's contemporary malaise by emphasizing the importance of civic associations and engagement in civil society, the question is the paradox upon which the utility of the concept is being built. That is, the paradox that social capital is declining in advanced capitalist societies "when liberal democracy has swept the battlefield, both ideologically and geopolitically" (Putnam, 1995: 78) is predicated on the concept of democracy as a method and not democracy as substantive content. The second irony for Putnam is that social trust is correlated with education. Yet social capital theorists worry that "because educational levels have risen sharply, the overall decrease in social trust is even more apparent if we control for education" (Putnam, 1995:78). This analysis is built on the simplistic premise that the educational experience is homogeneous for all individuals who have access to the educational institutions, and hence that education will always result (or should result) in increasing social trust. I will claim that there is no irony here; because the educational system is fragmented, the experience in education is not homogeneous: it depends on class, race, gender, geographical, and myriad other distinctions. Moreover, as a process of social and cultural reproduction, and given the important analytical conclusions advanced by the scholarship of race, class, gender, and the state, cultural politics intersects with the politics of identity, and the supposedly smooth, unitary, linear, and beneficial effect of education can be challenged from several perspectives.

For instance, from tracking and ability grouping as a way to attain resegregation of classrooms to the mismatch between the dynamics of the job market and the dynamics of educational reproduction, educational experiences are hardly the same for all members of a given population and do not produce the same effect of trust building. Perhaps a most important problem in social capital analysis is that cultural capital is not taken into account, nor is the idea popularized by Bourdieu and Passeron (1977) about the symbolic violence in the schools. This has all sorts of implications for multicultural education and democracy. In this light it is important to begin to address the connections between the crisis of democracy and education.

The Crisis of Liberal Democracy and the Role of Education

> Much of the present education fails because it neglects this fundamental principle of the school as a form of community life.
>
> —John Dewey, "My Pedagogic Creed"

The basis for establishing the relationship between education and democracy in Western societies has been the notion of democracy as political representation and the attempt to develop a political culture of citizenship based on the premises of the Enlightenment. Italian political scientist Roberto Bobbio has explained that the paradoxes of modern democracy make the connection between democracy and education more complex.

Bobbio argues, first, that "people are constantly asking for more democracy in objective conditions increasingly less favorable to it" (cited by Carnoy, 1984:160). That is to say, the objective conditions of modern capitalism are increasingly less democratic, and large organizations (and particularly capitalist corporations, from state organizations to multinational corporations to large research universities) find it more difficult to respect the rules of the democratic game. Second, the institution in charge of providing and overseeing the formal rationalization of the rules of the game, the state, has grown in size, becoming more hierarchical and certainly less democratic in terms of inviting more active participation from the citizenship. Third, and very important for education, capitalist societies have become so complex that problems require more and more technical solutions that, in turn, can only be found through resorting to a highly skilled technocracy. This poses the contradictions between democracy and technocracy, contradicting the letter and the spirit of Abraham Lincoln's famous words at the national cemetery of Gettysburg on 19 November 1863, "that the government of the people, by the people, and for the people shall not perish from the earth." Despite Lincoln's admonition, government is relying more and more on technocracy, specialized know-how, and esoteric knowledge that falls squarely outside popular control. Bobbio said it nicely: "The protagonist of industrial society is the scientist, the specialist, the expert; the protagonist of the democratic society is the common citizen, the man in the street, the *quisque e populo*" (cited by Carnoy, 1984: 160).

Here Bobbio finds in Weber a friendly companion in his critique of the connections between democracy and expert knowledge. Weber, discussing the rationalization of education and training, and particularly the role of special examinations (e.g., the bar exam), argues that

> Democracy also takes an ambivalent stand in the face of specialized examinations, as it does in the fact of all the phenomena of bureaucracy—although democracy itself promotes these developments. Special examinations, on the one hand, mean or appear to mean a 'selection' of those who qualify from all social strata rather than a rule by notables. On the other hand, democracy fears that a merit system and educational certificates will result in a privileged "caste." (Weber, 1958: 240)

Finally, Bobbio, echoing a long-standing preoccupation of Paulo Freire, suggests that democracy (and democratic education) supposes the full and free development of the human faculties, which is prevented by the effect of massification that suppresses the sense of individual responsibility, which is the

cornerstone of democratic decision making and democratic education.
Not only is the political culture that underscores democratic education
being eroded, but also its most "instrumental" goals are affected when commodity exchange weakens in capitalist societies. Offe (1984) argues that

> Schooling and training do not have the purpose of providing knowledge and
> abilities to young people; they have the purpose of putting individuals in the
> position to use their labor power as commodities on the labor market, and for
> this purpose knowledge and abilities are thought to be instrumental variables.
> How efficiently and effectively educational policies do operate can only be
> determined by looking at the increases in efficiency and effectiveness that appear
> in the private sector, that is, in the market interaction of the owners of labor
> power and the owners of money capital who are willing to pay wages for the use
> of this labor power. There is no "internal" criterion of "good" policy, indepen-
> dent of commodity interaction. (137)

While one need not be in total agreement with Offe's instrumentalism in
identifying the goals of schooling and training, there is no doubt that capitalism
can exist only because of its ability to deliver cost-effective commodities, making mass consumption affordable to a great majority of the citizens. To do this
for capitalism implies that wage laborers should be found in sufficient numbers,
at appropriate prices, and with the minimum appropriate qualifications. Unemployment, informal labor markets, growing poverty, and massive economic
downsizing undermine the connections between employment and education
and will undoubtedly deeply affect the impetus of democratic education.

Last but not least, democratic education can be affected by the growing
process of educational reform, which is part of school reform agendas that
have been launched in the United States and elsewhere focusing on "restructuring" rather than merely transforming the efficiency of existing systems.
Restructuring attempts the transformation of purposes, assumptions, and
methods of school systems (Darling-Hammond, 1993:xi). Not surprisingly,
this reform agenda is being implemented in times of serious financial retrenchment in public education everywhere, and there is a good deal of attention to
competency testing, certification, national exams—in short, diverse attempts
to improve excellence in instruction and learning.

Not only are technocratic proposals in direct contrast with public deliberation and increasing participation of the population in the process of reform, but
also some large and powerful associations or corporations are pursuing a
reform agenda that seeks to homogenize the goals and purposes of education,
producing a very specific educational model of research, policy, and practice
that falls outside the basic democratic accountability. An example at the
domestic level is the Business Roundtable in the United States, a national asso-

ciation of the chief executive officers (CEOs) of the largest transnational corporations, which pursues an agenda for public policy.

> Whereas more inclusive business organizations such as national chambers of commerce and national associations of manufacturers include both large and small firms representing many different interests and perspectives, the members of the Business Roundtables are all large transnational corporations aligned with the economic globalization agenda. . . . The Roundtable, surely one of America's most exclusive and least diverse membership organizations, has an unusually narrow notion of what constitutes a "cross" section of thinking on national issues. With few, if any, exceptions, its membership is limited to white males over fifty years of age whose annual compensation averages more than 170 times the U.S. per capita gross national product. Its members head corporations that disavow a commitment to national interests and stand to gain substantially from economic globalization. Once positions are defined, the Roundtable organizes aggressive campaigns to gain their political acceptance, including personal visits by its member CEOs to their individual senators and representatives. (Korten, 1996: 145–146)

At the international level we find the World Bank having an important impact particularly in the developing world. Thus, there is a conflict between technocracy and democracy in education, as well as a conflict between national sovereignty and autonomy in setting agendas and policy priorities, especially with respect to multilateral and bilateral international agencies, which fall outside democratic control and accountability.

Given these tensions and contradictions among education, democracy, and capitalism, a number of scholars have argued that it is necessary to reclaim a democratic education; Paulo Freire's contribution is particularly important here.

Reclaiming Democratic Education

> Maybe we have enjoyed our present democratic freedom so much that we are passionately dreaming about it. However, this taste and this passion for freedom coexist with authoritarian traditions and practices, resulting in one of our ambiguities.
>
> —Paulo Freire, *Pedagogy of the City*

Paulo Freire promotes a political anthropology of education, an anthropology that offers powerful perspectives for thinking about the democratization of educational practices and societies, in Latin America and elsewhere (Torres,

1980). Freire's political anthropology, which is based on blurring the positivist distinction between facts and values, as well as on advocating the view that education is not neutral, contributes to democratic education at two levels. First, he addresses a serious dilemma of democracy, the constitution of a democratic citizen. Second, he advanced in the 1960s—quite early compared with the postmodernist preoccupation of the 1980s—the question of border crossing in education. Freire (1998) says this very nicely in one of his last books translated into English:

> The comprehension of the limits of educational practice absolutely requires political clarity on the part of educators in relation to their project. It demands that the educator assumes the political nature of his/her practice. It is not enough to say that education is a political act, just as it is not enough to say that political acts are also educative. It is necessary to truly assume the political nature of education. I cannot consider myself progressive if I understand school space to be something neutral, with limited or no relation to class struggle, in which students are seen only as learners of limited domains of knowledge which I will imbue with magic power. I cannot recognize the limits of the political-educative practice in which I am involved if I don't know, if I am not clear about in whose favor I work. Clarifying the question of in whose favor I practice, puts me in a certain position, which is related to class, in which I devise against whom I practice and, necessarily, for what reasons I practice—that is, the dream, the type of society on whose behalf I would like to intervene, act, and participate. (46)

Let us discuss both contributions, beginning with the notion of democratic education. The notion of democracy entails the notion of a democratic citizenship where agents are responsible and able to participate, choose their representatives, and monitor their performance. These are not only political but also pedagogical practices, since the construction of the democratic citizen implies the construction of a pedagogic subject. Individuals are not by nature themselves ready to participate in politics. They have to be educated in democratic politics in a number of ways, including normative grounding, ethical behavior, knowledge of the democratic process, and technical performance. The construction of the pedagogic subject is a central conceptual problem, a dilemma of democracy. To put it simply: democracy implies a process of participation where all are considered equal. However, education involves a process whereby the "immature" are brought to identify with the principles and forms of life of the "mature" members of society. Thus, the process of construction of the democratic pedagogic subject is not only a process of cultural nurturing, but it also involves manipulating principles of pedagogic and democratic socialization in subjects who are neither tabula rasa in cognitive or ethical terms nor fully equipped for the exercise of their democratic rights and obligations.[2] Yet

in the construction of modern polities, the constitution of a pedagogical democratic subject is predicated on grounds that are, paradoxically, a precondition
but also the result of previous experiences and policies of national solidarity
(including citizenship, competence building, and collaboration).

A second major contribution of Freire, advanced in his *Pedagogy of the
Oppressed* and reiterated in countless writings, is his view that the pedagogical subjects of the educational process are not homogeneous citizens but culturally diverse individuals. From his notion of cultural diversity, he identifies
the notion of borders in education and suggests that there is an ethical imperative to cross borders if we attempt to educate for empowerment and not for
oppression. In my work with Adriana Puiggrós (1997), we argue that it was
Paulo Freire who, very early in his *Pedagogy of the Oppressed*, introduced if
not the concepts certainly the meanings of border crossings, otherness, hybrid
cultures, and asynchronic development in Latin America.

Freire's ways of theorizing education emphasize the political implications
of pedagogical work. Freire argues that notions of oppression and domination
are integral to the pedagogical relationship between teachers and pupils in traditional classrooms. Thus the notion of "extensionism," so popular in the
1960s and connected with the advances in the "green revolution" (i.e., the provision of the dominant educational discourse to peasants in the context of
agrarian reforms), was advanced not only as integral to a pedagogical discourse but also, and more relevant indeed, as integral to a political discourse
on development and agrarian modernization. A fundamental insight of Freire
is that the social and pedagogical subjects of education are not fixed, essential,
or inflexible "essences" but a set of mutually changing relationships given
their relational nature—that is, the teacher is a student and the student a
teacher. The cultural and pedagogical implications are that the place and role
of a teacher are not always or necessarily the extension of the role of the adult
white male or, conversely, a role performed by a female teacher subsumed
under the discourse of hegemonic masculinity (Connell, 1987; 1983). While
recognizing the importance of the subject matter and the need for the teacher
to be extremely competent in his or her knowledge, Freire does not see school
knowledge as only the product of European logocentric thought; he indicates
the importance of incorporating the experience and wisdom of the "pueblo"
and socially subordinate sectors. Moreover, school knowledge is not always
reproduced in schools but is also subject to contestation and resistance. While
Freire criticizes the Western school in Latin America as banking education and
as an authoritarian device (that is, as a device transmitting official knowledge
and, at the same time, eliminating the pupils as subjects of their own education), his pedagogy of liberation is an invitation to dialogue in the context of
multiple political and social struggles for liberation. Dialogue appears not only

as a pedagogical tool but also as a method of deconstruction of the way peda-gogical and political discourses are constructed.[3]

More than thirty years after Freire's main books were published (Gadotti et al., 1986; Torres, 1995), the concept of dialogical education, which challenges the positivistic distinction between value judgment and empirical judgment, may appear as a democratic tool for dealing with complex cultural conflicts in the context of unequal and combined development of Latin American educa-tion; its applicability in advanced industrial societies is well documented; and his message of a political democratic utopia in education is a political chal-lenge to the educational establishment.

The Political Challenge: Educational Utopia and Democratic Politics

> Educational practice is part of the superstructure of any society. For that very reason, educational practice, in spite of its fantastic importance in the socio-historical processes of the transformation of societies, is not in itself the key to transformation, even if it is fundamental... obviously, a power elite will not enjoy putting in place and practicing a pedagogical form or expression that adds to the social contradictions which reveal the power of the elite. It would be naive to think that a power elite would reveal itself for what it is through a pedagogical process that, in the end, would work against itself.
> —Paulo Freire, in Carlos A. Torres, *Education, Power, and Personal Biography*

Paulo Freire has argued that the connections between education and politics cannot be theorized only in terms of the intersections between power and edu-cation, or exclusively in terms of the relationships between power and knowl-edge—a theorizing that, to be sure, has permeated Freire's contributions. While Freire has tirelessly illuminated the "politicity of education," he has at the same time invited us to understand the relationships between education and citizenship training, particularly highlighting the historical, normative, and ontological foundations of democratic education and citizenship rights and responsibilities.

For Freire, debates about education and democracy should deal ultimately with the notion of utopia. Indeed, his proposal of an education for liberation still resonates for its boldness and utopian nature. Freire (1972) says, with Hegelian overtones:

> Truly, only the oppressed are able to conceive of a future totally distinct from their present, insofar as they arrive at a consciousness of a dominated class. The

oppressors, as the dominating class, cannot conceive of the future unless it is the preservation of their present as oppressors. In this way, whereas the future of the oppressed consists in the revolutionary transformation of society, without which their liberation will not be verified, the oppressor's future consists in the simple modernization of society, which permits the continuation of its class supremacy. (32)

This utopian factor implies a double tension: announcement and denouncement. Insofar as the teacher carries out his or her utopian role, he or she is turned into a dangerous prophet for the system. Rather than performing the role of the functionary who reproduces the elements of the ideological consciousness of the mode of production, the educator becomes a cultural critic and education becomes a public sphere, a theater for public deliberation controlled neither by the state nor by the market. Weffort'(1967), in reference to the beginnings of Freire's political philosophy of education and method, says:

> But, if a pedagogy of freedom outlines the germ of revolt, not for this reason would it be correct to affirm that revolt is found among the aims of the educator. If it happens, it is hardly and exclusively because conscientization discerns a real situation in which the most frequent givens are struggle and violence. To conscientize in no way means to ideologize or propose words of order. If conscientization opens the way to the expression of social insatisfactions it is because there are real components of a situation of oppression: many are the workers who, having just acquired literacy, join labor movements or unions, and this is because, to them, it seems to be the legitimate path for the defense of their interest and those of their workmates: finally, if conscientization of the popular classes signifies political radicalization, this is simply because the popular classes are radical. (13)

In Paulo Freire's early writings, education is seen as an instrumental factor to help man and woman reflect upon his or her ontological vocation of subject, to help build a critical consciousness of his or her reality (as much of its determinations as of its potentialities). However, the political implications of education were apparent yet contradictory. Let us explain ourselves. Freire, though totally aware of the political implications of a liberating education, is also aware of the contradictions of this education. On the one hand, there is always the possibility of the manipulation and ideologizing of consciousness, that is, placing education and methodologies at the service of a project of domination; on the other hand, Freire believes that a certain connection can be established between educational praxis and political praxis *stricto sensu*. It was incumbent on the educator, fundamentally, to develop a project of literacy training and conscientization, while the "professional" politician was in charge of realizing the task of organizing the oppressed sectors in terms of political structures. Weffort (1967) asserts, confirming our line of argument:

> This educator [Freire] knows that his task contains political implications and he knows, moreover, that these implications are in the interest of the common man and not of the elite. But he knows also that his field is pedagogy and not politics and that he cannot, as an educator, substitute the revolutionary politician interested in knowledge and structural transformation. He rejects the traditional notion of education as "lever for progress"; would it make sense to oppose to this the equally ingenuous thesis of "education as a lever for revolution"? A pedagogy of freedom can help popular politics since conscientization means an opening up to the comprehension of social structures as means of domination and violence. But the task of orienting this growth of awareness in a specifically political direction falls on the politician, not the educator. (16)

In countless interventions Freire postulates that there is no educational revolution without political revolution. No educational action can provoke a revolution of power. Education is not merely instrumental; it is, rather, a field of ideological struggles that must be waged, and the politicization of the citizenship is a possible outcome. Freire (1978a) argues that:

> When an illiterate from Angicos, speaking in front of President Goulart . . . declared that he was no longer "Masa" but "gente," that was not only a sentence: he consciously affirmed an option. He choose a decisive participation that only the people have and he rejected the emotional dimension of the masses. He was politicized. (145)

This politicization may help the people to begin the pronunciation of the word and the pronunciation of the world, a world increasingly more diverse and multicultural, and indeed it posits the need to revisit the interactions between democracy and education.

Democracy and Education

> Our civilization is wonderful, in certain spectacular and meretricious ways; wonderful in scientific marvels and inventive miracles; wonderful in material inflation, which it calls advancement, progress, and other pet names; wonderful in its spying-out of the deep secrets of Nature and its vanquishment of her stubborn laws; wonderful in its extraordinary financial and commercial achievement; wonderful in its hunger for money and its indifference as to how it is acquired. . . . It is a civilization which has destroyed the simplicity and

repose of life; replaced its contentment, its poetry, its soft romance dreams and vision with the money-fever, sordid ideals, vulgar ambitions, and the sleep which does not refresh.

—Mark Twain, *Letters from the Earth*

History shows clear linkages between public education as a function of the state, democracy, and the constitution of citizenship. For instance, Ted Mitchell (1997), in "The Republic for Which it Stands,"[4] offers a persuasive historical explanation of why in Revolutionary America public schools were designed to create citizens: "the period between the Revolution and the War of 1812 was a period of intense excitement over the potential of schooling to provide what the press could not and what standing armies would not: regular calibration of the balance between liberty and order within the breast of each child, building the state as it built citizens, a generation at a time" (5).

To do so, the Revolutionaries first embedded public education in the political philosophy of the new nation, creating a host of curricular materials that reflected the political values of the new Republic. But, above all, the founders of the American nation-state embraced the education of children as the standing solution for the foreseeable problems of law, order, and liberty. However, while this solution has been historically viable, it is not immutable: the definition of citizenship tends to change, and changes in the idea of citizenship lead to changes in schools (Mitchell, 1997:9).

These changes in schooling, however, are only loosely coupled with the needs of the nation-state, given the nature of local control of schooling in the United States and the fact that schools (and teachers in particular) retain important degrees of professional autonomy. Hence, "while schools have been in the orbit of the state, they have not been the creatures of the state" (Mitchell, 1997:10).

Mitchell (1997) offers a political argument about the functionality of schooling to the emerging Revolutionary state and its institutional aftermath. Rather than focusing on schooling exclusively as an instrument to promote the qualification of the labor force or as a principle of morality and ethics. Mitchell's political and historical analysis "seeks to put politics first, and to take seriously the rhetoric of identity between schooling and democracy, [and] to turn it inside out, demonstrating that the efficacy, indeed the acceptance of public schooling is contingent upon its ability and willingness to structure freedom and to swing the balance between liberty and order to the side of order" (13).

The corollary to this argument, according to Mitchell (1997), is that when the schools succeed in promoting the empowerment of the people, hence "weighing the balance on the side of liberty, their support among the elite diminishes and discussions once again turn to discussions over access" (14). Mitchell characterizes as typical examples of this phenomenon the backlash against immigrants in California and elsewhere in America at the end of this century, the perennial request by neoconservatives to abolish the Department of Education, and the policies of the English Only movement.

Two central goals provided the original impetus for the Revolutionary state to promote schooling in civil society: first, to avoid backsliding into monarchy—hence the need to create a new social consensus and new hegemony for the newly created Republic; and second, to prevent increased democratic participation from eventually tipping the balance between liberty and order and throwing the country into anarchy. James Madison (Hamilton, Madison, and Jay, 1961) was particularly keen in drawing a sharp distinction between pure democracy or direct democracy, which could eventually exist in a few restricted spatial domains, and the Republic. Moreover, he was extremely suspicious of direct democracy because of what he saw as deleterious trends of excess participation and factionalism, which renders pure democracy ineffectual: "pure democracy . . . can admit of no cure for the mischiefs of faction . . . as they have been as short in their lives as they have been violent in their deaths" (81).

Beyond building the Republic, schooling was also purported to serve in building the national character of Americans; hence the effort to create curricula and textbooks that, even in the domain of language, would differentiate Revolutionary America from England. Finally, the idea of promoting schooling for democratic citizenship in Revolutionary America was also prompted by the new Revolutionary elite's need to avoid educating their offspring in European (British) schools and colleges or—what would be a serious blow to the legitimacy of the Revolutionary elite—continuing the traditional practice of bringing tutors from Europe for their children.

The construction of a public educational system would, then, fulfill manifold functions: "In making education a part of the civil sphere rather than the private sphere, the revolutionary generation tied schools to the dynamic of the new political culture both as a creator of that culture and as a product of it" (Mitchell, 1997:35).

A central methodology implemented by the Revolutionaries to instill civic virtue through school practices was to resort to a pedagogy of heroes, with George Washington and Benjamin Franklin as key role models. This was an iconography that also transpired in the teaching of history in many Western countries, just changing the cast of characters of the story. The functionality of a pedagogy of heroes and heroism was clear: while repudiating the notion of self-interest as the sole (selfish) motive for social action, enhancing the virtues of some citizens, who become beacons (and icons) of a particular set of virtues, will still place—despite its seemingly contradictory orientations—the notion of the possessive individual and the pursuit of the common good as central to the construction of the new republican policy.

Mitchell's (1997) conclusion is telling and deserves to be quoted at length:

> The public school has become a central site for contests over the nature of citizenship and of the nature of the American nation state. It has also become the subject of scrutiny in ways that it has not been since the founding of the Republic. Debates over practice and access demonstrate a lack of consensus about the role of schools [a situation that cut across the analysis of the five critical periods that he selected]. . . . Questions about the nature of the history curriculum display a profound unease over issues of content. In the context of the argument of the book, these debates reveal the stakes involved in recasting the nation's history to become more inclusive of the agency of hitherto dispossessed groups and thereby expanding the boundaries of effective political action. Proposals to limit access to schooling among immigrants seem to acknowledge, for the first time in more than two hundred years, that schools are not effective mechanisms for political socialization. Finally movements to disestablish public schools, through vouchers and other means, as well as persistent proposals to disestablish the federal Department of Education, suggest that the state's role in providing schooling and in shaping political education is up for grabs. Again within the context of the argument of the book, this is the result of the failure of schools to serve as effective tools of social control, the "value" that originally built support for public schools. (22)

This historical experience of the American state is by no means idiosyncratic but, quite the contrary, has been very influential in the constitution of school systems in the postcolonial states, beginning with the independence of the Latin American countries. It is fundamental to keep in mind the tensions in the construction of democracy, citizenship, and education in capitalist societies before I address the multiculturalist answer to the problems of democracy and citizenship in the next chapter. However, while not the subject of this book, I cannot leave the conversation about democracy and education without making at least a reference to the possibility of democratic socialism as an alternative.

Postscript: Democracy and Socialism

> When yesterday's progressives, today's pragmatics, say that now our struggle is for democracy, they continue to set socialism and democracy against each other, repeating, thus, an old mistake: the mistake of assuming that democracy is the exclusive possession of the bourgeoisie. They demonstrate a profoundly mechanistic understanding of democracy, so mechanistic that it does not call

for questions about the world of values, beliefs, freedom, and being or not being.
—Paulo Freire, *Letters to Cristina*

No doubt, the world of "real" or "realist" socialism is dead and buried. For very good reasons, I doubt it will come back to haunt us. "Realist" socialism is indeed a historical category. There should be few people still mourning its passing beyond mourning the passing of their own lives in pursuing or supporting a bureaucratic nightmare, or the loss of their bureaucratic privileges. Few people may mourn "realist socialism" because, as Freire (1996) reminds us, "One of the reasons, as I see it, for the failure of 'realist socialism' was its lack of a taste for freedom, its authoritarianism, its mental bureaucratization, which reduced life to immobility. It was a mechanistic understanding of history which denied history a possibility and nullified freedom, choice, decision, and belief, and ended up terminating life itself" (165).

Yet the socialist impetus that animated the notion of an alternative mode of production, distribution, and politics to capitalism remains important for a number of reasons. Apple (1982c) reminds us that democratization implies "a practice that is based on the control of decisions about the majority of working people . . . one that is not limited to the political sphere but to, say economics and, critically, gender relations" (172).

In fact, Cerroni's (1976) distinction between democracy as method and democracy as content is important because it highlights the need to postulate, from a radical, socialist democratic perspective, a radical equality in racial, ethnic, class, and gender interactions, both in the public sphere and in the intimacy of the household. There is then no necessary contradiction between democracy and socialism, as Freire (1996) makes it patently clear with his passionate prose: "While I am a radical and substantive democratic, I am a socialist. There is no way of countering the one with the other. To do so is one of the tragic errors of so-called realist socialism" (114).

These are not only passionate words but also, and more important, programmatic words, reflecting Freire's experience when he became a policymaker in his city of residence, São Paulo, as secretary of education of the municipality of São Paulo, a megacity and the financial center of capitalist Brazil. This was a policy experiment in which Freire led a group of cultural workers, political activists, teachers, and parents in designing a fascinating model of educational and curriculum reform, literacy training, and school governance following democratic radical and socialist principles (O'Cadiz, Wong, and Torres, 1998).

Another important insight on the postsocialist condition is offered by Nancy Fraser (1997). She defines postsocialism as "an absence of any credible overarching emancipatory project despite the proliferation of fronts of struggle; a general decoupling of the cultural politics of recognition from the social politics of redistribution; and a decentering of the claims for equality in the face of aggressive marketization and sharply rising material inequality" (3).

Fraser offers three important suggestions. The first is to cultivate a skeptical distance "from the fashionable 'post-socialist' distrust in narrative, pragmatics, 'totalizing' thinking" (4). No doubt, any interest in linking in policy terms democracy, citizenship and multiculturalism in education demands an approach that is normative, ethically grounded, and politically pragmatic. A second insightful suggestion by Fraser is "to demystify 'post-socialist' ideologies manning the shift from redistribution to recognition" (4). This is a crucial observation. As I argued above, the social struggles in contemporary capitalism cannot be considered a zero-sum game. There is plenty of room for growth in the politics of alliances in multicultural coalitions without imagining that what one segment of the coalition appropriates or claims is lost by another segment. Finally, Fraser suggests that the gulf between impoverished masses and declining middle classes demands a distributional policy to make effective the claims of citizenship (5).

The experience of Latin America could indeed illuminate the connections between socialism and democracy. Radical experiences of democracies with socialist overtones have taken place in the region. For instance, notions such as popular democracy, based on the defense of popular sovereignty (the dignity and interest of the popular, socially subordinate social classes), the defense of national sovereignty (against the presence of metropolitan nation-states in the region that attempt to dominate given their imperialist power, and against the presence of multinational corporations that attempt to dominate given their mighty economic power), and the defense of the idea of public property as a common good, and the predominance of the right of collectivities over the right of individuals—all of these principles suggest a strong connection between socialism and democracy, or the connection between democracy as content rather than simply as a method of political representation. National experiences include the Mexican revolution (1911–1921), the Bolivian revolution of 1952, the early experiences of the Cuban revolution, the so-called peaceful transition to socialism in Chile under the leadership of Salvador Allende (1970–1973), and the Nicaraguan experience, particularly between 1979 and 1984, when the country became fully engulfed in a civil war stimulated and financed by the Reagan administration. Local experiences are many, from the Frente Zapatista uprising in Chiapas in 1994 to the agonizing experiences of the severe repression of indigenous community control by the Guatemalan army (Menchu, 1983) and the many microexperiences of community self-management and community education (Torres, 1980).

Quite consciously, I decided to write about democracy and socialism in the postscript of this chapter. Why? Not because socialism is a historical category, as neoliberals are proudly advocating with the theory of the end of ideologies and the end of history, but because the understanding of socialism in liberal societies, by liberals, conservatives, neoliberals, and neoconservatives has always implied a substantive, almost ontological differentiation between socialism and democracy, creating a popular schism that has made it very difficult for socialist intellectuals to bridge the gap between the two ideas by arguing that there is a substantive democratic impetus in the socialist project. I claim, however, that the notion of popular democracy or socialist democracy should be incorporated into the discussion. In fact, C. B. Macpherson's and Carole Pateman's notions of participatory democracy, for instance, are linked to a socialist-democratic tradition, as is, although more peripherally and critically, Ernesto Laclau and Chantal Mouffe's (1985) notion of radical democracy. Paulo Freire (1996) again shows the way: "If the dream of the emerging bourgeoisie was capitalism as the mark of bourgeois democracy, so the dream of the popular majorities today is socialism as the mark of popular democracy. The fundamental point is not to end democracy, but to perfect it and have not capitalism but socialism as its filling" (137).

In trying to rescue the important connections between democracy as the establishment of a universal system of government, tributary of the Enlightenment, promoting rules and standards of moral behavior embodied in laws, institutions, and states that respect life, liberty, the pursuit of happiness, equality, fraternity and sorority, and socialism, as a system of production, distribution, and political participation—connections that cannot be overlooked in discussing a notion of multicultural democratic citizenship—I want to make mine Eric Hobsbawm's (1997) words regarding Marx, words that can be easily transposed to the ideal of democratic socialism: "I would still continue to pay my respects, profound though not uncritical, to what the Japanese call a *sensei,* an intellectual master to whom one owes a debt that cannot be repaid" (ix).

Notes

1. See the insightful analysis of the parallels between the positions of Tocqueville and Kelsen in Umberto Cerroni, *La libertad de los modernos* (Barcelona: Martinez Roca, 1972) (1st Italian ed., 1968).

2. I am thankful to Walter Feinberg for this suggestion in a personal communication.

3. See Carlos Alberto Torres and Adriana Puiggrós, eds., *Latin American Education: Comparative Perspectives* (Boulder, Colo.: Westview, 1996). The notion of pedagogical subject is related to the notion of social subject developed by Ernesto Laclau in

several of his works. See, e.g., Ernesto Laclau and Chantal Mouffe, *Hegemonía y estrategía socialista* (Madrid: Siglo XXI, 1987); and Ernesto Laclau, *New Reflections on the Revolution of Our Times* (London: Verso, 1991).

4. Ted Mitchell, "The Republic for Which It Stands: Public Schools, the State, and the Idea of Citizenship in America" (Los Angeles, 1997). Mitchell explores five critical moments in the connection between schooling and citizenship: from the Revolutionary era up to the War of 1812; during the Civil War, in the development of the counterstate of the Confederacy; during Reconstruction, examining in particular the role of the Freedmen's Bureau in creating citizens of former slaves; during the expansion of the American empire at the end of the nineteenth century; and during World War I. He argues that by the end of that fifth critical moment, World War I, the fundamentals of the modern relationship between state, civil society, and citizenship had been institutionalized.

6

Multiculturalism

_____

This chapter discusses theories of multiculturalism in education. Starting with an exploration of some of the key themes of multiculturalism, I provide a critical reading of the multiculturalist movement as it is reflected in multicultural education through a relevant sample of criticisms from liberal quarters, from the neoconservative movement, and from the left. Focusing on the question of cultural difference, I show some of the contradictions associated with theories of multiculturalism in education. I focus on both multiculturalism as a social movement and multicultural education. Given the theoretical orientation and programmatic goals of this book, a discussion about citizenship education may benefit from the general arguments in this book but needs a specific analysis and curriculum criticism beyond the goals and available space of this book.[1]

Multiculturalism as Social Movement, as Multicultural Education, and as Citizenship Education: The Question of Whiteness

> The new cultural politics of difference are neither simply oppositional in contesting the mainstream (or malestream) for inclusion nor transgressive in the avant-gardist sense of shocking conventional bourgeois audiences. Rather they are distinct articulations of talented (and usually privileged) contributors to culture who desire to align themselves with demoralized, demobilized, depoliticized, and disorganized people in order to empower and enable social action and, if possible, to enlist collective insurgency for the expansion of freedom, democracy and individuality.
>
> —Cornel West, "The New Cultural Politics of Difference"

The epigram by Cornel West sets the right tone for the discussion. Multiculturalism in any form, shape, or color relates to the politics of difference and the emerging social struggles over racialized, gendered, and classist societies. Yet,

175

discussions on multiculturalism in the United States should start with a subtle but important differentiation between notions of multiculturalism as a social movement and a theoretical approach, multicultural education as a reform movement, and citizenship education as a curriculum-oriented specialty that, particularly given the characteristics of the U.S. racial makeup, needs to take into account issues of racial identity and cultural diversity for citizenship building as an antiracist pedagogy.

As a social movement, multiculturalism is a philosophical, theoretical, and political orientation that goes beyond school reform and tackles the issues of race, gender, and class relations in society at large.[2] Let us take, for example, the formulation that McLaren (1997) made of the challenges at hand for a critical multiculturalist movement:

> Our classroom investigations and discussions with urban educators in Los Angeles have also provoked us to rethink the issue of multicultural education. We have been distressed by the racial segregation that we see throughout the city at large, as well as in school playgrounds and lunchrooms. We link some of this to the politics of enforced assimilation reflected in the Proposition 187 legislation; the resurgent English Only movement; assaults on bilingual education in Republican legislation and by Republican spokespersons; the persistence of academic tracking; the Latinophobic, anti-immigration sentiment that has been growing since the early 1980s; deindustrialization; and the emergence of ethnic and racial movements that are demanding recognition. One also needs to view multiculturalism in terms of the larger picture, that is, from the reference point of the new world system of large-scale and continuous emigration flows, subaltern and transient cultures, stateless corporations, and the postindustrial labor force of women, racial minorities and immigrants from previously peripheral nations. (210)

As a programmatic reform movement, liberal multicultural education is oriented to ensure equity in schools. In this context, the most liberal segments of the movement consider that developing a notion of multicultural tolerance is central to their goals. Yet, as Fraser (1997: 174) analyzes, the fight for equity and recognition should be coupled with a fight for redistribution and equality, not only equity. This suggestion opens the way for a more radical understanding of the problem, that regarding multiculturalism the discussion should start with the question of whiteness.

The discussion about "whiteness" should be placed in the context of antiracist philosophies criticizing the notion of whiteness and white terror, looking at the construction of race, and particularly whiteness as a racial practice. The question is whether a discussion about whiteness can be used as a tool in the pursuit of antiracist policies. Giroux provides a subtle critique of bell hooks's (1990) position on this score. She argues that while whites see themselves as transparent and invisible—that is, they don't see themselves in racial terms—they are seen as a white terror in the way that interactions between blacks and whites are felt by blacks.[3] Yet, Henry Giroux (1997) suggests that the notion of whiteness cannot be understood exclusively in terms of the common experience of white domination and racism. Whiteness, for Giroux, should be rearticulated in antiessentialist terms. An antiracist pedagogy that takes seriously the nuances of the white experience should enable white students to move beyond positions of guilt and resentment. In fact, Giroux (1997) argues—and this is an important discussion for antiracist citizenship education—that "Whiteness needs to be theorized carefully in terms of its potential to provide students with a racial identity that can play a crucial role in refashioning an anti-racist politics that informs a broader, radical, democratic project" (16). Whiteness is for McLaren (1997b:237–293) an attribute of ethnicity, and white terror constitutes the leitmotif of critical multiculturalism as a social movement beyond the bounds of schooling.

McLaren (1997) links multicultural education to critical pedagogy, challenging the politics of "whiteness as a type of articulatory practice that can be located in the convergence of colonialism, capitalism and subject formation" (268). Interestingly enough, McLaren argues that whiteness is both mythopoetical, insofar as it constructs a collective social imaginary that hinges on the ontological superiority of the European and American social subject, and is metastructural, insofar as it links this collective imaginary to a cultural, social, and economic hegemony of capital at a global level including multiple layers of social differences.

In the same vein, Richard Dyer (1997) argues that "white discourse implacably reduces the non-white subject to being a function of the white subject, not allowing her/him space or autonomy, permitting neither the recognition of similarities nor the acceptance of differences except as a means for knowing the white self" (13). Whiteness, when equated to being human, "secures a position of power" (9), and therefore whites see themselves "not of a certain race, they're just the human race" (9).

Then the discourse and representation of whiteness as neutral serves the purpose of portraying a social group as the human ordinary, concealing relationships of power and privilege that the fact of being white mobilizes (indeed to the point that coalitions around whiteness seem to have been more powerful mobilizers than, say, class); and indeed whiteness appears as a symbol of aesthetic superiority, as the explicit ideal: "Though the power value of whiteness resides above all in its instabilities and apparent aneutrality, the colour does carry the more explicit symbolic sense of moral and also aesthetic superiority" (70).

Taking this critique of whiteness as a central "ontological" premise, a radical multiculturalism and a critical pedagogy should center on a political economy and critical pedagogy that, as McLaren (1997) argues, "What is essential for educators in this locus of struggle is to dismantle the discourses of power and privilege and social practices that have epistemically mutated into a new and terrifying form of xenophobic nationalism in which there is but one universal subject of history—the white, Anglo, heterosexual male of bourgeois privilege" (214).

There is no question that the presence of multicultural goals in the most recent discussions on citizenship education is at least challenging and at best changing the curriculum domain of citizenship education. Some scholars, most clearly James Banks (1997), argue that to educate citizens in a multicultural society demands a multicultural education.

Multiculturalism as Social Movement and as Theoretical Approach

> Who authenticates an authentic identity? Who is entitled to issue membership cards? Boundaries shift in time and space. Resemblance is relative to the culture and the purpose of classification. To a passerby or a census-taker, I am white. To an anti-Semite, I am simply a Jew. To a German Jew, I may be one of the Ostjuden; to Sephardim, an Ashkenazi Jew; to an Israeli Jew, American; to a religious Jew, secular; to a right wing Zionist, an apostate, or no Jew at all.
> —Todd Gitlin, *The Twilight of Common Dreams*

The question of identity is paramount in understanding the problems of education. However, identity and citizenship cannot be dissociated from the discussion of the state. The first duty of the state, as Ted Mitchell (1997) argues in his historical work, quoting DeWitt Clinton, governor of the state of New York in 1822, "is to render its citizens virtuous by intellectual instruction and moral discipline, by enlightening their minds, purifying their hearts, and teaching them their rights and obligations" (1).

Yet, as Mitchell makes painfully clear in his historical analysis, the notion of citizenship has taken different meanings over time for different groups of people in the United States and in different settings.

Mitchell's (1997) analysis shows that more than two hundred years ago, the new educational system created by the Revolutionary state tried to solve the tension between liberty and order. In Mitchell's (1997) words: "The problem, stated briefly here, was twofold, and lay, first, in finding an appropriate and durable equilibrium between liberty and order and second, in establishing institutional means by which that balance would hold" (3).

Mitchell's historical analysis, following the tradition of the new institutionalism in education, has shown that the Revolutionary American state aimed for an education that would provide an explicit focus on moral training, helping to establish the linkages between the individuals and the new state.[4] Expanding Mitchell's analysis, I shall argue that, the individual citizens that the Founders had in mind—not surprisingly, as it had previously been the case in England—were free white males. The education of Native Americans, African Americans—most of them living under conditions of slavery—and women was mostly neglected in the Revolutionary period.

The question of citizenship and democratic education cannot, and should not, be separated from the questions of who are the citizens to be educated, how these citizens change over time in terms of their own demographic, political, cultural, and even symbolic configuration, and, in turn, in terms of how citizens perceive these changes—what David Tyack (1993) called the public culture in the construction of difference. Moreover, it is fundamental to understand how the figure of the citizen itself changes in the context of the changes in the state and the process of globalization. Finally, it is fundamental to discover how the institutional settings in which citizens' virtues are played out change, implying, by definition, serious challenges to the role that the educational system and the political culture should play in citizenship building. In short, at least in the United States—and, I would argue, worldwide—the relationships between democracy, citizenship, and education cannot be treated in isolation from the question of multiculturalism.

With this historical word of caution in mind, it is safe to argue that while multiculturalism as a theoretical approach has taken a more vigorous shape in the 1980s and 1990s, the question of multiculturalism in the United States is as old as the country's attempts to establish mass, compulsory schooling. Unfortunately, the discussion about multiculturalism was framed in terms of the prevailing dominant-subordinate group relations where

> the dominant group used schools to integrate and socialize children from various ethnic groups; supported boarding schools to break the cultural and tribal bonds of Native Americans; excluded as much as possible African Americans, who sought entrance into the education system with hopes schooling could lead to good jobs and social mobility; and largely ignored three hundred years of Hispanic presence and influence in America. (La Belle and Ward, 1994:9)

At the turn of the century and perhaps even earlier, schooling was used to homogenize the language, experience, and values of diverse groups, ensuring that the large groups of immigrants coming to the United States would assimilate behavior, values, and customs in a "melting-pot society" as conceived of by the official knowledge and the official politics of culture in the emerging world power. As Tyack (1993) notes, citing J. F. McClymer, by 1916 "cultural diversity had come to be defined as a national crisis" (15).

The immediate postwar experience and the growing cultural struggles in the United States unleashed a series of debates on intergroup relations, diversity, and what was considered by education authorities as divisive struggles of different interest groups and ethnic constituencies competing to shape educational policy and practice. Tyack (1993) captures the dynamics of the confrontation, emphasizing that a competing construction of pluralism

> demanded a new definition of the public culture that did not simply celebrate cultural differences and then go on to prize a core of common values based on middle-class American individualism. The new version of pluralism was explicitly political and challenged not just the traditional academic canon but also entrenched interests that had sustained racism. Not surprisingly, this particular view has aroused far more controversy than did earlier forms of intercultural education. (19)

Given the ebbs and flows of social struggles in the United States, multiculturalism has not been a homogeneous social movement. Nor is it represented by a single theoretical paradigm, educational approach, or pedagogy. Therefore, despite the fact that they are often closely linked, the notion of multiculturalism as such cannot encapsulate the representation of the vast universe of the politics of cultural identity (Arthur and Shapiro, 1995). Some people see multiculturalism as an antiracist philosophy, others as a methodology for educational reform, others as a set of specific content areas within instructional programs. Multiculturalism means different things to different people.

Todd Gitlin (1995), in his elegant prose, points exactly to the versatility of the term "multiculturalism" and the ambivalence in its usage, aim, and leitmotif:

> The word is baggy, a melange of fact and value, current precisely because it is vague enough to serve so many interests. Partisans may use the term to defend the recognition of difference, or to resist policies and ideas imposed by conquerors, or to defend cosmopolitanism—the interest and pleasure that each may take in the profusion of humanity. The purists of identity politics use it to defend endless fission, a heap of monocultures. On the other side, multiculturalism and its demonic twin, "political correctness," serve conservatives as names for a potpourri of things they detest—including an irritating insistence on the rights of minorities. (228)

Any systematic analysis of the burgeoning multiculturalism literature will show that the major goals of multicultural education vary. First, they vary from developing ethnic and cultural literacy (e.g., expanding the degree of information about the history and contributions of ethnic groups that traditionally have been excluded from the curriculum) to personal development (e.g., developing pride in one's ethnic identity). Second, they vary from changing attitudes and clarification of values (i.e., challenging prejudices, stereotypes, ethnocentrism, and racism) to promoting multicultural competence (e.g., learning how to interact with people who are different from ourselves, or how to understand cultural differences). Third, they vary from developing proficiency in basic skills (e.g., improving reading, writing, and mathematical skills of people whose ethnic, racial, and/or class background is different from the mainstream cultural capital that predominates in formal schools) to striving to achieve simultaneously educational equity and excellence (e.g., developing learning choices that work across different cultures and learning styles). Fourth, they vary from pursuing individual empowerment to achieving social reform (e.g., cultivating in students attitudes, values, skills, habits, and discipline to become social agents committed to reforming schools and society with the goal of eradicating social disparities, racism, and gender and class oppression and therefore improving equality of educational and occupational opportunities for all).

Banks and Banks (1993), for instance, identify four approaches to multicultural education: (1) teaching about contributions of different cultural groups and individuals, an approach that can be called corporate conservative multiculturalism; (2) an additive approach that incorporates multicultural lessons as units of study that supplement or become appendixes to the existing curriculum, that is, a typical liberal multicultural approach; (3) a transformative approach that attempts to change the basic curriculum and instruction to reflect the perspectives and experiences of diverse cultural, ethnic, racial, and social groups—a social democratic multiculturalist approach; (4) a policymaking approach based on the history of social struggles in the country (e.g., women's movements, the civil rights movement, the Vietnam War movement, the free speech movement) that teaches students that intergroup relations are always an integral part of social and historical conflicts in society and that they should employ—in Bourdieu's terms—their cultural capital, habitus, and habitat to engage in political action for greater equality, freedom, and justice for everyone, while moving away from the principles of social organization of capitalism—a socialist multicultural approach.

This list, a slightly modified version of Banks's list, defines four organizing principles of multiculturalism as multicultural education. However, it is by no means the definitive classification of different types of multiculturalism.

Important work by Christine Sleeter and Carl Grant (1987) also identifies five prevailing categories that are useful for synthesizing the myriad multicultural approaches and curricula, teaching, and learning experiences being implemented in the United States. They include (a) teaching culturally different students to fit into mainstream society; (b) a human relations approach that emphasizes diverse peoples living together harmoniously; (c) the single-group-studies approach, which concentrates on developing awareness, respect, and acceptance of specific groups in society; (d) the focus on prejudice reduction and the provision of equality of educational opportunity and social justice for all; and, finally, (e) a social reconstructionist approach that promotes analytical and critical thinking focused on the redistribution of power, wealth, and other of society's resources among diverse groups.

Before we proceed with the critiques of multiculturalism and multicultural education, it is important to show the connections with democracy and citizenship education. In this regard, the contributions of James Banks are truly foundational.

Democracy, Multiculturalism and Citizenship Education: James Banks's Perspective

E pluribus unum

There are few, if any, analyses of the connections between democracy and multiculturalism. However, James Banks's (1997) recent work is an exception and deserves to be discussed as foundational work intimately linked to the liberal tradition.

Banks's (1997) starting point is the democratic gaps, that is, the difference between American ideals and American realities: "In a democratic curriculum, students need to be taught about and have opportunities to acquire American democratic values while at the same time learning about American realities that challenge these ideals, such as discrimination based on race, gender, and social class" (9).

Banks (1997) argues that multiculturalism is a growing development in the nation and that it will become more integrated into the social studies curriculum. As education for freedom, it is important to fill the gaps between democratic ideals and democratic practices in three important senses: (a) to allow students to affirm their gender, racial, and cultural identities; (b) to provide students with the freedom to function beyond ethnic and cultural boundaries; and (c) to allow students to obtain the necessary skills to live in a modern democratic society (26).

A central assumption of Banks's analysis is that because social science curricula reflect the major social, political, and economic developments in the United States, they will "continue to reflect the major issues and tensions within American life, as well as mirror the nation's ideals, goals, aspirations, and conflicts" (31). From a constructivist perspective,[5] knowledge can contribute to the creation of reflective citizens, a central goal of social science curricula and schooling (Banks, 1997: chaps. 4, 5).

For Banks (1997), multiculturalism offers a systematic answer to the question of citizenship education. It offers a systematic integration of content and a systematic approach to the process of knowledge construction, taking into account central categories such as class, race, and gender; aims at the reduction of individual and institutional prejudice; works through a pedagogy that emphasizes excellence and equality, and thus students of color find an equity pedagogy in their teachers that allows them to obtain better academic achievement; and, finally, contributes to the creation of an empowering school culture and social structure. Multicultural pedagogy is based on a multidimensional notion of knowledge, which Banks (1997:85) divides into three main areas: pedagogical knowledge, knowledge of the subject matter, and multicultural knowledge.

The construction of democratic citizenship for Banks implies not only that the teacher should possess a thorough knowledge in the three areas listed above but also that there is a set of pedagogical interventions specifically to modify students' racial attitudes. These interventions include reinforcement studies, that is, attempts to effect a change in the psychological profile of children by stressing positive reinforcement to combat racial prejudice; perceptual differentiation studies, including different types of interventions, particularly units and lessons that simulate experiences in the racial attitudes of students and teachers; and, finally, the promotion of cooperative learning and interracial contacts in schools. While he asserts the need for total school reform, Banks identifies as the key to multicultural education the role of the teacher in promoting racial tolerance and understanding and in creating multicultural classrooms (96–97).

To create democratic schools, teachers and administrators from diverse racial, ethnic, and cultural groups should examine their own cultural assumptions, biases, behaviors, knowledge, and paradigms on which their pedagogy is based and the subject matter that they teach. They also should help students identify how the knowledge embedded in the curriculum is constructed.

An undisputed premise of Banks's (1997) citizenship education model, based on a strong liberal foundation, is the presence of an American commonwealth to which every child, no matter of what ethnic, gender, or social group, should defer. Thus, a three-step process is recommended: first, ethnic identification; second, national identification; and based on these two, a third recommended step, global democratic identification. "As important as it is for the school to reflect cultural democracy and to understand the students' cultures, it is also vitally important for all American youth to develop a reflective and clarified national identification and a strong commitment to American political ideals" (129). There is a unity of purpose in these three steps, moving beyond ethnic and American identity, trying to reach a global identification: "I believe that cultural, national, and global identification are developmental in nature and that an individual can attain a healthy and reflective national identification only when he or she has acquired a healthy and reflective cultural identification; individuals can develop a reflective and positive global identification only after they have a realistic, reflective, and positive national identification" (139).

Hence, for Banks there are premises that should be followed in order to achieve a healthy democratic, pluralistic political culture and citizenship. Schools should make possible the linkages between these three sets of identifications or identities (i.e., ethnic, national, and global); the curriculum should teach both the prevalence of prejudice and democratic gaps, including exploitation and domination, and the achievements of different ethnic, social, and cultural groups and how all can contribute to *e pluribus unum*.

Even though Banks explores some of the dilemmas of democracy and citizenship, he tries to put a happy, optimistic face on the situation, using sociopsychological and curriculum tools to intervene, seeking the drastic reduction of racism and racial prejudice and the expansion of multiculturalism. Yet, his viewpoint, built as a combination of typologies, including an all-too-brief historical analysis about research, fails to take into account the complexities of the distance that I have identified between democracy as method and democracy as content (which goes much further than just the gap between democratic ideals and societal realities). Likewise, Banks fails to recognize the complexities associated with the notion of identity per se and how difficult it is to link identity(ies) to a theory of democracy. Because of this, his criticism of the capitalist nature of American society appears as ad hominem and cursory at best. Finally, despite his knowledge and good intentions, Banks's analysis of the complexities of citizenship and its linkages to multiculturalism fall short of addressing the key contradictions and dilemmas of democratic citizenship in multicultural societies.

Obviously, the divergent purposes and goals of multiculturalism outlined above, along with the variety of theoretical, epistemological, and political perspectives addressing multiculturalism as a social movement and multicultural education, create a cornucopia of responses from the left and the right, to traditional liberalism, critiques that I address in the next sections.

The Liberal Critique

> "Passionate detachment" requires more than acknowledged and self-critical partiality. We are bound to seek perspective from those points of view, which can never be known in advance, which promise something quite extraordinary, that is, knowledge potent for constructing worlds less organized by axes of domination.
>
> —Donna J. Haraway, *Simians, Cyborgs, and Women*

Liberalism has been at the heart of the multiculturalism movement, and sometimes is portrayed as the mainstay ideology of multicultural education. Yet, liberal scholars have voiced serious criticisms of what they perceive as the most radical liberal currents of multiculturalism. A central concern was portrayed by Arthur Schlesinger's (1991) defense of Europe against what he sees as the assault of multiculturalism and "ethnic" ideologies:

> Whatever the particular crimes of Europe, that continent is also the source—the unique source—of those liberating ideas of individual liberty, political democracy, the rule of law, human rights, and cultural freedom that constitute our most precious legacy and to which most of the world today aspires. These are European ideas, not Asian, nor African, nor Middle Eastern ideas, except by adoption. (76)

Schlesinger (1991) fears that multiculturalism may plunge American culture into incoherence and chaos. Schlesinger's central concern is how the emotional tenor of the debate and, more important, the quarrels about the question of culture diminish the stature of a common (Western) culture (and hence a common canon); undermine the solidity of the cultural bonds, already strained by the common conflicts of every culture; create a fragmentary culture full of ghettos, tribes, and enclaves, forcing the notion of a kind of cultural and linguistic "apartheid"; and hence deeply undermine the sameness and originality of American culture: "the bonds of cohesion in our society are sufficiently fragile, or so it seems to me, that it makes no sense to strain them by encouraging and exalting cultural and linguistic apartheid" (137–138). In so doing, Schlesinger (1990) argues, ethnic studies are un-American, because, in the end, they promote cultural balkanization of the population (A14).

A central player in liberal thought in the American academy, Gerald Graff (1992), disagrees with Schlesinger. Instead, Graff sides with most multiculturalist and feminist critics who would argue that these tensions, contradictions, and quarrels exist independently and certainly took place before a single movement called attention to them. More important, "the quarrel of these groups is not with the idea of shared cultural experience but with the use of that idea as an excuse for inequality and injustice" (46). As the subtitle of Graff's book reflects, going beyond the "Culture Wars" will show how "teaching the conflicts can revitalize American education."

Yet Graff is very much concerned about the politicization of education. While he thinks that the traditional analytical philosophy solution that calls for professors to leave their political views out of the classroom is unhelpful, and perhaps even simplistic, he is concerned about slogans like "all teaching is political," an oblique, if clear, reference to the analysis of cultural workers connected with critical pedagogy. For instance:

> The same problem holds for the growing body of writing that calls for an oppositional curriculum, a transformative educational practice, a "pedagogy of the oppressed." This radical educational writing never stops to ask what is to be done with those teachers and students who do not wish to be radicalized. (Graff, 1992:169).

Similar laments occur when he explores the growing popularity of "cultural studies programs," in fact not a simple a concept that allows for connecting and integrating disciplines but a field that

> has become a euphemism for leftist studies. Though cultural studies seems to me a highly promising umbrella concept for connecting and integrating the disciplines, it can hardly serve that purpose—and it can certainly not live up to its democratic pretensions—if it excludes everyone from its orbit who does not already agree with leftist postulates about the political nature of culture. (169)

Yet, for Graff the thrust of multiculturalism is correct: to enhance the ability of building a curriculum that is not the expression of an immutable canon. Graff, ironically, reminds us that when Mahatma Gandhi was asked what he thought about Western culture, he replied that it was a good idea. Loose canons, as the Afro-American writer and literary critic Henry Louis Gates (1992) reminds us, are paradoxical because, as Graff (1992) argues, following Gates:

> The criterion of group expression that legitimated the American canon was considered perverse and offensive, however, when used to justify the expression of minority cultures. And today when blacks, Third World people, and others invoke the representation of group experience to claim value for their own literatures, they are reproved for replacing literary value with politics and demographic clout. It is a classic case of pulling the ladder up behind us once we have made it ourselves. (155–156)

Graff's argument is a well-known liberal argument, which, like it or not, has been central in supporting the expansion of multicultural education and has been criticized by critical race theorists like Ladson-Billings and Tate (1995), who note that the multicultural paradigm is "mired in liberal ideology that offers no radical change to the current order" (62). Graff's (1992) argument is that "our subjects earned their way into the curriculum on their own merits, but theirs are getting in only through political pressure, on a free handout or dole" (156).

Not surprisingly, I myself have been confronted with this situation several times in my academic career in the United States. Just a couple of vignettes will suffice to illustrate. When I was offered my present position, after an open international academic competition at UCLA in 1990, a senior professor of higher education at the University of California-Berkeley, now retired, was reported to have commented that the other candidate, a white, conservative professor from the SUNY system, lacked the "proper ethnicity for the appointment."

It really did not matter to him that the Graduate School of Education at UCLA, which in the early 1990s could hardly have been considered by any stretch of the imagination as an institution representative of multicultural education, selected me over the other candidate by near unanimity of votes of the faculty because, as I was told, my dossier, publication record, and research agenda were more impressive and my agenda would fit better with the programmatic goals of some key faculty.

A similar, yet reversed incident occurred four years later, when a group of faculty in a leading public university tried to recruit me for a senior position in education, in what was termed (with the dubious wisdom of academics) "a star search." When I topped the list of candidates of the search committee, a faculty member who was supportive of my candidacy was reported to have remarked that it was quite a fortunate coincidence that they could get in that position an excellent scholar who, at the same time, could improve their record in affirmative action. Needless to say, several faculty at that institution who are my friends suggested to me at the time—I concurred with them—that under those circumstances, even under the symbolic veiled threat that my appointment would not be made under the criterion of scholarly merit, there was no point in my pursuing the appointment.

While I never lost any sleep over these incidents, reading a telling story of Henry Louis Gates's childhood, I somehow understood my own feelings about these situations. In a wonderful testimonial book, literary critic Gates (1992) reports an incident in his childhood. One afternoon, after a brief encounter in a cafeteria, he complained to his father, asking why his father had been called "George" by Mr. Wilson, a quiet white of Piedmont, West Virginia, whom they had just greeted; Gates's father's name was not George. His father's response was that Mr. Wilson called all colored people George.

Gates's remembrance is instructive because he tells us that after this conversation with his father, "A long silence ensued. It was 'one of those things,' as my mom would put it. Even then, that early, I knew when I was in the presence of 'one of those things,' one of those things that provided a glimpse, through a rent curtain, at another world we could not affect but that affected us" (131).

What I have learned from my little vignettes of living in the United States is that since race is a social construct, and given the history of the racial formation in the United States, I am always subject to "one of those things." Yet, I shall adopt as my own the words of Robert S. Chang, a professor of law at California Western School of Law and a Korean immigrant, who said, "In the same way that I inherit a legacy of discrimination against Asian Americans [a term that could be changed to reflect the experience of any person of color], I also inherit a legacy of struggle" (1995:331).

Returning to the liberal construction of multiculturalism, I think it is best summed up by Graff (1992) when he argues that:

> Perhaps we should try to think of American culture as a conversation among different voices—even if it's a conversation that some of us weren't able to join until recently . . . [and education as] an invitation into the art of this conversation in which we learn to recognize the voices, each conditioned by a different perception of the world. Common sense says that you don't bracket 90 percent of the world's cultural heritage if you really want to learn about the world. . . . Common sense (Gramscian and otherwise) reminds us that we're all ethnic, and the challenge of transcending ethnic chauvinism is one we all face. (175)

Thus, the call for schools to provide the opportunity for dialogue across, among, and between different tribes. And the need to promote cultural tolerance based on cultural understandings: "the challenge facing America in the next century will be the shaping, at long last, of a truly common culture, one responsive to the long-silenced cultures of color. If we relinquish the ideal of America as a plural nation, we've abandoned the very experiment that America represents" (176).

Yet dialogue implies risks, including the possibility of the end of dialogue and thus the endless continuation of the conflict. The continuation of dialogue implies, at some point, an understanding that the premises that may have originated the dialogue are different—materially and symbolically—and that the locations of the different interlocutors in this dialogue are not only merely distinct but hierarchically different in terms of power, wealth, and prestige.[6] Indeed, to understand the act of dialogue is also to recognize the possibility of the incommensurability of discourses and the potential contradictions of self-interest. Finally, the very possibility of dialogue implies going beyond the need for cultural tolerance based on cultural understanding. It is imperative to situate such dialogue, tolerance, and understanding in the context of the political economy of the limits as well as the possibilities of citizenship, and in the context of the limits and possibilities of democracy in capitalist societies.

The public culture that Graff hopes to uphold, rebuild, and honor in multiculturalist America, which is becoming as transnational as the "Californian-ization" of youth taste, may in fact undermine the criticism that the ritualized invocation to "otherness" may be losing its capacity to engender new forms of knowledge, or that the critical position that Graff (1992) so easily classifies at the margins, "may have exhausted its strategic value as a position from which to theorize the very antinomies that produced it as an object of study" (192).

While intriguing, Graff's argument is self-defeating, first and foremost because critical studies are no longer at the fringes of the educational establishment in the United States. It is clear that their contributions are impacting quite heavily several arenas of educational intervention—more clearly in teacher education, for example, than in policymaking within the establishment. Additionally, if at worst the critical argumentation is losing ground, as Graff seems subtly to imply, or at best has reached its ceiling, there is no reason to believe that the political debates will continue to be confined to traditional schisms or that the political activism of social movements, community organizations, NGOs, and all sorts of institutions of civil society can be contained within the framework of the end of history that somebody like Fukuyama (1992) has advanced. Nor is there any indication that the political narratives of social movements should follow the same rules of logic, tolerance, and cultural understanding that Graff is calling for.

Despite his hypothesis that "teaching the conflicts can revitalize American education," Graff doesn't seem to recognize that the art of politics does not always follow the same rules as the art of education. While the overarching purpose in education is to persuade by using the best argument, theoretical reasoning, and available data, the overarching purpose of politics is to win, using the most effective means, whatever they are. Therefore, the dispute about multiculturalism is a dispute about the politics of identity and the politics of culture, and the neoconservative critique has taken on a life of its own, almost as a crusade against multiculturalism as a social movement.

Multiculturalism as Crusade: The Neoconservative Critique

> From the bottom to the top of the system, professional social reformers abound.
> They are more interested in equality than in excellence. . . . The war for the
> public school will be fought at the local level, where parents and back-to-basics
> educators find themselves in alliance with a conservative White House.
> —Peter Brimelow, "Shock Waves from Whoops Roll East"

Neoconservatives would argue that multiculturalism is a plot against the dominant cultural canon and a crusade for the fulfillment of key demands of ethnic groups. Right-wing academics and politicians usually link debates about political correctness with what they consider to be a homogeneous program of multiculturalism. Similarly, other enemies of multiculturalism argue against a "cult of multiculturalism," which they consider a representative of the cultural politics of identity (of different ethnicities or special interest groups). Moreover, the critics charge that the multiculturalism movement displays a strong "Europhobia" that will undermine the unity and common culture of the American nation.

As is clear, in a neoconservative analysis of social science curriculum in the United States, liberal and progressive intellectuals are blamed for the ills of American society and for the perception that multiculturalism undermines the basis of American civilization by focusing on the needs of a specific social group:

> Progressive and New Deal intellectuals adopted the working class as their
> favorite underdog group and, as we saw in the case of Herbert Croly, John
> Dewey, Charles A. Beard, and V. L. Parrington, favored democratic socialism as
> the embodiment of a fulfilled promise of American life and as the cure for the
> capitalist disease. More recently, as the socialist dream has faded, but the hostility to our civilization remains, we witness the promotion of race and sex as
> defining the key underdog groups meriting special support and reward. (Lerner,
> Nagai, and Rothman, 1995:155)

Indeed, insists Giroux (1988), the critics usually embrace a form of nationalism, and "rather than analyzing multiculturalism as a complex, legitimate, and necessary on-going negotiation among minorities against assimilation . . . see in the engagements of cultural difference less a productive tension than a debilitating divisiveness" (50).

The least extreme forms of the antimulticulturalism movement see the politics of difference as a threat to patriotism, nationalism, national unity, and traditional values, while the most extreme forms see the politics of difference as a threat to the Christian values of the American nation or to the immaculate white European racial heritage of the country (Giroux, 1997).

Thus the critique of multiculturalism is part of the program of the New Right. If choice is the knight in shining armor of the neoconservative state, as I argued in chapter 2, multiculturalism is its nemesis. It is common knowledge that in the 1980s in the United States, race was effectively used by the Reagan and Bush administrations to construct and hold together a new neoconservative majority. In education, this strategy involved addressing the intractable issues of multiculturalism. No doubt many neoconservatives are "Eurocentric" in that they deny or place in secondary positions the legitimacy of historical and symbolic constructions of ethnic and national groups other than the dominant white or European culture. However, as West (1993a) so persuasively argues, opposing multiculturalism to Eurocentrism obscures the theoretical and political treatment of the issue.

West (1993a) argues, with his textured and knowledgeable style, that we must move beyond the debate about multiculturalism and Eurocentrism

> because it means from the very beginning we must call into question any notions of pure traditions or pristine heritage, or any civilization or culture having a monopoly on virtue or insight. . . . the very terms themselves, multiculturalism and Eurocentrism, are not analytical categories, they are categories to be analyzed with a nuanced historical sense, and also a subtle social analysis. (4)

Traditional arguments define the sources of Western thought in the production of European, male, and heterosexual thinkers; their basic premise is the call for canonical texts as the foundation of liberal education. One may expect that after much public debate, recalcitrant, one-sided, and unidimensional versions of Eurocentrism once prominent in the neoconservative movement will lose ground to the neoconservative positions on cultural diversity and multiculturalism in the United States. Yet, hints of Eurocentrism flare up occasionally in movements like the English Only movement in California. However, the dispute, even within neoconservative quarters, is not clear-cut given that neoconservatism is an unstable amalgam of diverse groups and an alliance of diverse constituencies. For instance, debates in the Republican Party about Propositions 187 and 209 in California, which limit illegal immigrants' access to public services, are a good example of the complexity of the issues involved and the different positions taken in neoconservative quarters.

Neoconservative intellectuals have tried to address the importance of multiculturalism for American education, opposing ethnic multiculturalism to cultural pluralism and arguing for the advantages of the latter over the dangerous trends of the former. While accepting that multiculturalism in the United States is a "recognition of the sensitivities of ethnic or racial minorities, [it should not] be confused with cultural pluralism. . . . [E]thnic groups should be maintained as identifiable constituents of the American nation because of the unique contributions they make to the richness and variety of American culture" (Safran, 1994:69).

Although neoconservatives accept that notions of cultural pluralism may have a racialist dimension because they blur together race, culture, and nationality, they do not find cultural pluralism, unlike the majority of approaches to multiculturalism, ethnoracial. As William Safran (1994) says:

> While most proponents of cultural pluralism fully accept a "national" culture—usually that of the majority—as superordinate, that is, as one that serves a vehicle of interethnic communication, multiculturalism often tends to be culturally isolationist or "separatist." Moreover, many proponents of multiculturalism believe that their minority ethnic culture is not only equal but superior to that of the majority. While cultural pluralism is conservative, multiculturalism is radical in that it rejects long-established cultural traditions that the dominant as well as minority elites have wished to conserve. Yet cultural pluralism may be a force for modernity because it accords a place to ethnic minority cultures that may in certain instances be more advanced than the culture of the majority, whereas multiculturalism is antimodern to the extent that it stresses affirmative action and ascriptive (as opposed to merit-based) recruitment. (69–70)

Needless to say, this position contrasts starkly with James Banks's (1993, 1997) argument that multicultural education strives to provide all students— regardless of their gender, ethnicity, race, culture, social class, religion, or exceptionality—with educational quality in the schools. In addition, multicultural education, as predicated by Banks, seeks to eliminate school discrimination, placing multiculturalism as a reform movement growing out of the civil rights and protest movements of the 1960s and 1970s, and constituting an international reform movement that tries to help students and teachers "develop positive attitudes toward racial, cultural, ethnic, and language diversity" (Banks, 1993:3).

Not surprisingly, in the neoconservative vision, multiculturalism is a unified movement. This view contrasts sharply with the typical liberal analysis of multi-culturalism as expression of cultural diversity and political programs and an arena for confrontation of alternative views between agency and structural relationships, particularly the dynamics of race, ethnicity, culture, class, and gender in American education. Thus, for neoconservatives, ethnoracial multiculturalism (i.e., a view of multiculturalism anchored in notions of the social construction of ethnicity, race, culture, and nationality) is antimodern because it skews meritocracy and credentialism and states its claims based on ascriptive status, tradition, and the politics of identity rather than merit. Safran's (1994) remarks resonate with the common neoconservative complaint advanced by Lerner, Nagai, and Rothman (1995) that multiculturalism is parochial, lacks universalism, and constitutes another instance of the force of the political correctness movement in academia and educational settings:

> During the late 1960s, student uprisings and university disruptions permanently transformed the American university. The growth and spread of the New Left on the United States's college and university campuses helped legitimate the sense that all American institutions, including education, suffered from major failings, which required radical change. In response to the protest, many policies were adopted by colleges and universities: codes allowing much greater student self-expression, grade inflation, less regard for traditional academic standards, the abolition of requirements, the near abolition of general education, and the creation of new departments of black, and, later, women's studies. These measures assumed that if universities abolished requirements and lowered grading standards, primary and secondary schools might as well follow suit. And so they did. (Safran, 1994:44)

Multiculturalism is also seen as an expression of the excessive power of the women's movement and feminism in undermining a common curriculum in schools, but above all it is seen as undermining the very quality of education. Empirical research on the issue by Lerner, Nagai, and Rothman (1995) concludes, from a typical neoconservative approach, that:

> Textbooks changed rapidly. Michael Kirst, in describing his experiences as a member of the California State Board of Education who wanted to raise the level of textbooks, reported that as of 1980, no publisher had a book both exhibiting high academic standards and meeting feminist criteria: The old books were sexist, while the newer books were dumbed down. (43)

For neoconservatives, the groups responsible for promoting multiculturalism are the same classroom teachers who have become extremely proactive in American education, lacking constraints on their actions. As Lerner, Nagai, and Rothman (1995) argue: "The issues we examine, together with the evidence we record, suggest the presence of a factor of enormous importance in shaping America's political and civil culture: The outlook and convictions of the nation's educators. If only by default, American educators have assumed great powers that deserve public scrutiny." (5)

Feminism, for neoconservatives, is certainly responsible for this situation:

> The findings of Diane Ravitch and Chester E. Finn Jr. (1987) suggest a considerable feminist influence over what high school students in the United States

read. The paradox is that Americans believe that education is controlled at the local level. And yet, clearly, the push for feminist changes did not come from parents and local school board members. (Lerner, Nagai, and Rothman, 1995:55)

Moreover, the problem is seen as a "technical" historical problem. That is, there are not enough examples of female presence in history because history has been made mostly by males (who are the heroes, soldiers, statesmen, etc.). From this standpoint, neoconservatives regret that with the overreaching power of the political correctness movement, they have attempted to solve this lack of female presence in history through a simplistic political solution that Lerner, Nagai, and Rothman call "filler feminism," ignoring the historical fact or truth of the workings of males in history:

> There is one major problem, however, in writing nonsexist history textbooks. Most of American history is male-dominated, in part because women in most states were not allowed to vote in federal elections or hold office until the twentieth century. This is regrettable, but it is still a fact. What, then, is the "nonsexist" writer of the American history textbook to do? The answer is "filler feminism"—accentuating the importance of minor characters and events without completely limiting coverage of the major persons and events of the standard panorama of American history. (56)

Multiculturalism is seen not only as a crusade but also as an attempt to develop workforce diversity, which is seen as the political correctness movement's final frontier (Lynch, 1995:32).

Linda Chavez has written extensively in her attempt to demystify multiculturalism. For Chavez (1994), multiculturalism is based on a wrong demographic premise, that the white population is rapidly declining compared to the nonwhite population. Second, there is also a blurring of the distinction between race and culture: "multiculturalists insist on treating race and ethnicity as if they were synonymous with culture" (26). A central assumption of multiculturalism—thoroughly rejected by neoconservatives like Chavez—is that there is no common American culture. In fact, she sees as a distinguishing characteristic of this culture the ability to incorporate many disparate groups, creating a new whole from separate parts. For Chavez, this culture has proven so powerful that the several waves of immigrants who have come to the United States have adapted and assimilated to the point that in their second or third generation they no longer conserve the language of, or even strong ties with, their nations of origin: "Ironically, the multiculturalists' emphasis on education undercuts their argument that culture is inextricable from race or national origin. . . . [T]hey seem to believe that without a heavy dose of multicultural indoctrination, immigrants won't be able to resist" assimilation to American culture" (30).

While blaming some multiculturalists for their strategies and end result, the disuniting of America, Chavez believes that multiculturalism is not an autonomous grassroots movement. On the contrary, it "was created, nurtured, and expanded through government policy" (32). That is to say, multicultural-ism is also another creature, or at least a by-product, of the welfare state and the excesses of liberalism in the Democratic Party. She states unequivocally that "it is easy to blame the ideologues and radicals who are pushing the dis-uniting of America, to use Arthur Schlesinger's phrase, but the real culprits are those who provide multiculturalists the money and the access to press their cause" (32).

The use of race as part of the divide-and-conquer strategy of the neocon-servative state has not been subtle. Given the complexities of curricula in mul-tilingual, multiethnic, and multicultural societies like the United States, neo-conservatives had to agree at some point that teaching about heroes, holidays, and achievements of ethnic minorities has a wide appeal to ethnic pride. Yet, the debate on multiculturalism and the promotion of a multicultural curricu-lum is, in the view of neoconservatives (Safran, 1994), purely self-serving and opportunistic:

These policies may provide jobs for ethnic minority intellectuals and adminis-trators; in order to justify their positions—and the maintenance of the new eth-nic minority bureaucracy—they may seek to attract a large enough clientele by appealing to the lowest common denominator, for example, by offering courses on Chicano cuisine and dance (vestigial or nostalgic ethnicity) and socioeco-nomic problems in the *barrio* (oppression studies) rather than the Spanish lan-guage and literature. In order to gain tactical allies, the purveyors of multicul-turalism often make common cause with non-ethnic multiculturalists by mixing courses on ethnic culture with those on gender-specific (for example, feminist) culture and the culture of alternative life styles. While these approaches seek to undermine the dominance of the majority culture, they are ultimately counter-productive for the ethnic minority because they may cancel each other out and undermine the clarity and prestige of its culture. (69–70)

Lamenting the loss of "purity" and "prestige" of a culture, or the decline in its social efficacy, the multicultural strategy of neoconservatives highlights dif-ferences and accepts the notion of diversity as long as these different cultural groups agree to shape their identities in reference to an acceptable canon. This canon can be defined either in terms of prescribed cultural literacy, a superor-dinate culture, or acceptable and recommended political fervor and behavior, such as patriotism. Borrowing a page from the liberal prescription on tolerance in cultural encounters, pragmatic/utilitarian neoconservatives (as opposed to doctrinaire ones) define the war of cultures in the United States as creating insurmountable contradictions in the construction of uniform identities, unless we choose the only option to avoid the chaos resulting from cultural strife: identifying firm principles or foundations that every culture may refer to in the national context.

The neoconservative argument welcomes internal and self-destructive strife among minority groups, as well as any attempt to define monolithic, singular cultural identities. Borrowing from Tocqueville's most conservative views, neoconservatives lament the loss of purity in the culture and the fact that no bulwarks remain:

> In aristocratic societies, the ruling class, the one that gives the tone to opinion and takes the lead in public affairs, is placed above the crowd and thinks highly of itself. These opinions and the honor associated with them impel men of learning toward learning for its own sake—what Tocqueville calls "a sublime, almost a divine love of truth." (Lerner, Nagai, and Rothman, 1995:462)

Neoconservatives would argue that in the United States today, the teaching profession, dominated by liberal and egalitarian ideologies, has taken an adversarial stance towards the American canon. At the same time, the country lacks some of the tools that Tocquevillians imagine would avoid the proliferation of the vices of democracy. Thus "the teaching of history, at least from the evidence of high school history texts, is increasingly dominated by radical egalitarians. Given recent changes in American society and culture, this is not likely to change in the near future" (Lerner, Nagai, and Rothman, 1995:157).

The latest rendition of the neoconservative critique, however, has turned the tables of the discourse, arguing, from a neoconservative pragmatic perspective, that the problem has gone away because, as the title of Nathan Glazer's (1997) new book so clearly puts it, "we are all multiculturalists now." And so, it seems, a neoconservative crusade against multiculturalism is a futile effort, and systemic co-optation may run its course. When a concept is threatening or points to dangerous tides that some people may try to stem, there are few better strategies than co-optation and incorporation into the mainstream discourse of choice.

Nathan Glazer starts with the assumption that, after a historical push for cultural recognition, multiculturalism is here to stay. Indeed, in pushing to accept the notion of cultural diversity, Glazer (1997) contends that "black students are the heart of the matter" (9). His argument is that

When I say multiculturalism has won, and that "we are all multiculturalists now," I mean that we all now accept a greater degree of attention to minorities and women and their role in American history and social studies and literature classes in schools. Those few who want to return American education to a period in which the various subcultures were ignored, and in which America was presented as the peak and end-product of civilization, cannot expect to make any progress in the schools. (14)

Yet, the idea of America has been a complete success in the view of Glazer, and he can but state as forcefully as he can, though with a nostalgic edge:

I emphasize the inescapability of the phase we are now through in American education and society in our centuries-old encounter with the questions of American racial and ethnic difference. It is not a phase we can embrace wholeheartedly, and I hope my own sense of regret that we have had to come to this will not escape the reader. (21).

The devil of implementing multiculturalism in the school curriculum is, therefore, in the details. Glazer (1997) concludes that after the emotional tenor of the discussion is abandoned, in the end certain objectives of education are pursued by both multiculturalist advocates and their opponents. These include "higher educational achievement for all groups, a measure of civil harmony, competence in performing the tasks that are basic to economic productivity. All of these require other qualities such as truthfulness, responsibility, ability to communicate" (83).

One may hardly disagree with these laudable goals, and yet Glazer's pragmatic neoconservatism needs further refinement to be fully accepted by the most liberal and radical factions of the multiculturalist movement. A premise of the analysis is that the movement previously known as cultural pluralism is now called multiculturalism. This is, from a political, ethical, and epistemological perspective, simply an illusion (Glazer, 1997:97). The issue now is not that the politics of identity leads to politics of recognition but that there is an important difference between tolerance of difference and the acceptance of the politics of identity, including growing demands of social movements for changes in the social power structure (in terms of class, gender, and race) to accommodate the demands of the feminist movement, subaltern spaces, or critical race theory, as I discussed in chapter 4.

A careful exploration of theories of the state in education helps us to identify and criticize the pitfalls and analytical gaps of positions embraced by neoconservative intellectuals. It is particularly instructive to see how multiculturalism in education is considered by neoconservatives a separatist movement damaging the social fabric of American society. And more instructive is to compare this argument with the arguments of the left (which I outline below) and critical race theorists (explained in chapter 4) that, on the contrary, see the dominant liberal multiculturalism movement as working on behalf of the white, conservative establishment.

Taking into account these weak aspects of the neoconservative argument, it is clear how neoconservatives see cultural pluralism as making use of the resources of multicultural societies while still selecting individuals by achievement and performance. What is fascinating about the secular and moderate neoconservatives is that, like neoliberals, they favor free trade and advocate the globalization of cultures and economies because globalization improves the mobility of capital. But to their dismay, globalization—as I explained in chapter 3—also increases the mobility of labor. Thus, it is paradoxical that they resent immigration and multiculturalism, which are the other side of the coin of promoting the globalization of economies. Yet globalization definitely does not necessarily mean global-mindedness. Moreover, for Christian fundamentalists and other extremely conservative factions within neoconservatism, globalization is not always a welcome process—another expression of the contradictions within the neoconservative movement.

Yet, multiculturalism as a vehicle of selective social mobility cannot be avoided in the logic of the neoconservative state. For neoconservatives, the resolution of the debate on multiculturalism cannot, ironically, be left to the operation of the logic of the market. Neoconservatives seek to establish a basic knowledge, an official knowledge to which all cultures should be exposed in order to mold their cultural understandings while keeping their folkloric character. However, as one critic has said, every definition of knowledge is a site for conflict "over the relations between culture and power in class, race, gender, and religious terms" (Apple, 1993a:5). For neoconservatives, individual responsibility and choice are the basis for cultural performance in dynamic markets. There is, however, an important tension: If the market is left unchecked and a vigorous debate occurs in the different scenarios of culture, the moral commitments of different cultures could eventually mold individual responsibility and choice.

Because neoconservatives have used the politics of race as an effective tool for disintegration and fragmentation and as a policy of divide and conquer in U.S. politics, the notion of "otherness" has been employed as a wild card in "exporting" the blame for the failure of neoconservative policies to less powerful communities. Fragmentation and conflict between different factions of multicultural movements is acceptable and even encouraged in neoconservative quarters; multiracial coalitions and social movements for equality and radical democracy are not.[7] Critical multiculturalists would be deemed separatists by neoconservatives.

Moreover, there is reluctance in many parts of the establishment as outlined in the work of Therstrom and Therstrom (1997) to accept that racial segregation still exists in schools, that domination and oppression are pervasive in America society, and by implication, in schools, and that domination and oppression affect not only blacks but also a large variety of social and racial groups.

The discussion on whiteness outlined earlier, following the analyses of Giroux, McLaren, and others, is anathema in many neoconservative quarters. Likewise, the notion, propagated by Therstrom and Therstrom (1997), for instance, that America in black and white is one and indivisible is nothing but another exercise in historical consciousness building trying to show how a successful society can be built without considering that institutional racism has played a major role in the constitution of American capitalism. Therstrom and Therstrom's (1997) argument overlooks the fact that the democratic ethos has been thwarted by capitalist social relations and hierarchies. Finally, they do not seem to recognize that, in the end, social movements are not only trying to accommodate specific demands within the established structures (e.g., the politics of recognition of specific ethnic groups, or the politics of identity), and therefore simply enhancing the quality of educational opportunity, but that several factions of the multiculturalist movement are arguing for radical democracy and substantive systemic change, as outlined in chapter 5, with the notion of democracy as content and participatory democracy. The liberal response, therefore, has not been much different from neoconservative pragmatism. The critics on the left, however, blame multiculturalists for conflating race, class, and gender and for overlooking the contributions of the Enlightenment.

Class, Race, and Enlightenment: Critiques from the Left

The far ranging investigation of university practices—curricular change, admissions standards, financial aid, fellowship awards, disciplinary codes, hiring and tenure procedures, teaching loads, time spent on research, accreditation standards, even, I would argue, the investigation of the misuse of overhead funds—are all attempts to delegitimize the philosophical and institutional bases from which social and cultural criticism have traditionally come. We are experiencing another phase of the ongoing Reagan-Bush revolution which, having packed the courts and privatized the economy, now seeks to neutralize the space of ideological and cultural nonconformity by discrediting it. This is the context within which debates about political correctness and multiculturalism have taken shape.

—Joan W. Scott,"Multiculturalism and the Politics of Identity"

It would be impossible to try to synthesize the vast gamut of criticisms from the left to the key brands of multiculturalism, both within and outside the multiculturalism movement. I have selected only a few examples representing diverse positions illustrating the kinds of criticisms that multiculturalism, both as a social movement and as multicultural education, face from the new and the old left.

Some critics from the left, such as Cameron McCarthy, present a critical assessment of conservative and liberal, multicultural, and neo-Marxist approaches to the problem of racial inequality in education, emphasizing the nonsynchronous and even contradictory relationships between class, race, and gender (McCarthy and Apple, 1988:9–39). McCarthy (1993:289–305) argues that "multiculturalism is not a solution to the race problem, boldly stating that multiculturalism is the product of a particular historical conjuncture of relations among the state, contending racial minority and majority groups, and policy intellectuals in the United States when the discourse over schools became increasingly racialized" (289).

McCarthy recognizes that multiculturalism as a social movement is grounded on the legitimate desires of people of color to overcome the perils of assimilation into the dominant culture while addressing the risks that people of color have in facing the barriers of discrimination, oppression, and domination.[8] He also agrees with the best intentions of the proponents of multiculturalism and addresses head-on the reconstruction of the curriculum that challenges the official knowledge that ignores the history of, and symbolic production by, people of color. For McCarthy, multicultural education as curriculum reform "must address issues of representation as well as issues of unequal distribution of material resources and power outside the school door" (291).

Yet, multiculturalism is faulted because some factions in the movement have been "sucked back" into the system, as McCarthy (1993) so candidly says: "proponents of multicultural education 'claw back' from the radical themes associated with subaltern challenges to the white dominated school curriculum and school system, emphasizing instead a normative rhetoric that accepts the broad structural and cultural parameters and values of American society and the American way" (290).

Hence, mainstream multicultural traditions do not challenge the capitalist organization of society. Instead, "It is the nonthreatening social centrality of the 'good bourgeois' life for the minority poor that the multiculturalist ultimately seeks to promote" (290).

This criticism is similar to the one pronounced by critical race theorists such as Ladson-Billings and Tate (1995), who criticized multiculturalism as having been sucked back into the system and having the same deficiencies as traditional civil rights law. They claim that multiculturalism's liberal foundations offer no challenge to the existing social order and therefore offer no radical solutions to the social, economic, and political problems associated with discrimination, inequality, and exploitation. Current practices of multiculturalism, the criticism goes, reduce the model to trivial cultural examples promoting respect and tolerance; but few discussions, if any, take place that identify the growing tensions that exist between and among the various groups professing a multiculturalist affiliation. Therefore, for Ladson-Billings and Tate (1995) two problems remain. First, is the fact that "the ever-expanding multicultural paradigm follows the traditions of liberalism—allowing a proliferation of difference. Unfortunately, the tension between and among these differences is rarely interrogated, presuming a 'unity of difference'—that is, that all difference is both analogous and equivalent" (62).

Second, there is a parallel analogy between multiculturalism and traditional civil rights law. Critical race theorists have doubts about the foundations of traditional civil rights law and multiculturalism because they do not challenge property rights. Thus, "without disrespect to the pioneers of civil rights law, critical race legal scholars document the ways in which civil rights law is regularly subverted to benefit whites. We argue that the current multicultural paradigm functions in a manner similar to civil rights law" (Ladson-Billings and Tate, 1995:62).

Examples of this position abound. For instance, a few years ago, a multiculturalist organization from East Los Angeles, the Boyle Heights Elementary Institute, was funded through private philanthropy and operated by enthusiastic promoters of equality of educational opportunity for Latino children. It turned out to be an efficient, self-sustaining operation, and a number of undergraduate and graduate students at UCLA work at Boyle Heights either as volunteers or as staff. One of the goals of the institute is to enhance the ability and opportunity of fifth- and sixth-graders to meet, upon graduation from high school, the standards of the University of California system, which takes, by law, 12.5 percent of California high school graduates, although first choice of campus is not guaranteed.

A group of Spanish-speaking parents from the institute were invited to join an academic event coordinated by UCLA graduate students and including faculty participation and the participation of tutors from the institute. The astonishment of the several Spanish-speaking Latino mothers and the single father who attended the event was evident. In her opening comments, the spokesperson for the group, a humble but vibrant woman from El Salvador, told us that although they were coming from East Los Angeles—UCLA is located in west Los Angeles, in one of the most expensive real estate areas of southern California, and the rumor is that this district has the highest concentration of Rolls-Royces per capita in the world—they were not thugs but honest people. After asserting her dignity as a working woman, she told us that immediately upon entering the campus, she felt the need to kiss the ground she was walking on, because she never thought that a person of her origins would even be able to come to UCLA. She then confessed a deep desire that her children would be able to attend such a prestigious university, that being the reason she was involved with the Boyle Heights Elementary Institute.

The conversation, conducted in Spanish, turned to analysis of what would make it possible for children from poor, immigrant, and Spanish-speaking Latino backgrounds to attend the university and why obtaining a university education was important. Another mother from East Los Angeles stood up and said that she always told her son that her neighbor who went to the university has a wonderful, brand-new, red sports car. She emphasized to him that by going to the university, he would have the opportunity to reach the neighbor's level of consumption and buy a similar fancy car.

Nobody challenged the assumption, not even I. For a long time I have been pondering why some of us who were present in that room, and who consider that higher education is not merely a ticket to the "capitalist good life" (although it is certainly a key element in the social mobility for people of color in the United States, as Martin Carnoy [1994] has empirically documented), did not challenge her views in a democratic conversation.

Perhaps it was the celebration of popular knowledge *tout court* and the sense that academics in the United States are, in fact, enjoying the benefits of managerial capitalism that may blind us to the possibility of challenging her views. After all, why deny to the rest of the world what one can indeed obtain with an acceptable credit record and a permanent job?

Perhaps it was that many of us in that room had had a brand-new sports car, red or otherwise, like the one she wanted for her son, and therefore the prevailing assumption was not to challenge capitalism as a system of commodity production and consumption but to enhance the ability of the poor to consume along the same lines as the middle class does—as McCarthy believes of some brands of multiculturalism do. Perhaps it was the expectation that the motivation of buying a brand-new red car at the end of his university studies would encourage the son of a poor, Spanish-speaking immigrant from East Los Angeles to enter the public democratic sphere of the university and encounter the kind of democratic discourse that some of us hope to promote and that could indeed change the world.

Perhaps nobody challenged her because there was the important obstacle of the "symbolic" social distance between university professors and people from the popular sectors, as Freire (1997a) has argued. Had the event taken place in Latin America, most likely the people from socially subordinate sectors would have been collaborating with some university professors in projects of popular education,[9] which is not unlike the case of some of us working with community organizations in the greater Los Angeles area, and hence faculty and parents would have a different conversation, one based on a notion that while they were not equals (a liberal dream), they were *compañeros* in the same process of struggle. Under those conditions, dialogue and open exchange might be facilitated and the "symbolic" distance bridged to the point that academic authority, while included in popular education, is not without checks and balances and becomes just another resource in the democratic conversation.

Whatever the explanation, I am still haunted by this image of a red, brand-new sports car as a multicultural device to create incentives for increased academic performance of male Latino students.

McCarthy (1993) argues that multiculturalists vary in the way representatives of the movement understand the connections between race, culture, and diversity. He identifies three key brands. The first, which he links with a relativistic perspective, is interested mainly in promoting cultural understanding and awareness. The second, which he identifies with a cultural pluralist perspective, mainly sees multiculturalism as a movement engaged in enhancing cultural competence. A third brand, which goes beyond the previous two, is identified as "cultural emancipation," similar to the Boyle Heights Elementary Institute's aims. It tries to bolster the educational success and economic future of youth through a reformist multicultural curriculum. Without denying the potential (yet limited) benefits of these strategies, McCarthy (1993) still notes critically that: "Multicultural educators who promote the idea of cultural emancipation . . . hold a great deal of faith in the redemptive qualities of the educational system and its capacities to influence positive changes in the job market and in the society" (292).

McCarthy's central criticism is that the three types of multicultural discourse mentioned above, while differing in emphasis, still place an enormous significance on the role of attitudes in the constitution and reproduction of racism. Attitudinal and cognitive behavioral change is what is sought, but for McCarthy these aims fall short of what is needed.

McCarthy (1993) argues that schools should, first of all, be conceptualized as sites of power and contestation in which different racial groups have differential access: "In significant ways, too, the proponents of multiculturalism fail to take into account the differential structure of opportunities that helps to define race relations in the United States" (293). Second, he points out that the complexity of coding and decoding race relations occasionally causes cognitive and attitudinal changes through sensitivity training to backfire, so that they do not produce the intended goals. Third, a focus on attitudinal change does not pursue the goal that, for McCarthy (1993), should be the starting point in rethinking multiculturalism: "the interrogation of the discourse of the Eurocentric basis of the American school curriculum that links the U.S. to Europe and to 'Western Civilization'" (294).

Endorsing what he terms a "critical emancipatory multiculturalism," McCarthy (1993, 1998) suggests several avenues to accomplish this model. First and foremost, a thorough critique of the Eurocentrism and Western-ness of the American school curriculum is required. Next, it is necessary to insist on both the centrality of the notion of diversity for the school curriculum and the inherent relationality of diversity. School curriculum is deeply linked to human interests and implicated in unequal social relations. American schools, while immersed in local dynamics, benefit from the global dynamics of inequity that characterize the workings of an increasingly globalized world system, in which there are privileged actors who have unequal relationships with peripheral nations.

Without considering the issue of ideological representation of dominant and subordinate groups in education and popular culture (particularly the media), a task that McCarthy has undertaken in his recent book *The Uses of Culture* (1998), a true multicultural curriculum cannot be accomplished. This issue of ideological representation must take into account the important conditions that: (a) "minority cultural identities are not fixed or monolithic but multivocal, and even contradictory" (McCarthy, 1993:290); and (b) there are issues related to the contradictory location, particularly with the emergence of a "new" black and brown middle class (for instance, the discussions about the "black bourgeoisie"), and the role of neoconservative black and white intellectuals (Lawrence-Lightfoot, 1994: 5–9, 296). McCarthy (1993) is very clear about the fact that "you cannot read off the political behavior of minority groups from assumptions about race pure and simple. Different class interests within minority groups often cut at right angles to racial politics" (298).

Following the works of Bob Connell,[10] McCarthy (1993) comes to the conclusion that a standpoint theory should be used to articulate a critical emancipatory multicultural curriculum and draw from common learning:

> A critical multicultural curriculum, which emphasizes anti-racist and anti-sexist change and social reorganization and utilizes the points of view and experiences of oppressed minorities and working-class women and men as the primary bases for a core curriculum, would constitute a fundamental step in the direction of preparing students for democratic participation in a complex and differential world. (301)

However, McCarthy's "common learning" approach should be mindful of Freire's word of caution in *Pedagogy of the Oppressed,* that the oppressor also resides in the consciousness of the oppressed.[11] Hence multicultural educators should not reify the oppressed through an activism that alienates them by telling through "communiqués"—so brilliantly criticized by Paulo Freire (1973) in his work on extensionism—what they are, who they are, and how they can overcome their condition. Nor should multicultural educators acritically celebrate popular knowledge and popular wisdom as if the weltanschauung of the subordinate sectors is immune to capitalist hegemonic common sense and meritocratic ideology, an approach that Freire (1997a) defined as "basism." Moreover, for McCarthy, a critical emancipatory multicultural curriculum built on standpoint theory should recognize that knowledge is socially constructed and relational in nature and heterogeneous and that the interconnections between knowledge and power should be assessed through deconstructive and relational analysis.

In critical dialogue with some of the key insights of McCarthy, Peter McLaren proposes a project of critical multiculturalism that he calls revolutionary multiculturalism. In a chapter suggestively entitled "Unthinking Whiteness, Rethinking Democracy," McLaren postulates revolutionary multiculturalism not just as multicultural education but as a whole social movement that aims to recognize the political economy that materially structures our lives, the relations of production in which we are all situated, and the material and symbolic conditions that produce our subjectivity and are reflected in our lived experience. In language reminiscent of the discussions in the 1960s about the need to change revolutionarily rather than to reform social relations, McLaren (1997b) claims:

> Revolutionary multiculturalism is a socialist-feminist multiculturalism that challenges those historically sedimented processes through which race, class, and gender identities are produced within capitalist society. Therefore, revolutionary multiculturalism is not limited to transforming attitudinal discrimination but is dedicated to reconstituting the deep structures of political economy, culture, and power in contemporary social arrangements. It is not about reforming capitalist democracy but rather transforming it by cutting at its joints and then rebuilding the social order from the vantage point of the oppressed. (287)

This perspective is based on a reading of the contradictions between the local and the global in the new political economy with a post-Fordist mode of industrial organization and on a belief that racial formations like the United States, particularly in some localities like Los Angeles, are ready to blow up. A major flaw in McLaren's analysis is his equating the process of globalization with neoliberal capitalism and globalization with post-Fordism. With this blanket assessment of the complexities of the political economy of capitalism, he is left with virtually no political options other than a call for revolution and apocalypse. For McLaren, the time is ripe for the construction of a new language that will help not only in constituting new identities but also in transforming—perhaps even through violence—the actual conditions of racial, gender, and class exchanges in capitalist societies. McLaren wants to move multiculturalism and critical pedagogy beyond the threshold of liberal pluralism in the direction of a revolutionary democracy, and he sees the contradictions and dynamics of class, race, and gender as contributors to this revolutionary end (see McLaren, 1997b:294–304). However, the political conditions that will facilitate this revolution, the sociological analysis of which actors are pursuing revolutionary options in the context of a society like the United States, and what policy options for educational reform can be pursued are all but ignored. Good intentions, I am afraid, do not guarantee good theory.

A very different perspective from the old New Left is presented by Todd Gitlin (1995). Arguing that the dynamics of identity politics are self-confirming, Gitlin claims that there is a tendency towards a fundamentalist identity culture and that "today's cultivation of cultural difference tends to detract from majoritarian thinking" (163). Moreover,

> many exponents of identity politics are fundamentalists—in the language of the academy, "essentialists"—and the belief in essential group differences easily swerves toward a belief in superiority. In the hardest version of identity thinking, women are naturally cooperative, Africans naturally inventive, and so on. . . . Essentialists, when they secede from the commons, dismantle it. (165)

This criticism of the politics of identity as essentialist is supplemented by a harsh view of standpoint theory. This approach, standpoint theory, an epistemological perspective nourished in the ranks of the feminist movement, is defined by Nel Noddings (1995) as follows:

> Many feminists deny that knowledge claims are somehow vitiated when they are colored by the personal aims and interests of the knower. Often called "standpoint" epistemologists, these thinkers insist that a certain privilege is acquired by those who experience oppression. Thus, women have access to privileged knowledge with respect to issues of gender, the poor with respect to poverty, blacks and other ethnic minorities with respect to race, and perhaps students with respect to schooling. Notice that whereas many philosophers agree that scientific knowledge can be and probably is contaminated with such influences, standpoint theorists do not believe that we get closer to "truth" by confessing our biases and rooting them out. On the contrary, they claim that such standpoint-laden claims and reports are epistemically richer and more accurate than those generated through traditionally objective methods. (183)

Gitlin (1995), offering exactly the reverse criticism of what McCarthy sees as the only choice for a radical critical emancipatory multicultural curriculum, argues that even though the politics of identity, in the words of Canadian philosopher Charles Taylor, "grow organically out of the politics of universal dignity," standpoint theory deeply undermines the notion of universality that it tries to rescue. Gitlin (1995) continues:

> The most common form of this argument today is so-called standpoint feminism, the idea that so-called objectivity and so-called emancipation are nothing but the trappings of the imperial masculine ego at work, consuming, obliterating, or paving over everything in its path. In this view, patriarchy's rage to rule is the inevitable consequence of the Cartesian illusion that the mind is separate from the body and hovers in free space, like God's eye, treating the world as an object. At the root of male supremacy and ecological disaster alike lies the false assumption that the world has no life of its own but exists for the pleasure and conquest of the (white, Western, heterosexist) male ego. (214)

Perhaps Gitlin's criticism is too one-sided, conflating standpoint theory into a tool of feminism when in fact it can be used as an epistemological tool per se, asking "who is speaking?" As Noddings (1995) notes, black feminists put greater emphasis on the experiential credentials of the speaker/knower and correspondingly less on the speaker's argument (183).

Thus, the argument is judged not only in terms of its internal logic or verisimilitude but also in terms of its commitment and engagement of the speaker. This viewpoint may lead to a serious conundrum: how to weigh experience vis-à-vis traditional argument or objectivity and what place logic, internal articulation, coherence, the connection between claims and evidence should have in light of the importance of lived experience. Yet, not all lived experience has been by definition well comprehended. We all know that experience is a source of knowledge, but we don't know how to make easily the transition between the source and a more elaborated explanation of the experience. To put it differently, we may have experienced something but still not know what it is; yet we can recognize some of the contours of the impression the experience has made upon our multiple identities.

This question of the relationship between knowledge and experience presents serious epistemological problems that run throughout any research process from the selection of the research problem, to the selection of theory and methods, to the process of sampling, data collection, and data analysis, and to the connections between research findings and policy implications—including choices regarding strategies of presentation and dissemination/devolution of the research. Providing a lukewarm defense of another kind of standpoint theory, which I would like to term "maternal feminism," Noddings (1995), try- ing to stay away from any form of essentialism, still argues that "centuries of experience have left their mark on women's way of thinking and on the values they espouse, and not all of these ways and values are to be rejected as part of the legacy of oppression" (180). Not to recognize experience as a source of knowledge is, epistemologically speaking, debilitating of theory and practice; yet not to recognize the connections between experience and knowledge and the need to develop the analytical categories that may facilitate the translation of experience to knowledge and thus to practice is, politically speaking, de- empowering and demobilizing.

Coming back to Gitlin's agenda, next in importance to his criticism of stand- point theory is the political criticism of identity politics. A possible perverse out- come of the politics of identity—which Gitlin blames for not pursuing a common cause—is separatism. Gitlin distinguishes between the old New Left, with its deep beliefs of universalist hope, and the most recent New Left politics of sepa- ratist rage (146). Moreover, he is concerned with the ironic reversal of postures in political struggles not only within the left itself, but also between the left and the right: "The oddity is that the Left, which once stood for universal values, seems to speak today for selected identities, while the Right, long associated with privileged interests, claims to defend the common good" (36). Ironically, as Gitlin argues, the current state of public policy demonstrates that "While the Right was occupying the heights of the political system, the assemblage of groups identified with the Left were marching on the English Department" (148).

The experience of political reform in the United States and most liberal democracies, in Gitlin's view, is based on coalition building, including the ability to persuade and negotiate towards the creation of majority alliances that could, in electoral competition, successfully carry an idea of reform with its implementation. Separatism, as a risk in the politics of identity, conspires against coalition building, particularly in a diverse society like the United States, which includes a vast gamut of interest and power groups: "Politics in a multiracial society is alliance-making, and the work of alliance-making is not accomplished by adding up numbers. . . . The assumption among identity politics militants that natural alliances exist on the basis of nonwhiteness is purely sentimental" (114, 117).

But beyond the criticism of identity politics in terms of politics and epis- temology, the key element continues to be multiculturalists' lack of a com- mon dream. Yet, as Gitlin (1995) himself asked, if we are at the twilight of the common dream, how has that common dream been articulated? The basis, at the most abstract, epistemological level, is easy to identify. It is the Enlightenment. At a concrete, political, and historical level, the notion of a common culture in America is more difficult to identify.

Perhaps, as Gitlin muses, it all boils down to the notion of an American dream rather than an American culture; but, "to paraphrase Lippman: America is not yet. It is a collective anticipation. But how does one identify with a potential?" (47). The common culture is not yet more than a sense of universal rights for all people, or, to put it in Gitlin's terms, looking at the Jeffersonian preface to the American Constitution, it is based on the notion of the search for "life, liberty and the pursuit of happiness," a phrase that Gitlin, notwithstanding his conviction of the importance of the Universal Declaration of Human Rights, finds "at war with itself" (48).

Thus, Gitlin is not advocating a particular common culture to retain or to reinvigorate through a cultural canon. In fact, he argues that one of the few things that runs throughout the U.S. experience or political culture is perhaps not so much Whitman's dictum of a "nation of many nations" but what seems to be unique to the U.S. experience, and typical of the preponderance of a liberal philosophy with strong libertarian overtones, "the widespread respect for the disrespect of authority" (43). Gitlin is advocating a particular dream to relive and perhaps to reinvent individually and collectively in the pursuit of democratic civic virtues.

What follows from his analysis is that the Enlightenment is the appropriate bedrock for this dream, despite the fact that standpoint theories (what he calls "perspectivism") "fail or refuse to recognize that their preoccupation with multiculturalism, identities, perspectives, incommensurable world views, and so forth would be unimaginable were it not for the widespread acceptance of Enlightenment principles: the worth of all individuals, the right to dignity, and to a social order that satisfies it" (214). Yet, the Enlightenment, Gitlin cautions, "erected great structures of thought but also manufactured the acid to dissolve them" (216).

In short, it is the enduring legacy of universal rights that gives epistemological foundations to the politics of identity, because the right to be different is a human right. In this sense, multiculturalism will show the limits of citizenship, but it will also show the limits of the state, along the lines of our discussion on human rights and globalization in chapter 3.

What, then, according to Gitlin's reconstructed critical modernism, are the alternatives to multiculturalism as the politics of identity? Gitlin (1995) seems to be engulfed in despair when he writes: "The question is how to cultivate the spirit of solidarity across the lines of difference—solidarity with 'anyone who suffers.' For surely that spirit cannot be expected to generate spontaneously inside fortified groups, each preoccupied with refining its differences from other groups" (217).

Clearly, Gitlin's criticisms of multiculturalism are completely different from McCarthy's. Gitlin provides an indictment of multiculturalism not only because its aims are vague, its politics divisive, and its logic reductionist, promoting "perspectivistic" or standpoint theories that are based on particular rather than universal traits; but also, taking a classic position, because diversity cannot be separated from a notion of the commons. Gitlin (1995) claims: "if multiculturalism is not tempered by a stake in the commons, then centrifugal energy overwhelms any commitment to a larger good" (236).

In his conclusion, Gitlin is not grandiose or apocalyptic but self-restrained and cautious, perhaps feeling overwhelmed by the magnitude of the task ahead. Gitlin (1995) concludes:

> Make no mistake—the path of commonality offers no utopian destination. It offers, in fact, difficulties galore. Majorities come and go; they are not easy to stitch together under the best of circumstances. A diversity of customs and races is here to stay—and nowhere more than in amazingly profuse, polychrome, polyglot America. Plainly people are motivated by loyalties to clan, religion, race. Meanwhile, capital moves across frontiers at the speed of light as labor lumbers along at a human pace. (237)

Gitlin's position contrasts sharply, for instance, with the concluding paragraphs of Peter McLaren's *Revolutionary Multiculturalism* (1997b). Its postscript starts as follows: "The smell of blood lingers in the air. A regime of madmen watch from the darkness that is preparing to descend. It is a darkness brought by the false promises of neoliberalism and the false hopes of liberal democracy" (301). It concludes: "South of la linea, in Mexico, vatos locos from Nezahualcoyotl, powered by La Banda and political fearlessness, walk through streets paved with block and dreams. It is the stuff of which corridos are made. . . . And capitalism's pinstriped gangsters would do well to tremble before its humble grandeur and to drive their Bentleys out of town before the apocalypse strikes" (301).

Despite this apocalyptic warning by McLaren, Gitlin's defense of the Enlightenment opens the door to a most suggestive indictment of multiculturalism (including the notions of cultural diversity and cultural pluralism) in the United States offered by Russell Jacoby (1994). He boldly states that multiculturalism is nothing but a myth and an ideology, a new cant:

> multiculturalism and the kindred terms of cultural diversity and cultural pluralism are a new cant. Incessantly invoked, they signify anything and everything. This is not simply an example of sloppy terms; these phrases have become a new ideology. To put it more provocatively: multiculturalism flourishes as a program

while it weakens as a reality. The drumbeat of cultural diversity covers an unwelcome truth: cultural differences are diminishing, not increasing. For better or worse only one culture thrives in the United States, the culture of business, work and consuming. (121–122)

For Jacoby, the diversity of cultures in the United States exists within a single consumer society. These diverse cultures do not offer an alternative to consumerism and capitalism, and the proponents of the ideology of multiculturalism simply seek "the best way to enter and prosper in the American mainstream" (123). Because of their propensity to consumerism and the fact that we are all molded by our exposure to the globalization of cultural politics through mass media (which many would claim is simply the "Americanization" of culture worldwide), Jacoby is skeptical that the cultural heterogeneity of America reflects the interaction of distinct cultures, even for African American communities where "the cult of consumption has permeated the emotional and cultural life for the urban African-American kids with devastating consequences" (124).

Politically, Jacoby's (1994) critique to some extent overlaps with Gitlin's and McCarthy's criticisms, especially when he argues that multiculturalism is

a genteel phrase for ethnic and racial disparity and sometimes for affirmative action . . . [but that as such may not be useful to argue for proportional representation of racial groups]. To read racial and ethnic inequalities as cultural difference is not only inaccurate, but makes a bad situation worse. It fosters group chauvinism and enmities; it infers every group has a special perspective and intelligence, which each member represents. An African-American is hired, then, not from simple justice but for cultural reasons: he or she carries a distinctive sensibility. (126)

In short, for Jacoby, this ideology of multiculturalism speaks not so much of different lives in different cultures but of different lifestyles in American society, which all strive to enjoy the same American capitalist and consumerist mainstream lifestyles. Despite its clear-cut class orientation and the criticism of the alienation of multiculturalism for lacking an understanding of class and capitalism, some of Jacoby's criticism would, in the end, overlap with key components of the neoconservative critique of multiculturalism.

Whichever version of multiculturalism one cares to endorse or consider from a critical perspective, it is clear that debates about multiculturalism are related to new forms of theorizing about globalization, immigration, border identities, politics, race, ethnicity, and postcolonial literature. Perhaps, and ironically, as I have outlined above, nowhere is that more clear than in the neoconservative critique of multiculturalism as a social movement and as multicultural education, a critique that, on occasion, has turned into a crusade against multiculturalism.

Crucially Disputed Issues of Identity and Multiculturalism: Conclusion

> Who must ask for forgiveness and who can grant it? Those who, during so many years, sat in front of a full table and satiated themselves while we sat with death, so daily, so ours, that we are no longer afraid of it? Those who filled their pockets and their souls with formal statements and promises? The dead, our dead, so deadly dead of "natural" death, that is, of measles, flu, dengue, cholera, typhoid, mononucleosis, tetanus, pneumonia, malaria, and other gastrointestinal and pulmonary goodies? Our dead, so completely dead, so democratically dead. Our dead who died without anyone counting, without anyone saying at last "That's enough?" That would give meaning back to those deaths so that someone would ask of the common dead, our dead, that this time they come back to live rather than to die again? Those who denied the right and the ability of our people to govern? Those who denied the respect to our customs, our color, our language? Those who treated us as strangers in our own land and who asked us for papers and to obey a law whose existence and righteousness we ignore? Those who tortured us, imprisoned us, and disappeared us for wanting a piece of land, not a large piece, not a small piece, only a piece where we could reap something to fill the stomach? Who must ask for forgiveness and who can grant it?
>
> —Subcomandante Marcos, "¿De que nos van a perdonar?"
> *(trans. Julie Ann Thompson)*[12]

The epigraph, taken from a famous letter of Zapatista Subcomandante Marcos to the journal *Proceso* in Mexico shortly after the Zapatista insurgency in 1994, makes the limits of liberalism painfully clear and chastises its outcomes. The proponents of liberal multiculturalism argue that it will: (1) increase fairness (by representing the range and richness of America's different ethnicities), and (2) increase tolerance (by exposing students to multiple perspectives on the meaning of history). "In this view, multiculturalism pluralizes the notion of an American identity by insisting on attention to African-Americans, Native Americans, and the like, but it leaves in place a unified concept of identity" (Scott, 1992:13).

I have argued that the most important, and indeed an original, strand of multiculturalism is based on a liberal pluralist perspective, well represented in its critical approach in the work of James Banks and associates (1993). Within the pluralist framework, identity "is taken as the referential sign of a fixed set of customs, practices, and meanings, an enduring heritage, a readily identifiable sociological category, a set of shared traits and/or experiences" (Scott, 1992:14).

From an existentialist and not merely a sociological standpoint, identity is also related to key feelings and experiences of protection, association, and recognition. As Cornel West (in West, Klor de Alba, and Shorris, 1991) so forcefully claims:

> People identify themselves in certain ways in order to protect their bodies, their labor, their communities, their way of life; in order to be associated with people who ascribe values to them; and for purposes of recognition, to be acknowledged, to feel as if one actually belongs to a group, a clan, a tribe, a community. So that any time we talk about the identity of a particular group over time and space, we have to be very specific about what the credible options are for them at any given moment. (57)

Yet, diversity as a process of learning continuously surprises the learner, creating conditions for experiencing identity and knowledge in diverse ways, not only as protection, association, and recognition—truly existentialist demands—but also as a way to find the true, evolving self that many of us find so difficult to really understand, to capture, or even to name.

Without falling into a Kantian perception that we cannot ever fully understand the enacted narrative of our own individual life as embedded in the history of the diverse communities to which we belong, there is something ineffably personal in the recognition of identity as a process of individual (and collective, as well) learning, better captured in poetry, perhaps, than in analytical philosophy. The following poem, composed by a Berkeley student after writing a senior paper on Chicano literary works, is quite telling of the importance of experiencing identity as a lifelong, surprising revelation. Identity is a journey of learning, knowledge, and recognition.

> Looking through my Kaleidoscope I ask :
> —Do I know you?
> I stutter to respond searching for myself,
> —Well . . . ,
> I don't think there IS a "Me".
> To identify who I am is to limit myself from experiencing who
> I am
>   Tomorrow
>
> I can tell you what I've Learned about me, and what I
>   THINK constitutes my entity,

But, who "I AM",
  my identity,
  is a life long
    daily
    surprising
    Revelation;
It exists as I exist
in a changing time and space
in varying ways
  Never quite settled but grounded in life,
    to earth
  I am here and now.

I once wanted to cling to an identity
  "Latina", or "woman", or... whatever—but now,
I cling to the Truth of myself;
  a constituted work of time,
a "post-structuralist" notion of me,
    a culmination of various elements that
      Don't fit neatly in a box;
    I can't check it off when asked: Identify yourself as:
    Latina?
      —Okay,
  Hispanic?
      —uh, I guess...
  Non-white Hispanic?
      —uhmm . . . What does this mean?
    Female?
    —Yes.
  Woman?
    —I'd say so, but what do you mean by that
anyway . . . ?

So many unarticulated elements find their way
in me and express themselves
  daily.
They converge without my knowledge
  Yet, not without my recognition—
I appreciate their journeys into myself and the subsequent
discovery;
  Elements that brush against me—
    Unintelligibly,
      through their determination
Continually giving me a name,

> giving me a heart, a Soul
>   A Life.
>   I appreciate the learning,
>   the experience—
>   the desire to laugh
>   and be loved,
>   to love and live
>   with endless wonder of
>   Who I am.[13]

Identity is a process of discovery and learning. In my conversation with Gloria Ladson-Billings, she made this very clear in thinking about the connections with national identity: "What came out of the study is that there does have to be a kind of ethnic affiliation before one can make the connection to a national identity. Part of what happens in schools is a denial of ethnicity and a denial of racial difference. And the presumption we're 'all Americans'" (Torres, 1998a:193). Diversity, on the other hand, as Scott (1992) argues: "refers to the plurality of identities, and it is seen as a condition of human existence rather than as the effect of an enunciation of differences[14] that constitute hierarchies and asymmetries of power" (14).

"Analytical agony" is the term used to describe best the complexity of this process: identity and diversity can neither be subsumed under, nor separated from, class supremacy. Cornel West (in West, Klor de Alba, and Shorris, 1996) would agree, since he argues that "this historical process of naming is part of the legacy not just of white supremacy but of class supremacy" (57).

To show how intractable the issue of identity can be, let us get back to Gitlin's (1995) analysis. Noting that some terms quickly become clichés and that categories become overstated, Gitlin criticizes Scott's position. Gitlin begins by quoting Scott as follows:

> [D]ifferences and the salience of different identities are produced by discrimination. . . . [D]ifference has to do with something that's vital to the sense of self of an individual or a group, and it constitutes a power relationship with a set of interests and problems that are not easily resolved or given over by the notion of universalism. (204)

Yet, Gitlin argues:

> If the first sentence in Scott's second quotation means that differences are reducible to power relationships, it is demonstrably false. (Russians perceive that Africans are "different," but not because they necessarily have any power over the Africans, or because the Africans have any power over them.) If the

first clause of the sentence means that difference automatically creates a power relationship, it is demonstrably false. (The Kurds and the Tutsi are different, but they have very little if any relationship at all.) If it means that difference creates nothing but a power relationship, it is demonstrably false. (If I like the raps of Sister Souljah, it is not because she has the power to compel me to buy her compact disc.) If it means that there are no power relationships without difference, it is tautological. . . . The unexamined use of these terms presumes that life experience amounts to nothing but the language and institutions of the milieu. Likewise, to say that identities (for example, women or homosexuals) are "constructed" in history catches the truth that labels shift and categories come and go but is frequently stretched so far as to presume that they are constructed out of thin air. (204)

Power and difference in multiculturalism narratives are always interrelated with a discussion of identity. Yet, *national identity,* the most important form of territorial solidarity, based on notions of a single nation-state and the experience and feeling of patriotism and a common cultural heritage, is not a fixed marker that guides citizens in their choices of loyalties and solidarities.[15] National identity, as Giroux (1992) so clearly states, "is always a shifting, unsettled complex of historical struggles and experiences that are cross-fertilized, produced, and transacted through a variety of cultures. As such it is always open to interpretation and struggle" (53).

Not surprisingly, then, the concept of national identity is better defined historically in opposition to "others" (e.g., another national identity or an enemy of the nation) than in reference to a set of uncontested historical properties of the nation and the national experience of its people as a homogeneous group. This question invites a discussion of the relationship between canon and culture that I will undertake in the next chapter.

Therefore, identities are constructed in a process of contestation and struggle and are subject to multiple interpretations; identity is a journey of learning, knowledge, and recognition. Identities are social constructions with material and historical bases, and indeed they are based on (or, if one allows for the Althusserian lapse, are interpellated by) perceptions of knowledge, ways of seeing and feeling, and lived experience of power, particularly what knowledge is (or should be considered) legitimate and should count, what experience should be celebrated and learned from, and how power can be negotiated among different knowledges and experiences. Yet, the same notion of experience that seems to underlie the notion of identity, as Joan Scott has so forcefully argued, is something historically, culturally, and discursively produced. There are, to be sure, dominant views of national identity that "have been developed around cultural differences constructed within hierarchical relations of power that authorize who can or cannot speak legitimately as an American" (Giroux, 1992, 53).

As Michael Apple (1982b, 1986b, 1993, 1997) has so aptly argued for more than two decades, the connections between power and knowledge become central to any practical agenda of research and policymaking in education, particularly in this new phase of the conservative restoration.

Identity, as I have argued, is not a fixed marker, an essential substance that some people share in virtue of their origin, race, religious affiliation, sexual preference, gender, or class, but a process of learning that is context dependent and indeed open to interpretation. As such, it also depends on the historicity of the struggles that impinge upon social consciousness at a given point in time, making experience, and the consciousness of the experience, a salient process of understanding and meaning-making by the individuals attempting to understand the conditions of their—our—lives. However, it would be naïve to understand identity simply as an evolving narrative, as an endless play of words in the social construction of the self. There is much more to identity than just rhetoric, argumentation, or an evolving social (and individual) "text" constructed by, and through, different sets of experiences and knowledge.

Poet T. S. Eliot (1934) said that "we have the experience but we missed the meaning, and approach to the meaning restores the experience." Eliot's dictum tells us that the notion of identity built on a given experience is as elusive as the notion of identity consciousness, which in itself, presupposes some sense of completion of the journey having achieved some measure of self-identification. Yet—and this is a premise of my analysis—the process of symbolic meaning-making or consciousness cannot be separated from processes of oppression, discrimination, and exclusion that constitute people's lives, whether we are able to recognize this process or not. This observation is even more important when some cultural forms attempt to establish themselves as the universal form, as the metaphysical canon by which to judge all other social formations or consciousness, as Scott (1992) cautions us: "a process that establishes the superiority or the typicality or the universality of some in terms of the inferiority or atypicality or particularity of others" (14–15).

The discussion of multiculturalism and multicultural education is a discussion not only about canon and culture but also about the future of citizenship and democracy in culturally diverse capitalist societies—a discussion that shows, with unusual clarity, the incommensurability of discourses and the limitation of technical responses to political problems. Once again, the shadow of John Dewey comes alive in the critical dialogue that Paulo Freire proposes. For Dewey, education requires "doing" because knowledge, as the grasping of essences, is rejected in favor of a view that ties knowing to manipulating reality. When we know something, we have come to understand its connections to other experiences and we are able to relate it to our own interests. Hence, education involves appealing to the students' interest not simply as a device to recall knowledge better but as a means of intricately connecting knowing and interest.

Freire introduces an epistemological perspective to pedagogy. Like Dewey, he believes that "knowing" emanates from lived experiences and not merely from rational, "abstract" understanding—which, if properly recognized and implemented, certainly can do nothing but enrich lived experience. Problem-posing education, which is at odds with problem-solving educational models, starts by discovering the theory hidden in the practice of human agency and social movements. Freire's epistemological perspective seeks, in turn, to produce new knowledge that will guide, inspire, redefine, and assist in the comprehension of praxis. However, this unknown theory has not yet been elaborated. It has to be discovered, invented, constructed, or re-created in an intelligent dialogue between the logic of critical social theory and/or the aesthetics of poetry and literature and the demands of tension-ridden, complicated, and contradictory practices.

No doubt Freire's epistemology of curiosity has recognized (from the very beginnings of the political-pedagogical paideia that animated his work) the notion of multiple identities as a journey of learning, and hence his epistemological stance, which has at least two major implications for pedagogy. On one hand, critical pedagogy emerging from Freire's contribution is concerned with how emancipatory education can validate learners' own cultures and discourses while at the same time empowering them. On the other hand, Freire's recognition of the tensions between objectivity and subjectivity, between theory and practice—as autonomous and legitimate spheres of human endeavor—lead him (departing once again from Dewey) to recognize that these dichotomies and tensions cannot be overcome, nor can they be captured in their entire complexity through mainstream methodologies.

Identity formation is an agonic process, with a complex, convoluted mixture of pleasure and pain involving meaning-making at the individual level, but it also can be predicated at the level of communities and social movements. Indeed, the process of knowledge construction and learning that may help to recognize the experience shares the same "norms" as identity learning. (Here I follow Paulo Freire's understanding that consciousness is constituted as a deliberate whole that temporally symbolizes-signifies.) Hence conscientization exceeds in amplitude the mark of individual psychological consciousness; it is in fact a phenomenon (for lack of a better word) that goes beyond Freud's psychological consciousness (the Über-ich), beyond individual consciousness itself, being fully concerned with historical or collective consciousness, that is, the so-called field of intersubjectivity. The implications of this conceptualization of consciousness for identity formation—fully understood within a critical modernist analysis—are too many simply to be sketched here in rough form.

The epigraph that animates the conversation in this conclusion, taken from the indictment by Subcomandante Marcos of the Ladino Mexican system and written in the Lacandona tropical rain forest of Chiapas, is a sobering reminder of what is at stake in considering multiculturalism and the political challenges to the politics of culture and identity.

Notes

1. Citizenship education entails what traditionally was called civic education, i.e., the teaching of constitutional democracy. Three categories are usually associated with civic education: (a) *civic knowledge,* which in the context of constitutional democracy usually entails the knowledge of basic concepts informing the practice of democracy, such as public elections, majority rule, citizenship rights and obligations, constitutional separation of powers, and the placement of democracy in a market economy, which are used as the basic premises of civil society; (b) *civic skills,* which usually mean the intellectual and participatory skills that facilitate citizens' judgment and actions; and (c) *civic virtues,* usually defined around liberal principles such as self-discipline, compassion, civility, tolerance, and respect. It is important, therefore, to emphasize that citizenship education is wedded to politics and by implication is a contested concept, one that relates to the notion that sociologists call "'political socialization,'" a notion that, in turn, links the formation of individuals to state policies. There are questions of whether citizenship education should emphasize civic knowledge, civic skills, and civic virtues as defined by the political establishment. "If they conceptualize the citizen role mainly as one of compliance and cooperation, they may reward these behaviors and teach about law and government; if they define the role in more participatory terms, however, educators might teach students how to influence public affairs and deliberate public policy. Both viewpoints are plentiful in U.S. citizenship education literature" (W. C. Parker, "Citizenship Education," in *Dictionary of Multicultural Education,* ed. C. A. Grant and G. Ladson-Billings. Phoenix: Oryx, 1997.)

2. This is not the place to criticize the discussion of homogeneity and heterogeneity as it has been advanced, in my opinion in quite simplistic and reductionist ways—Manichean ways is perhaps a better formulation—by Theo Goldberg in his otherwise excellent introduction to *Multiculturalism: A Critical Reader* (Oxford: Blackwell, 1996).

3. See her *Black Looks: Race and Representation* (Boston: South End Press, 1992). For an alternative sociological view, see Ruth Frankenberg, *The Social Construction of Whiteness* (Minneapolis: University of Minnesota Press, 1993).

4. Ted Mitchell and the new institutionalist school in the history of education have tried to challenge the notion of inevitability in the history of educational institutions with a focus on the struggles that constitute the dynamics of transformation of reality.

In Mitchell's view, these struggles mediate, give shape to, and underscore the institutionalization of social action in educational institutions. Institutions are built around routines, rules, norms, and structures, and they guide action within certain limits and frames of behavior. Institutional theory tries to understand the historical and sociological configuration of the rationalization of social action in educational institutions. Its proponents see education—particularly political socialization—as a tool to increase purposive rational democratic action. Hence the role of the state is central for institutional theory.

As Professor Mitchell claims, any study of the history of educational institutions should consider "the real struggles that created the structures and practices that we have subsequently come to take for granted. Why is schooling maintained at public expense? Why do we have grades and grade levels? For many professionals and most of the public, answers to this kind of question tend to rely on universals, on varieties of developmental or institutional determinism. Yet each of these features has a particular, time-bound history and set of causes. Recovering these histories and the conflicts surrounding them is critical to appreciating the specificity of causation, and that appreciation is essential for anyone, lay or professional, with an interest in understanding or improving our educational institutions" (Los Angeles: UCLA, 1986, manuscript, p. 1). Thus, a central concern for institutionalist theorists is the expansion of state authority and the role of education as a contemporary initiation ceremony. They conceptualize state building and the incorporation and expansion of public systems of education as a central part of the national construction of citizenship and the extension of state authority through the population. For instance, Ted Mitchell, drawing on the work of Michael Katz, David Tyack, Bernard Bailyn, Lawrence Cremin, Michael Apple, and other cultural critics of educational institutionalization, has tried to "restore the consciousness, agency, and functionality of decisions that were made and that shaped our educational institutions. [Hence] showing how certain decisions reflected specific interests at specific times, one may be liberated to make very different decisions as times, circumstances, and power relations change. It is in this way, by recreating agency and struggle for the past, that history can become relevant to present policy choices" (ms., p. 2). A fascinating early example of this work is Mitchell's first book, *Political Education in the Southern Farmers' Alliance* (Madison: University of Wisconsin Press, 1987).

5. See the conclusion for a discussion of constructivism.

6. It is useful to remember that Saussure makes a distinction between the arbitrary or conventional nature of signs and the motivated nature of symbols. For Saussure, the notion of the value of a sign is a function of its position in an associate network, or paradigmatic and contrastive relations existing between all signs in a set. Language, therefore, in Saussure's model, is simply a system of interdependent terms in which the value that each term acquires results from the simultaneous presence of the other.

7. For positions critical of neoconservatism, see Cameron McCarthy and Warren Crichlow, "Theories of Identity, Theories of Representation, Theories of Race," in *Race, Identity, and Representation in Education,* ed. Cameron McCarthy and Warren Crichlow (New York: Routledge, 1993), xiii–xxix; Michael W. Apple, "Constructing the Other: Rightist Reconstructions of Common Sense," in *Race, Identity, and Representation,* ed. McCarthy and Crichlow, 24–39; Cornel West, *Race Matters* (Boston,

Beacon Press, 1993); bell hooks and Cornel West, *Breaking Bread: Insurgent Black Intellectual Life* (Toronto: Between the Lines, 1991); Cornel West, "The Postmodern Crisis of the Black Intellectual," in *Cultural Studies*, ed. Lawrence Grossberg, Cary Nelson, and Paula Treichler (New York: Routledge, 1992), 689–705; Cornel West, "Marxist Theory and the Specificity of Afro-American Oppression," in *Marxism and the Interpretation of Culture*, ed. Larry Grossberg and Cary Nelson (Urbana: University of Illinois Press, 1988), 17–29; Antonia Darder, *Culture and Power in the Classroom: A Critical Foundation for Bicultural Education* (New York: Bergin & Garvey, 1991).

8. I hope my discomfort with terminology that is descriptive in general terms but faulty analytically has been clear throughout this book. It is important to qualify the terminology while trying to address analytically its potential horizon. I have steadfastly refused in this book to use the term "minority" to refer to nonwhite or non-Caucasian populations, simply because this is a term overcharged with racist values and emotional connotations. What is termed a minority in the United States is, from the perspective of global populations, the majority, and "whites" or Caucasians definitely remain, demographically, a minority in the world system. In some states like California, it is estimated that by the year 2025 the majority (understood as 51 percent or more of the population) will be people of Latino/a or Chicana/o origin. Thus the term "minority," under which Latinos are usually subsumed, will not apply, in the strict demographic sense, to Latinos living in California by the first quarter of next century. "People of color" is also a problematic category, because the color white cannot be used as a noncolor nor as the reference against which all other "colors" can be measured. Yet "people of color" can be made a political symbol since all of us are people of color, and if we learn how to respect, learn about, and celebrate the difference and take advantage of the diversity, both at the level of production and at the level of distribution in the political economy, then we can make possible the adage of the civil rights movement, widely popularized by Martin Luther King, that we should be judged by the content of our character and not by the color of our skin. Finally, I should say that Richard Dyer's (1997) solution to refer to people of nonwhite origins as "nonwhite" in the end is self-defeating because it uses the standard "white" terminology as the rule by which to judge the exceptions.

9. The paradigm of popular education, one of the most important contributions of Latin America to educational reform and intimately related to pedagogy of the oppressed, has been a source of intellectual and political inspiration for a host of reformers. A great many of Latin America's micro experiments, and to a lesser extent its large-scale experiments, can be counted among the most intellectually and politically vigorous reform experiments in the world. For a good, concise text with most of the theoretical and some practical experiences, see Moacir Gadotti and Carlos Alberto Torres, eds., *Educação popular: Utopia latinoamericana (ensaios)* (São Paulo: Cortez Editora–Editora da Universidade de São Paulo, 1994). Translation is under way for publication by Zed Books, England.

10. For instance, McCarthy quotes Connell's argument: "Different standpoints yield different views of the world and some are more comprehensive and powerful than others. . . . If you wish to teach about ethnicity and race relations, for instance, a more comprehensive and deeper understanding is possible if you construct your curriculum from

the point of view of the subordinated ethnic groups than if you work from the point of view of the dominant one. . . . The standpoint of the least advantaged in gender relations, articulated in feminism, has transformed that. Modern feminism has produced a qualitatively better analysis of a large domain of social life through a range of new concepts (sexual politics, patriarchy, the sexual division of labor, etc.) and new research informed by them." R. W. Connell, "Curriculum, Politics, Hegemony, and Strategies of Change." (New South Wales: Macquarie University, Department of Sociology), 16–18.

11.   See my analysis of Freire's Hegelian leanings in "Education and the Archeology of Consciousness: Hegel and Freire," *Educational Theory* 44, no. 4 (Fall 1994): 429–445.

12.   "¿Quien tiene que pedir perdón y quién puede otorgarlo? ¿Los que, durante años y años, se sentaron ante una mesa llena y se saciaron mientras con nosotros se sentaba la muerte, tan cotidiana, tan nuestra que acabamos por dejar de tenerle miedo? ¿Los que llenaron las bolsas y el alma de declaraciones y promesas? ¿Los muertos, nuestros muertos, tan mortalmente muertos de muerte 'natural, es decir, de sarampión, tosferina, dengue, cólera, tifoidea, mononucleosis, tétanos, pulmonía, paludismo y otras lindezas gastrointestinales y pulmonares? ¿Nuestros muertos, tan mayoritariamente muertos, tan democráticamente muertos, nuestros muertos que se iban nomás, sin que nadie llevara la cuenta, sin que nadie dijera, por fin, el 'YA BASTA!' que devolviera a esas muertes su sentido, sin que nadie pidieran a los muertos de siempre, nuestros muertos, que regresaran a morir otra vez pero ahora para vivir? ¿Los que nos negaron el derecho y don de nuestras gentes de gobernar y gobernarnos? ¿Los que negaron el respecto a nuestra costumbres, a nuestro color, a nuestra lengua? ¿Los que nos tratan como extranjeros en nuestra propia tierra y nos piden papeles y obediencia a una ley cuya existencia y justeza ignoramos? ¿Los que nos torturaron, apresaron, asesinaron y desaparecieron por el grave 'delito' de querer un pedazo de tierra, no un pedazo grande, no un pedazo chico, sólo un pedazo al que se le pudieran sacar algo para completar el estómago? ¿Quién tiene que pedir perdón y quién puede otorgarlo?" Subomandante Marcos, "¿De que nos van a perdonar?"

13.   Laura Silvina Torres, Berkeley, 9 December 1997, manuscript.

14.   On difference as a process of *enunciation,* see Homi Bhabha, "The Commitment to Theory," in *Third Cinema Reader,* ed. J. Pines and P. Willemen (London: British Film Institute, 1989), 111–132, esp. 125.

15.   A Kantian understanding in the realm of moral philosophy of the incompatibilties between liberal thought and patriotic thought (nationalism) suggests that it is important to understand that they constitute in fact two contrasting (and perhaps incompatible) moralities. On the one hand is the morality of liberal impersonality (i.e., to judge from a moral standpoint is to judge impersonally, independent of the individual's social interests, social positions, or affections). On other hand is the morality of patriotism (i.e., that precisely because it is framed in terms of membership in some particular social community, the nation must be excepted from criticism, particularly at times of national crisis, and thus patriotic loyalty is unconditional). For a detailed analysis, see Alasdair MacIntyre, "Is Patriotism a Virtue?" Lindley Lecture, University of Kansas, 1984.

7

Toward a Theory of Democratic Multicultural Citizenship

From Los Angeles to Boston: A Vignette

> Meditate on virtue within yourself,
> and you will find the benefit of virtue.
> Use it as the ground for the family,
> and your virtue will last for generations.
> Take it as your guidance for the village,
> and the place will blossom for years to come.
> Use it to guide the nation,
> and the nation will create abundance.
> Be guided by it for the Whole and it will flood its way over the world.
> —*Tao Te Ching*

There is nothing like lived experience to show the practical implications of social theory for education. This is particularly so, as Gitlin (1995) has so eloquently argued, when a central aim in the construction of a democratic multicultural citizenship is to understand the importance of cultivating "the spirit of solidarity across the lines of difference" (217).

When I was writing this final chapter, I couldn't help thinking about an experience I had in Boston a few years ago. Let me start from the beginning. After finishing, at 10 p.m., my course on the scholarship of class, race, gender, and the state, which I taught jointly with Ted Mitchell at UCLA, I left for Boston on a midnight flight affectionately known as the red-eye. Tired but happy after having enjoyed a wonderful class interaction, I arrived at Boston's Logan Airport at 7 A.M., ready to get to the hotel for a brief rest before my academic activities. I hired a taxicab at the airport, indicating to the driver, an Irish Bostonian, the address of a hotel in Cambridge. Silent, I decided to take advantage of the trip in the early Boston fall, ready to delight in the multicolored leaves of the trees and to derive pleasure from the gray skies struggling with the sun to create a choreography of aesthetics deeply marked by a peculiarly Bostonian life on the banks of the Charles River.

The driver inquired right away, "Where did you come from?" I am not sure what the experience of other immigrants is, but for me that is an uncomfortable question. This question, rather than resulting simply in information for a civilized and usually inconsequential chat, always makes me feel uncomfortable because I am aware that my appearance and my accent are "different." For me, this question is more than just a question about geographical origin. It is a question about ethnic and racial location. It is a question that, in the context of that taxicab ride, made me feel different, made me think about "otherness."

Without much enthusiasm, I replied that I was coming from Los Angeles. In terse confirmation of a certainty, the driver told me that my accent was not from Los Angeles—as if the human community that makes up the megalopolis of Los Angeles can be easily identified by a distinctive, single, and homogeneous accent! I replied, without giving much explanation, that before Los Angeles, I used to live in Canada. Again, showing how persistent this cabdriver could be, he insisted that my accent was neither Chicano nor French Canadian. Annoyed and tired, I replied, intending to end the conversation right there, that I was born in Argentina. A short silence followed my answer until the taxi driver inquired again; "Argentina is in South America, isn't it?" he asked. I answered yes, and without hesitation he told me that he had always thought that the people born south of the Rio Grande were intellectually inferior.

I paused for a moment and thought how paradoxical the whole situation was. There I was, tired and until that moment happy, sitting in a cab going to a hotel in Cambridge to get ready to lecture, all expenses paid, at Harvard, the oldest and one of the finest universities in the United States. And here was this white taxicab driver, who may have just finished high school at best, who was telling me that he considered me "intellectually inferior" to him by birth, because of my national origin and, no doubt, because of my ethnicity. Leaving the insult aside and trying to forget about the whole episode, I just murmured that "people are people." I tried to go back to my own ruminations, when the taxi driver charged again, this time by saying, "Hey, you know, I don't understand the Latino family." As a friend of mine said when I told him the story, this cabdriver was pushing all my buttons. I could have let him go on with his personal attack on my intellectual abilities, but this reference to the Latino family had just crossed the line. I braced myself for a verbal fight in that cab, and, needless to say, I couldn't have cared less about the beautiful Boston we were crossing.

When I asked why he couldn't understand the Latino family, to my surprise, he started to tell me his love story. His girlfriend from the Dominican Republic had just left him to go with her mom, who had moved to Massachusetts.

The cabdriver couldn't understand why Latinos have such strong family ties and loyalties. I suspected that there was more to it than just his "culturally biased" comment, and I asked, "Do you still love her?" He waited a few seconds to reply, and his reply showed to me not only that he loved her but also that he missed her tremendously. I immediately asked, "What do your friends say about her?" He replied, emphatically this time, that he paid no attention to what his friends told him. As I suspected, he had encountered criticism from his friends for going out with a Latino woman. We were getting closer to my hotel when I suddenly asked him, "Do you care for her?" He replied that he cared for her very deeply. Then I candidly asked, "Have you tried to contact her, to call her after she moved out?" To my surprise he told me that he had not, asking me, "Do you think I should?"

We arrived at my destination, and I told him that Latino families are tightly knit because there is a sense of intimacy, loyalty, and love that is shared and openly discussed. He should, I said, try to contact her and tell her how much he loved and cared for her. When I paid the fare, he looked at me and said something like, "Thank you very much, Doctor, you have helped me a lot."

Cultivating "the spirit of solidarity across the lines of difference" could be the motto of this conversation. I have thought long and hard about that conversation that impressed me so much. I am still amazed at how schizophrenic the whole episode was. In our (forced) dialogue, we moved from prejudice and perhaps insult into a conversation about love relationships. In the end, I was granted some authority to help him with his problem because I was a Latino male who—obviously, in his view—could help him relate to a Latino woman and the Latino family, as if there is one "typical" answer that encapsulates the complexity of the issues involved. Not only that, but when he thanked me, he granted me some "esoteric" expertise by referring to me as "Doctor," despite the beginning of our conversation.

This vignette is telling of the many issues involved in social interactions, particularly when issues of race and ethnicity are involved, and more so in the context of the racial formation of the United States. I chose to tell the story in the opening pages of this concluding chapter because I think it exemplifies most of the dilemmas that we deal with in addressing the question of a multicultural democratic citizenship and the virtues of civility.

The Challenges of Democratic Multicultural Citizenship

Where there is no vision, the people perish.

—Proverbs 29:18

The ancient wisdom of the book of Proverbs teaches us that without a vision, we cannot accomplish our dreams, and without dreams, we cannot survive the contradictions in which we, as creators of culture and inhabitants of nature, are immersed. With this admonition in mind, in this concluding chapter I shall discuss at length three main theses to advance a theory of democratic multicultural citizenship.

First, only by considering the importance of theories of the state in education will we be able to understand the "politicity" of the educational act—as Freire has so persuasively argued—and hence the political implications of understanding the connections between citizenship and education.[1]

Second, by focusing on the contradictions reflected in the three theoretical approaches analyzed in this book—theories of citizenship, theories of democracy, and theories of multiculturalism—I will show how these contradictions have made the goal of achieving a democratic multicultural citizenship difficult and how the democratic conversation should address topics that are indeed seemingly intractable.

Finally, I outline some of the main challenges that we need to confront, both theoretically and politically, in discussing the contradictions of a democratic multicultural citizenship. I do so considering the context of theories of the state and of education and the growing process of globalization of technology, markets, and cultural politics.

As Paulo Freire has consistently taught us with his epistemology of curiosity, we should always explore the relationships between education, politics, and power if we really want to understand and act upon the educational dilemmas of our time. So the question is, Why should educational researchers think politically about education?

Implications of Theories of State and Education: Why Educational Researchers Should Think Politically about Education

During the nineteenth and, especially, the twentieth centuries, education has been increasingly and overwhelmingly a function of the state. Education is sponsored, mandated, organized, and certified by the state. Indeed, public education is not only a state function in terms of legal order or financial support: the specific requirements for degrees, teacher requirements and qualifications, mandated textbooks, and required courses for basic curriculum are controlled by state agencies and designed under specific public policies of the state.

—Raymond Morrow and Carlos Alberto Torres,
Social Theory and Education

A Troubled Beginning

The state is a myth. It is nothing "but the sancta simplicitas of the human race" (Cassirer, 1969:4). This warning by neo-Kantian German political philosopher Ernst Cassirer appeared in the opening pages of his last book, *The Myth of the State*, posthumously published in 1946. Cassirer, having witnessed the rise of the totalitarian state in Germany, saw the emergence of the power of mythical thought undermining rational thought as the most alarming feature of the time. As a myth, the state is nothing but the *Urdummheit* of man, the product of "primeval stupidity" (Cassirer, 1969:4).

Whether the state is myth or rational creation, writing this book posed serious concerns for me. How should I approach the elusive state-education relationship, and how should I account for all the nuances (historical as well as theoretical) involved? Coming full circle, I shall argue, reformulating Cassirer's claim, that the state is not a myth, but educators find ways to mythologize and mystify the relationships between the state and education. I could have started from Theodore R. Sizer's (1992) remark that "the major elements of schooling are controlled outside the teachers' world. The state, or its contractor firms, writes the tests. The state mandates when each subject is to be taught; it and the district control that key coinage of school, the time of teachers and students. Evaluations of schools and teachers, the union contract, the departmental division, all run according to traditional formulas" (8). However, rather than looking at the empirical expressions of state action in schooling or educational policies, I have chosen to look at the state from the perspective of a political philosophy of education informed as well by a political sociology of education, considering the connections between democracy, citizenship, and multiculturalism.

Pressing Questions

What kind of heuristic construct or notion of the state is implied when educators blame the state for educational problems? What type of state do they have in mind when they think of educational reform seeking to improve the quality of education, testing, curriculum, or instruction? How do educational theorists, researchers, and teachers perceive the interplay of power, politics, and education in the context of educational reform? These are some of the questions that are implicit in the discussion in the previous chapters. I am aware that I have not offered a systematic answer to each one of them, knowing very well that most of the answers need to be elaborated in contextual rather than normative ways. Answers to these questions are not exclusively political-philosophical, but they are historical, dependent on ideological debates, shifting intellectual paradigms, the constitutions of intellectual communities, and conjunctural and structural changes occurring simultaneously at the levels of the nation-state and the global economy. I believe a thorough review of theories of the state-education relationship is helpful to lay the groundwork for addressing these questions. Here is a summary of the arguments regarding the politicity of education outlined throughout this book.

Argument 1: The Classics

The question of why educational researchers should think politically about education and why they should consider theories of the state can be answered in part by listening to the voices of the classics of political philosophy. For the authors of the classics, the question of education has never been separated from the question of power. Paideia, pedagogy, and politics have always gone hand-in-hand. Education has always—from Plato to Aristotle to Jean-Jacques Rousseau to John Dewey and Paulo Freire, to name but a few—been considered an extension of a political project (Apple, 1982a; Gadotti et al., 1996). The failure to recognize the intersections of education and power (and in practical terms, the role of the state) is the result of the failure to consider the relevance of theories of the state for education and, of course, of ignoring the classics of political philosophy.[2]

Argument 2: Metanarratives

Theories of the state are interwoven with any attempt to constitute a pedagogical subject, even in the most radical postmodernist expressions of the constitution of decentered subjects. Likewise, theories of the state give substance to the range of moral and ethical dimensions (and roles) attributed to education and schooling in the process of cognitive socialization and construction of cultural identities. Moreover, theories of the state (and their precepts regarding the linkages between power, state, and society) will guide the constitution of national, regional, and local educational policies of schooling including job-training programs and on-the-job skill-training programs, and the knowledge that is deemed legitimate and official.

The construction of metanarratives (with the playfulness of colorful rhetorics interplaying in the debates about dichotomous choices,[3] with questions of emphasis, direction, and scope) is all marked by political rationales of education and power explicit and implicit in theories of the state. In simpler terms, debates about dichotomous choices for educational reform include excellence versus equity; educational quality versus educational expansion;

centralization versus decentralization; and privatized and market-oriented versus state-sponsored programs. Despite their apparent pragmatic or technical nature, all rest on different (sometimes antagonistic) theories of the state and education. What is at stake here is a discussion about the only organized set of state institutions in capitalist societies—schooling and nonformal education—where dexterity and practical skills, key moral and ethical values, and official and counterhegemonical knowledge are negotiated as an integral component of the democratic political accord. To ignore the importance of theories of the state underlying these debates is dangerous for any serious attempt to advance educational theory and practice.

Debates about theories of the state should be undertaken with serious consideration of the importance of cultural studies. The notion of growing fragmentation (cultural as well as political) of the polity should direct our attention to curriculum, teaching, and learning in schools. These are also contested terrains of social regulation. The notion of autonomy, so entrenched in the discourse of liberalism, is either neglected or criticized in the neoconservative and neoliberal approaches to state and education. For these reasons, a metatheoretical framework of theories of the state and education helps to identify the normative-ethical, practical-political, and epistemological-philosophical issues involved (Morrow and Torres, 1995).

Any systematic criticism of social theory resting on a metatheoretical framework will identify critical theoretical transformations in the sociology of education. Theories of the state and education are crucial for a discussion of social and cultural reproduction theories that remain extremely relevant to any analysis of education. First, though the actual term "reproduction" has tended to slip out of sight in recent work, Morrow and Torres (1995) have suggested that the basic problematic of social and cultural reproduction remains a central preoccupation of critical theories of the relationships among state, school, and society. Second, a new model, the parallelist strategy (social action as the product of parallel determinations stemming from class, gender, and race), while highly sensitive to history, agency, and social practices, still employs structuralist methodological strategies. Nevertheless, the parallelist models have effectively encouraged the exploration of the independent effects of class, gender, race, and other forms of domination in the context of schooling. Third, despite the progress made by parallelist models of analysis, they have failed to address adequately three fundamental issues: (a) that each of these forms of domination has a significantly different systemic character with crucial consequences for their conceptualization as forms of domination; (b) that the analysis of the interplay of these "variables" has been obscured by the language of "relative autonomy" left over from structuralist Marxism; and (c) that even though the explanatory objectives of parallelist reproduction theory are necessarily more modest and historically contingent than envisioned by classic structuralist reproduction theories, they avoid the postmodernist tendency to fragment endlessly and pluralize conflicts and differences as if no systematic links exist among them (Morrow and Torres, 1994:43–61).

Argument 3: Power

I have already argued, drawing from critical traditions in the sociology of education, that a critical theory of power and the state is a necessary starting point for studying policymaking, "hence moving the analysis from the strict realm of individual choice and preference somehow modeled by organizational behavior, to a more historical-structural approach where individuals indeed have choices, but they are prescribed or constrained by historical circumstances, conjunctural processes, and the diverse expressions of power and authority (at the micro and macro level) through concrete rules of policy formation" (Morrow and Torres, 1995:343). The relationships between power, complex organizations such as schooling, and the state should be understood from a combined perspective of the political economy and political sociology of education. A case in point is the development of the neoconservative movement.

The influence of neoconservative policies extends well beyond the U.S. borders and, through neoliberal policies of economic stabilization, have reached the so-called Third World. The role of international organizations such as the World Bank in setting the agenda for educational reform worldwide has called into question the autonomy of the nation-state and has projected neoliberalism as the standard, mainstream ideology in education. There is, however, growing contestation over the politics of education, textbooks, and teaching. These struggles are also molding the political discussions in nation-states regarding the role of education for democracy and, indeed, are molding the dominant discourse of educational research.

Contestation from below and conflict and contradictions from above mark the life of neoconservative and neoliberal states. A most prominent contradiction in the political philosophy of neoconservatism and neoliberalism is the dilemma of promoting individual autonomy while simultaneously supporting public obligations. In terms of economic rationality, a similar dilemma occurs between individualistically conceived preferences and rational social choice. These dilemmas add complexity to the nature of the state as an arena displaying interactions of domestic and international actors. The state then is a microcosmic condensation of power relations in society. Schools are also part of these dynamics, subject to changes in state policies and in the division of labor. Educational systems and settings, however, also develop, with relative autonomy from the state and the division of labor, their own institutional and political behavior and governability.

Argument 4: New Departures

As outlined in chapter 2, nonsynchronous parallelist and relational theories, neo-Marxism, postmodernism, and feminism offer alternative views to traditional political philosophy. The state seen as a historical, multilayered, and relational concept is at the center of the production of social relationships in education. A multilayered concept of the state will consider not only the action of actors but also the deployment of strategies of power, including expert knowledge.

Capitalism, while historically specific, has intertwined with patriarchy, and the capitalist state can be defined as a patriarchal state. According to feminism, the patriarchal state encapsulates and/or does not adequately challenge conventional gender representations and specific sexist (and racist and classist) practices in education.

Whether we move towards a new institutionalized form of the nation-state in the context of capitalist globalization or towards a model of interdependency where the nation-state will be gradually muted, theories of the state continue to be decisive in understanding changes in the division of labor, society, and education.

Argument 5: Nuanced Historical Sense or Depoliticization

The apparent yet elusive relationships between theories of the state and educational reform have convinced Martin Carnoy and Henry Levin (1985), in their analysis of the U.S. educational system, that learning about previous struggles for equity and democracy will guide educational reform from progressive perspectives. Their words, written more than a decade ago, provide inspiration for people who care about the democratic education of children, youth, and adults:

> Continuing struggle, together with the failures of existing policies to meet the larger concerns of a democracy, will increase the power of democratic coalitions for fairness, equity, and participation. Democratic struggles for just and meaningful schooling are effective counters to the economic forces that are attempting to gain primacy over American schools and the formation of our youth. A study of the past supports our optimism for the future. (267)

In addition to the arguments listed above, I find another reason that educational researchers should think politically about education. If our goal is an education for political and economic democracy and community empowerment, theories of the state and education should be continually revisited, in theoretical and practical terms, and actively employed in educational research. Herbert Marcuse's eloquent analysis in the mid-1960s criticizing the fetishism of technology and the unidimensionalization of politics in late capitalism warns about the risk of depoliticization of educational researchers dominated by instrumental reason.[4] This is so because—to paraphrase Held (1989:104)—researchers obsessed with technique, productivity, and efficiency are likely to consider their work free of any political interest and independent of the state and the forces of civil society. Unfortunately, the consequences of depoliticization are not better research findings but the eventual eradication of political and moral questions from schools and public life, which is deeply marked by contradictions and dilemmas.

Contradictions, Dilemmas, and Challenges

> The American dream is a complex and cogent idea that millions of individuals have come to the United States seeking—and that pulls to America each year thousands of immigrants who hope to realize it. This fact is especially significant because the material aspects of the American dream are becoming increasingly elusive for most Americans.
> —James A. Banks, *Educating Citizens in a Multicultural Society*

Challenges

For the constitution of a theory of democratic multicultural citizenship, it is imperative to face the key contradictions, challenges, and dilemmas of citizenship, democracy, multiculturalism, and education. These challenges are incorporated, first and foremost, in the new scholarship of class, race, gender, and the state, including the most serious challenges that emerge from feminist theories criticizing the construction of the political from patriarchal frameworks (McClafferty, Torres, and Mitchell, forthcoming). Likewise, the challenge of postcolonialism cannot be ignored, particularly when multicultural societies are constituted, by and large, by the presence of large masses of immigrants, many of them linked to previous colonial experiences. While feminism and postcolonialism address the importance of alternative "voices" and experience frameworks in the constitution of critical citizenship, the location of those voices and frameworks in the context of the international system of power and of the hierarchies within nation-states constitutes a new challenge: the challenge of subaltern spaces, only occasionally addressed by the new social movements. In some historical contexts, these challenges highlight the need to resort to critical race theory to expose the importance of racism for the constitution of social relationships in many metropolitan and peripheral societies. Along with this is the challenge of globalization as a counterpart to the rise and decline of the nation-state. In this context, the constitution of citizenship faces diverse constraints. Last but not least, all of these challenges boil down to the challenges of utopian politics and education; the work of Paulo Freire continues to be a most inspiring source for understanding democracy, multiculturalism, and citizenship. These challenges need to be understood in the context of the contradictions of democracy and capitalism, the dilemmas of citizenship and multiculturalism.

Contradictions and Dilemmas

> In the social production which men carry on they enter into definitive relations that are indispensable and independent of their will; these relations of production correspond to a definite stage of development of their material forces of production. The sum total of these relations of production constitute the economic structure of society—the real foundation, on which rises the legal and political superstructure and to which correspond definite forms of social consciousness. The mode of production in material life determines the social, political and intellectual life in general. It is not the consciousness of men that determines their being, but, on the contrary, their social being that determines their consciousness.
>
> —Karl Marx, *Grundrisse*

The notion of contradictions, taken from the theoretical arsenal of neo-Marxism, may prove useful in helping to understand the dilemmas and tensions in citizenship, democracy, and multiculturalism. Michael Apple (1988c) has argued from a neo-Marxist perspective that a focus on contradictions is important, "especially if they have been articulated through the State, are the results of conflicts, compromises, and accords within various levels of the State, and between the State and a wide array of social movements and forces in the wider society" (36–37). Hence, the call is for a more subtle analysis of the state, which should include the advances made in the political economy of gender, class, and race as outlined in the previous chapters and as so eloquently suggested by Fraser (1997): "the politics of recognition is becoming increasingly dissociated from the politics of redistribution, and the former is increasingly eclipsing the latter. The result is a truncated problematic, which is impeding efforts to develop a credible vision of radical democracy"

(180–181). This is certainly an analysis that complements discussions of the central place of democratic conflicts in the state itself in the face of policies of privatization, centralization, vocationalization, and differentiation (Ball, 1993; Dale, 1989).

A more subtle analysis of state theory should stress that there are many contradictions and dilemmas in citizenship theory. First is the dilemma, outlined in chapter 4, of understanding citizenship in terms of legal foundations versus understanding citizenship as a set of civic virtues. This, in essence, creates a first set of problems when we consider citizenship only in terms of its legal conditions and not, as we should, in terms of its ability to construct a moral, socially viable, politically effective, and economically responsible polity in the context of the political economy.

A second dilemma of citizenship is the fact that for neoconservatives in the end citizenship is regulated by market relationships; that is to say, citizenship rests on the ability to compete successfully in the (international) markets. Hence the citizen appears as a consumer. Therefore, corporations, state institutions, capital, and labor are important in specifically identified local spaces (in the global system) rather than the nation-state. Only those individuals who as producers and consumers can participate in the logistics of this global arrangement via productivity can acquire citizenship. The rest are merely ignored because they lack a hegemonic economic niche.

From the left, however, the limits of citizenship emerge with the notion of human rights, which, when fully explored, supersede all other acquired status rights (by birth or adoption).[5] In fact, the notion of human rights, promoted internationally, challenges the premise of nationalism as well as of the nation-state and of statehood as the institutional basis for the sole organization of citizenship. For human rights advocates, the question of citizenship is in fact one of planetary rather than national citizenship.

Finally, citizenship has been predicated in liberal democracies as the keystone for the incorporation of individuals into the polity despite the fact that several processes are fragmenting the polity. This applies to the exclusion of individuals who, while nominally citizens, cannot fully exercise their rights. More often than not, they are coerced to exercise their responsibilities and obligations, yet their full access to entitlements is thwarted. This has been the case, for instance, for the Native American people, who were stripped of their land and colonized by the white immigrants. Confining them to reservations clearly separated them from the dynamics (and benefits) of citizenship.

Like citizenship, democracy is marked by several contradictions and dilemmas. First and foremost is the fact that democracy (as a political system) has become intertwined with capitalism (as a mode of production). This situation has resulted in a most substantive democratic contradiction of free individuals who lack substantive equality, thus creating the need for successive democratic accommodations. The important political and theoretical distinction of democracy as content versus democracy as a method of political representation appears central in the discussion of citizenship building. After the contributions of political theorists C. B. Macpherson and T. H. Marshall, it is clear that the notion of democracy as a political and social right cannot be excluded from the notion of democracy as an economic right—what Fraser (1997) called radical democracy: "I assume that to be a radical democrat today is to appreciate—and to seek to eliminate—two different kinds of impediments to democratic participation. One such impediment is social inequality; the other is the misrecognition of difference. Radical democracy, on this interpretation, is the view that democracy today requires both economic redistribution and multicultural recognition" (173–174).

Finally, multiculturalism, like democracy and citizenship, is marked by egregious contradictions. The first one is the distinction between universality and identity. That is to say that knowledge as a universal domain constitutes the basis for rationality, drawing upon the logic of the Enlightenment, and that the politics of identity reflects a localized set of struggles defying any possible notion of universalism—that is, standpoint theory as strongly criticized by Gitlin (1995) or mildly questioned as epistemology by Noddings (1995). Secondly, similar to the contradiction of democracy is the fact that ethnic, racial, and cultural distinctions in societies that are not fully egalitarian persist, creating a serious tension between freedom and equality.

These contradictions and dilemmas underscore serious challenges to a theory of democratic multicultural citizenship and therefore the need to reevaluate the key theoretical developments in social theory that affect our understanding of multiculturalism, democracy, and citizenship.

A Theory of Democratic Multicultural Citizenship

> The single-minded pursuit of production for profit by large and small business, and the state's unquestioned support for this objective in the name of economic growth, sets a highly limited political agenda: it creates a situation in which public affairs become concerned merely with debating different means—the end is given, that is, more and more production. Depoliticization results from the spread of "instrumental reason"; that is, the spread of the concern with the efficiency of different means with respect to pre-given ends.
> —David Held, *Political Theory and the Modern State*

A premise underlying this book is that the new scholarship of class, race, gender, and the state offers integrated perspectives, answering postmodernist criticisms and clarifying some of the dilemmas of democracy, citizenship, and multiculturalism (McClafferty, Torres, and Mitchell, forthcoming).

Morrow and Torres (1995), among others, have advanced the proposition that the scholarship of race, class, gender, and the state, as integrated perspectives, has emerged from the tradition of critical modernism and constitutes a response to the excesses of postmodernism while constituting, in itself, a systematic criticism of instrumental rationality.

How can we link postmodernism to theories of democracy, citizenship, and multiculturalism? Moreover, how can we relate postmodernist theories to a discussion of power in capitalist societies?

As argued in previous chapters, according to postmodernism, there is a "new" epoch in society and a new cultural paradigm. Some of the key sociological implications of postmodern society and culture can be summarized as a situation involving various processes of fragmentation including: (1) decentering and fragmentation of power that calls into question theories of domination and hegemony; (2) an uncoupling of material interests and subjective expressions in collective action, resulting in the shift of the demands of social movements from distributional to cultural-ethical issues; (3) the emergence of heterogeneity as opposed to the homogenization that has been previously characteristic of the world system; (4) a growing distrust of, and disillusionment with, democracy resulting from the fragmentation of political communities and identities (Torres and Mitchell, in press).

Concluding my analysis of postmodernism from a political perspective of critical modernism, I have argued in chapter 2 that a more obvious failure of postmodernism is the lack of direction and the absence of a political program. Moreover, the politics of postmodernism may turn out to be a false radicalism that challenges all viewpoints without advancing a clear political program and that, in the end, doesn't challenge the fragmented politics of divergent special and regional interest groups. This situation, added to the secular, internecine struggles of progressive groups; the structural and historical action of the capitalist state; and actions from the Right, undermines the constitution of communities of learning and political action, hindering the ability of progressive groups to challenge differential access to influence, power, and wealth resources of elites and dominant classes in most areas, including education. In short, this call echoes Nancy Fraser's (1997) belief that a radical democracy demands the incorporation of a political economy alongside the proposals for critical multiculturalism.

This "transgressive" activism of postmodernism may challenge the narratives of neoconservative and neoliberal projects in education, which is not a minor accomplishment considering the power of the "common sense" narrative of the Right, but it offers few if any guidelines for practical politics. It is worthwhile to reiterate Gitlin's (1995) admonition:

> Those postmodernists who propose to discard the Enlightenment as an excrescence of male, imperialist, racist, Western ideology are blind to their own situation. For all their insistence that ideas belong to particular historical moments, they take for granted the historical ground they walk on. They fail, or refuse, to recognize that their preoccupation with multiculturalism, identities, perspectives, incommensurable world views, and so forth would be unimaginable were it not for the widespread acceptance of Enlightenment principles: the worth of individuals, their right to dignity, and to social order that satisfies it. (214)

The problem is compounded when social subjects are considered to be politically decentered. A central undertaking of the new scholarship of class, race, gender, and the state is to explore the analytical possibilities as well as the limits of critical race theory, one of its central theoretical approaches. Alongside critical race theory, the challenge of feminism to social and political theory is central. The epistemology of feminism focuses on the constitution of "the other." Does "the other" exist per se, independent of "us," or is it always a socially constructed category? If the notion of "the other" is socially constructed, to what extent does the constructing of "the other" rest on notions of generalization and universality that are deeply marked by a male perspective? Constructivism has struggled for a long time to deal with the implications of constructing "the other." Feminism's epistemological criticisms of notions of universality should invite researchers to be extremely cautious and, especially, all-inclusive in looking at pedagogical discourses, needs assessment, and particularly the simplistic distinctions of who are "we" and "the other." Thus, constructivism is an epistemological and ethical alternative to positivism.

The polar opposite of positivism is a constructivist model of social science that reflects a strong alternative vision in which reality appears as a product of discontinuities and unpredictable effects. Learners, in the view of constructivists, actively participate in learning, a notion that applies to both the most elementary forms of learning and the most advanced forms of research. Viewing all knowledge and learning as a social activity does not necessarily mean, as some postmodernists argue, that we cannot potentially represent reality; but it does imply that we must acknowledge the diversity of perspectives involved in the formation of a community, and especially of a community of inquirers and teachers. Abandoning the quest for certainty does not require abandoning the search for knowledge.

Methodological pluralism follows from a constructivist conception of scientific knowledge. This does not mean that anything goes but that we must acknowledge that there are diverse logics-in-use that make up inquiry. Accordingly, the key issue for policy research is the development of coherent research designs that link theory and research techniques appropriate to the questions asked and problems to be solved.

A third premise, in stark contrast with positivism, is that knowledge cannot be separated from meaning and value; hence education is necessarily a moral enterprise. But in a culturally diverse society, this does not imply an absolute moral code, as opposed to procedural principles for guiding ethical thinking and action. In the context of education, caring, justice, and individual responsibility are central principles of moral action that should complement each other.

As feminist theorists have reminded us, the nurturing principle of caring is at the heart of all learning, which is an interactive process that must respect the dignity of others. In the context of male-dominated culture, an ethics of caring can emerge only through a feminist approach that can provide the foundations for change. Feminist scholars have argued that the male experience is overwhelmingly reflected in public policy, including education. In schools, we need to take very seriously the culture of "otherness," specifically women's culture and the cultures of people of color, broadening the perspectives of citizenship education to include responsible and mutually respectful behavior in the family and in interpersonal relationships in society at large. Further, principles of social justice provide rational grounds justifying criticism of social relations that undermine caring and the equitable fulfillment of human needs. Finally, a notion of individual responsibility is central for the constitution of morality and ethics in education.

Learning is also an interactive process that should be organized around dialogical principles. Although they do not necessarily undermine the importance of intellectual authority and leadership, dialogical principles as predicated by John Dewey and Paulo Freire, among others, do pose the question of the education of the educators and researchers and the need for self-reflexivity about what is to be taught and what are the social uses of research (Burbules, 1993).

Finally, constructivists recognize that research and education are socially and historically situated activities in institutions that are constrained and enabled by the power relations in the society around them. For this reason, the role of expert knowledge, research, and education should be considered from the point of view of a political sociology of education, paying attention to the relationships of the ideals and values embodied in researchers and research practices that seek to inform and guide educational policies.

The constructivist perspective has been struggling with this issue for a long time and is able to offer a legacy of understanding and ways of seeing that is very compelling when compared to positivism. Indeed, as Mouffe (1993) has explained, it is not useful to consider the category "women" as a unified and unifying essence:

> The central issue becomes: How is "woman" constructed as a category within different discourses? How is sexual difference made a pertinent distinction in social relations? And how are relations of subordination constructed through such distinctions? The whole false dilemma of equality-versus-difference is exploded since we no longer have a homogeneous entity "woman" facing another homogeneous entity "man," but a multiplicity of social relations in which sexual difference is always constructed in very diverse ways and where the struggle against subordination has to be visualized in specific and differential forms. To ask whether women should become identical to men in order to be recognized as equal, or whether they should assert their difference at the cost of equality, appears meaningless once essential identities are put into question. (78)

From a critical theory perspective, the tension that we face is between the increasing globalization of the economy, culture, and the polity and the revitalization of local dynamics (e.g., the old adage that "all politics are local"). While some dynamics are totally imbricated in the dynamics of globalization, many others emerge that resist practices of globalization (Mander and Goldsmith, 1996). What, in fact, globalization seems to represent is the reverse of the Trotskyist slogan of international proletarianism, that is, planetarian capitalism and the internationalism of capitalism on a scale never seen before. Yet, with the cohabitation of capitalism and democracy, it is not unthinkable to believe in the need for a global citizen, one who can rely on mutual loyalties and solidarities, and one who can ignore the national frontiers, crossing borders that, while legal, are also historical and thus can be redefined in the context of a new historical epoch. It seems that globalization is shaping particularly ethnic and racial borders in unexpected ways. Yet, social movements are emerging as central actors promoting democratic citizenship.

As if all these theoretical and practical challenges were not enough, any serious redefinition of the linkages between education, citizenship, democracy, and multiculturalism underscores the question of the independence of science as a neutral arbiter of social conflict and as a key tool for social engineering. With these challenges, science appears to be related to power (Harding, 1996). For instance, if we take a perspective of science close to Foucault's view, science will be an essential part of disciplinary forms of power. Its strategic aim is to increase social productivity and utility. The attempt to "remake and reconceptualize the world on the model of laboratory microworlds is neither a fully coherent project deliberately imposed from above nor an irresistible force that cannot be countered from below by those it affects" (Rouse, 1987:244). Thus a dialectical view of science as power sees science, power, and resistance as naturally interlinked and invites researchers to take ethical positions and to consider two-way relationships (e.g., external assistance/research and local communities), three-way relationships (external assistance/research, local communities, bureaucratic legal domination) and the degree of contradictions and ethics involved in each interaction. Who profits, who pays, and who benefits from science as power should be perennial questions for people and institutions involved in multiculturalism, the formation of democratic communities, and citizenship building.

Therefore, if science cannot be accepted as the firm ground to settle, once and for all, the social and political disputes, we need to go back to the source of this inquiry. Here the contribution of Paulo Freire acquires gigantic dimensions, because he told us that freedom is still to be conquered. Freire's contribution to understanding education as the act of freedom is an invitation to see the interminable dialectics in the struggle to free ourselves and others from constraints of freedom. In and of itself, the struggle for liberation is another form of intervention that can be considered as part of the ethics of intervention. Certainly, education as the act of freedom implies a different perspective on local, socially constructed, and generationally transmitted knowledge. It also implies a perspective that challenges normal science and nonparticipatory planning and implies the construction of a theoretical and methodological perspective that is always suspicious of any scientific relationship as one that conceals relationships of domination. At the same time, while freedom is still to be conquered, freedom can be conquered because unequal, exploitative relationships are built by human beings and can be changed by human beings.

In sum, these dilemmas and contradictions of normal science show that research always moves between moral imperatives, ethical choices, and amoral realities. Researchers cannot avoid this fact, although we can deceive ourselves by adopting a cynical perspective and thinking that we only propose technical solutions while others are making the difficult political and ethical decisions. It is not that easy, particularly when we face political challenges.

The Political Challenge: Educational Utopia and Democratic Politics

Educational practice is part of the superstructure of any society. For that very reason, educational practice, in spite of its fantastic importance in the sociohistorical processes of the transformation of societies, is not in itself the key to transformation, even if it is fundamental. Dialectically, education is not the key to transformation, but transformation is in itself educational. The question that you raise, Carlos, also seems to me to be founded on another problem, which is the problem of political options and decisions. In the first place, with respect to a democratic pedagogy, there is no reason why it cannot be applied simply because we are dealing with the first world. Secondly, what is needed is to deepen the democratic angle of this pedagogy which I am defending. This deepening and widening of the horizon of democratic practice will necessarily involve the political and ideological options of the social groups that carry out this pedagogy. So, obviously, a power elite will not enjoy putting in place and practicing a pedagogical form of expression that adds to the social contradictions which reveal the power of the elite classes. It would be naive to think that a power elite would reveal itself for what it is through a pedagogical process that, in the end, would work against itself.

—Paulo Freire, in Carlos Alberto Torres,
Education, Power, and Personal Biography

Paulo Freire has argued that the connections between education and politics cannot be theorized only in terms of the intersections of power and education, or exclusively in terms of the relationships between power and knowledge—a theorizing that, to be sure, has permeated Freire's contributions. While Freire has tirelessly illuminated the "politicity of education," he has at the same time invited us to understand the relationships between education and citizenship training and particularly to highlight the historical, normative, and ontological foundations of democratic education and citizenship rights and responsibilities.

For Freire, debates about education and democracy should deal, ultimately, with the notion of utopia. Indeed, his proposal for an education for liberation still resonates for its boldness and utopian nature. Freire (1972), in a passage I have already quoted, says, with Hegelian overtones:

Truly, only the oppressed are able to conceive of a future totally distinct from their present, insofar as they arrive at a consciousness of a dominated class. The oppressors, as the dominating class, cannot conceive of the future unless it is the preservation of their present as oppressors. In this way, whereas the future of the oppressed consists in the revolutionary transformation of society, without which their liberation will not be verified, the oppressor's future consists in the simple modernization of society, which permits the continuation of its class supremacy. (32)

This utopian factor implies a double tension: announcement and denouncement. Insofar as the teacher carries out his or her utopian role, he or she is turned into a prophet who is dangerous for the system. Rather than performing the role of the functionary who reproduces the elements of the ideological consciousness of the mode of production, the educator becomes a cultural critic and education becomes a public sphere, a theater for public deliberation controlled neither by the state nor by the market. Weffort (1967), in reference to the early beginnings of Freire's political philosophy of education and method, says:

> But, if a pedagogy of freedom outlines the germ of revolt, not for this reason would it be correct to affirm that revolt is found among the aims of the educator. If it happens, it is hardly exclusively because conscientization discerns a real situation in which the most frequent givens are struggle and violence. To conscientize in no way means to ideologize or propose words of order. If conscientization opens the way to the expression of social insatisfactions it is because there are real components of a situation of oppression: many are the workers who, having just acquired literacy, join labor movements or unions, and this is because, to them, it seems to be the legitimate path for the defense of their interest and those of their workmates: finally, if conscientization of the popular classes signifies political radicalization, this is simply because the popular classes are radical. (13)

Freire, though totally aware of the political implications of a liberating education, is also aware of the contradictions of this education. On the one hand, there is always the possibility of the manipulation and ideologizing of consciousness, that is, promoting education and methodologies in the service of a project of domination. On the other hand, Freire believes that a certain connection can be established between educational praxis and political praxis *stricto sensu*. For instance, it is incumbent on the educator, fundamentally, to develop a project of literacy training and conscientization, while the "professional" politician is in charge of realizing the task of organizing the oppressed sectors in terms of political structures.[6]

In countless interventions, Freire postulates that there is no educational revolution without political revolution. No educational action can provoke a revolution of power. Education is not merely instrumental; it is, rather, a field of ideological battles that must be fought, and the politicization of the citizenry is a possible outcome.

This politicization may help the citizenry begin the pronunciation of the word and the pronunciation of the world, a world increasingly more diverse and multicultural; a world that is structuring the life of schools.

The Contradictions and Challenges of Diversity: Multiculturalism, Citizenship, and Democracy in Education

> We should not call the people to school to receive instructions, prescriptions, recipes, threats, reprimands and punishments, but moreover to participate in

the collective construction of knowledge, which goes beyond the knowledge of past experience, and that takes into account the necessities of the people and turns that knowledge into an instrument of struggle, making possible the people's transformation into subjects of their own history. The popular participation in the creation of culture and of education breaks with the tradition that only the elite is competent and knows what are the necessities and interests of the society. The school should also be a center for the dissemination of popular culture, at the service of the community, not to consume it but to create it.

—Paulo Freire, *Diário Oficial*

Let us take as a premise of the analysis that the suffrage movement at the turn of the century, the civil rights movement in the 1960s, and the affirmative action statutes, as well as the constitutional amendment guaranteeing freedom of speech, helped the renewal of citizenship in the United States, enhancing the existing democracy.[7] As Walter Feinberg (1996) rightly points out, affirmative action "uses group membership to identify and correct past acts of discrimination against individuals, acts that have resulted in inadequate educational, economic, and social positioning" (378).

It is not risky, then, to assume that the suffrage, civil rights, and free speech movements, and indeed affirmative action, even with their multiple contradictions and limitations, have contributed to create better conditions for the practice of democracy, because these movements understand diversity as a central component of citizenship in the United States.

Attacks on affirmative action and cultural diversity, particularly in the realm of higher education, may undermine the foundations of citizenship in the United States. Why? First because, as Feinberg (1996) claims, affirmative action reminds us of a historical debt that needs to be repaid to specific groups. Second, race-based affirmative action needs to be complemented with need-based affirmative action, because there cannot be equality of political opportunity without equality of social opportunity. This idea of citizenship is as old as the radical democratic ideal espoused by two figures as different as Plato and Jean-Jacques Rousseau, who, in fact, argued that economic democracy must go hand-in-hand with political democracy—that is, democracy as content and not merely as a method of political representation.

Rousseau (1980) theorized about the conditions that would assure the existence of democracy and freedom. To achieve these objectives, he recommended reducing the differences between the "extreme classes" as much as possible, to prevent the existence of both beggars and magnates. These social groups, two sides of the same coin, were considered threats to the future of democracy because "it is between them that public liberty must be firm: some of them buy and some of them sell" (292–293). Nothing else is what the Western political tradition demands. As Gitlin (1995) suggests, "The right to a job, education, medical care, housing, retraining over the course of life—these are the bare elements of an economic citizenship that ought to be universal" (254).

Finally, in the context of U.S. democracy, affirmative action reaffirms the importance of the critique to public policy and the history of a given society. Not surprisingly, many people have identified African Americans as the preeminent subject of affirmative action (though they have not, as a group, become the principal beneficiaries of these policies, who have been white women).[8] Cornel West (in West, Klor de Alba, and Shorris, 1996) said it very passionately: "One of the reasons why black people are so integral a part of American civilization is because black people have raised a lot of hell. That is very important, especially in a society in which power and pressure decide who receives visibility. By raising hell I mean organization, mobilization, chaos-producing capacity, as in rebellion" (58). The black struggle in the United States shows that criticism and rebellion emerge as two key factors in the constitution of citizenship for a democracy of content and not merely a democracy of method.

No doubt criticism and rebellion against mainstream ideas that may represent the powers that be have long been central components of any political democratic education for citizenship. In fact, we cannot understand the construction of multicultural citizenship without understanding the role that education, particularly higher education, plays in the constitution of the democratic pact. Moreover, I contend that we cannot attain a progressive understanding of the democratic pact without considering affirmative action policies and cultural diversity as indissolubly linked.[9]

Universities are seen by Giroux (1996a) and others in the field of critical pedagogy as a public sphere. As such, universities are responsible for creating critical citizens, and professors are seen as public intellectuals. From a moral rather than an instrumental perspective, Giroux (1996) would argue that universities should accentuate the imperative of public service rather than "the dynamics of professionalism, competition, and social mobility" (124). Giroux would even go so far as to argue that universities and institutions of higher learning should be defended as a public resource that is vital to the moral life of a nation.

Yet, for this to happen, I contend that some conditions should be met. First and foremost, universities should allow improved access by working-class people, people of color, women in nontraditional professions, and members of marginalized communities, particularly people living in subaltern spaces. Second, with this constituency in mind—and not merely the representatives of the dominant cultural capital or individuals from marginal habitats and habitus who have managed to make a successful transition (or perhaps we should say "mutation") to higher learning—knowledge itself needs to be democratized, in a broader reconstruction of what knowledge is valuable, whose knowledge counts, and how knowledge, skills, dexterities, and learning relate to power, wealth, and prestige.

This redemocratization of access and knowledge entails, in the view of Giroux (1996a) and a large number of critical pedagogues, that "the political" and not merely a "politicizing" education becomes a unifying principle of the university. Challenging the liberal establishment and the neoconservative reformers alike, Giroux (1996a) argues that "the political in this sense rejects the language of normalization and universalization for the discourse of contingency and the constitutive role of difference and conflict. For it is precisely through the revival of the political that democracy is bolstered—through competing conceptions of the common good, a range of possible identities to define what it means to be a citizen, and a reassertion of the important relationships between ethics and public life" (125).

The tradition of critical pedagogy inspired by critical theory, the work of Paulo Freire, and a critical reading of John Dewey, among other sources, have long criticized the instrumental notion of politics (i.e., politics as manipulation of civic virtues and public opinion). Critical theorists endorse a notion of politics understood as both oppositional practices and enlightened critical judgment about the question of the polis. Likewise, they challenge traditional distinctions between fact and value, alleging that the "imperatives of objectivity" attempt to reduce the whole political debate in universities to the question of academic standards and insist that university practices should remain neutral and apolitical. Critical pedagogy would argue instead, with Paulo Freire and a whole generation of cultural critics, that we cannot easily dissociate politics and education. Early on in his research, Freire studied the organization of the class consciousness of the oppressed, focusing on concrete social processes while at the same time searching for an effective transformation of the structures of oppression. In so doing, his focus was always educational and cultural. While Freire's thought requires a number of historical (theoretical and strategic) mediations for its implementation in pedagogical, organizational, and political terms, it is, from its very beginnings, an eminently political thought. For Freire, politics, power, and education are an indissoluble unity. As a set of relationships, they interpenetrate each other (Torres, 1978).

Freire (1998) says this very nicely in one of his last books to be translated into English, shortly before his death:

The comprehension of the limits of educational practice absolutely requires political clarity on the part of educators in relation to their project. It demands that the educator assumes the political nature of his/her practice. It is not enough to say that education is a political act just as it is not enough to say that political acts are also educative. It is necessary to truly assume the political nature of education. I cannot consider myself progressive if I understand school space to be something neutral, with limited or no relation to class struggle, in which students are seen only as learners of limited domains of knowledge which I will imbue with magic power. I cannot recognize the limits of the political-educative practice in which I am involved if I don't know, if I am not clear about in whose favor I work. Clarifying the question of in whose favor I practice puts me in a certain position, which is related to class, in which I devise against whom I practice and, necessarily, for what reasons I practice—that is, the dream, the type of society on whose behalf I would like to intervene, act, and participate.

In this tradition, Giroux (1996a) distinguishes between political education and politicizing education. The former teaches students how to exercise power and responsibility in a democracy and how to exercise the distinguished tradition of critiquing the status quo, posing embarrassing questions, confronting dogmas and orthodoxies, and avoiding being co-opted by corporations, governments, or the temptations of power networks. The latter "is a form of pedagogical terrorism in which the issue of what is taught, by whom, and under what conditions is determined by a doctrinaire political agenda that refuses to examine its own values, beliefs, and ideological constructions. While refusing to acknowledge the social character of its own claims to history, knowledge, and values, a politicizing education silences in the name of a specious universalism and denounces all transformative practices through an appeal to a timeless notion of truth and beauty" (127).

Indeed, recognizing that relations of domination are central to public life, as Freire so insightfully and persistently argues, critical pedagogy argues that domination, aggression, and violence are an intrinsic part of human and social life, and any political education nourishing the construction of a public sphere should recognize that overcoming oppression, domination, and exploitation is a central goal of any project of democratic citizenship building.

As I argue in discussing the connections between democracy and education in chapter 5, the central question of education today is what role, if any, educational institutions and practices should play in the constitution of the social pact that articulates democracy. This brings us to the dilemma of a democratic culture that I have outlined before but want to reiterate now, the construction of a democratic citizen. To put it simply: democracy implies a process of participation where all are considered equal. However, education involves a process whereby the "immature" are brought to identify with the principles and forms of life of the "mature" members of society. Thus, the process of constructing the democratic citizen is a process not only of cultural nurturing but of articulating principles of pedagogic and democratic socialization in individuals who are neither tabula rasa in cognitive or ethical terms nor fully equipped for the exercise of their democratic rights and obligations. The central problem of education is how to contribute to the democratic pact and how we can build an approach to multicultural democratic citizenship. I have argued that citizenship can be predicated in terms of civic virtues or legal status but that we need to stress as well the political economy of citizenship. Civic virtues point to a sense of solidarity that unites individuals around common goals. These goals are, at the very least, how to survive and live together in our contemporary, diverse society. These goals, however, can also be accomplished as part of a more ambitious agenda: learning to thrive as a community of communities, as a culture of cultures drawing from our cultural diversity as a cultural strength, and promoting affirmative action, broadly understood, as a useful policy.

Surely, as Gitlin (1995) cautions us, and I quoted before, "The question is how to cultivate the spirit of solidarity across the lines of difference—solidarity with 'anyone who suffers.' For surely that spirit cannot be expected to generate spontaneously inside fortified groups, each preoccupied with refining its differences from other groups" (217). For frameworks of solidarity and common ground across cultures, ethnicities, classes, and gender differences, the goals of cultural diversity are central. We need to develop flexible frameworks for solidarity in schools that take seriously the need for democratic reform. Cultural diversity is a major by-product of the growing process of economic, cultural, and political globalization with an intensity which has no parallel in the history of humankind. Globalization produces all sorts of implications for the multicultural, multilingual, and multiethnic configuration of local communities in the United States and elsewhere. In terms of the social covenant, not surprisingly, diversity is a key challenge for any institution of higher education in complying with federal statutes for affirmative action and in facing growing social and educational demands.

Yet, we cannot accomplish this without, paradoxically, a culture of commonality: "To be active citizens of the whole, they must also spend time Monday through Saturday fraternizing across the lines, cultivating cultural hybrids, criticizing the narrowness of the tribe, working up ideas that people 'unlike' themselves might share. One may respect the democratic rights of distinct groups to organize as they choose and still argue vigorously against the aggrandizement of difference" (Gitlin, 1995:218).

Higher-education institutions are at the center of the storm in terms of diversity and affirmative action and, I must say, in terms of promoting a renewal of citizenship. A commitment to diversity and multiculturalism implies a commitment to diversify the faculty so that it resembles, to the extent possible and given the available resources, the demographic traits of society in schools and universities in the United States. Diversity also implies diversifying the student body so that students will be able to appropriately address in their classrooms demands from different intellectual, ethnic, gender, and underrepresented groups and constituencies. To achieve the goals of diversity and multiculturalism, universities should be able to attract the best and brightest, the most qualified scholars, undergraduates, and graduate students, who can explore the frontiers of knowledge in their teaching, research, and outreach without prejudice but with creativity, joy, enthusiasm, and dedication and with a sense of utopian hope.

Achieving diversity and developing a multicultural academic environment are not easy tasks. Tensions will always arise between growing social and intellectual demands and diminishing fiscal resources. There are also tensions among diverse intellectual, ethnic, and social constituencies and between faculty desires to serve the ideals of equity and the imperatives of equality and the perennial academic quest for excellence and community. There are also serious criticisms of policies oriented to equity and equality in education, including affirmative action policies.[10] Despite recent setbacks to the gains of the civil rights movement, affirmative action cannot be considered wiped out from public policy nor from the public imagination or our moral commitments. Yet, affirmative action should not be considered as a moral absolute but should be included in a democratic conversation on how affirmative action and cultural diversity enhance citizenship and the role that higher-education institutions should play in this respect.[11]

I believe that in order to achieve the mission of higher education, it is essential to construct an academic consensus based on the notion of diversity. This consensus building, however, should begin with a recognition of the importance of these tensions, should take into account the precariousness of many of the managerial solutions available, and should recognize the limitations of the many intellectual paradigms in vogue. These are some of the intellectual challenges of discussing citizenship, cultural diversity, and affirmative action in higher education. However, in terms of the politics of culture, the sticky distinction between culture and canon needs to be addressed.

Canon and Culture

> The impossibility of an uncontested canon results from the impossibility of defining a single, integrated, nonproblematic, and descriptive social and pedagogical identity in the culture of the West.
>
> —Raymond Morrow and Carlos Alberto Torres,
> *Social Theory and Education*

In a sense, this is a game of never-ending mirrors.
—Immanuel Wallerstein, "Social Science
and the Quest for a Just Society"

Canon and culture are not, in principle, opposed, but they have a difficult time cohabiting, especially when a given canon (which is in principle a social construction accepted as foundation of a given identity, be it national, cultural, or otherwise) is regarded as a set of metaphysical principles that cannot be historically examined or challenged but must be preserved at any cost. Metaphysical canons become, in principle, opposed to cultural negotiation.

Foundational canons, however, are ongoing processes of cultural negotiations, taking as their precedents key foundations for dialogue and open-ended interpretations of history and community experiences. They also enjoy what Freire calls an epistemology of curiosity: an endless need to define what cultural principles make the life of people more harmonious, cultural exchanges more self-reflective, and the ethical underpinnings of the culture closer to the cultural imperatives of social justice, individual responsibility, and caring.

Foundational canons are changed through cultural negotiation. As Gitlin put it in a personal communication to me: "Negotiation may take place—does take place—on the edges of a canon, so that Whitman was brought in the '40s, while Whittier was booted out (Leo Marx has made that point), and during recent years Ellison's *Invisible Man* is effectively canonized. In other words, once a foundation is clear, there's plenty of room for divergences and plurality."

Any cultural canon, as long as it is made into a metaphysical condition of being, is in principle opposed to cultural negotiation. As such, a metaphysical cultural canon, a canon revered as the encapsulation of virtue, wisdom, and truth, must have several authority sources or legitimacy claims, which may include, for instance, the sheer power of a given group to establish legal restrictions that become the law of the land (e.g., the South African white power before the establishment of racial democracy in 1994, or the legislation of slavery in the American South); claims to enjoy racial purity (e.g., Nazism); claims to being the original founding fathers of the nation (e.g., Caucasian and Eurocentric immigrant-bashing groups); claims to control the language that constitutes identity and regulates and makes possible social, political, and economic exchanges (e.g., English-only movements); or a claim to moral or ethical superiority based on a religious mandate, "Beruf," or "call" (e.g., Christian bigotry, movements to establish the biblical superiority of men over women, and homosexual-bashing movements based on Christian faith).

The liberal pluralist call to recognize the richness of "otherness" and diversity in a society otherwise characterized by shared historical foundations identified on the basis of cultural consensus (e.g., the notion of "togetherness" as an essential pragmatic principle for the social pact to work) can be confronted with a more radical, historically nuanced perception of multiculturalism: "Oddly enough, given the charges of incoherence and anarchy made against multicultural approaches, historicizing the question of identity also offers the possibility of a more unified view than that of the liberal pluralists. . . . Alternative to pluralism is to make difference and conflict the center of a history 'we' all share" (Scott, 1992:16).

Now, if national identity is a not a fixed marker but a process of learning as I have argued in chapter 6, this creates another conundrum.[12] The first question to consider is, Is it possible that exposure to similar processes of learning creates different conclusions? This is certainly the drama of democratic education and democratic life. What we pursue in democracy is to allow the process of learning to go on and, at the same time, to accept that the conclusions could, and indeed will, be divergent. People will have different views, and political disagreements will be the bread and butter for education as much as coalition and alliance politics is for democratic governance.

This has implications at the level of the knowledge base of the society and the democratization of knowledge. The next question is, Are some explanations more powerful than others? In other words, is one type of social science more useful (I am tempted to say more truthful) than others? Discussing the impact of deconstructionism in the social sciences, Immanuel Wallerstein (1997) warns us that "We are clearly involved here in a very complex activity, one in which equilibria (canons) are at best transient and one in which there can be no determinate future, since the aleatory elements are too vast" (1253).

The problem, it seems, is the tendency to consider that because reality is a social construction, everything goes, and therefore every explanation is as valuable as the next, that there are no particular criteria upon which to ascertain which explanation is more truthful or explanatorily powerful, or which is a better approach to understanding and explaining the complexity of reality. Wallerstein (1997) is very clear in this respect:

> The role of the scholars is not to construct reality but to figure out how it has been constructed and to test the multiple social constructions of reality against each other. In a sense, this is a game of never-ending mirrors. We seek to discover the reality on the basis of which we have constructed reality. And when we find this, we seek to understand how this underlying reality has in turn been socially constructed. In this navigation amidst the mirrors, there are however more correct and less correct scholarly analyses. Those scholarly analyses that are more correct are more socially useful in that they aid the world to construct a substantively more rational reality. Hence the search for truth and the search for goodness are inextricably linked the one to the other. We are all involved, and involved simultaneously, in both. (1254)

Three points should be stressed here. First, despite the deconstructionist storm and the fact that we can think of reality as a social construction, this social construction is not just the product of our imagination but the product of real people interacting in complex ways, and hence not all explanations have the same quality (e.g., logical coherence, analytical insight, empirical documentation), explanatory power, or truthfulness. Second, even if all explanations, by their very nature, are transient—that is, they are works in progress until a better explanation is constructed—they are all to be judged by their ability to explain and, in turn, their ability to help construct a more rational society. Hence, there is an element of usefulness in each validity construct that cannot be overlooked. While the previous comment can be read as overtly pragmatic, it in itself points to the third implication of Wallerstein's analysis, that the notion of the truth and the goodness in society are intimately and inextricably intertwined. Constructive, useful, rational society, refers to Wallerstein's suggestion of looking at the social sciences as part of the quest for a just society. Hence, Wallerstein is proposing a categorical imperative of justice and goodness to inspire if not to guide the analytical endeavor.

In politics and social struggles, however, disagreements could be even more drastic than the implications of debates in the social sciences about causality or explanatory validity. Consider, for instance, the situation in Algeria. If democratic elections are granted (as in 1992), the fundamentalist Islamic movements will win the elections. Considering their platform of basing the social order on a peculiar vision of strict literal adherence to the Koran and their practice of intimidating citizens, mostly displayed lately with massacres in small towns in Algeria (with a toll, according to journalistic sources, of 100,000 dead in the last five years) and sporadic violence in Egypt, this victory not only will result in many people, particularly women, as demonstrated in the Taliban government in Afghanistan, losing their civil liberties but also will imperil the democratic structure. Here the government of the majority that could be achieved through democracy as a method will undoubtedly destroy democracy as practice and content. The constitution of a democratic political culture is then a foundational premise for the continuation of democracy and the exercise of democratic life.

The idea of democracy is to learn to live with challenges and tensions and to learn about the process of learning about democratic differences. Democratic disagreements will take place everywhere, from dinner-table discussions in which families disagree passionately over public and private issues to the political pulpits in which leaders and coalitions try to capture the imagination of most people and to constitute electoral majorities. These coalitions, however, will always be temporary, fragile, and subject to disintegration—in a word, ephemeral.

The notion of democracy as a method facilitates the process of differential representation and participation in which, through the voting process, alliance making, and majority coalitions, some conclusions may prevail at a particular point in time. Thus, some majorities may push for a particular vision that is not, by definition, shared by all the members of the given polity. I have argued in this book, however, that democracy as a method does not and cannot totally encapsulate the notion of democracy as content.

The notion of democracy as content, however, places some limits on what is expected and acceptable democratic behavior and highlights civil minimums that go beyond the formalities of the democratic methodology, reaching a more radical understanding of democratic representation and participation—in short, of democratic interactions in the public and private spheres.

Thus, considering identity as a process of learning, we are back to the unpleasant question of how to establish that some views are more plausible than others. This question is made even more uncomfortable if, as I have discussed above, science can be related to power and therefore cannot be used without qualification to settle the disputes. There is no metaphysical answer to this question, but there are procedural and methodical as well as historical answers. The procedural and methodical answers attempt to expand, to push the democratic envelope to its limits, while respecting the rules of confrontation and negotiation, trying to understand how democratic life may accommodate a diversity of interests, identities, experiences, and ideologies without damaging the fabric of the democratic discourse and without accepting the premise that a final solution for a problem will be reached in the deliberations. We know the implications of metaphysical notions such as a "final solution."

The historical answer is partly what we have defined as historical accommodations between capitalism and democracy. The period in which we are living shows that the process of globalization may in fact be creating the conditions for a new historical accommodation. Yet, as has been clear with previous historical accommodations, the viability of the social pact is always suspect with sizable segments of the population. Tensions and conflicts will continue to arise, more prominently where the ability to redistribute resources diminishes. Consensus building and consensus politics are always fragile, and democracy continues to be a dream as much as a system of radical political representation and participation.

The notion of consensus should indeed be differentiated from the notion of the democratic social pact. Social pacts are more enduring than historical consensuses, which are by nature ephemeral. The paradox is that social pacts are made up of historically consensual agreements that generations create, sustain, and transform into laws, routines, customs, practices, habits, regulations, and even cultures. What cannot be changed, unless we are willing to do away with the notion of democracy, is the notion of a prevailing social pact that, by its mere existence, will in the long run prevent the polity from falling into chaos or authoritarianism—a social pact that strives to accommodate as the keystone of the government of the people, by the people, and for the people. As Freire has so often reminded us, the ability to agree to disagree is as fundamental for a politics of democratic dialogue as the ability to live with tensions and contradictions is fundamental for democratic politics.

Another important question falls squarely in the domain of education: Is there an opposition between identity formation (which should be a significant part of the educational agenda) and the formation of citizenship through establishing a knowledge floor? Identity formation has always been part of the liberal state ideology; as historian Ted Mitchell reminds us, Governor DeWitt Clinton of New York told his constituency in 1822 that it is the first duty of the state. Paradoxically, identity building has always been (consciously or unconsciously) blended in educational policy with the notion of citizenship building, as if identity and citizenship are fixed markers that will always coincide, assuming that citizenship can be predicated as a cultural representation with an acute degree of homogeneity and historical accuracy.

Towards the end of the millennium, it is clear that identity formation takes place in many spheres, including education, but that citizen building has been mostly confined formally to the educational domain.[13] The issue, which certainly goes beyond the limits of this work, is whether both identity formation and citizen building should be treated as processes of life-long learning (with the potential divergent conclusions); whether they should be treated as discrete theoretical entities that may intersect at some point, giving rise to the need to rethink their contradictions and correspondences; and whether this interaction between identity and citizenship can be accomplished at all in the context of late capitalism and the criticism of democratic ungovernability.

Thus, identity, as I have argued in chapter 6, is a never-secured effect of a process of enunciation of cultural difference.[14] Taken to the extreme, however, this epistemological premise may seem impractical for pedagogy or political mobilization.[15] Yet, from a progressive perspective, it would be simplistic to think of cultural differences as differences between dominant and subordinate cultures. The fact is that critical multiculturalism should also address the ideological cleavages and differences within subordinate cultures, not only as the negotiation between people of color and the oppressive networks of power but also among people of color themselves. Here, the words of critical race theorists resonate with peculiar force: "Unfortunately, the tension between and among these differences is rarely interrogated, presuming a 'unity of difference'—that is, that all difference is both analogous and equivalent" (Ladson-Billings and Tate, 1995:62).

Membership and experience in a given identity do not guarantee the accurate recollection of the experience—for instance, using the analytical tools of social sciences and humanities—and hence the political risks are many, including the fact that in many multiculturalist quarters, as Scott has reminded us, "Personal testimony of oppression replaces analysis, and this testimony comes to stand for the experience of the whole group" (1992:18).

Despite the growing literature on multiculturalism, only recently has the discussion shifted to address the connections between multiculturalism and citizenship, exploring the limits and possibilities of multiculturalism in democratic societies.[16] Perhaps it is fair to argue that the multitude of tasks confronting multiculturalism is overwhelming. Those tasks include the attempt to develop a sensible, theoretically refined, and defensible new metatheoretical and theoretical territory that would create the foundations for multiculturalism as a paradigm; the attempt to establish its epistemological and logical premises around the notions of experience, narrative, voice, agency, and identity; the attempt to pursue empirical research linking culture/power/knowledge with equality/inequality/discrimination; and the need to defend multiculturalism from the conservative right, which has demonized multiculturalism as an antipatriotic movement that opposes the need for a canon that can regulate cultural exchanges from a principle of order.[17] These multifaceted tasks and the concrete political experience of the 1980s and 1990s in the United States have forced the proponents of multiculturalism into the defensive, in both theoretical and political terms. This means that they have so far been unable to address fully the need for a theory of multicultural citizenship, a theory that should be instrumental in advancing democratic goals in the context of theories of democracy, despite the fact that they operate within the capitalist framework. A final dilemma for multiculturalism is the understanding of the connections between diversity and commonality, that is, the question of unity in diversity.

There are certainly many analytical and political alternatives to confront the dilemma of unity in diversity. First is the need to explore the degree of hybridization of cultures and the notion that every social subject is constituted by multiple identities and multiple affiliations.[18] Recognition of the complexities posed by the process of hybridization and the notion of multiple identities in the social and psychological construction of the pedagogical subject should challenge any attempt to essentialize differences based on race, gender, class, nationality, ethnic, religious, or sexual preferences. Second, rather than dealing with differences in ethical and political commitments as primary contradictions, one may see them as secondary contradictions or as conflicting loyalties in the social construction of identity. This opens up areas of negotiation in the context of progressive alliances based on multiple identities and learning communities.[19] A fundamental premise is to avoid any essentialization of cultural struggles. Yet it is also important to recognize that there are a number of insights in neoconservative and neoliberal arguments. For instance, from a very different vantage point than neoconservatives, Cornel West (1993a), along with a number of black intellectuals, is concerned with "Cultural breakdown and escalating self-destructive nihilism among the poor and very poor" (196). Nihilism certainly offers poor foundations for the advancement of democracy and the attainment of citizenship. Civic virtues, then, emerge as key notions in the constitution of a democratic citizenship.

Civic Virtues and Multicultural Democratic Citizenship

> I speak here of poetry as a revelatory distillation of experience, not the sterile word play that, too often, the white fathers distorted the word poetry to mean—in order to cover a desperate wish for imagination without insight.
> —"Poetry Is Power" bulletin board

A central tenet of my analysis has been that citizenship should be understood as civic virtues in the context of distributional policies and not merely as the conferring of status. At the invitation of Professor Pedro Noguera, I presented my analysis in his graduate course on race and class at the University of California–Berkeley in September 1997. Towards the end of the question-and-answer period, a black student challenged me, arguing that I had been discussing citizenship as civic virtues but I had not outlined the principles of civic virtues for a multicultural democratic citizenship. The question was a revelatory experience because I had not thought about that at all. The words, used here as an epigraph, that I read on a bulletin board labeled "Poetry Is Power" minutes before entering the classroom popped into my head the moment I heard the question, because it was as insightful as it could be.

Multicultural citizenship should not be considered a "supplement" to "ordinary" citizenship. On the contrary, the argument is that no real citizenship as civic virtues can be achieved unless contemporary capitalist societies and liberal democracies solve the problem of democratic multicultural citizenship. It is because of the pitfalls of liberal democracy that we need to advocate a democracy with adjectives, a radical democracy. Similarly, it is the pitfalls of traditional theories of citizenship with which we are concerned in developing a theory of multicultural citizenship. In short, the adjective matters. Ideally, we should be discussing a notion of citizenship or democracy without adjectives or qualifications, but we all know how far away reality can be from our own desires.

Having said these words of epistemic and political caution, I shall now discuss the principal virtues of multicultural citizenship, virtues that should be nurtured in families, churches, and the principal organizations that socialize our children and youth, and, very importantly, in schools and citizenship education.

The first virtue coincides with the greatest learning of liberalism, the virtue of tolerance. Liberalism emerged as the political philosophy that upheld freedom over any other categorical imperative as a normative condition for all social interactions and as an antidote to absolutism, authoritarianism, and despotism. In the context of contemporary discussions, the civic virtue of tolerance is essential to a flourishing diversity, since we are continually crossing the lines of diversity in our societies. Tolerance requires a systematic process of self-vigilance and self-consciousness, of revisiting the constitution of our own consciousness—which is never a fully accomplished outcome but a lifelong learning process—to identify the sources of preconcepts and prejudice. For instance, while individual racism can be confronted through permanent discussion and education (that is, knowledge matters), confronting institutional racism—practices, rituals, routines, and mores that are more pervasive than sporadic individual acts—requires a systematic, legal/judicial, and political vigilance by individuals, communities, and social movements.

Tolerance also requires knowledge and discipline: knowledge to challenge ignorance, which is no doubt one of the bases of racial, sexual, gender, religious, and class prejudice; discipline, because only through a systematic exercise of introspection and research can we discover that while social representations are socially constructed, they are based on historical processes that need to be examined as evidence for understanding. Hobsbawm (1997) is very clear about this: "without the distinction between what is and what is not, there can be no history. Rome defeated and destroyed Carthage in the Punic Wars, not the other way around. How we assemble and interpret our chosen sample of verifiable data (which may include not only what happened but what people thought about it) is another matter" (viii). Actually, Hobsbawm's point that the most common "ideological abuse of history is based on anachronism rather than lies" (7) is a basic premise of knowledge for enhanced tolerance.

Tolerance based on knowledge, discipline, and self-reflection is not sufficient for the exercise of democratic multicultural citizenship. An epistemology of curiosity, as outlined by Paulo Freire, is an important virtue to cultivate. Freire's (1997b) last book, released in Portuguese less than a month before his death, offers a decalogue of virtues for teachers—a set of ethical principles for teaching—and constitutes the heart of a project of multicultural citizenship. Freire's decalogue is based on the notion of autonomy, a notion that is also very precious to liberalism, but which Freire extends with his critical modernist perspective and his constant flirting with libertarian philosophy. Here is his list of virtues for a teacher:

1. Teaching requires respect for the student's knowledge.

2. Teaching requires aesthetics and ethics.

3. Teaching requires setting an example.

4. Teaching requires respect for the autonomy of the student.

5. Teaching requires good judgment.

6. Teaching requires curiosity.

7. Teaching requires self-confidence, professional competence, and generosity.

8. Teaching requires freedom and authority.

9. Teaching requires knowing how to listen.

10. Teaching requires loving the students.

A third virtue I would like to emphasize to avoid the twin positions of cynicism and nihilism is hope. Cynicism is the absence of hope, the conviction that since nothing can or will fundamentally change, the only option is to pursue a "business as usual" approach. As such, cynicism is an antiutopian philosophy of brutal adaptation to reality, trying to take advantage of benefits without exercising rights and obligations. The other side of the coin is nihilism, a morbid experience of giving up, accepting that since there is no hope, there is no need to change the social order, nor even the slim possibility of doing so. Taking Ilya Prigogine's apothegm, "The possible is richer than the real," Immanuel Wallerstein (1997) offers an important point for civic virtues:

> The possible is richer than the real. Who should know this better than social scientists? Why are we so afraid of discussing the possible, of analyzing the possible, of exploring the possible? We must move not utopias, but utopistics, to the center of social science. Utopistics is the analysis of possible utopias, their limitations, and the constraints on achieving them. It is the analytic study of real historical alternatives in the present. It is the reconciliation of the search for truth and the search for goodness. (1254–1255)

In short, only hope is an antidote for cynicism and nihilism.

A fourth virtue is a secular, or nonreligious, spirituality of love. Nothing is more powerful than love to guide decision making based on community and compassion. A spirituality of love, as Eric Fromm (1986) argued thirty years ago, does not have to be based on transcendental faith, but it needs to be based on faith in human nature and on the need to reconcile reason and passion in our actions.

A fifth virtue is the ability to dialogue. No multicultural citizenship can be accomplished without the ability to dialogue, even when the positions of the people in the dialogue are remote or distinct, even when there is an incommensurability in the languages involved, even when open-ended dialogues are risky. The ability to dialogue is the basic principle of Habermas's social construct of ideal speech and communicative rationality. In dialogue we can construct a communicative rationality, that is, the ability to communicate and accept validity claims, a factor in communication that goes beyond simple coherence. Three elements intervene in this notion of dialogue as communicative rationality: first, the notion of intersubjectivity in the validity claims (the position of the person in the dialogue is relevant); second, the mode of argumentation (which varies by discipline, set of interactions, professions, etc.); and, finally, the idea of the possibility of reaching a rational agreement. Thus dialogue entails mutual recognition of diverse individuals, the ability to evaluate validity claims and modes of argumentative interactions, and the objective of reaching a rational attitude and understanding in the whole exchange.

This process of symbolic production presupposes a form of rationalization of human life and hence, I may say with a Durkheimian bent, a notion of systemic integration and not merely mechanical integration of social action. It presupposes that human beings come of age as individuals not only through their exchanges with nature and with other human beings for the possession of nature, abilities, skills, and social benefits (that is, moving beyond the notion of work as humanization) but that they come of age as individuals because of their ability to develop their communicative competence and communicative rationality. Communicative rationalization, which emerges not only as a precondition for the dialogue but also as one of its most important outcomes, is a central claim and virtue of a multicultural democratic citizenship (Burbules, 1993).

In summary, an antiracist, antisexist, and anticlassist philosophy based on tolerance, an epistemology of curiosity à la Freire, a rejection of cynicism and nihilist postures, a secular spirituality of love, and skillful engagement in dialogue as a method but also as process of cognition constitute central virtues of a democratic multicultural citizenship, a bridge between foundational canons and cultures.

Epilogue

The present cannot be the measure of happiness, because happiness is simply a collection of images that vanish with distance and become distorted with proximity.

—Carlos Alberto Torres

The central concern for us is education for democracy: how to build better schools, intellectually richer schools, particularly for those who are at the bottom of the society; how to build a democratic multicultural curriculum where everybody learns from the rich diversity of the society and where the trends toward balkanization and growing separatism in modern societies can be prevented and even reversed. Schools should play a central role in the constitution of democratic discourse and citizenship. I am convinced that the Bosnian syndrome in the polarization of social classes and ethnic or racial groups can be prevented.

We can do a much better job in preparing for the twenty-first century teachers who are capable of working in school settings that can become the center of collective expertise and solidarity. We need to prepare professionals who understand the importance and contradictions of cultural diversity and affirmative action. We need to move back and forth between theoretical and applied research in real school settings without neglecting the importance of nonformal education, adult education, and the role of grassroots organizations, social movements, and communities in cultural revival, democracy, and production. After all, if identity is a process of learning, it is lifelong learning.

Democracy is a messy system, but it has survived because there is a sphere for debates and a set of rules that people follow even if they don't benefit from them. Schools and universities for democratic communities cannot be less committed to expanding the democratic discourse and to challenging the political economy of capitalism. Without a serious exploration of the intersections between cultural diversity, affirmative action, and citizenship, the plural bases for democracy and the democratic discourse per se are at risk. Without a technically competent, ethically sound, spiritually engaging, and politically feasible theory and practice of democratic multicultural citizenship, the people will perish: Where there is no vision, the people perish. I shall conclude with Friedrich Nietzsche ([1983] 1991) that "I know of no better aim of life than of perishing, *animae magnae prodigus,* in pursuit of the great and the impossible" (112). The call for a democratic multicultural citizenship implies the pursuit of the great and the impossible, even at the risk of perishing.

Notes

1. I concur with Theo Goldberg when he states: "So multiculturalism is a political commitment. But it is no more political than monoculturalism, and for similar reasons" D. T. Goldberg, ed. *Multiculturalism: A Critical Reader* (Oxford: Blackwell, 1996), 28.

2. While I am aware that "the classics" of political philosophy reflect by and large male, European, and heterosexual views and therefore cannot be made uncritically a

cultural canon of any sort, I contend that, properly deconstructed and analyzed with a nuanced historical sense, they continue to be an invaluable source for thinking and praxis. A similar argument is made by Carole Pateman discussing the pertinence of the classics for feminist political science: "it is impossible completely to turn our backs on the classics or on contemporary methodology, because all modes of discourse reflect and are implicated in the past to a greater or lesser degree. Moreover, there are valuable insights to be gained and lessons to be learned from male-stream theory." Carole Pateman, "Introduction: The Theoretical Subversiveness of Feminism," in *Feminist Challenges. Social and Political Theory,* ed. Carole Pateman and Elizabeth Gross (London: Allen & Unwin, 1986), 3.

3. A good example of dichotomous choices is Goldberg's analysis counterpointing heterogeneity and homogeneity. Another is his suggestion of displacing Afrocentricity "by self-critical Afromodalities, the heterogeneous modes of African seeing, knowing, and doing that serve notice on the parochialism of Euromotivated vision, epistemologies, and practices." Goldberg, *Multiculturalism,* 39.

4. The notion of instrumental rationality is central to critical theory. It is defined here combining Weber's notion of rationality as purposive-instrumental action and Habermas's notion of instrumental action. For Max Weber, purposive-instrumental action is "determined by expectations as to the behavior of external objects and of other men, and making use of these expectations as 'conditions' or 'means' for the rational success-oriented pursuit of the agent's own rationally considered ends" (T. McCarthy, *The Critical Theory of Jürgen Habermas.* [Cambridge: MIT Press, 1979], 28). The notion of instrumental action in Habermas "is governed by technical rules based on empirical knowledge. In every case they imply empirical predictions about observable events, physical or social" (391). I shall add, following Herbert Marcuse's criticism of technical reason, that every form of instrumental rationality, insofar as it represents an adequate means to a given end and is governed by technical rules based on empirical knowledge seeking to forecast and control social and physical events, involves a substantive purpose of domination exercised through methodical, scientific, calculating, and calculated control.

5. C. B.Macpherson in his essay "The Real World of Democracy" (the Massey Lectures, in *The Real World of Democracy* [Oxford: Oxford University Press, 1966], 56–67), and particularly in his essay on human rights as citizenship rights, shows that in the proposal of possessive individualism exemplified in the political philosophical contributions of Hobbes and Locke, human rights included the right to life, body, capacities, the members of the family, liberties, and land. In his view, democratic theory should recognize that human rights and freedom are not mutually exclusive and that the attainment of the former does not preclude the attainment of the later and vice versa.

6. Weffort ("Educação e politica: Reflexões sociológicas sobre una pedagogia da liberdade," in *Educação como prática da liberdade* [Rio de Janeiro: Paz e Terra, 1967), 56–67) asserts, confirming our line of argument, that "this educator [Freire] knows that his task contains political implications and he knows, moreover, that these implications are in the interest of the common man and not of the elite. But he also knows that his field is pedagogy and not politics and that he cannot, as an educator, substitute the rev-

olutionary politician interested in knowledge and structural transformation. He rejects the traditional notion of education as 'lever for progress'; would it make sense to oppose to this the equally ingenuous thesis of 'education as a lever for revolution'? A pedagogy of freedom can help popular politics since conscientization means an opening up to the comprehension of social structures as means of domination and violence. But the task of orienting this growth of awareness in a specifically political direction falls on the politician, not the educator" (16).

7. "Affirmative action began with Title VII of the Civil Rights Act of 1964, which prohibited discrimination on the basis of race and sex and which was later augmented by a number of executive orders that regulate federal contracts and set goals and timetables for hiring minorities." Walter Feinberg, "Affirmative Action and Beyond: A Case for a Backward-Looking Gender- and Race-Based Policy," *Teachers College Record* 97, 3 (Spring 1996): 363.

8.. E.g., while "blacks represent over 12 percent of the population in the United States, they comprise only 4.2 percent of doctors, 3.3 percent of the lawyers, 5 percent of the university teachers, 3.7 percent of the engineers. . . . [However,] the percentage of women lawyers and judges increased from a mere 3.8 percent in 1972 to 22.8 percent in 1993 and women faculty members rose from 28 percent in 1972 to 42.5 percent in 1993." (Feinberg, "Affirmative Action and Beyond," 366–367).

9. Let me be very clear on this point. I believe democracy can result only from a social contract that establishes a system of cooperation through a legal framework and an equally responsible enforcing administration, hence the importance of a democratic state to achieve a democratic social contract and to facilitate the creation of a democratic public sphere. Yet, with Jean-Jacques Rousseau, I believe that only this social contract creates the possibility of self-regulation or self-government and that the governed should in fact be the governors!

10. The Supreme Court on Monday, 10 November 1997, rejected a broad challenge to California's Proposition 209. Following this lead, the House Judiciary Committee announced that it would vote on a bill (HR1909) modeled after Proposition 209, the Civil Rights Act of 1997. "The bill would prohibit the government from discriminating against or granting preferential treatment to anyone on the basis of race or gender in connection with federal contracts, employment or other programs and activities" (*Los Angeles Times,* 4 November 1997, A12). Subsequently, showing how divisive the issue of affirmative action could be, the GOP leadership chose to table the affirmative action bill initiated by Republican Rep. Charles T. Canady. Four Republicans joined the 13 Democrats in the House Judiciary Committee to vote to table the bill, while a host of supporters of affirmative action cheered the action from the galleries. This decision means that this bill, or a similar one, will not be discussed in Congress until 1998, and most likely, with the approach of national elections for president and Congress, action will again be postponed for some time (*Los Angeles Times,* 7 November 1997, A23).

11. After the meeting mentioned in note 10, in a press release, Rep. George Gekas (R-Pa.) explained why he offered a motion to table the bill: "I do not believe that voting on this legislation at this time will help us, but will actually hinder the achievement of the ideals espoused by one of our nation's greatest presidents [Lincoln]. The concept of racial preferences, set-asides, and quotas clash with the foundation on which our

country was built. However, rushing head-long into the issue without building a national consensus will only be seen as political and divisive. American society is moving toward that consensus as evidenced by decisions by the United States Supreme Court, state initiatives and public opinion. Let me make it clear that I am adamantly opposed to all forms of discrimination and I am committed to eliminating policies which favor people on the basis of immutable characteristics. The offering of this bill today will not speed up the correction of the current injustices, nor will it narrow the racial divide. The thrust of this bill is commendable but I fear that forcing the issue at this time could jeopardize the daily progress being made in ensuring equality." To underscore the point, Rep. John Conyers (D-Mich.), the ranking minority member of the House Judiciary Committee, issued a press release that hailed the committee's action in tabling consideration of HR 1909. The press release noted, "The admission results from California and Texas law schools provide stark evidence that ending affirmative action will return us to the days of segregated—and unequal—education. African-American admissions to UCLA and Berkeley Law School have dropped by more than 75%, while the University of Texas Law School faces the specter of an almost all white freshman class."

12. Todd Gitlin, in a personal communication to the author, challenged the view that identity is a process of learning. The following analysis was elicited by his insightful challenge.

13. Despite the importance of mass media and the symbolic cultural apparatus of capitalism, the notion of citizenship has been pushed along by national states, while the notion of citizen as consumer has been predicated mostly by capitalist factions and eventually by neoliberal government coalitions departing significantly from the politics of the traditional liberal state.

14. Joan W. Scott ("Multiculturalism and the Politics of Identity," *October* 61 [Summer 1992]:12–19) is right when she argues that identities are historically conferred, that this conferral is ambiguous, and that subjects are produced by multiple identifications, some of which become politically salient for a time in certain contexts (16).

15. A central question is how to understand, in a postnational era, the relationships between citizenship and nationality. Giroux ("National Identity and the Politics of Multiculturalism," *College Literature* 22, no. 2 [June1992]:54) argues that in practical terms: "(1) educators must address critically how national identity is constructed in the media, through the politics of state apparatuses, and through the mobilization of material resources and power outside of the reach of the state. . . . [and] (2) national identity must be inclusive and informed by a democratized pluralization of cultural identities. If the tendency towards a universalizing, assimilative impulse is to be resisted, educators must ensure that students engage varied notions of an imagined community by critically addressing rather than excluding cultural differences."

16. James Banks's new book, *Educating Citizens in a Multicultural Society* (New York, Columbia University, Teachers College Press, 1997), is one of the few examples of its kind.

17. Examples of this relentless critique from the right are Allan Bloom, *The Closing of the American Mind: How Higher Education Has Failed Democracy and Impover-*

ished the Souls of Today's Students (New York: Simon & Schuster, 1987); and Dinesh d'Souza, *Illiberal Education: The Politics of Race and Sex on Campus* (New York: Free Press, 1991). For a very insightful response from the liberal camp, see Gerald Graff, *Beyond the Culture Wars: How Teaching the Conflicts Can Revitalize American Education* (New York: W. W. Norton, 1992). In turn, for a serious countercriticism to Graff's liberal perspective from a critical pedagogy advocate, see Henry Giroux, *Fugitive Cultures: Race, Violence, and Youth* (New York: Routledge, 1996), 126.

18. A central conjecture about the multiplicity of hybrid cultures that coexist today in many places, e.g., in Latin America, speaks of the multitemporal heterogeneity of cultures. The notion of hybrid cultures emerges as a trademark for the complex (and often confusing) array of expressions of cultural modernity, cultural tradition, and survival strategies of popular groups. See Nestor García Canclini, *Cultural hibridas: Estrategias para entrar y salir de la modernidad* (Buenos Aires: Editorial Sudamericana, 1992). For a different take on the subject of multiple identities, see Nancy Fraser, *Justice Interruptus: Critical Reflections on the "Postsocialist Condition"* (New York: Routledge, 1997), 179.

19. This is exactly the spirit that animates the richly textured dialogue between J. Jorge Klor de Alva and Cornel West, "Black-Brown Relations: Are Alliances Possible?" *Social Justice* 24, no. 2 (Summer 1997): 65–83.

References

Adler, M. 1982. *The Paideia Proposal.* New York: Macmillan.

Almond, G., and Sydney Verba. 1963. *The Civic Culture.* Princeton, N.J.: Princeton University Press.

Altbach, P., ed. 1990. *International Handbook, Student Movement.* New York: Greenwood Press.

Althusser, L. 1971. *Lenin and Philosophy and Other Essays,* translated by Ben Brewster. New York: Monthly Review Press.

Anderson, P. 1978. *Las antinomias de Antonio Gramsci.* Barcelona: Fontanara.

Andrews, F. E. 1956. *Philanthropic Foundations.* New York: Russell Sage.

Anzaldúa, Gloria. 1997. "La Conciencia de la Mestiza: Towards a New Consciousness." Pp. 765–775 in *Feminisms: An Anthology of Literary Theory and Criticism,* edited by R. Warhol and D. Price Herndl. New Brunswick, N.J.: Rutgers University Press.

Apple, M. W., ed. 1982a. *Cultural and Economic Reproduction in Education: Essays on Class, Ideology, and the State.* London: Routledge & Kegan Paul.

———. 1982b. "Curricular Form and the Logic of Technical Control: Building the Possessive Individual." Pp. 247–274 in *Cultural and Economic Reproduction in Education: Essays on Class, Ideology, and the State,* edited by M. W. Apple. London: Routledge & Kegan Paul.

———.1982c. *Education and Power.* Boston: Routledge.

———. 1986a. "Curriculum, Capitalism, and Democracy: A Response to Whitty's Critics." *British Journal of Sociology of Education* 7, no. 3:320–321.

———. 1986b. *Teachers and Text: A Political Economy of Class and Gender Relations in Education.* New York: Routledge.

———. 1988a. "Facing the Complexity of Power: For a Parallelist Position in Critical Educational Studies." Pp. 112–130 in *Bowles and Gintis Revisited: Correspondence and Contradiction in Educational Theory,* edited by M. Cole. Philadelphia: Falmer Press.

———. 1988b. "Standing on the Shoulders of Giants: Class Formation and Capitalist Schools." *History of Education Quarterly* 28, no. 2:231–241.

———. 1988c. *Teachers and Texts: A Political Economy of Class and Gender Relations in Education.* New York: Routledge.

———. 1989. "The Politics of Common Sense." Pp. 32–49 in *Critical Pedagogy, the State, and Cultural Struggle,* edited by H. Giroux and P. McLaren. Albany: State University of New York Press.

265

———. 1992. "Education, Culture, and Class Power: Basil Bernstein and the Neo-Marxist Sociology of Education." *Educational Theory* 42, no. 2:143.

———. 1993a. *Official Knowledge: Democratic Education in a Conservative Age.* New York: Routledge.

———. 1993b. "What Post-Modernists Forget: Cultural Capital and Official Knowledge." *Curriculum Studies* 7, no. 3:301–315.

———. 1997. *Teoría crítica y educación.* Buenos Aires: Miño y Dávila Editores.

Apple, M. W., and L. Weiss. 1986. "Seeing Education Relationally: The Stratification of Culture and People in the Sociology of School Knowledge." *Journal of Education* 168, no. 1:7–33.

Archibugi, Daniele, and David Held, eds. 1995. *Cosmopolitan Democracy: An Agenda for a New World Order.* Cambridge, England: Polity Press.

Arnot, M. 1994. "Male Hegemony, Social Class, and Women's Education." Pp. 84–104 in *The Education Feminism Reader,* edited by L. Stone. New York: Routledge.

Arnove, R. F., ed. 1980. *Philanthropy and Cultural Imperialism: The Foundations at Home and Abroad.* Bloomington: Indiana University Press.

Arthur, J., and A. Shapiro. 1995. *Campus Wars: Multiculturalism and the Politics of Difference.* Boulder, Colo.: Westview Press.

Ashcroft, B., Gareth Griffiths, and Helen Tiffin, eds. 1995. *The Post-Colonial Studies Reader.* New York: Routledge.

Ayers, W. C., and J. L. Miller, eds. 1998. *A Light in Dark Times: Maxine Greene and the Unfinished Conversation.* New York: Teachers College Press, Columbia University.

Ball, S. J. 1993. "Educational Markets, Choice, and Social Class: The Market as a Class Strategy." *British Journal of Sociology of Education* 14, no. 1: 3–19.

Ball, T. 1992. "New Faces of Power." Pp. 14–31 in *Rethinking Power,* edited by T. E. Warteberg. Albany: State University of New York Press.

Banks, J. A. 1989. "Multicultural Education: Characteristics and Goals." Pp. 3–28 in *Multicultural Education: Issues and Perspectives,* edited by J. A. Banks and C. A. McGee Banks. Boston: Allyn & Bacon.

———. 1993. "Multicultural Education: Historical Development, Dimensions, and Practice." *Review of Research in Education* 19: 3–49.

———. 1997. *Educating Citizens in a Multicultural Society.* New York: Teachers College Press, Columbia University.

Banks, J. A., and C. A. McGee Banks. 1989. *Multicultural Education: Issues and Perspectives.* Boston: Allyn & Bacon.

Bardis, P. D. 1985. *Dictionary of Quotations in Sociology.* Westport, Conn.: Greenwood Press.

Barnet, R., and J. Cavanagh. 1996a. "Electronic Money and the Casino Economy." Pp. 360–371 in *The Case against the Global Economy and for a Turn toward the Local,* edited by J. Mander and E. Goldsmith. San Francisco: Sierra Club Books.

———. 1996b. "Homogenization of Global Culture." Pp. 71–77 in *The Case against the Global Economy and for a Turn toward the Local,* edited by J. Mander and E. Goldsmith. San Francisco: Sierra Club Books.

Baron, S., et al. 1981. *Unpopular Education: Schooling and Social Democracy in England*. London: Hutchinson.

Bashevkin, S. 1994. "Confronting Neo-Conservatism: Anglo-American Women's Movements under Thatcher, Reagan, and Mulroney." *International Political Science Review* 15, no. 3:275–296.

Bell, D. 1987. *And We Are Not Saved: The Elusive Quest for Racial Justice*. New York: Basic Books.

———. 1995. "Racial Realism—After We're Gone: Prudent Speculations on America in a Post-Racial Epoch." Pp. 2–8 in *Critical Race Theory: The Cutting Edge,* edited by Richard Delgado. Philadelphia: Temple University Press.

Bendix, R. 1962. *Max Weber: An Intellectual Portrait*. New York: Doubleday/Anchor Books.

———. 1977. *Nation-Building and Citizenship: Studies of Our Changing Social Order*. Berkeley and Los Angeles: University of California Press.

Berman, M. 1982. *All That Is Solid Melts into Air: The Experience of Modernity*. New York: Simon & Schuster.

Bernstein, B. 1973. *Class Codes and Control*. Vol. 1, *Theoretical Studies Towards a Sociology of Language*. London: Paladin.

———. 1977. *Class Codes and Control*. Vol. 3, *Towards a Theory of Educational Transmission*. 2nd ed. Boston: Routledge & Kegan Paul.

Bernstein, R. J. 1983. *Beyond Objectivism and Relativism: Science, Hermeneutics, and Praxis*. Philadelphia: University of Pennsylvania Press.

Bérubé, M. 1994. *Public Access: Literary Theory and American Campus Politics*. London: Verso.

Bhabha, H. 1989. "The Commitment to Theory." Pp. 111–132 in *Third Cinema Reader,* edited by J. Pines and P. Willemen. London: British Film Institute.

Block, F. 1989. *Revising State Theory: Essays in Politics and Postindustrialism*. Philadelphia: Temple University Press.

Bloom, A. 1987. *The Closing of the American Mind: How Higher Education Has Failed Democracy and Impoverished the Souls of Today's Students*. New York: Simon & Schuster.

Bobbio, N. 1995. "Democracy and the International System." Pp. 17–41 in *Cosmopolitan Democracy: An Agenda for a New World Order,* edited by Daniele Archibugi and David Held. Cambridge, England: Polity Press.

———. 1996. "Intelectuales." *La Gaceta de la UNAM*. Mexico: UNAM.

Bobbio, N., Nicola Matteucci, and Gianfranco Pasquino. 1987–1988 (1976). *Diccionario de Política*. Mexico City: Siglo XXI Editores.

Boli, J., and F. Ramirez. 1992. "Compulsory Schooling in the Western Cultural Context." Pp. 25–38 in *Emergent Issues in Education: Comparative Perspectives,* edited by G. P. Kelly, Robert Arnove, and Philip P. Altbach. Albany: State University of New York Press.

Borges, J. L. 1996. *Otras Inquisiciones*. Buenos Aires: EMECE.

Boron, A. A. 1981. "La crisis norteamericana y la racionalidad neoconservadora." *CIDE Cuadernos Semestrales* 9:31–58.

————. 1990–91. "Estadolatria y teorías 'estadocéntricas': Notas sobre algunos análisis del estado en el capitalismo contemporáneo." *El Cielo por Asalto* 1, no. 1: 97–124.

————. 1994a. "The Capitalist State and Its Relative Autonomy: Arguments regarding Limits and Dimensions." Los Angeles: UCLA, manuscript.

————. 1994b. *The State, Capitalism, and Democracy in Latin America.* Boulder, Colo.: Lynne Rienner.

Boron, A. A., and C. A. Torres. 1996. "The Impact of Neoliberal Restructuring on Education and Poverty in Latin America." *Alberta Journal of Educational Research* 42, no. 2:102–114.

Boudon, R., and F. Bourricaud. 1989. *A Critical Dictionary of Sociology.* London: Routledge.

Bourdieu, P. 1968. "Structuralism and Theory of Sociological Knowledge." *Sociological Research* 35:681–706.

————. 1977. *Outline of a Theory of Practice.* Translated by Richard Nice. Cambridge: Cambridge University Press.

Bourdieu, P., and J.-C. Passeron. 1967. "Sociology and Philosophy in France since 1945: Death and Resurrection of a Philosophy without a Subject." *Social Research* 34:162–212.

————. 1977. *Reproduction in Education, Society, and Culture.* Translated by Richard Nice. London: Sage.

Bowles, Samuel, and Herbert Gintis. 1976. *Schooling in Capitalist America; Educational Reform and the Contradictions of Economic Life.* New York: Basic Books/Harper.

————. 1981. "Education of a Site of Contradictions in the Reproduction of the Capital-Labor Relationship: Second Thoughts on the 'Correspondence Principle.'" *Economic and Industrial Democracy* 2:223–242.

————. 1986. *Democracy and Capitalism: The Contradictions of Modern Political Life.* New York: Basic Books.

Braverman, H. 1974. *Labor and Monopoly Capital.* New York: Monthly Review Press.

Burbules, N. 1993. *Dialogue in Teaching: Theory and Practice.* New York: Teachers College Press, Columbia University.

Butler, J. P. 1993. *Bodies That Matter: On the Discursive Limits of Sex.* New York: Routledge.

Caldéron Gutierrez, F., and Mario R. dos Santos, 1987. "Movimientos sociales y democracia: Los conflictos por la constitución de un nuevo orden." Pp. 11–32 in *Los conflictos por la constitución de un nuevo orden.* Buenos Aires: Consejo Latinoamericano de Ciencias Sociales.

Carens, J. H., ed. 1993. *Possessive Individualism and Democratic Theory: Macpherson's Legacy.* Albany: State University of New York Press.

Carlson, Dennis. 1997. *Making Progress: Education and Culture in New Times.* New York: Teachers College Press, Columbia University.

Carnoy, M. 1977. *Education and Employment: A Critical Appraisal.* Paris: UNESCO, International Institute for Educational Planning.

————. 1984. *The State and Political Theory.* Princeton, N.J.: Princeton University Press.

————. 1992. "Education and the State: From Adam Smith to Perestroika." Pp. 143–159 in *Emergent Issues in Education: Comparative Perspectives,* edited by Philip G. Altbach, Robert F. Arnove, and G. P. Kelly. Albany: State University of New York Press.

————. 1994. *Faded Dreams: The Politics and Economics of Race in America.* New York: Cambridge University Press.

Carnoy, M., and H. M. Levin. 1985. *Schooling and Work in the Democratic State.* Stanford, Calif.: Stanford University Press.

Carnoy, M., and J. Samoff, eds. 1990. *Education and Social Transition in the Third World.* Princeton, N.J.: Princeton University Press.

Carnoy, M., and C. A. Torres. 1994. "Educational Change and Structural Adjustment: A Case Study in Costa Rica." Pp. 64–99 in *Coping with Crisis: Austerity, Adjustment, and Human Resources.* London: Cassell and UNESCO.

Carnoy, M., et al. 1979. *Can Educational Policy Equalize Income Distribution in Latin America?* London: Saxon House.

————. 1982. "The Political Economy of Financing Education in Developing Countries." Pp. 39–68 in *Financing Educational Development,* edited by International Development Research Center (IDRC). Ottawa: IDRC.

————. 1993. *The New Global Economy in the Information Age: Reflections on Our Changing World.* University Park: Pennsylvania State University Press.

Cassirer, E. 1969. *The Myth of the State.* New Haven: Yale University Press.

Castañeda, Carlos. 1973. "Sorcery: A Description of the World." Ph.D. diss., University of California–Los Angeles.

Cerroni, U. 1972. *La libertad de los modernos.* Barcelona: Martinez Roca.

————. 1976. *Teoría política y socialismo.* Mexico City: ERA.

————. 1992. *Política: Método, procesos, sujetos, instituciones, y categorías.* Mexico City: Siglo XXI.

Chang, R. S. 1995. "Toward an Asian American Legal Scholarship: Critical Race Theory, Post-Structuralism, and Narrative Space." Pp. 322–356 in *Critical Race Theory: The Cutting Edge,* edited by Richard Delgado. Philadelphia: Temple University Press.

Chapman, W. 1956. *Rousseau: Totalitarian or Liberal?* New York: Columbia University Press.

Chavez, L. 1994. "Demystifying Multiculturalism." *National Review,* 21 February, 26–32.

Chávez Candelaria, C. 1997. "The 'Wild Zone' Thesis as Gloss in Chicana Literary Study." Pp. 248–256 in *Feminisms: An Anthology of Literary Theory and Criticism,* edited by R. R. Warhol and D. Price Herndl. New Brunswick, N.J.: Rutgers University Press.

Chirot, D. 1977. *Social Change in the Twentieth Century.* New York: Harcourt Brace Jovanovich.

Chomsky, Noam. 1987. *The Chomsky Reader.* Edited by James Peck. New York: Pantheon Books.

Chubb, J. E., and T. M. Moe. 1990. *Politics, Markets, and America's Schools.* Washington, D.C.: Brookings Institution.

———. 1993. "The Forest and the Trees: A Response to Our Critics." Pp. 219–239 in *School Choice: Examining the Evidence,* edited by E. Rasell and R. Rothstein. Washington, D.C.: Economic Policy Institute.

Clark, T. N., Seymour Martin Lipset, and Michael Rempel. 1993. "The Declining Political Importance of Social Class." *International Sociology* 8, no. 3:293–316.

Clarke, S. 1990. "New Utopias for Old: Fordist Dreams and Post-Fordist Fantasies." *Capital and Class* 42 (Winter):131–155.

Cohen, J. L., and A. Arato. 1992. *Civil Society and Political Theory.* Cambridge: MIT Press.

Cole, M., ed. 1988. *Bowles and Gintis Revisited: Correspondence and Contradiction in Educational Theory.* Philadelphia: Falmer Press.

Coleman, J. S. 1988. "Social Capital in the Creation of Human Capital." *American Journal of Sociology* 94:95–120.

———. 1990. *Foundations of Social Theory.* Cambridge: Harvard University Press, Belknap Press.

Collier, D., ed. 1979. *The New Authoritarianism in Latin America.* Princeton, N.J.: Princeton University Press.

Connell, R. W. 1983. *Which Way Is Up? Essays on Sex, Class, and Culture.* Sydney: George Allen & Unwin.

———. 1987. *Gender and Power: Society, the Person, and Sexual Politics.* Stanford, Calif.: Stanford University Press.

———. 1996. "Curriculum, Politics, Hegemony, and Strategies of Change." Macquarie University, Department of Sociology, New South Wales. Manuscript.

Connolly, W. E. 1993. "Democracy and Contingency." Pp. 193–220 in *Democracy and Possessive Individualism: The Legacy of C. B. Macpherson,* edited by J. H. Carens. Albany: State University of New York Press.

Coole, D. 1993. *Women in Political Theory: From Ancient Misogyny to Contemporary Feminism.* Boulder, Colo.: Lynne Rienner.

Coraggio, J. L., and R. M. Torres. 1997. *La educación según el Banco Mundial: Un análisis de sus propuestas y métodos.* Buenos Aires: Miño & Davila and Centro de Estudios Multidisciplinarios Fundación.

Coser, L., and I. Hower, eds. 1977. *The New Conservatives: A Critique from the Left.* New York: New American Library.

Culp, Jerome McCristal, Jr. 1995. "Autobiography and Legal Scholarship and Teaching: Finding the Me in the Legal Academy." Pp. 409–429 in *Critical Race Theory: The Cutting Edge,* edited by Richard Delgado. Philadelphia: Temple University Press.

Culpitt, I. 1992. *Welfare and Citizenship: Beyond the Crisis of the Welfare State?* London: Sage.

Dahl, R. 1956. *Preface to Democratic Theory.* Chicago: University of Chicago Press.

Dahrendorf, R. 1975. *The New Liberty: Survival and Justice in a Changing World.* Stanford, Calif.: Stanford University Press.

Dale, R. 1983. "The Political Sociology of Education." *British Journal of Sociology of Education* 4, no. 2:185–202.

———. 1989. *The State and Education Policy.* Philadelphia: Open University Press.

Dalton, R. J., Manfred Kuechler, and Wilhelm Búrklin. 1990. "The Challenge of New Movements." Pp. 1–20 in *Challenging the Political Order,* edited by R. J. Dalton and Manfred Kuechler. New York: Oxford University Press.

Darder, A. 1991. *Culture and Power in the Classroom: A Critical Foundation for Bicultural Education.* New York: Bergin & Garvey.

Darling-Hammond, L. 1993. Introduction to *Review of Research in Education* 19. Washington, D.C.: American Educational Research Association.

De Tommasi, L., M. J. Warde, and S. Haddad, eds. 1996. *O Banco Mundial e as políticas educacionais.* São Paulo: Cortes, PUC-UP-Ação Educativa.

Delgado, Richard, ed. 1995. *Critical Race Theory: The Cutting Edge.* Philadelphia: Temple University Press.

Dewey, J. 1954. *The Public and Its Problems.* Chicago: Swallow Press.

———. 1981. *The Philosophy of John Dewey.* Edited by J. J. McDermott. Chicago: University of Chicago Press.

———. 1993. *Philosophy and Education in Their Historic Relations.* Edited by J. J. Chambliss. Boulder, Colo.: Westview Press.

Dore, R. 1976. *The Diploma Disease: Education, Qualification, and Development.* Berkeley and Los Angeles: University of California Press.

d'Souza, D. 1991. *Illiberal Education: The Politics of Race and Sex on Campus.* New York: Free Press.

Dyer, R. 1997. *White.* New York: Routledge.

Easton, D. 1981. "The Political System Besieged by the State." *Political Theory* 9, no. 3 (August):303–325.

Eder, K. 1993. *The New Politics of Class: Social Movements and Cultural Dynamics in Advanced Societies.* London: Sage.

Eisenstein, Z. R., ed. 1979. *Capitalist Patriarchy and the Case for Socialist Feminism.* New York: Monthly Review Press.

Evans, M. 1991. "The Classical Economists, Laissez-Faire, and the State." Pp. 1–23 in *The Market and the State: Studies in Interdependence,* edited by M. Moran and M. Wright. New York: St. Martin's Press.

Everman, R. S., G. Lennart, and Thomas Söderqvist, eds. 1987. *Intellectuals, Universities, and the State in Western Modern Societies.* Berkeley and Los Angeles: University of California Press.

Eyerman, R., and A. Jamison. 1991. *Social Movements: A Cognitive Approach.* Cambridge, England: Polity Press.

Fagerlind, I., and L. Saha. 1983. *Education and National Development: A Comparative Perspective.* Oxford: Pergamon Press.

Farber, D. A., and S. Sherry. 1995. "Telling Stories Out of School: An Essay on Legal

Narratives." Pp. 283–292 in *Critical Race Theory: The Cutting Edge,* edited by Richard Delgado. Philadelphia: Temple University Press.

Featherstone, M. 1991. *Consumer Culture and Postmodernism.* London: Sage.

Feinberg, W. 1996. "Affirmative Action and Beyond: A Case for a Backward-Looking Gender- and Race-Based Policy." *Teachers College Record* 97, no. 3 (Spring): 363–397.

Flora, P., and J. Alber. 1991. "Modernization, Democratization, and the Development of Welfare States in Western Europe." Pp. 37–80 in *The Development of Welfare States in Europe and America,* edited by P. Flora and A. J. Heidenheimer. New Brunswick, N.J.: Transaction Books.

Fortune. 1992. "Your New Global Workforce." 14 December, 52–66.

Foucault, M. 1980. *Power/Knowledge: Selected Interviews and Other Writings, 1972–1977.* Edited and translated by Colin Gordon. New York: Pantheon Books.

Foweraker, J. 1995. *Theorizing Social Movements.* London: Pluto Press.

Fox, J. 1997. "Chretien: No Cover-up over Somalia Mission." *Miami Herald,* 6 July, 12A.

Fraser, N. 1989. *Unruly Practices: Power, Discourse, and Gender in Contemporary Social Theory.* Minneapolis: University of Minnesota Press.

———. 1994. "Rethinking the Public Sphere: A Contribution to the Critique of Actually Existing Democracy." Pp. 74–98 in *Between Borders: Pedagogy and the Politics of Cultural Studies,* edited by H. Giroux and P. McLaren. New York: Routledge.

———. 1997. *Justice Interruptus: Critical Reflections on the "Postsocialist Condition."* New York: Routledge.

Freire, P. 1972. "La misión educadora de las iglesias en América Latina." *Perspectivos de Dialogo* 7, nos. 66–67 (August): 172–179, 201–209.

———. 1973. *¿Extensión o comunicación? La concientización en el medio rural.* Buenos Aires: Siglo XXI and Tierra Nueva.

———. 1978a. *Educación como práctica de la libertad.* Buenos Aires: Siglo XXI.

———. 1978b. *Pedagogía del oprimido.* Buenos Aires: Siglo XXI.

———. 1993. *Pedagogy of the City.* New York: Continuum.

———. 1994. *Cartas a Cristina.* São Paulo: Paz e Tierra.

———. 1996. *Letters to Cristina.* New York: Routledge.

———. 1997a. "Interview." Pp. 89–106 in *Education, Power, and Personal Biography: Dialogues with Critical Educators,* edited by C. A. Torres. New York: Routledge.

———. 1997b. *Pedagogia da autonomia: Saberes necessários à prática educativa.* São Paulo: Paz e Tierra.

———. 1998. *Politics and Education,* translated by P. L. Wong. Los Angeles: UCLA Latin American Center.

Fromm, Eric. 1986. *For the Love of Life,* translated by Robert Kimber and Rita Kimber, edited by H. J. Schultz. New York: Free Press.

Fukuyama, F. 1992. *The End of History and the Last Man.* New York: Free Press.

Fuller, B. 1991. *The Western State Builds Third-World Schools.* New York: Routledge.

Gadotti, M. 1996. *Pedagogy of Praxis: A Dialectical Philosophy of Education.* Preface by Paulo Freire, translated by John Milton. Albany: State University of New York Press.

Gadotti, M., et al. 1996. *Paulo Freire: Uma Biobibliografia.* São Paulo: CORTES— Instituto Paulo Freire and UNESCO.

Gadotti, M., and C. A. Torres, eds. 1994. *Educação popular: Utopia latinoamericana (ensaios).* São Paulo: Cortez Editora–Editora da Universidade de São Paulo.

Garcia Canclini, N. 1992. *Cultural hibridas: Estrategias para entrar y salir de la modernidad.* Buenos Aires: Editorial Sudamericana.

———. 1993. "Una modernización que atrasa: La cultura bajo la regresión neoconservadora." *Revista de Casa de las Américas* 193 (October–December):3–12.

Garda, H. P. 1981. *América Latina 80: Democracia y movimiento popular.* Lima: Centro de Estudios y Promoción del Desarrollo, DESCO.

Gates, Henry Louis. 1992. *Loose Canons: Notes on the Culture Wars.* New York: Oxford University Press.

Gerson, M. 1996. *The Neoconservative Vision: From the Cold War to the Culture Wars.* Lanham, Md.: Madison Books.

Giddens, A. 1991. *Modernity and Self-Identity: Self and Society in the Late Modern Age.* Stanford, Calif.: Stanford University Press.

Giroux, H. 1988. *Schooling and the Struggle for Public Life: Critical Pedagogy in the Modern Age.* Minneapolis: University of Minnestoa Press.

———. 1992. "National Identity and the Politics of Multiculturalism." *College Literature* 22, no. 2 (June):42–57.

———. 1996a. *Fugitive Cultures: Race, Violence, and Youth.* New York: Routledge.

———. 1996b. "White Noise: Racial Politics and the Pedagogy of Whiteness." Pennsylvania State University, College Park. Manuscript.

———. 1997. "Memories of Whiteness." Pennsylvania State University, College Park. Manuscript.

Giroux, H., and P. McLaren, eds. 1989. *Critical Pedagogy, the State, and Cultural Struggle.* Albany: State University of New York Press.

———. 1994. *Between Borders: Pedagogy and the Politics of Cultural Studies.* New York: Routledge.

Gitlin, T. 1995. *The Twilight of Common Dreams: Why America Is Wracked by Culture Wars.* New York: Henry Holt.

Glazer, N. 1997. *We Are All Multiculturalists Now.* Cambridge: Harvard University Press.

Goldberg, D. T., ed. 1996. *Multiculturalism: A Critical Reader.* Oxford: Blackwell.

Goldsmith, E. 1996. "The Last Word: Family, Community, Democracy." Pp. 501–514 in *The Case against the Global Economy and for a Turn toward the Local,* edited by J. Mander and E. Goldsmith. San Francisco: Sierra Club Books.

Gordon, L. 1989. "Beyond Relative Autonomy: Theories of the State in Education." *British Journal of Sociology of Education* 10, no. 4:435–448.

———, ed. 1990. *Women, the State, and Welfare.* Madison: University of Wisconsin Press.

Gourevitch, P. A. 1986. *Politics in Hard Times: Comparative Responses in International Economic Crisis.* Ithaca, N.Y.: Cornell University Press.

Graff, G. 1992. *Beyond the Culture Wars: How Teaching the Conflicts Can Revitalize American Education.* New York: W. W. Norton.

Gramsci, A. 1971. *Selections from the Prison Notebooks.* Translated by Quintin Hoare and Geoffrey Nowell Smith. New York: International Publishers.

Grant, C. A., and C. E. Sleeter. 1986. "Race, Class, and Gender in Education Research: An Argument for Integrative Analysis." *Review of Educational Research* 56:195–211.

———. 1988. "Race, Class, and Gender and Abandoned Dreams." *Teachers College Record* 90:19–40.

Grant, C. A., and G. Ladson-Billings, eds. 1997. *Dictionary of Multicultural Education.* Phoenix, Ariz.: Oryx Press.

Gutmann, A. 1987. *Democratic Education.* Princeton, N.J.: Princeton University Press.

Habermas, J. 1985. "Psychic Thermidor and the Rebirth of Rebellious Subjectivity." Pp. 67–77 in *Habermas and Modernity*, edited by R. J. Bernstein. Cambridge: MIT Press.

———. 1989. *The Structural Transformation of the Public Sphere: An Inquiry into a Category of Bourgeois Society.* Translated by Thomas Burger and Frederick Lawrence. Cambridge: MIT Press.

———. 1990. "Modernity versus Postmodernity." Pp. 345–354 in *Culture and Society: Contemporary Debates*, edited by J. C. Alexander and S. Seidman. Cambridge: Cambridge University Press.

———. 1992. "Citizenship and National Identity: Some Reflections on the Future of Europe." *Praxis International* 12:1–19.

Hage, G., J. Hage, and B. Fuller. 1988. "The Active State, Investment in Human Capital, and Economic Growth: France, 1825–1975." *American Sociological Review* 53, no. 6:824–837.

Hall, J. A., and G. J. Ikenberry. 1989. *The State.* London: Open University Press.

Hall, Stuart. 1996. "When was 'the Post-Colonial'? Thinking at the Limit." Pp. 242–260 in *The Post-Colonial Question: Common Skies, Divided Horizons*, edited by Ian Chambers and Lidia Curti. New York: Routledge.

Halsey, A. H., ed. 1961. *Education, Economy, and Society: A Reader in the Sociology of Education.* New York: Free Press.

Hamilton, Alexander, James Madison, and John Jay. 1961. *The Federalist Papers.* Introduction by Clinton Rossiter. Chicago: New American Library.

Haney López, Ian F. 1997. "White by Law." Pp. 542–550 in *Critical Race Theory: The Cutting Edge*, edited by Richard Delgado. Philadelphia: Temple University Press.

Hanushek, E. A. 1986. "The Economics of Schooling: Production and Efficiency in the Public Schools." *Journal of Economic Literature* 24:1141–1178.

Haraway, D. 1991. *Simians, Cyborgs, and Women: The Reinvention of Nature.* New York: Routledge.

———. 1992. "Ecce Homo, Ain't (Ar'n't) I a Woman, and Inappropriate/d Others: The

Human in a Post-Humanist Landscape." Pp. 86–100 in *Feminists Theorize the Political*, edited by J. Butler and J. W. Scott. New York: Routledge.

Harding, S. 1996. "Is Science Multicultural? Challenges, Resources, Opportunities, Uncertainties." Pp. 344–370 in *Multiculturalism: A Critical Reader*, edited by D. T. Goldberg. Oxford: Blackwell.

Harding, S., and M. Hintikka, eds. 1983. *Discovering Reality: Feminist Perspectives on Epistemology, Metaphysics, Methodology, and Philosophy of Science*. London: D. Reidel.

Hartmann, H., et al., eds. 1981. *The Unhappy Marriage of Marxism and Feminism: A Debate of Class and Patriarchy*. London: Pluto Press.

Harvey, D. 1989. *The Condition of Postmodernity*. Oxford: Blackwell.

Hegel, G. W. F. 1857. *Lectures on the Philosophy of History*. Translated by J. B. Baillie. London: Henry G. Bahn.

———. 1976. *The Phenomenology of Mind*. Translated by J. B. Baillie. 2nd ed. London: Allen & Unwin/ New York: Macmillan.

Held, David, ed. 1983. *States and Societies*. Oxford: Martin Robinson in association with Open University.

———. 1989. *Political Theory and the Modern State*. Stanford, Calif.: Stanford University Press.

———. 1995. "Democracy and the New International Order." Pp. 97–120 in *Cosmopolitan Democracy: An Agenda for a New World Order*, edited by Daniele Archibugi and David Held. Cambridge, England: Polity Press.

———, ed. 1991. *Political Theory Today*. Stanford, Calif.: Stanford University Press.

Hennessy, R. 1993. *Materialist Feminism and the Politics of Discourse*. New York: Routledge.

Hirst, P., and J. Zeitlin. 1991. "Flexible Specialization versus Post-Fordism." *Economy and Society* 20, no. 1:1–56.

Hobsbawm, E. 1997. *On History*. New York: New Press.

hooks, b. 1990. *Yearning: Race, Gender, and Cultural Politics*. Boston: South End Press.

hooks, b., and Cornel West. 1991. *Breaking Bread: Insurgent Black Intellectual Life*. Toronto: Between the Lines.

Hulme, P. 1986. *Colonial Encounters: Europe and the Native Caribbean, 1492–1797*. London: Methuen.

Inter-American Foundation. 1990. *1990 Annual Report*. Rosslyn, Va.: Inter-American Foundation.

Jacoby, R. 1994. "The Myth of Multiculturalism." *New Left Review* 208:121–126.

Jelin, E. 1987. "Movimientos sociales en Argentina: Una introducción a su estudio." *Cuestión de Estado* 1:28–37.

———. 1990. "Citizenship and Identity: Final Reflections." Pp. 184–207 in *Women and Social Change in Latin America*, edited by Elizabeth Jelin. London: Zed Books.

Jencks, C., et al. 1972. *Inequality: A Reassessment of the Effect of Family and Schooling in America*. New York: Harper & Row.

Jessop, B. 1983. "Accumulation Strategies, State Forms, and Hegemonic Projects." *Kapitalistate* 10/11:89–111.

———. 1988. "Regulation Theory, Post-Fordism, and the State." *Capital and Class* 34:147–168.

Johnson, T. 1993. "Expertise and the State." Pp. 139–152 in *Foucault's New Domains*, edited by M. Gane and T. Johnson. London: Routledge.

Karabel, J., and A. H. Halsey, eds. 1977. *Power and Ideology in Education*. New York: Oxford University Press.

Keane, J., ed. 1988. *Civil Society and the State*. London: Verso.

Kellner, D. 1997. "Globalization and the Postmodern Turn." University of California–Los Angeles. Manuscript.

Kennedy, Randall L. 1995. "Racial Critiques of Legal Academia." Pp. 432–450 in *Critical Race Theory: The Cutting Edge*, edited by Richard Delgado. Philadelphia: Temple University Press.

Klor de Alva, G., and Cornel West. 1997. "Black-Brown Relations: Are Alliances Possible?" *Social Justice* 24, no. 2 (Summer):65–83.

Korten, D. C. 1995. *When Corporations Rule the World*. West Hartford, Conn.: Kumarian Press and Berrett-Koehler.

Kymlicka, W., and W. Norman. 1994. "Return of the Citizen: A Survey of Recent Work on Citizenship Theory." *Ethics* 104 (January):352–353.

LaBelle, T. J., and C. R. Ward. 1994. *Multiculturalism and Education: Diversity and Its Impact on Schools and Society*. Albany: State University of New York Press.

Laclau, E. 1985. "New Social Movements and the Plurality of the Social." Pp. 27–42 in *New Social Movements and the State in Latin America*, edited by D. Slater. Amsterdam: Centrum voor Studie en Documentatie vans Latijns Amerika.

———. 1991. *New Reflections on the Revolution of Our Times*. London: Verso.

Laclau, E., and C. Mouffe. 1985. *Hegemony and Socialist Strategy: Towards a Radical Democratic Politics*. London: Verso.

Ladson-Billings, G., and W. F. Tate. 1995. "Toward a Critical Race Theory of Education." *Teachers College Record* 97, no. 1 (Fall):47–68.

Lawrence-Lightfoot, S. 1994. *I've Known Rivers: Lives of Loss and Liberation*. Reading, Mass.: Addison-Wesley.

Lechner, N., ed. 1987. *Cultura política y democratización*. Santiago: Facultad Latinoamericana de Ciencias Sociales and Instituto de Cooperación Iberoamericana.

Lengermann, P., and J. Niebrugge-Brantley. 1992. "Contemporary Feminist Theory." Pp. 308–357 in *Contemporary Sociological Theory*, edited by G. Ritzer. 3rd ed. New York: McGraw-Hill.

Lerner, R., Althea K. Nagai, and Stanley Rothman. 1995. *Molding the Good Citizen: The Politics of High School History Texts*. Westport, Conn.: Praeger.

Levin, H., Martin Carnoy, Suleman Sumra, Reggie Nuget, Jeff Unsicker, and C. A. Torres. 1986. *La economía política del financiamiento educativo en países en vías de desarrollo*. Mexico City: Gernika.

Lipset, S. M. 1972. *Rebellion in the University*. Boston: Little, Brown.

Lomnitz, L., and A. Melnick. 1991. *Chile's Middle Class: A Struggle for Survival in the Face of Neoliberalism.* Boulder, Colo.: Lynne Rienner.

Lorde, A. 1984. *Sister Outsider.* Trumansburg, N.Y.: Crossing Press.

Lynch, F. R. 1994. "Workforce Diversity: PC's Final Frontier?" *National Review,* 21 February, 32–34.

———. 1995. *Workforce Diversity.* New York: Free Press.

Machiavelli, N. 1993. *The Prince.* Ware, England: Wordsworth Editions.

MacIntyre, A. 1988. *Whose Justice? Which Rationality?* London: Duckworth.

MacKinnon, C., et al. 1985. "Feminist Discourse, Moral Values, and the Law: A Conversation." 1984 James McCormick Mitchell Lecture. *Buffalo Law Review* 34, no. 1 (Winter):25–75.

Macpherson, C. B. 1962. *The Political Theory of Possessive Individualism: Hobbes to Locke.* Oxford: Oxford University Press.

———. 1966. *The Real World of Democracy.* Oxford: Oxford University Press.

———. 1968. *The Life and Times of Liberal Democracy.* New York: Oxford University Press.

———. 1973. *Democratic Theory: Essays in Retrieval.* Oxford: Oxford University Press.

———. 1977. "Do We Need a Theory of the State?" *Archives Européennes de Sociologie* 18, no. 2:223–244.

Madison, J., A. Hamilton, and J. Jay. 1961. *The Federalist Papers.* New York: Mentor Books.

Mainwaring, Scott, and Eduardo Viola. 1984. "New Social Movements, Political Culture, and Democracy in Brazil and Argentina in the 1980s." *Telaso* 61:17–54.

Manacorda, M. A. 1977. *El principio educativo en Gramsci: Americanismo y conformismo.* Translated by Luis Legaz. Salamanca: Ediciones Sígueme.

Mander, J., and E. Goldsmith, eds. 1996. *The Case against the Global Economy and for a Turn toward the Local.* San Francisco: Sierra Club Books.

Mann, M. 1987. "Ruling Class Strategies and Citizenship." *Sociology* 21:339–354.

———. 1989. *The Sources of Social Power.* New York: Routledge.

Mannheim, K. 1953. *Essays on Sociology and Social Psychology.* London: Routledge & Kegan Paul.

———. 1960. *Ideology and Utopia.* London: Routledge & Kegan Paul.

Mansbridge, J. 1993. "Macpherson's Neglect of the Political." Pp. 155–173 in *Democracy and Possessive Individualism: The Intellectual Legacy of C. B. Macpherson,* edited by J. Carens. Albany: State University of New York Press.

Marcos, S. 1994. "Marcos:¿De qué nos van a perdonar?" *Proceso* 1, 21 July, 13.

Marcuse, H. 1987. *Hegel's Ontology and the Theory of Historicity.* Translated by S. Benhabib. Cambridge: MIT Press.

———. 1989. *Reason and Revolution: Hegel and the Rise of Social Theory.* 2nd ed. Atlantic Highlands, N.Y.: Humanities Press.

Marshall, T. H. 1950. *Citizenship and Social Class and Other Essays.* Cambridge: Cambridge University Press.

———. 1963. *Sociology at the Crossroads.* London: Heinemann Educational Books.

———. 1965. *Social Policy in the Twentieth Century.* London: Hutchinson.

———. 1981. *The Right to Welfare and Other Essays.* Cambridge: Cambridge University Press.

———. 1983. "Citizenship and Social Class." Pp. 248–260 in *States and Societies,* edited by David Held et al.

Marx, K. 1973. *Grundrisse.* New York: Vintage Books.

McCarthy, C. 1990. *Race and Curriculum: Social Inequality and the Theories and Politics of Difference in Contemporary Research on Schooling.* London: Falmer Press.

———. 1993. "After the Canon: Knowledge and Ideological Representation in the Multicultural Discourse on Curriculum Reform." Pp. 289–305 in *Race, Identity, and Representation in Education.* New York: Routledge.

———. 1998. *The Uses of Culture: Education and the Limits of Ethnic Affiliation.* New York: Routledge.

McCarthy, C., and M. W. Apple. 1988. "Race, Class, and Gender in American Educational Research: Toward a Nonsynchronous Parallelist Position." Pp. 9–39 in *Class, Race, and Gender in American Education,* edited by L. Weiss. Albany: State University of New York Press.

McCarthy, C., and Warren Crichlow. 1993. "Theories of Identity, Theories of Representation, Theories of Race." Pp. xiii–xxix in *Race, Identity, and Representation in Education.* New York: Routledge.

McCarthy, T. 1979. *The Critical Theory of Jürgen Habermas.* Cambridge: MIT Press.

McClafferty, K., C. A. Torres, and T. Mitchell, eds. Forthcoming. "Urban Education: Challenges for the Sociology of Education." Los Angeles: UCLA.

McLaren, P. 1989. *Life in Schools.* White Plains, N.Y.: Longman.

———. 1991. "Schooling the Postmodern Body: Critical Pedagogy and the Politics of Enfleshment." Pp. 144–173 in *Postmodernism, Feminism, and Cultural Politics: Redrawing Educational Boundaries,* edited by H. A. Giroux. Albany: State University of New York Press.

———. 1994. "Critical Pedagogy, Political Agency, and the Pragmatics of Justice: The Case of Lyotard." *Educational Theory* 44, no. 3 (Summer): 319–340.

———. 1995. *Critical Pedagogy and Predatory Culture: Oppositional Politics in a Postmodern Era.* London: Routledge.

———. 1997a. "Critical Pedagogy and Globalization: Thirty Years after Che." Los Angeles. Manuscript.

———. 1997b. *Revolutionary Multiculturalism: Pedagogies of Dissent for the New Millennium.* Boulder, Colo.: Westview Press.

McNeil, L. M. 1988. *Contradictions of Control: School Structure and School Knowledge.* New York: Routledge.

Meehan, J. 1995. *Feminists Read Habermas.* New York: Routledge.

Menchú, R. 1983. *Me llamo Rigoberta Menchú y así me nació la conciencia.* Barcelona: Argos Vergara.

Merton, R. 1968. *Social Theory and Social Structure.* New York: Free Press.

Meyer, J. 1977. "The Effects of Education as an Institution." *American Journal of Sociology* 83, no. 4:55–57.

Miliband, R. 1969. *The State in Capitalist Society.* New York: Basic Books.

Mitchell, T. R. 1987. *Political Education in the Southern Farmers' Alliance.* Madison: University of Wisconsin Press.

———. 1998. "The Republic for Which It Stands: Public Schools, the State, and the Idea of Citizenship in America." University of Calfiornia–Los Angeles. Manuscript.

Mollis, M. 1996. "The Paradox of the Autonomy of Argentine Universities: From Liberalism to Regulation." Pp. 219–235 in *Latin American Education: Comparative Perspectives,* edited by C. A. Torres and Adriana Puiggrós. Boulder, Colo.: Westview Press.

Monsivais, C. 1987. *Entrada Libre.* Mexico City: Era.

Morales-Gómez, D., and C. A. Torres. 1990. *The State, Corporatist Politics, and Educational Policy-Making in Mexico.* New York: Praeger.

Moran, M., and M. Wright. 1991. *The Market and the State: Studies in Interdependence.* New York: St. Martin's Press.

Morley, D. 1992. *Television Audiences and Cultural Studies.* New York: Routledge.

Morrow, R. A., and C. A. Torres. 1994. "Education and the Reproduction of Class, Gender, and Race: Responding to the Postmodern Challenge." *Educational Theory* 44, no. 1:43–61.

———. 1995. *Social Theory and Education: A Critique of Theories of Social and Cultural Reproduction.* Albany: State University of New York Press.

———. In press a. *Critical Theory and Education: Freire, Habermas, and the Dialogical Subject.* New York: Teachers College Press, Columbia University.

———. In press b. "Education, the State, and Social Movements." In *Comparative Education: The Dialectics of the Global and the Local,* edited by R. Arnove and C. A. Torres. Lanham, Md.: Rowman & Littlefield.

Mouffe, C. 1993. *The Return of the Political.* London: Verso.

Myrdal, G. 1960. *Beyond the Welfare State: Economic Planning and Its International Implications.* New Haven: Yale University Press.

———. 1973. *Against the Stream: Critical Essays on Economics.* New York: Pantheon Books.

National Commission on Excellence in Education. 1983. "A Nation at Risk: An Imperative for Educational Reform." *Education Week,* 27 April, 12–16.

Nietzsche, F. 1967. *The Birth of Tragedy and the Case of Wagner.* New York: Vintage Books.

———. [1983] 1991. *Untimely Meditations.* Translated by R. J. Hollingdale. Cambridge: Cambridge University Press.

Noddings, Nel. 1995. *Philosophy of Education.* Boulder, Colo.: Westview Press.

Nordlinger, E. A. 1981. *On the Autonomy of the Democratic State.* Cambridge: Harvard University Press.

Nuhoglu Soysal, Y. 1994. *Limits of Citizenship: Migrants and Postnational Membership in Europe.* Chicago: University of Chicago Press.

Oakes, J. 1985. *Keeping Track: How Schools Structure Inequality.* New Haven: Yale University Press.

O'Cadiz, P., P. L. Wong, and C. A. Torres. 1998. *Education and Democracy: Paulo*

Freire, Social Movements, and Educational Reform in São Paulo. Boulder, Colo.: Westview Press.

O'Donnell, G., P. C. Schmitter, and L. Whitehead, eds. 1986. *Transitions from Authoritarian Rules: Comparative Perspectives.* Baltimore: Johns Hopkins University Press.

Offe, C. n.d. "Notes on the Laws of Motion of Reformist State Policies." Mimeographed.

———. 1973. "The Capitalist State and the Problem of Policy Formation." Pp. 125–144 in *Stress and Contradiction in Modern Capitalism,* edited by R. A. Leon, N. Lindberg, Colin Crouch, and C. Offe. Lexington, Mass.: Heath.

———. 1984. *Contradictions of the Welfare State,* edited by J. Keane. London: Hutchinson.

———. 1985. *Disorganized Capitalism: Contemporary Transformation of Work and Politics.* Cambridge, England: Polity Press.

Offe, C., and U. K. Preuss. 1991. "Democratic Institutions and Moral Resources." Pp. 143–171 in *Political Theory Today,* edited by David Held. Stanford, Calif.: Stanford University Press.

Ohmae, K. 1990. *The Borderless World: Power and Strategy in the Interlinked World Economy.* New York: Harper Business.

———. 1995. *The End of the Nation-State: The Rise of Regional Economies.* New York: Free Press.

Olivas, M. A. 1995. "The Chronicles, My Grandfather's Stories, and Immigration Law: The Slave Trader's Chronicle as Racial History." Pp. 9–20 in *Critical Race Theory: The Cutting Edge,* edited by Richard Delgado. Philadelphia: Temple University Press.

Oliver, N., and B. Wilkinson. 1988. *The Japanisation of British Industry.* London: Basil Blackwell.

Oxenham, J., ed. 1984. *Education versus Qualifications? A Study of Relationships between Education, Selection for Employment, and the Productivity of Labour.* London: George Allen & Unwin.

Paine, T. 1953. *Common Sense and Other Political Writings.* Indianapolis: Bobbs-Merrill.

Parker, W. C. 1997. "Citizenship Education." Pp. 39–40 in *Dictionary of Multicultural Education,* edited by C. A. Grant and G. Ladson-Billings. Phoenix, Ariz.: Oryx.

Pateman, C. 1970. *Participation and Democratic Theory.* Cambridge: Cambridge University Press.

———. 1985. *The Problem of Political Obligation: A Critique of Liberal Theory.* Cambridge, Mass.: Polity Press.

———. 1986a. "Feminism and Participatory Democracy." Paper presented at the meeting of the American Philosophical Association, St. Louis Missouri, May.

———. 1986b. "Introduction: The Theoretical Subversiveness of Feminism." Pp. 1–10 in *Feminist Challenges: Social and Political Theory,* edited by C. Pateman and E. Gross. Boston: Northeastern University Press.

———. 1988. *The Sexual Contract.* Stanford, Calif.: Stanford University Press.

————. 1992. "Equality, Difference, Subordination: The Politics of Motherhood and Women's Citizenship." Pp. 17–31 in *Beyond Equality and Difference: Citizenship, Feminist Politics, and Female Subjectivity,* edited by G. Bock and S. James. London: Routledge.

————. 1995. "Democracy, Freedom, and Special Rights." University of Wales, Swansea.

————. 1996. "Democratization and Citizenship in the 1990s: The Legacy of T. H. Marshall." Wilhelm Aubert Memorial Lecture. Institute for Social Research and Department of Sociology, University of Oslo.

Peters, M. In press. *Introduction to Lyotard Education and the Postmodern Condition.* Westport, Conn.: Bergin & Garvey.

Picciotto, S. 1991. "The Internationalism of the State." *Capital and Class* 43 (Spring):43–63.

Piore, M., and C. Sabel. 1984. *The Second Industrial Divide.* New York: Basic Books.

Pitelis, C. 1991. "Beyond the Nation-State? The Transnational Firm and the Nation-State." *Capital and Class* 43 (Spring):131–152.

Plant, R. 1990. "Citizenship and Rights." In *Citizenship and Rights in Thatcher's Britain: Two Views.* London: Institute of Economic Affairs.

Plato. 1941. *Republic.* Translated by F. M. Cornford. Oxford: Clarendon Press.

Pooley, S. 1991. "The State Rules, OK? The Continuing Political Economy of Nation-States." *Capital and Class* 43 (Spring):65–82.

Popkewitz, T. S. 1987. "Knowledge and Interest in Curriculum Studies." Pp. 335–354 in *Critical Studies in Teacher Education: Its Folklore, Theory, and Practice.* London: Falmer Press.

————. 1991. *A Political Sociology of Educational Reform: Power/Knowledge in Teaching, Teachers Education, and Research.* New York: Teachers College Press, Columbia University.

————. 1994a. "Decentralization, Centralization, and Discourses in Changing Power Relationships: The State, Civil Society, and the Educational Arena." Madison, Wisconsin. Mimeographed.

————. 1994b. "Systems of Ideas in Historical Spaces: Vigotsky, Educational Constructivism, and Changing Patterns in the Regulation of the Self." Madison, Wisconsin. Mimeographed.

————. 1996. "Rethinking Decentralization and State/Civil Society Distinctions: The State as a Problematic of Governing." *Journal of Education Policy* 11, no. 1:27–51.

————, ed. 1993. *Changing Patterns of Power: Social Regulation and Teacher Education Reform.* Albany: State University of New York Press.

Popkewitz, T. S., and M. A. Pereira. 1993. "An Eight-Country Study of Reform Practices in Teacher Education: An Outline of the Problematic." Pp. 1–52 in *Changing Patterns of Power: Social Regulation and Teacher Education Reform,* edited by T. S. Popkewitz. Albany: State University of New York Press.

Portes, A., and P. Landolt. 1996. "The Downside of Social Capital." *American Prospect* 26 (May-June): 18–21, 94.

Przeworski, A. 1991. *Democracy and the Market: Political and Economic Reforms in Eastern Europe and Latin America.* New York: Cambridge University Press.

Psacharopoulos, G. 1988. "Critical Issues in Education and Development: A World Agenda." *International Journal of Educational Development* 8, no. 1: 1–7.

Puiggrós, A. 1990. *Sujetos, disciplina, y curriculum en los orígenes del sistema educativo argentino.* Buenos Aires: Galerna.

Pusey, M. 1980. "The Legitimation of State Education Systems." *Australian and New Zealand Journal of Sociology* 16 (July): 45–52.

Putnam, Robert D. 1993. *Making Democracy Work: Civic Traditions in Modern Italy.* Princeton, N.J.: Princeton University Press.

———. 1995. "Bowling Alone: America's Declining Social Capital." *Journal of Democracy* 6, no. 1 (January):65–78.

Reich, R. B. 1991. *The Work of Nations.* New York: Vintage Books.

Ricupero, Rubens. 1994. "Eu não tenho escrúpolos. O que é bom a gente fatura; o que é ruim, esconde." *Journal ISTOE,* 7 September, 21.

Rocco, R. A. 1997. "Reframing Postmodernist Constructions of Difference: Subaltern Spaces, Power, and Citizenship." Paper presented at the Symposium on the Challenge of Postmodernism to the Social Sciences and the Humanities, University Complutense, Somosaguas campus, Madrid, 22–25 April.

Rodriguez Brandão, C. 1982. *Lutar com a palavra.* Rio de Janeiro: Graal.

Rouse, J. 1987. *Knowledge and Power: Toward a Political Philosophy of Science.* Ithaca, N.Y.: Cornell University Press.

Rousseau, J.-J. 1967. *The Social Contract and Discourse on the Origin of Inequality.* Edited by L. G. Crocker. New York: Washington Square Press.

———. 1980. *The Social Contract.* Baltimore: Penguin Books.

Ruccio, D., S. Resnick, and R. Wolff. 1991. "Class Beyond the Nation-State." *Capital and Class* 43 (Spring):25–42.

Russell, D. G. 1989. *Planning Education for Development.* Cambridge: Harvard University Press.

Safran, W. 1994. "Non-separatist Politics Regarding Ethnic Minorities: Positive Approaches and Ambiguous Consequences." *International Political Science Review* 15, no. 1:61–80.

Saldivar-Hull, Sonia. 1994. "Feminism on the Border: From Gender to Politics to Geopolitics." Pp. 203–220 in *Criticism in the Borderlands: Studies in Chicano Literature, Culture, and Ideology,* edited by H. Calderón and J. D. Saldivar. Durham, N.C.: Duke University Press.

Samoff, J. 1990. "More, Less, None? Human Resource Development: Responses to Economic Constraint." Palo Alto, Calif. Mimeograph.

Sarup, Madan. 1989. *An Introductory Guide to Post-Structuralism and Postmodernism.* Athens: University of Georgia Press.

Schlesinger, A. 1990. "When Ethnic Studies Are Un-American." *Wall Street Journal,* 23 April.

———. 1991. *The Disuniting of America.* Knoxville, Tenn.: Whittle Direct Books.

Scott, A. 1990. *Ideology and the New Social Movements.* London: Unwin Hyman.

Scott, J. W. 1992. "Multiculturalism and the Politics of Identity." *October* 61 (Summer): 12–19.

Selowsky, M. 1980. "Preschool Age Investment in Human Capital." Pp. 97–111 in *The Educational Dilemma,* edited by J. Simmons. London: Pergamon Press.

Shapiro, J. A., and A. Shapiro, eds. 1995. *Campus Wars: Multiculturalism and the Politics of Difference.* Boulder, Colo.: Westview Press.

Simon, B. 1965. *Education and the Labour Movement: 1870–1920.* London: Lawrence & Wishart.

———. 1987. *The Rise of the Modern Educational System.* Cambridge: Cambridge University Press.

Sizer, T. R. 1992. *Horace's School: Redesigning the American High School.* Boston: Houghton Mifflin.

Skocpol, T. 1979. *States and Social Revolutions: A Comparative Analysis of France, Russia, and China.* Cambridge: Cambridge University Press.

Slater, D., ed. 1985. *New Social Movements and the State in Latin America.* Amsterdam: Centrum voor Studie en Documentatie vans Latijns America.

Sleeter, C. E., and C. A. Grant. 1987. "An Analysis of Multicultural Education in the United States." *Harvard Educational Review* 57: 421–444.

Smelser, N. 1994. "Contested Boundaries and Shifting Solidarities." *International Sociological Association Bulletin* 60, no. 5 (Spring): 1–2.

Smith, D. E. 1987. *The Everyday World as Problematic: A Feminist Sociology.* Boston: Northeastern University Press.

Smith, S. B. 1989. *Hegel's Critique of Liberalism.* Chicago: University of Chicago Press.

Smith, T., and M. Noble. 1995. *Education Divides: Poverty and Schooling in the 1990s.* London: Child Poverty Action Group.

Solorzano, D. G., and O. Villalpando. In press. "Marginality and the Experience of Students of Color in Higher Education." In *Sociology of Education: Emerging Perspectives,* edited by C. A. Torres and T. Mitchell. Albany: State University of New York Press.

Somers, M. 1992. "Narrativity, Narrative Identity, and Social Action: Rethinking English Working-Class Formation." *Social Science History* 16, no. 4 (Winter): 591–630.

———. 1993. "Citizenship and the Place of the Public Sphere: Law, Community, and Political Culture in the Transition to Democracy." *American Sociological Review* 58 (October): 587–620.

Sonntag, H. R., and H. Valecillos. 1977. *El estado en el capitalismo contemporáneo.* Mexico City: Siglo XX Editores.

Stanton-Salazar, R., and S. Dornsbusch. 1995. "Social Capital and the Reproduction of Inequality: Information Networks among Mexican-Origin High School Students." *Sociology of Education* 68:116–135.

Stepan, A. C. 1988. *Rethinking Military Politics: Brazil and the Southern Cone.* Princeton, N.J.: Princeton University Press.

Sternbach, N. S., M. Navarro-Arangurn, P. Chuchryk, and S. Alvarez. 1992. "Feminisms in Latin America: From Bogotá to San Bernardo." *Signs: Journal of Women in Culture and Society* 17 (no. 2): 393–433.

Stockman, D. A. 1986. *The Triumph of Politics: Why the Reagan Revolution Failed.* New York: Harper & Row.

Stoer, S. R., and R. Dale. 1987. "Education, State, and Society in Portugal, 1926–1981." *Comparative Education Review* 31, no. 3: 405.

Stromquist, N. 1991. "Educating Women: The Political Economy of Patriarchal States." *International Studies in Sociology of Education* 1:111–128.

Sujstorf, M. E., Amy Stuart Wells, and Robert L. Crain. 1993. "A Final Word on Chubb and Moe." Pp. 245–246 in *School Choice: Examining the Evidence,* edited by E. Rasell and R. Rothstein. Washington, D.C.: Economic Policy Institute.

Therborn, G. 1979. *What Does the Ruling Class Do When It Rules?* London: Verso.

———. 1989. "Los retos del estado de bienestar: La contrarevolución que fracasa, las causas de su enfermedad, y la economía política de las presiones del cambio." Pp. 81–99 in *Crisis y futuro del estado de bienestar,* edited by R. M. de Bustillo. Madrid: Alianza Universidad.

Therstrom, S., and A. Therstrom. 1997. *America in Black and White: One Nation, Indivisible.* New York: Simon & Schuster.

Thomas, G. M., and J. M. Meyer. 1984. "The Expansion of the State." *Annual Review of Sociology* 10:461–482.

Thurow, L. 1992. *Head to Head: The Coming Economic Battle among Japan, Europe, and America.* New York: William Morrow.

Tilly, C. 1978. *From Mobilization to Revolution.* New York: Random House.

Tocqueville, A. de. 1969. *Democracy in America.* Edited by J. P. Maier; translated by G. Lawrence. Garden City, N.Y.: Anchor Books.

Tomaney, J. 1990. "The Reality of Workplace Flexibility." *Capital and Class* 40:29–60.

Torres, C. A. 1976a. "A dialética Hegeliana e o pensamento lógico-estrutural de Paulo Freire: Notas para uma análise e confrontaçáo dos pressupostos filosóficos vigentes na dialética da pedagogia dos oprimidos e do pensamento freireano em geral." *Sintesa, nova fase* 3, no. 7 (April–June):61–78.

———. 1976b. "Servidumbre, autoconciencia, liberación: La solución dialéctica Hegeliana y la filosofía de la alfabetización problematizadora de Paulo Freire: Notas provisorias para su confontación." *Franciscanum* 18, no. 54:405–478.

———. 1978. *Leitura crítica de Paulo Freire.* São Paulo: Loyola.

———. 1980. *Paulo Freire: Educación y concientización.* Salamanca: Ediciones Sígueme.

———. 1985. "State and Education: Marxist Theories." Pp. 4793–4798 in *International Encyclopedia of Education: Research and Studies,* vol. 8, edited by T. Husén, and T. N. Postlethwaite. Oxford: Pergamon Press.

———. 1986. "Nation at Risk: La educación neoconservadora." *Nueva Sociedad* 84: 108–115.

———. 1989. "The Capitalist State and Public Policy Formation: A Framework for a Political Sociology of Educational Policy-Making." *British Journal of Sociology of Education* 10, no. 1:81–102.

———. 1990. *The Politics of Nonformal Education in Latin America.* Westport, Conn.: Praeger.

———. 1991. "State Corporatism, Education Policies, and Students' and Teachers' Movements in Mexico." Pp. 115–150 in *Understanding Reform in Global Context: Economy, Ideology, and the State.* New York: Garland.

———. 1992. *The Church, Society, and Hegemony: A Critical Sociology of Religion in Latin America.* Translated by Richard A. Young. Westport, Conn.: Praeger.

———. 1994. "La universidad latinoamericana: De la reforma de 1918 al ajuste estructural de los 1990." Pp. 13–54 in *Curriculum universitario siglo XXI,* edited by R. C. F. Torres, M. Albornoz, S. Duluc, and L. Petrucci. Paraná, Argentina: Facultad de Ciencias de la Educación, Universidad Nacional de Entre Rios.

———. 1995a. "The State and Education Revisited, or Why Educational Researchers Should Think Politically about Education." *AERA, Review of Research in Education* 21:255–331.

———. 1995b. *Estudios Freiranos.* Buenos Aires: Libros del Quinquincho.

———. 1996a. "Adult Education and Instrumental Rationality: A Critique." *International Journal of Educational Development* 16, no. 2:195–206.

———. 1996b. *Pedagogia da luta.* São Paulo: Cortez Editores.

———. 1998a. *Education, Power, and Personal Biography: Dialogues with Critical Educators.* New York: Routledge.

———. 1998b. "The Political Pedagogy of Paulo Freire." Introduction to *Paulo Freire, Politics and Education.* Los Angeles: UCLA, Latin American Center.

Torres, C. A., Rajinder S. Pannu, and M. Kazim Bacchus. 1993. "Capital Accumulation, Political Legitimation, and Education Expansion." Pp. 3–32 in *International Perspective on Education and Society 3,* edited by A. Yogev and J. Dronkers. Greenwood, Conn.: JAI Press.

Torres, C. A., and A. Puiggrós, eds. 1995. *Comparative Education Review* 39, no. 1 (February). Special issue on education in Latin America.

———. 1997. *Latin American Education: Comparative Perspectives.* Boulder, Colo.: Westview Press.

Torres, C. A., and T. Mitchell, eds. In press. *Introduction to Sociology of Education: Emerging Perspectives.* Albany: State University of New York Press.

Touraine, A. 1981. *The Voice and the Eye: An Analysis of Social Movements.* Translated by A. Duff. Cambridge: Cambridge University Press.

Tucker, R. C., ed. 1978. *The Marx-Engels Reader.* New York: W. W. Norton.

Tully, J. 1993. "The Possessive Individualist Thesis: A Reconsideration in the Light of Recent Scholarship." Pp. 19–44 in *Possessive Individualism and Democratic Theory: Macpherson's Legacy.* Albany: State University of New York Press.

Turner, B. 1986. *Citizenship and Capitalism: The Debate over Reformism.* London: Allen & Unwin.

———. 1990. "Outline of a Theory of Citizenship." *Sociology* 24, no. 2:189–217.

Tussie, Diana. 1997. *El Banco Interamericano de Desarrollo.* Buenos Aires: Facultad Latino-americana de Ciencias Sociales and Universidad de Buenos Aires.

Twain, Mark. 1962. *Letters from the Earth.* New York: Harper & Row.

Tyack, D. 1990. "Restructuring in Historical Perspective: Tinkering toward Utopia." *Teachers College Record* 92, no. 2 (Winter): 170–191.

―――. 1993. "Constructing Difference: Historical Reflections on Schooling and Social Diversity." *Teachers College Record* 95, no. 1 (Fall):8–34.

Vincent, A. 1987. *Theories of the State.* Oxford: Basil Blackwell.

von Hayek, F. A. 1960. *The Constitution of Liberty.* Chicago: University of Chicago Press.

von Ketteler, W. E. 1981. *The Social Teachings of Wilhelm Emmanuel von Ketteler, Bishop of Mains, 1811–1877.* Translated by Rupert J. Ederer. Washington, D.C.: University Press of America.

Wallerstein, I. 1979. *The Capitalist World Economy.* Cambridge: Cambridge University Press.

―――. 1991. "The National and the Universal: Can There Be Such a Thing as World Culture?" Pp. 91–106 in *Culture, Globalization, and the World System.* Binghamton: State University of New York at Binghamton.

―――. 1997. "Social Science and the Quest for a Just Society." *American Journal of Sociology* 102, no. 5 (March): 1241–1257.

Walsh, C. E. 1996. *Education Reform and Social Change: Multicultural Voices, Struggles, and Visions.* Albany: State University of New York Press.

Wartenberg, T. E., ed. 1992. *Rethinking Power.* Albany: State University of New York Press.

Weber, M. 1958. *From Max Weber: Essays in Sociology.* Edited by H. H. Gertz and C. W. Mills. New York: Oxford University Press, Galaxy Books.

―――. 1964. *The Theory of Social and Economic Organizations,* edited by T. Parsons. New York: Free Press.

―――. 1966. *The City.* Glencoe, Ill.: Free Press.

Weffort, F. 1967. "Educação e politica: Reflexões sociológicas sobre una pedagogia da liberdade. Pp. 3–26 in *Educação como prática da liberdade.* Rio de Janeiro: Paz e Terra.

Weiler, H. N. 1983. "Legalization, Expertise, and Participation: Strategies of Compensatory Legitimation in Educational Policy." *Comparative Education Review* 27:259–277.

Weinstein, W. L. 1971. "The Private and the Public: A Conceptual Inquiry." Pp. 88–104 in *Privacy,* edited by J. R. Pennock and J. W. Chapman. New York: Atherton.

Wells, A. S. 1993. "The Sociology of School Choice: Why Some Win and Others Lose in the Educational Marketplace." Pp. 47–48 in *School Choice: Examining the Evidence,* edited by E. Rasell and R. Rothstein. Washington, D.C.: Economic Policy Institute.

West, C. 1988. "Marxist Theory and the Specificity of Afro-American Oppression." Pp. 17–29 in *Marxism and the Interpretation of Culture,* edited by L. Grossberg and C. Nelson. Urbana: University of Illinois Press.

―――. 1992. "The Postmodern Crisis of the Black Intellectual." Pp. 689–705 in *Cultural Studies,* edited by L. Grossberg, C. Nelson, and P. Treichler. New York: Routledge.

———. 1993a. *Prophetic Thought in Postmodern Times.* Monroe, Maine: Common Courage Press.

———. 1993b. *Race Matters.* Boston: Beacon Press.

———. 1993c. "The New Cultural Politics of Difference." Pp. 11–23 in *Race, Identity, and Representation in Education,* edited by C. McCarthy and W. Crichlow. New York: Routledge.

West, C., J. Klor de Alva, and E. Shorris. 1996. "Colloquy: Our Next Race Question. The Uneasiness between Blacks and Latinos." *Harper's Magazine,* April, 55–63.

West, G. W. 1981. "Education, Moral Reproduction, and the State: Some Implications of Activistic Interpretations of Recent European State Theories for Canadian Educational Policy." *Interchange* 12, nos. 2–3:86–101.

Wexler, P. 1987. *Social Analysis of Education: After the New Sociology.* London: Routledge & Kegan Paul.

Whitty, G. In press. "Citizens or Consumers? Continuity and Change in Contemporary Education Policy." In *Critical Educational Theory in Unsettling Times,* edited by D. Carlson and M. W. Apple. Minneapolis: University of Minnesota Press.

Wilensky, H. L. 1975. *The Welfare State and Equality: Structural and Ideological Roots of Public Expenditures.* Berkeley and Los Angeles: University of California Press.

———. 1976. *The New Corporatism: Centralization and the Welfare State.* Beverly Hills, Calif.: Sage.

———. 1994. "Tax and Spend: The Political Economy and Performace of Rich Democracies." Berkeley, Calif.

Willener, A. 1970. *The Action-Image of Society: On Cultural Politicization.* London: Tavistock.

Williams, M., and G. Reuten. 1993. "After the Rectifying Revolution: The Contradictions of the Mixed Economy." *Capital and Class* 49 (Spring):77–112.

Wilms, W. W. 1996. *Restoring Prosperity: How Workers and Managers Are Forging a New Culture of Cooperation.* New York: Random House.

Wolin, S. S. 1960. *Politics and Vision: Continuity and Innovation in Western Political Thought.* Boston: Little, Brown.

Wrigley, J. 1982. *Class Politics and Public Schools.* New Brunswick, N.J.: Rutgers University Press.

Zaretsky, E. 1983. "The Place of the Family in the Origins of the Welfare State." Pp. 290–305 in *States and Societies,* edited by David Held. Oxford: Martin Robertson in association with Open University.

Zeitlin, I. 1968. *Ideology and Sociological Theory.* New York: Prentice Hall.

Index

About the Author

 Carlos Alberto Torres, a political sociologist of education, is a professor at the Graduate School of Education and Information Studies and director of the Latin American Center at the University of California–Los Angeles. He was educated in Argentina, Mexico, Canada, and the United States. He has written extensively on social theory and education, the work of Paulo Freire, and Latin American education in comparative perspective. Among his books are *Social Theory and Education* and *Education, Power, and Personal Biography*, both with R. A. Morrow. He is also coeditor, with T. Mitchell, of *Sociology of Education: Emerging Perspectives* and, with P. O'Cadiz and P. L. Wong, of *Education and Democracy: Paulo Freire, Social Movements, and Educational Reform in São Paulo.*